A Functional Discourse Grammar for English

Oxford Textbooks in Linguistics

PUBLISHED

A Functional Discourse Grammar
for English
by Evelien Keizer

Pragmatics
Second edition
by Yan Huang

Compositional Semantics
An Introduction to the Syntax/Semantics
Interface
by Pauline Jacobson

The Grammar of Words
An Introduction to Linguistic Morphology
Third edition
by Geert Booij

A Practical Introduction to Phonetics
Second edition
by J. C. Catford

Meaning in Language
An Introduction to Semantics
and Pragmatics
Third edition
by Alan Cruse

Natural Language Syntax
by Peter W. Culicover

Principles and Parameters
An Introduction to Syntactic Theory
by Peter W. Culicover

A Semantic Approach to English Grammar
by R. M. W. Dixon

Semantic Analysis
A Practical Introduction
by Cliff Goddard

The History of Languages
An Introduction
by Tore Janson

Diachronic Syntax
by Ian Roberts

Cognitive Grammar
An Introduction
by John R. Taylor

Linguistic Categorization
Third edition
by John R. Taylor

IN PREPARATION

Lexical Functional Grammar
by Mary Dalrymple, John Lowe,
and Louise Mycock

The Lexicon
An Introduction
by Elisabetta Ježek

Translation
Theory and Practice
by Kirsten Malmkjaer

Speech Acts and Sentence Types in English
by Peter Siemund

Linguistic Typology
Theory, Method, Data
by Jae Jung Song

A Functional Discourse
Grammar for English

Evelien Keizer

OXFORD
UNIVERSITY PRESS

OXFORD

UNIVERSITY PRESS

Great Clarendon Street, Oxford, OX2 6DP
United Kingdom

Oxford University Press is a department of the University of Oxford.
It furthers the University's objective of excellence in research, scholarship,
and education by publishing worldwide. Oxford is a registered trade mark of
Oxford University Press in the UK and in certain other countries

First Edition published in 2015
Impression: 1

Published in the United States of America by Oxford University Press
198 Madison Avenue, New York, NY 10016, United States of America

British Library Cataloguing in Publication Data
Data available

Library of Congress Control Number: 2014940244

ISBN 978–0–19–957186–4 (Hbk)
ISBN 978–0–19–957187–1 (Pbk)

Printed and bound by
CPI Group (UK) Ltd, Croydon CR0 4YY

Contents

Acknowledgements   x
List of tables   xi
List of abbreviations and symbols   xii

1. **Why Functional Discourse Grammar?**   1
    1.1.   Introduction   1
    1.2.   Why linguistic theory?   2
    1.3.   Why functional?   5
           1.3.1.   Some fundamental theoretical issues   5
           1.3.2.   Formal and functional approaches   10
    1.4.   Why discourse?   13
    1.5.   What is (in) a grammar?   14
    1.6.   Summary   15
    Exercises   16
    Suggestions for further reading   19

2. **The general architecture of FDG**   20
    2.1.   Introduction   21
    2.2.   FDG in its wider context   23
           2.2.1.   The Conceptual Component   23
           2.2.2.   The Contextual Component   25
           2.2.3.   The Output Component   28
    2.3.   The Grammatical Component   28
           2.3.1.   Operations   28
           2.3.2.   Primitives   30
           2.3.3.   Levels of representation   31
    2.4.   Summary   39
    Exercises   40
    Suggestions for further reading   42

3. **The Interpersonal Level**   43
    3.1.   Introduction   44
    3.2.   The organization of the Interpersonal Level   45

3.3.   The Move   48
    3.3.1.   General characterization   48
    3.3.2.   The head   49
    3.3.3.   Modifiers   50
    3.3.4.   Operators   51
3.4.   The Discourse Act   52
    3.4.1.   General characterization   52
    3.4.2.   The head   57
    3.4.3.   Modifiers   58
    3.4.4.   Operators   59
3.5.   The Illocution   60
    3.5.1.   General characterization   60
    3.5.2.   The head   61
    3.5.3.   Modifiers   66
    3.5.4.   Operators   68
3.6.   The Speech Participants   68
    3.6.1.   General characterization   68
    3.6.2.   The head   70
    3.6.3.   Modifiers   71
    3.6.4.   Operators   71
3.7.   Communicated Content   72
    3.7.1.   General characterization   72
    3.7.2.   The head   73
    3.7.3.   Modifiers   79
    3.7.4.   Operators   82
3.8.   Ascriptive Subacts   83
    3.8.1.   General characterization   83
    3.8.2.   The head   85
    3.8.3.   Modifiers   87
    3.8.4.   Operators   89
3.9.   Referential Subacts   90
    3.9.1.   General characterization   90
    3.9.2.   The head   92
    3.9.3.   Modifiers   94
    3.9.4.   Operators   95
3.10.   Summary   96
Exercises   97
Suggestions for further reading   101

4. The Representational Level   102

4.1.   Introduction   103

4.2.   The organization of the Representational Level   104

4.3.   The Propositional Content   108

4.3.1.   General characterization   108

4.3.2.   The head   109

4.3.3.   Modifiers   113

4.3.4.   Operators   116

4.4.   The Episode   117

4.4.1.   General characterization   117

4.4.2.   The head   119

4.4.3.   Modifiers   121

4.4.4.   Operators   123

4.5.   The State-of-Affairs   124

4.5.1.   General characterization   124

4.5.2.   The head   125

4.5.3.   Configurational heads: number and roles
of the participants   127

4.5.4.   Copular and existential constructions   136

4.5.5.   Complex SoAs   140

4.5.6.   Modifiers   142

4.5.7.   Operators   143

4.6.   The Property   146

4.6.1.   General characterization   146

4.6.2.   The head   148

4.6.3.   Modifiers   150

4.6.4.   Operators   151

4.7.   The Individual   152

4.7.1.   General characterization   152

4.7.2.   The head   154

4.7.3.   Modifiers   156

4.7.4.   Operators   158

4.8.   Locations and Times   159

4.8.1.   General characterization   159

4.8.2.   The head   162

4.8.3.   Modifiers   164

4.8.4.   Operators   166

4.9. Summary   166

Exercises   167

Suggestions for further reading   171

5. **The Morphosyntactic Level**   172

5.1. Introduction   173

5.2. The organization of the Morphosyntactic Level   175

5.3. Transparency and synthesis   178

5.4. Linguistic Expressions   181

5.5. Clauses   184

5.5.1. Introduction   184

5.5.2. The ordering of non-core units   186

5.5.3. Alignment   191

5.5.4. The ordering of core units   199

5.5.5. Dummy elements   204

5.5.6. Agreement   207

5.5.7. Subordination   208

5.6. Phrases   218

5.6.1. Introduction   218

5.6.2. The ordering of units within the Phrase   220

5.6.3. Dummy elements   225

5.6.4. Agreement   227

5.6.5. Subordination   229

5.7. Words   231

5.7.1. Introduction   231

5.7.2. Words vs. lexemes   232

5.7.3. Lexical and Grammatical Words   235

5.7.4. The ordering of non-core units   237

5.7.5. Alignment   240

5.7.6. The ordering of core units   242

5.7.7. Dummy elements   243

5.7.8. Compounding, derivation, and affixation: summary   244

5.8. Summary   246

Exercises   247

Suggestions for further reading   250

6. The Phonological Level   251
    6.1.   Introduction   252
    6.2.   The organization of the Phonological Level   255
    6.3.   Utterances   257
    6.4.   Intonational Phrases   259
    6.5.   Phonological Phrases   263
    6.6.   Phonological Words   269
    6.7.   Feet and Syllables   273
    6.8.   Summary   279
    Exercises   280
    Suggestions for further reading   282

7. Sample representations   283
    7.1.   Example 1   283
            7.1.1.   Interpersonal Level   284
            7.1.2.   Representational Level   285
            7.1.3.   Morphosyntactic Level   286
            7.1.4.   Phonological Level   288
    7.2.   Example 2   290
            7.2.1.   Interpersonal Level   290
            7.2.2.   Representational Level   290
            7.2.3.   Morphosyntactic Level   292
            7.2.4.   Phonological Level   293
    7.3.   Example 3   294
            7.3.1.   Interpersonal Level   294
            7.3.2.   Representational Level   295
            7.3.3.   Morphosyntactic Level   296
            7.3.4.   Phonological Level   297

Glossary   298
List of languages   317
Bibliography   319
Index   329

Acknowledgements

I would like to express my gratitude to a number of colleagues, students, and friends who have contributed to this first textbook on Functional Discourse Grammar. My thanks go, first of all, to Kees Hengeveld and Lachlan Mackenzie, for encouraging me to write the book, for their support and advice throughout the writing process, and for their invaluable feedback on earlier versions. I am also grateful to the other members of the Functional Discourse Grammar research group, Marize Dall'Aglio Hattnher, Mike Hannay, Wim Honselaar, Lois Kemp, Kasper Kok, Arjan Nijk, Hella Olbertz, and Ewa Zakrzewska, who discussed and commented on various chapters of the manuscript; a special word of thanks is owed to Hella Olbertz for initiating and organizing these meetings, and for providing me with the feedback. I would also like to thank María-Jesús Pérez Quintero, who at the early stages helped to give shape to the project. I'm indebted to my student assistants Udo Schimanofsky and Iris Vukovics for their perceptive comments and for the enthusiasm with which they suggested many useful ideas for exercises. Further I would like to thank the students of the FDG linguistics seminar at the University of Vienna (winter semester 2013) for their feedback and suggestions, and in particular Elnora ten Wolde for going through the whole manuscript once again. Thanks are also due to Victoria Hart and Kate Gilks at OUP for their patience and support, and to my copy-editor, Kim Allen. Finally, I'm grateful to Lotti Viola for preparing and proofreading the manuscript and to Maria Valencia Cuberos and Annemarie Rapberger for their help in correcting the proofs. It goes without saying that any remaining errors and shortcomings are entirely my own.

This book is dedicated, with heartfelt thanks and much love, to my partner Norval.

Evelien Keizer

Vienna

List of tables

4.1. Basic semantic categories   105
4.2. Further semantic categories   106
4.3. Different types of representational head
(layer of the Individual)   107
4.4. Different types of head: Propositional Contents   113
4.5. Different types of head: Episodes   121
4.6. Different types of head: States-of-Affairs   127
4.7. Predication frames in English   131
4.8. Possible combinations of basic semantic functions in English   135
4.9. Further types of SoA in English   138
4.10. Different semantic classes (parts-of-speech)   146
4.11. Different types of head: Properties   150
4.12. Different types of head: Individuals   156
4.13. Different types of head: Locations and Times   163
5.1. Possible configurations of Linguistic Expressions   183
5.2. Nominative–accusative alignment   195
5.3. Absolute–ergative alignment   197
5.4. Syntactic function assignment in three-place predication
frames, Type I   197
5.5. Syntactic function assignment in three-place predication
frames, Types I and II   198
5.6. Types of subordinate Clauses   208
5.7. Matrix verbs and their complements   209
5.8. Matrix verbs and their complements: representations   210
5.9. Grammatical Affixes in English   238

List of abbreviations and symbols

Abbreviations used in representations

Interpersonal level

1	singular
[±A]	± involving the Addressee
[±S]	± involving the Speaker
±id	± identifiable
±s	± specific
A	Addressee
A_1	Discourse Act
approx	approximative
Aside	Aside
C_1	Communicated Content
Con	Contrast
Conf	Confirmation
DECL	declarative
emph	emphasis
exact	exactness
F_1	Illocution
Foc	Focus
h	higher social status
ILL	variable for an Illocution
IMP	imperative
INTER	interrogative
INTERP	interpellative
m	plural
M_1	Move
Motiv	Motivation
P_1	Speech Participant
R_1	Subact of Reference
Reinf	Reinforcement

rep	reportative
S	Speaker
SA	Subact
T_1	Subact of Ascription
Π	operator
Π^A	operator of the Discourse Act (etc.)
Σ	modifier
Σ^A	modifier of the Discourse Act (etc.)
Φ	pragmatic or rhetorical function
Φ^A	function of the Discourse Act (etc.)

Representational level

♦	lexeme
$\forall$	universal quantifier operator
$\exists$	existential quantifier operator
$\varnothing$	zero
1	singular / one
A	Actor
ant	anterior
Ass	Associative
coll	collective
Com	Comitative
comp	comparative
dis	distance
distr	distributive
e_1	State-of-Affairs
ep_1	Episode
f_1	Property
hab	habitual
hyp	hypothetical
L	Locative
l_1	location
LEX	lexeme
m	plural
p_1	Propositional Content
past	past

perf	perfect
pop	pop marker
pres	present
prog	progressive
prox	proximity
Rec	Recipient
Ref	Reference
Res	Resultative
sgltv	singulative
sim	simultaneous
So	Source
t_1	Time
U	Undergoer
x_1	Individual
$^c x_1$	countable Individual
$^{coll} x_1$	collective Individual
$^m x_1$	mass Individual
α_1	variable at the relevant layer
π	operator
π^e	operator of the State-of-Affairs (etc.)
σ	modifier
σ^e	modifier of the State-of-Affairs (etc.)
ϕ	semantic function
ϕ^e	semantic function of the State-of-Affairs (etc.)

Morphosyntactic level

1	first person
2	second person
3	third person
$Aaff_1$	Adjectival Affix
$Adpp_1$	Adpositional Phrase
$Adpw_1$	Adpositional Word
Ads_1	Adpositional Stem
$Advaff_1$	Adverbial Affix
$Advp_1$	Adverbial Phrase

$Advs_1$	Adverbial Stem
$Advw_1$	Adverbial Word
Aff_1	Affix
Ap_1	Adjectival Phrase
As_1	Adjectival Stem
Aw_1	Adjectival Word
Cl_1	Clause
$^{dep}Cl_1$	Dependent Clause
def	definite
Gw_1	Grammatical Word
indef	indefinite
Le_1	Linguistic Expression
$Naff_1$	Nominal Affix
Np_1	Noun Phrase
Ns_1	Nominal Stem
Nw_1	Nominal Word
Obj	Object
past	past
past-part	past-participle
P^{centre}	position of Clause with respect to pre- and postclausal positions
P^F	final position
P^{F-n}	position situated n places before the final position
P^I	initial position
P^{I+n}	position situated n places after the initial position
pl	plural
P^M	medial position
P^{M+n}	position situated n places after the medial position
P^{M-n}	position situated n places before the medial position
P^{post}	postclausal position
P^{pre}	preclausal position
pres	present
sg	singular
Subj	Subject
sup	superlative
$Vaff_1$	Verbal Affix
Vp_1	Verb Phrase
Vs_1	Verbal Stem
Vw_1	Verbal Word

$^{fin}Vw_1$	finite Verbal Word
$^{nonf}Vw_1$	finite Verbal Word
Xp_1	Phrase of type X
Xs_1	Stem of type X
Xw_1	Word of type X

Phonological level

f	fall
F_1	Foot
h	high
IP_1	Intonational Phrase
l	low
PP_1	Phonological Phrase
PW_1	Phonological Word
r	rise
s	stress
S_1	Syllable
U_1	Utterance
π	operator

Parts-of-speech

A	Adjective
Ad	Adposition
Adv	Adverb
N	Noun
V	Verb

Abbreviations used in glosses

1	first person
2	second person
3	third person
ABL	ablative

ABS	absolutive
ACC	accusative
ADMON	admonitive
AUX	auxiliary
CAUS	causative
COLL	collective
COMM	commissive
CONTR	contrastive
COP	copula
DAT	dative
DECL	declarative
DEF	definite
DEM	demonstrative
DUB	dubitative
EMPH	emphasis
ERG	ergative
EXACT	exactly
F	feminine
FINAL	final (independent) verb
FOC	focus
FORMAL	formal
FUT	future
GEN	genitive
IMM	immediate
IMP	imperative
INF	inferential
INTER	interrogative
M	male, masculine
NEG	negative, negation
PERC	perceived
PFV	perfective
PL	plural
PROG	progressive
PROH	prohibitive
PRS	present tense
PST	past

REP	reportative
SEQ	sequence
SG	singular
SGLTV	singulative
Q	question marker
U	undergoer

1

Why Functional Discourse Grammar?

1.1. Introduction   1   1.5. What is (in) a grammar?   14

1.2. Why linguistic theory?   2   1.6. Summary   15

1.3. Why functional?   5   Exercises   16

1.4. Why discourse?   13   Suggestions for further reading 19

The aim of this chapter is to give a first impression of the assumptions and principles underlying the theory of Functional Discourse Grammar and to indicate its position in the larger context of linguistic research. After a brief introduction (Section 1.1), we will address the question of why many linguists wish to go beyond the level of language description and why, in doing so, they wish to make use of theoretical models (Section 1.2). Next, a very general characterization of Functional Discourse Grammar will be provided by discussing each of the words that make up its name:

- Why functional? (Section 1.3)
- Why discourse? (Section 1.4)
- What is (in) a grammar? (Section 1.5).

1.1. Introduction

Linguistics is all about trying to increase our knowledge of and insight into human language—how it is organized, used, and acquired and how it develops over time. This is something linguists on the whole agree on. Linguists disagree, however, on what is the best way to achieve this. Some maintain that a systematic and detailed description and comparison of individual languages is, ultimately, all that is needed, while others believe that a certain degree of generalizing and theorizing is required, which often results in the use of linguistics models. Those who agree that theoretical models can be useful often disagree, however, on the shape and organization of such models, and the kind of phenomena they ought to represent and explain. Before embarking on a detailed description of Functional Discourse Grammar (FDG), we will use this introductory chapter to address the question of why linguistic models in general, and FDG in particular, can help us understand how language works.

1.2. Why linguistic theory?

All linguistic research is first and foremost based on observation and description—it will be clear that it is no use trying to analyse linguistic expressions and to theorize about them unless we get the data right. This may sound simple, but performing the tasks of observation and description already involves a number of important decisions on the part of a linguist. First of all, a linguist has to decide what or who to observe, that is, which sources to use. In the first half of the twentieth century, linguists (or grammarians, as they are usually referred to) largely confined themselves to published texts (mostly of a literary or journalistic nature) and introspection. This choice was partly dictated by the circumstances in which these grammarians worked: published written sources were the only external sources that were readily available for examination. Partly, however, the restrictions were deliberately imposed by these grammarians themselves, since many of them believed that grammars ought to fulfil not only a **descriptive** but also a **prescriptive** function: their aim was not so much to describe which linguistic expressions were used in a language, but which linguistic expressions *ought* to be used. These expressions, they reasoned, were primarily to be found in published, edited texts. In the second half of the twentieth century, however, both the circumstances of linguistic research and the attitude of linguists towards the function of linguistic description changed. Technological developments made it possible to examine all kinds of language: written as well as spoken, formal and informal, different geographical varieties (**dialects**) and social varieties (**sociolects**), while linguists, on the whole, opted for a more purely descriptivist approach, in which all these different sources were, indeed, considered relevant.

Another choice that descriptive grammarians were faced with was that of selecting the relevant information from the huge amount of raw data they had at their disposal: a principled choice needed to be made as to which data to describe and which not. For a long time these were the tasks linguists set themselves: in the so-called descriptive tradition linguists were, on the whole, content to give as comprehensive and systematic a description of one particular language as possible.

In the course of the twentieth century, however, linguists increasingly felt the need not only to describe what was and was not acceptable in a particular language, but also to reveal the rules and principles underlying the construction of linguistic expressions. This meant the description of languages was no longer seen as the ultimate aim of linguistic research, but as a basis for tackling such questions as why languages are organized the way they are, how they are acquired, and why and how they change. In other words, the linguist's aim was now to discover the system behind language and the general principles underlying this system. To perform this new task, linguists began to develop theoretical models which would allow them to compare (sometimes widely) different languages in a systematic manner, to make intra-linguistic and cross-linguistic generalizations, to recognize—perhaps not eas-ily nor directly observable—deeper patterns, and to ensure consistency and efficiency in analysis. Rather than having to rely on ad hoc explanations, linguists were now able to develop a well-grounded, unified approach, using clearly defined concepts and unambiguous underlying representations.

Once the idea of using models to represent the internal organization of languages, as well as the relations between different languages, had gained a foothold, linguists became more ambitious. As the first models became more and more sophisticated, there was a growing awareness that these models could be used for other ends as well. Subsequently, these models came to be applied in a large number of areas, including:

- *Language processing*. This is where theoretical linguistics meets such disciplines as psycholinguistics and neurolinguistics. Some theories, for instance, claim to describe or represent the way human beings produce and process language, or the way (linguistic) knowledge is represented in the mind. These models go beyond the description and explanation of the language system; they are meant to describe the actual processes of production and/or interpretation and are as such based on theories about how knowledge is stored, activated, and retrieved. Other theories take a more modest position in this respect, merely claiming to be compatible with what is at present known about language production and comprehension (see also Section 1.5).

- *Language acquisition*. Language models could also be applied in research on both first and second language acquisition. One of the fundamental questions in this area is that of how much (and which) linguistic knowledge is genetically determined (innate) and how much is acquired through exposure to linguistic input (see also Section 1.3).

- *Language change*. Just as theoretical models can help to describe, explain, and represent languages in their present form, they can do the same for the earlier stages of each language. This, in turn, can help us to chart the changes (in individual languages, but also in groups of languages) that have taken place over time; moreover, it enables linguists to demonstrate affinities that existed between now perhaps hugely differing languages at earlier stages of their development. Of particular interest in this respect is the process of **grammaticalization**. Most theories make a distinction between lexical elements (elements with semantic content, lexemes) and grammatical elements (semantically empty elements, e.g. inflections, auxiliaries, determiners, etc.). Since these two groups of elements behave differently (semantically, morphosyntactically, and phonologically), they are analysed and represented in different ways. Diachronic research has shown abundantly that most grammatical elements have developed out of lexical ones, and that, since this change is gradual, many elements are in the process of becoming grammatical at any point in the history of a language. It is this final point in particular that forms a challenge for linguistic models, which typically rely on a strict categorization of elements, and as such are ill-equipped to deal with this kind of in-between stage. At the same time, this particular feature of linguistic models may prove to be useful, as it forces the linguist to describe well-defined criteria for distinguishing lexical and grammatical elements (see also Section 1.3 and Section 2.3.2).

- *Language evolution.* In recent years, there has been an increasing interest in the evolution of language, as linguists (as well as psychologists, cognitive scientists, biologists, anthropologists, neuroscientists, mathematicians, and many others) started to ask such questions as how did language emerge, did it emerge suddenly or gradually, how did it evolve, why is it structured the way it is, what is its relation to biological evolution, and why is it that only humans possess it? Thus far, much of the work is speculative, but it is clear that here, too, theoretical considerations will play a role.

Altogether, there seem to be good reasons for wanting to couch one's linguistic research in some kind of theoretical framework. FDG is one such framework. This, of course, leads us to the question of which framework or model to use, and, more specifically, why use FDG?

1.3. Why functional?

1.3.1. Some fundamental theoretical issues

Although many linguists agree that some kind of theoretical basis is required in order to gain more insight into the way language is organized, there is at the same time considerable disagreement about what linguistic theories and the models they use should look like, which questions they should seek to answer, and on which underlying assumptions and beliefs they ought to be based. As a result, a great many theoretical models have been developed, each with their own specific object of study, their own aims and underlying principles, and their own concepts, terminology, and way of representing linguistic structure. Broadly speaking, it is possible to distinguish two main paradigms: the formal paradigm and the functional paradigm. Although the distinction is far from clear-cut, theories belonging to these paradigms tend to differ along a number of (sometimes interrelated) parameters. Let us consider some of these parameters in some detail.

1.3.1.1. The purpose of language

Whenever we use language, we do so for a reason, even if we are not always aware of the exact function of our linguistic utterances at a particular moment. Although in most cases the average speaker can identify some direct purpose (to give or obtain information, to get something done, or to express surprise or anger), speakers normally do not realize how many different functions language can serve. For a linguist, however, the question of why people use language is a crucial one, since, as we will see in what follows, the answer may determine which areas of linguistic description are considered to be central, which in turn will determine the exact object of study. The following list, although not exhaustive, gives an impression of the wide range of functions that have been identified (based on Finch 2003: 21–40, cf. Jakobson 1960):

(i) Physiological function

At moments of extreme excitement, anger, pain, etc., language may simply serve to release nervous/physical energy. Linguistic expressions fulfilling this function often take the form of 'bad language' (*Damn! Yuck!*)

(ii) Phatic function

Language may serve a purely social function: we are not conveying information, but are merely being polite or sociable. Commenting on the weather may have this function, as well as other conventionalized phrases like *How do you do?* when used as a greeting or *Dear John* at the beginning of a letter.

(iii) Recording function

People everywhere use language to note down things that they want to remember, from shopping lists, to minutes of a meeting, journals, and even epic stories.

(iv) Identifying function

Language is constantly used to name things: by using a particular word to describe an object they want to talk about, people categorize that object as belonging to a particular class. One of the functions of such categorization is that it helps us to identify objects, thereby enabling hearers to pick out the object that I, as the speaker, have in mind (see also the discussion of linguistic categorization in subsection 1.3.1.5).

(v) Reasoning function

Although not all of our thought processes make use of words, much of what we think already takes the shape of (more or less) complete linguistic constructions. As such, language can be seen as an instrument to express thoughts and ideas (sometimes also referred to as the symbolic function of language, e.g. Evans and Green 2006: 6–9).

(vi) Communicating function

In the eyes of many people this probably constitutes the most crucial function of language, and perhaps even the *raison d'être* for the existence of language. People use language to communicate, to get their meaning across. Language, on this view, codes a speaker's intentions; the hearer's job is that of decoding the utterance and of deducing the intended message on the basis of the form of the linguistic expressions used by the speaker.

(vii) Pleasure function

In some cases, language is primarily used to give delight: in poetry, for instance, certain combinations of sounds (different forms of rhyme), and the use of special rhythms, neologisms, and unusual syntactic constructions may be used to give pleasure to the hearer or reader.

Not all of these functions are considered equally crucial. Generally speaking, linguistic theories tend to be based on one of only two of these functions: either it is believed that the main purpose of language is to express thought, or that language first and foremost serves the purpose of communication. Other functions are either subsumed under these two main functions (e.g. the identifying function can easily be seen as resulting from a need to communicate), or regarded as derivative, in the sense that the function may have arisen after language had come to exist (e.g. the phatic or the pleasure function).

1.3.1.2. The object of study
(i) Central area of interest
The grammar of a language is generally assumed to consist of a number of different areas, traditionally referred to as phonology (the study of sounds, stress, and intonation), morphology (the study of the internal structure of words), syntax (concerned with the structure of clauses and phrases, and the order of elements within clauses and phrases), semantics (the study of meaningful elements within a language), and pragmatics (concerned with the way in which speakers use language in order to communicate their intentions). In addition, grammars do not operate in isolation: there is continuous interaction between the grammar and a language user's conceptualization of the world, between the grammar and previous discourse, between the grammar and the immediate discourse situation (including the speech participants), and between the grammar and the society in which it is used. Different theoretical frameworks focus on different areas and relations, which inevitably leads to differences in the overall organization of the models used, as well as to differences in concepts, terminology, and representation.

(ii) Competence vs. performance
Many theoretical linguists (as well as prescriptivist grammarians through the ages) choose to concentrate on **competence** in their study of language,

that is, on a speaker's abstract, tacit knowledge about the structure of his/
her (native) language. Within the heterogeneous phenomenon of human
speech, De Saussure, for instance, made a distinction between *langue* and
parole. *Langue* is defined as 'both a social product of the faculty of speech
and a collection of necessary conventions that have been adopted by a social
body to permit individuals to exercise that faculty'; it is 'a self-contained
whole and a principle of classification' (De Saussure 1974 (1915): 9). *Parole*,
on the other hand, is the executive side of human speech, the actual mani-
festations of language; as such, it is always individual (De Saussure 1974
(1915): 13). For De Saussure *langue* was the essential part of human speech:
to master a language is to master its *langue*, that is, the system of signs that
make up the language. Unlike *parole*, *langue* is homogeneous; as such it is
the only part that can be studied separately. *Langue*, therefore, is the only
possible object of study for the linguist.

One might, on the other hand, also argue that performance forms the only

Chomsky (1965, 1986) made a similar distinction. For him the two funda-
mentally different concepts are those of (grammatical) competence and **performance** (later I-language and E-language). Performance equals De
Saussure's *parole*: it is defined as 'the actual use of language in concrete
situations' (Chomsky 1965: 4) and is characterized by false starts, deviating
forms, hesitation markers, and all kinds of other speech errors which speakers,
on reflection, will identify as 'mistakes'. Performance, therefore, cannot be
regarded as a direct reflection of a speaker's competence, that is, of 'the
speaker-hearer's knowledge of his language' (Chomsky 1965: 4). According
to Chomsky, '[a] grammar of a language purports to be a description of the
ideal speaker-hearer's intrinsic competence' (Chomsky 1965: 4). Linguistic
theory is, in other words, mentalistic, 'since it is concerned with discovering a
mental reality underlying actual behaviour' (Chomsky 1965: 4).

One might, on the other hand, also argue that performance forms the only
objective and directly accessible source available; for empirical researchers
(strongly represented in the discipline of corpus linguistics), it is therefore
the only legitimate object of study. Moreover, it has turned out that from
the point of view of language change, performance cannot be dismissed:
what may be considered as ungrammatical or deviating use of language
may, in fact, turn out to signal a change in progress.

1.3.1.3. Innateness
With regard to the issue of **innateness**, two different camps can be identified
(although in-between positions also exist). On the one hand, there are the

nativists, who believe that children are born with a highly abstract knowledge of language (in the form of **language universals**). The most important reason for assuming the presence of such knowledge is the fact that children can learn their native language(s) very rapidly, at a very early age, and only before a certain age (the critical, or sensitive, period). Moreover, children manage to do this on the basis of incomplete and often incorrect input (often referred to as the 'poverty of stimulus' argument). This has led many linguists to believe that language must, to a large extent, be innate; that is, that knowledge about language, in a very abstract form, is there when we are born, as a kind of linguistic blueprint (the **language faculty** or **language acquisition device**). This abstract knowledge, in the form of language universals, needs to be activated by input, which then triggers the correct, language specific forms.

On the other hand, there is the cultural camp, or the emergentists, who claim that linguistic knowledge is acquired just like any other kind of knowledge. They do not believe in a separate language acquisition device, but maintain that children learn language through 'emergence' (Sampson 2005: 179–84) or 'construction' (Butler 2003: 26–7); that is to say, they gradually build up their knowledge of language on the basis of general cognitive abilities and linguistic input (see also Dik 1997a: 6–7).

1.3.1.4. The role of context

Some theories emphasize the importance of the context of a linguistic utterance, while in other theories the role of context is (at most) marginal. Whether or not context is considered to be important depends on what is regarded as the purpose of language and what forms the object of study. If the purpose of language is the expression of thought, we are dealing with a purely individual, mentalistic phenomenon, for which a study of context is irrelevant. Likewise, it will be clear that theories which focus entirely on grammatical competence will pay little or no attention to the context of use, whether linguistic or extra-linguistic: all that matters is that the expressions produced are grammatical according to a speaker's internalized grammar. If, on the other hand, language is first and foremost seen as a means of communication, linguistic knowledge must include not only purely grammatical knowledge, but will also have to include knowledge of which expressions are most appropriate, effective, or efficient in a particular context. Similarly, if a theory is based on the idea that the form of linguistic utterances is (directly or indirectly) related to, or derived from, the way these expressions are used (i.e. their communicative function), the context in which these utterances are used cannot be ignored.

1.3.1.5. The nature of linguistic categorization

Man is often described as a categorizing animal in the sense that all human activity involves categorization: without the ability to recognize objects as belonging to a particular class, we could not survive (e.g. Labov 1973: 342; Lakoff 1987: 5–6). Similarly, both the use and the study of language cannot do without categorization. As Aarts et al. (2004) put it:

> Categorization is a notion that lies at the heart of virtually all approaches to grammar, be they descriptive, theoretical, or cognitive. All linguists would agree that you cannot do linguistics without assuming that grammatical categories exist in some shape or other. What linguists disagree about is the nature of those categories. Are they discrete, as the classical Aristotelian tradition has it, or are they blurred at the edges, as has been argued more recently, especially by cognitive linguists?
>
> (Aarts et al. 2004: 1)

Naturally, it would be most convenient for linguists if the classical view could be upheld and categories could be assumed to have strict boundaries, with each and every linguistic item clearly belonging to one, and only one class. As many linguists have pointed out, however, even the most basic distinctions in linguistics (say between verbs and nouns, or between lexical and grammatical elements) are not always clear cut (e.g. Crystal 1967; Taylor 2003; Aarts 2007; Keizer 2007a, 2007b). This means that we have to accept that linguistic categories may have fuzzy boundaries, while category membership may be graded, in that some elements may be better (more central) members of a category than others). To accommodate the idea of **gradience** in linguistic categorization, theories often appeal to **prototype theory** (e.g. Rosch 1978; Lakoff 1987).

1.3.2. Formal and functional approaches

Formal and functional approaches tend to take opposite stands on each of these issues. A very general characterization of the two perspectives will suffice to illustrate, in a somewhat black-and-white manner, the different choices they make. We will then proceed by giving a more detailed description of the FDG position.

The formal paradigm	
Purpose of language	Instrument for thought
Object of study	Morphosyntax and phonology (i.e. the formal aspects of language); in particular the ideal native speaker's knowledge of those formal aspects (grammatical competence).

Innateness	Human beings have an innate knowledge of a 'universal grammar', i.e. the very abstract features that all languages have in common. This knowledge is located in a separate part of the brain (the language faculty), which functions autonomously from other types of knowledge.
Role of context	Very small. Typically limited to immediate linguistic context (the clause).
Categorization	Strict, on the basis of well-defined necessary and sufficient features.

The functional paradigm

Purpose of language	Instrument for communication
Object of study	All aspects of language that ultimately dictate the use and form of linguistic expressions, e.g. pragmatics, semantics, morphosyntax, and phonology, whereby pragmatics and semantics (intention and meaning) are more central than syntax and phonology (form). Focus of interest is the speaker's communicative competence (Hymes 1972), i.e. all the knowledge required for successful linguistic communication.
Innateness	The acquisition of language develops as the result of communicative interaction; what is needed, apart from linguistic input, are the general cognitive abilities that also form the basis for the acquisition of many other forms of knowledge and skills.
Role of context	Essential. Since the form of linguistic expressions is regarded as being shaped by their use, they can only meaningfully be studied within the context in which they are used.
Categorization	Gradual, due to the interaction of several, sometimes competing, factors; definitions based on prototypical instances.

Functional Discourse Grammar, as the name clearly indicates, belongs to the functional paradigm. Within the functional paradigm, however, we find a wide range of different approaches, ranging from moderate to extreme (see discussion in Butler 2003: 28–31). Extreme functionalists, according to Butler (2003: 30) 'not only claim that grammatical phenomena and categories emerge from the requirements of discourse, but also go on to reject the concept of grammar as a structural system'. Moderate functionalists, on the other hand, do recognize that, at any particular point in time, a grammar is indeed a structural system—a system shaped by use, and therefore to be described in relation to language use. FDG, Butler argues, belongs to the latter category; using Van Valin's (1993) terminology, FDG can be charac-terized as a 'structural-functional' theory of language. A closer look at the FDG stand on some of the issues mentioned above seems to support this view:

- FDG 'seeks to reconcile the patent fact that languages are structured complexes with the equally patent fact that they are adapted to function as instruments of communication between human beings' (Hengeveld and Mackenzie 2008: ix; cf. Dik 1997a: 3).
- FDG believes in a functional explanation of the form of linguistic expres-sions. FDG takes, in other words, a 'function-to-form' approach: taking as its input a speaker's communicative intentions, a process of formula-tion takes place which translates these intentions into two functional representations (one containing pragmatic, the other semantic informa-tion); in turn, these representations form the input to a process of encod-ing, which determines the morphosyntactic and phonological form of the utterance (e.g. Hengeveld and Mackenzie 2008: 39).
- FDG tries to attain pragmatic adequacy. FDG takes a top-down, modu-lar approach, starting with the speaker's communicative intention. The basic unit of analysis is, therefore, not the clause or the sentence, but the Discourse Act, as expressing this communicative intention. In doing so, FDG 'takes the functional approach to language to its logical extreme in that "pragmatics governs semantics, pragmatics and semantics govern morphosyntax, and pragmatics, semantics and morphosyntax govern phonology"' (Hengeveld and Mackenzie 2008: 13; see also 37–8).
- FDG takes a discourse-oriented approach, acknowledging the fact that certain formal properties of a linguistic expression can only be explained when taking into account the discourse of which this expression forms part (see also Section 1.4). It is, however, not only the previous discourse

(textual information) which may determine the form of a linguistic utterance: in addition, the situational context (providing physical and social information about, for instance, the speech participants, the time and place in which the speech event takes place, any other entities), as well as long-term (cultural) knowledge need to be consulted at various times during the production of a linguistic expression (see e.g. Connolly 2004, 2007, 2014; Rijkhoff 2008; Cornish 2009; Alturo et al. 2014a).

- Finally, as far as the acceptance of gradience in linguistic categorization is concerned, the position taken by FDG clearly tends towards the structural (formal) position. Thus, although it is acknowledged that '[t]he analysis of linguistic data does not always lead to clear-cut results', FDG does not regard this gradience to be part of the grammar: whereas the cognitive and acoustic information is analogue in nature, the grammar itself is digital (Hengeveld and Mackenzie 2008: 9). Where the distinction between lexical and grammatical elements is concerned, for instance, there is no denying that from a diachronic point of view, the distinction is a gradual one, with the large majority of grammatical elements being derived, through a gradual process, from lexical elements. Synchronically, however, FDG insists on a sharp distinction between the two categories— a distinction which, as we will see, plays a crucial role in the analysis of any linguistic utterance (see Section 2.3.2; see also Keizer 2007b, 2013).

From the preceding, it will have become clear that, although definitely belonging to the functional paradigm, FDG certainly does not take a radical position within this paradigm. In fact, it would be more correct to characterize FDG as occupying a position halfway between functional and formal approaches to grammar.

1.4. Why discourse?

One important feature of FDG is that it acknowledges the fact that some grammatical phenomena can only be explained by taking into consideration units higher than the individual clause or sentence. Consider the following simple exchange:

(1) A: Where does your brother live?
     B: He lives in London.

At least two formal features of B's answer depend on the previous discourse context (in this case A's question): the choice of pronoun (*he*) and the prosodic prominence of *in London* as the most important part of B's answer). In FDG, these formal aspects are accounted for by allowing the grammar to interact with the (textual, situational, cultural, etc.) context in which the discourse takes place.

The view that linguistic utterances need to be considered in the larger discourse context also allows FDG to accept that units smaller than the clause can make up complete Discourse Acts. Examples of such units are vocatives (*Peter!*, *Doctor!*), answers to questions (A: *Where does he live?* B: *In London*), or conventionalized phrases (*Thanks*, *Good luck*). In FDG such units are not analysed as reduced clauses: as long as these units, by themselves, constitute complete contributions to the ongoing discourse, they will be analysed as (non-clausal) Discourse Acts. It is, in other words, the discourse-oriented nature of FDG that inevitably leads to the conclusion that the clause cannot be the basic unit of analysis (Hengeveld and Mackenzie 2008: 4).

Despite this attempt to integrate FDG into a larger discourse context, Hengeveld and Mackenzie emphasize that

FDG, despite its name, is not a functionally oriented Discourse Grammar (in the sense of an account of discourse relations). Rather, it is an account of the inner structure of Discourse Acts that is sensitive to the impact of their use in discourse upon their form. (2008: 42)

As we will see in the following section, this position is consistent with the FDG conception of what constitutes a grammar.

1.5. What is (in) a grammar?

We have seen that, as a functional theory, FDG does not analyse linguistic utterances in isolation, but also takes into account conceptual aspects (e.g. speakers' intentions) and contextual aspects (the discourse context and the immediate situation). In other words, FDG regards the grammar of a language as interacting with a conceptual and a contextual component in a wider theory of verbal communication. Nevertheless, it makes a clear distinction between the grammar and these other components, in that it only considers those linguistic phenomena that are encoded in the grammar of a language. Thus, unlike in cognitive linguistics, a sharp distinction is made between cognitive (conceptual) and semantic information: the former is preverbal in nature, and although it may trigger the use of specific linguistic forms, it is not in itself linguistic; semantic information, on the other hand, is part of the grammatical system, and includes only those parts of a speaker's conceptualized knowledge of the world that are linguistically expressed. Thus, although FDG is functional in that it takes a 'function–form' approach, it is, as Hengeveld and Mackenzie (2008: 38–9) point out, at the same time 'form-oriented': it only provides an account of those pragmatic and semantic, as well as conceptual and contextual phenomena which are reflected in the morphosyntactic and phonological form of an utterance. We will refer to this as the **Principle of Formal Encoding** (see also Section 2.2.2).

Another important issue concerns the relation between the FDG model and the actual, online process of language production. One of the distinctive features of FDG is that it is a top-down model, starting with the formulation of the speaker's intention and from there progressing to articulation. It needs to be emphasized, however, that this should not be interpreted as meaning that FDG is a model of the speaker, that is, a model faithfully reflecting the steps taken by the speaker in the production of a linguistic utterance. Although FDG seeks to be psychologically adequate in that it tries to make use of evidence from psycholinguistic studies of language production (Levelt 1989), it remains a grammar, that is, an account of linguistic phenomena. FDG is thus a model of language, of 'encoded intentions and conceptualizations', not a model of the language user (see Hengeveld and Mackenzie 2008: 2). Instead, the grammar must be seen as mimicking the process of language production by modelling 'the sequence of steps that the analyst must take in understanding and laying bare the nature of a particular phenomenon' (Hengeveld and Mackenzie 2008: 2).

1.6. Summary

This chapter has provided a general characterization of the theory of FDG by describing the underlying aims and principles of the theory and by indicating its position in the spectrum of functional approaches. The main points can be summarized as follows:

- FDG is a functional theory in that it regards the form of a language as being shaped by its use. As such, FDG does not look at linguistic utterances in isolation, but also takes into consideration the cognitive, discourse, and interactional aspects of such utterances.
- FDG is at the same time form-oriented in that its aim is to capture all and only the formal properties of linguistic units, taking into consideration,

however, the communicative intentions with which these units where produced and the context in which they were uttered. This means that FDG only includes in its grammar those cognitive, discourse, and interactional aspects that are systematically reflected in the form (morphosyntax or phonology) of a language.

• Despite the fact that FDG is speaker-oriented and modular, it is not intended as a model of language production. Instead, FDG is first and foremost an attempt to describe and explain linguistic facts in a way compatible with what is known about language processing.

• It is believed that only through this specific combination of features and assumptions will it be possible to offer a unified and comprehensive account of the use, meaning, and form of all linguistic utterances.

Exercises

1. One prescriptive rule for English is that double negations are not allowed. Now consider the examples in (ia) (from Chaucer's *The Canterbury Tales*) and (ib) (from Spanish):

(i) a. Ther *nas no man nowher so vertuous.   *was not
        He was the beste beggere in the hous.
                (Chaucer, *The Canterbury Tales*, General Prologue 251–252)

    b. No   sé   nunca   nada   de   nada.
       not   know   never   nothing   about   nothing
       'I never know anything (about anything).'

How many negations do these examples contain? What does this tell you about the nature of prescriptive rules?

    Now compare the following two examples:

(ii) I don't use bloody carbolic soap, I, don't never use nothing like that.
      (BYU-BNC, spoken, conversation)

Find similar examples from a corpus (for instance the BNC or COCA) and/or the Internet and see if you can find patterns in the use of these double/triple negations (who uses them, under which circumstances, what is their function).

    If such patterns exist, what does that mean for the validity of this prescriptive rule?

2. Using the list of functions of language in Section 1.3.1, try and identify the main function(s) of the examples in (i). Is it always easy to determine the (possible) function(s) of an utterance? Are there any (major) functions that you feel should be added to the list?

(i) a. My Christmas wish list: pony, Resident Evil 4, no socks!!!
   b. Brrr, bit nippy today.
   c. Joe Bloggs 1941–2012 | No pain, no grief, no anxious fear | can reach our loved one sleeping here.
   d. Ouch!
   e. Why is the number six so scared? Because seven eight nine!
   f. Big deal. | Whatever. | Yeah, right.

3.* As pointed out in Section 1.3.1, linguistic elements may not always be easy to categorize, for instance in terms of syntactic category (verb, noun, adjective, preposition, etc.).
   Consider the examples in (i) and (ii):

(i) a. The dog was tired.
   b. The dog was very tired.
   c. the tired dog

(ii) a. The dog was asleep.
   b. *The dog was very asleep.
   c. *the asleep dog

a. What kind of words are *tired* and *asleep* (verb, noun, adjective, etc.). Are both equally good examples of the category they belong to? Why (not)?
b. Look up the origin of the word *asleep*. What form did it have in Old English? Does this help us to explain the syntactic behaviour illustrated in (ii)?

Changes in the syntactic category of a word also take place in Present-day English, as illustrated in example (iii):

(iii) a. Many companies attempted to justify the dismissals by saying employees were *absent*. (COCA, written, newspaper)
   b. But it is still clear that *absent* this program, thousands of Georgia students would still be attending public schools their parents felt—for whatever reason—were not serving their children's needs. (COCA, written, newspaper)
   c. *In the absence of* better public transportation, some teens would like to skateboard from place to place . . . (COCA, written, newspaper)

c. Comment on the use and syntactic category/form of the italicized elements in examples (iiia–c). How do you think these elements are related?

4. Consider the following quotes and try to determine which paradigm they represent. Use the parameters given in Section 1.3 to support your answer.

(i) When we communicate, we do not, in general, use isolated sentences. Rather, communication takes place through multi-propositional discourse, organised into structures we now recognise as characterising conversations, lectures, committee meetings, formal and informal letters, and the like. These categories recognise the important relationship between (both written and spoken) texts and the contexts in which they are created and understood. (Butler 2003: 28)

(ii) Syntactic investigation of a given language has as its goal the construction of a grammar that can be viewed as a device of some sort for producing the sentences of the language under analysis. (Chomsky 1957: 11)

(iii) [A] language is in the first place conceptualized as an instrument of social interaction among human beings, used with the intention of establishing communicative relationships. (Dik 1997a: 3)

(iv) Syntax is not radically arbitrary, in this view, but rather is relatively motivated by semantic, pragmatic and cognitive concerns. (Van Valin 1991: 9)

(v) The structure of language can truly serve as a 'mirror of mind,' in both its particular and its universal aspects. (Chomsky 1968: 67)

(vi) [T]he construction of meanings is rule-governed, in the same way that the construction of the well-formed syntactic expressions of a language is rule-governed. (Cann 1993: 4)

5.* Section 1.5 addresses the question of what is in a grammar. The concepts listed below can all be said to influence in some way the form of a linguistic utterance. In view of the form-oriented function–form approach of FDG, which of these concepts would you consider to be part of grammar, and why?

gestures	pauses	intonation	semantic roles
emotion	background knowledge	word choice	stress
style/genre	speed of delivery	discourse situation	volume (e.g. whispering)
word order	tense	stammering	intention
irony			

Suggestions for further reading

For a comprehensive overview of the most important linguistic theories and models, students are referred to Heine and Narrog (2010), which also includes a very useful introduction. The question of why linguistic theory is useful is also addressed in Börjars (2006). A detailed comparison of three major functional theories (Systemic Functional Grammar, Role and Reference Grammar, and Functional Grammar) can be found in Butler (2003), the introductory chapter of which provides an excellent characterization of functionalism. Other useful discussions of functional (vs. formal) linguistics can be found in Croft (1995, 1999). Simon-Vandenbergen et al. (1997), Butler et al. (2007), and Hannay and Steen (2007) all present collections of papers applying different functional approaches to a range of linguistic issues; introductions to and applications of specific functional theories can be found in Halliday (1978, 1994, 1997; Systemic Functional Grammar), Dik (1997a, 1997b; Functional Grammar) and Van Valin and LaPolla (1997; Role and Reference Grammar). Finally, Butler and Gonzálvez-García (2005) is specifically devoted to the discussion of where to situate Functional Discourse Grammar in the functional-cognitive paradigm.

Students interested in the subject of linguistic categorization are referred to Taylor's highly informative and very accessible textbook (Taylor 2003); a collection of seminal papers on the subject can be found in Aarts et al. (2004). A detailed discussion of syntactic gradience is provided by Aarts (2007), while gradience within the English noun phrase is discussed in Keizer (2007a).

For students interested in grammaticalization and lexicalization, a good place to start would be Hopper and Traugott (1993) and Brinton and Traugott (2005). A very useful collection of papers on grammaticalization from different (theoretical) approaches can be found in Heine and Narrog (2011), which also includes a chapter on the grammaticalization of tense and aspect in Functional Discourse Grammar (Hengeveld 2011). Finally, the question of how to deal with grammaticalization and lexicalization processes in FDG is addressed in Keizer (2007b) and Pérez Quintero (2013) (on English), Olbertz (2007) (on Spanish), and Van de Velde (2009) (on Dutch).

2

The general architecture of FDG

2.1. Introduction   21   2.4. Summary   39

2.2. FDG in its wider context   23   Exercises   40

2.3. The Grammatical Component   28   Suggestions for further reading   42

In this chapter we will look at the overall organization of FDG, paying particular attention to those features that set it apart from other linguistic theories. We will start by looking at some of FDG's distinctive underlying principles, before discussing some of the specific features of the model:

- the four components, more specifically the interaction between the Grammatical Component (the FDG) and a Conceptual, a Contextual, and an Output Component;
- the primitives: frames and templates, lexemes and morphemes, operators;
- the four different levels of analysis: the Interpersonal Level, the Representational Level, the Morphosyntactic Level, and the Phonological Level.

A note of warning may be in place here. Since the aim of this chapter is to give an outline of the theory of FDG, the information provided will, of necessity, be rather abstract. In the chapters that follow, however, the concepts introduced rather sketchily here will gradually be fleshed out.

2.1. Introduction

In the previous chapter we saw that, as a 'structural-functional' theory of language, FDG has a number of general features in common with other functional approaches, including its predecessor FG (Dik 1997a, 1997b). If, however, we look at the more specific intentions and assumptions of FDG, and at the way these are reflected in the organization of the model, we find that FDG differs from these other approaches in a number of respects (Hengeveld and Mackenzie 2008: 1–12):

(i) FDG has a top-down organization, starting with the encoding of the Speaker's intention and then working its way down to articulation.

(ii) FDG takes the Discourse Act as its basic unit of analysis. As such, FDG can accommodate regular clauses, as well as units larger than the clause (e.g. sequences of sentences), and units smaller than the clause (incomplete utterances and interjections).

(iii) FDG analyses Discourse Acts in terms of independent pragmatic, semantic, morphosyntactic, and phonological modules, which interact to produce the appropriate linguistic forms. Although still primarily a semantically and pragmatically oriented theory of grammar, FDG thus aims at being comprehensive by dealing with all levels of grammatical organization.

(iv) FDG is envisaged as a Grammatical Component interacting systematically with a Conceptual, a Contextual, and an Output Component within an overall model of verbal communication. The Conceptual Component contains the prelinguistic conceptual information relevant for linguistic analysis and is regarded as the driving force behind the Grammatical Component. The Output Component turns the output of the Grammatical Component into acoustic, orthographic, or signed output. The Contextual Component contains non-linguistic information about the immediate discourse context that affects the form of a linguistic utterance.

A general outline of the model is given in Figure 2.1.

It is important to realize that it is only the Grammatical Component (the shaded area in Figure 2.1) that constitutes the FDG of a language, and that only those aspects of verbal interaction that are formally reflected in linguistic structure are considered to be part of the grammar (the Principle of Formal Encoding, see Section 1.5). At the same time, FDG acknowledges that most of these aspects can only be properly accounted for by taking into

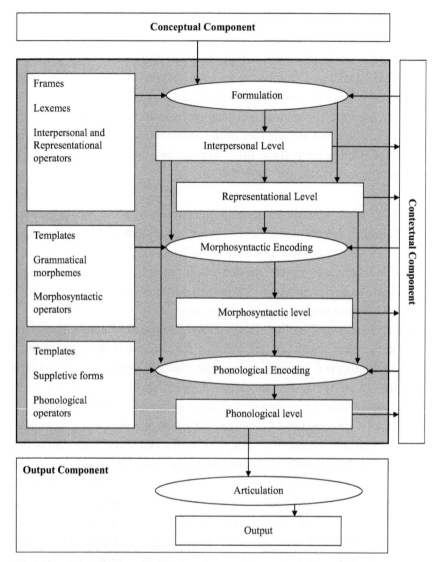

Figure 2.1 General layout of FDG
(Hengeveld and Mackenzie 2008: 13)

account the interaction between the grammatical component and the other three components.

In what follows we will first consider the four components that make up the entire model. We will begin by examining the way in which the Grammatical Component interacts with the Conceptual, Contextual, and Output Components. Subsequently, we will concentrate on FDG itself—that is, the Grammatical Component—and its internal organization.

2.2. FDG in its wider context

As can be seen from Figure 2.1, the Grammatical Component of a language does not function in isolation. Instead, it continually interacts with relevant conceptual and contextual information, and ultimately yields the physical product (the output) of this interaction. In this section, we will describe the non-grammatical components of the model in Figure 2.1 in terms of the nature of the information they contain and the way in which this information interacts with the grammar. The Grammatical Component itself will be the topic of Section 2.3.

2.2.1. The Conceptual Component

Every linguistic communication starts with a Speaker's communicative intention and its corresponding mental representation at the prelinguistic conceptual level. In FDG this mental representation of the Speaker's intention is located in the Conceptual Component. This component can therefore be seen as the driving force behind the Grammatical Component, triggering the operation of Formulation which converts the prelinguistic conceptual information into the linguistically relevant pragmatic and semantic representations allowed by the grammar of a language. Efficiency dictates that the Conceptual Component does not contain all conceptual information required for the production of a linguistic utterance, but only those cognitive aspects directly related to the communicative intention of the Speaker that trigger the use of a particular linguistic utterance.

Let us consider some examples to illustrate the kind of information that is contained in the Conceptual Component and the way this information may affect the form of a linguistic utterance. Say a Speaker of English wants to convey the news that a good friend is ill. He/she can simply do so by saying *Tom is ill*. Realizing, however, that this will be bad news for the Addressee, the Speaker may want to mitigate the statement, in which case he/she may say *I'm afraid that Tom is ill*. It will be clear that the Speaker is not really 'afraid' when he/she utters the statement: what he/she is trying to do is reduce the impact the news may have on the Addressee. Both these aspects—the conveying of the news itself and the act of mitigation—are seen as part of the communicative intention of the Speaker. Note that the same bit of news could also have been delivered in an entirely different way. The Speaker might, for instance, have used the sentence *I hear Tom is ill*. Here the Speaker conveys exactly the same information ('Tom is ill'), this time, however, indicating that he/she did not receive this news first-hand, possibly with the intention of inviting the Addressee to confirm the news and to provide further details. Since all these aspects are part of the Speaker's immediate communicative intention, they are represented in the Conceptual Component.

As pointed out, not all conceptual information forms part of the Conceptual Component. At any given moment in a discourse (or any other waking moment, for that matter), certain parts of a Speaker's or Addressee's knowledge are activated (in various degrees). Mention of the name *Tom*, for instance, may activate certain knowledge associated with Tom: what he looks like, what he does, where he lives, or what he said the last time we saw him. Uttering or hearing a simple statement like *Tom is ill* may also evoke all kinds of information related to the concept of illness: different kinds of illness, people who are or have been ill, possible consequences of being ill, etc. Although all this information is represented conceptually in the minds of Speaker and Addressee, only those parts that a Speaker intends to communicate (and to code linguistically) will enter the Conceptual Component.

The Conceptual Component also plays a role in the use of indirect speech acts (e.g. Searle 1969) or implicatures (in the sense of Grice 1975). One important guiding principle of FDG is that whether a particular phenomenon is to be dealt with in the Grammatical Component depends on whether its grammatical effect on the language is systematic, that is, subject to grammatical rules (as dictated by the Principle of Formal Encoding). This means that indirect speech acts and implicatures are not regarded as belonging to the Grammatical Component. After all, in both cases the intention of the Speaker is, by definition, not systematically coded in language; instead, the intended interpretation relies entirely on the Addressee's ability to infer the Speaker's intention within the given discourse context. Consider, for instance the following examples:

(1) It is hot in here.

(2) a. Yes, it is.
     b. Oh, I'm sorry, I'll open the window.
     c. In that case, I think I'll wait outside.

Sentence (1) can be interpreted in a number of ways. First of all, it can be regarded as a simple statement, intended to inform the Addressee of a certain fact. The Addressee, when he/she agrees, might react as in (2a). Sentence (1) may, however, also be intended as a request. When the Addressee recognizes it as such, a plausible reaction would be (2b). In other circumstances, the same sentence might also be intended as a warning, which may trigger the response in (2c). It is, however, only the intention to inform that is coded in the language: by choosing the form of a declarative sentence, Speakers normally express their intention to inform the Speaker of some fact. The two other (additional) intentions (request, warning) are not coded as such; the Speaker expects the Addressee to recognize his/her intention in the given discourse situation, but does not use any linguistic means to indicate this intention. Since FDG is concerned only with those aspects of communication that are explicitly and systematically coded in the language, indirect speech acts and other kinds of implicatures are not regarded as forming part of the grammar (i.e. the Grammatical Component). However, since even in the case of an implicature, the Speaker's intention (to express a warning or request) triggers a linguistic utterance (the declarative in (1)), this intention is regarded as being part of the Conceptual Component.

2.2.2. The Contextual Component

One of the basic principles of FDG is that language is first and foremost a means of communication. It is therefore not surprising that in its analysis of linguistic utterances, FDG takes the communicative context into consideration; at least those elements of the communicative context that have a systematic impact on the form of the linguistic utterance (see also Hengeveld and Mackenzie 2014: 205). These linguistically relevant aspects of the communicative context are part of the Contextual Component (see Figure 2.1), which can be described as capturing the interplay between grammatical organization and (long-term or short-term) memory. The Contextual Component contains various types of information; broadly speaking, a distinction can be made between situational information (about non-linguistic entities in the immediate discourse context) and textual information (about linguistic antecedents in the immediate discourse context). Let us consider both types of information in some more detail.

Situational information obviously plays a role when the form of a linguistic expression is licensed by the physical presence of an entity in the immediate situation. An example is the use of deictic expressions. Thus, a Speaker can only felicitously use a deictic pronoun when the entity (object, event) referred to can be assumed to be perceptible to the Addressee, as in *Look at **her**!* when a female human entity is visible to the Addressee. It will be clear that in such cases, the pronoun in question will be selected on the basis of contextual information concerning the gender and number of the referent, as well as its relative distance from the Speaker and/or Addressee (e.g. *he* vs. *she*; *it* vs. *they*, *this* vs. *that*). It will also be clear that this kind of contextual information is dynamic and will be updated when changes in the immediate surroundings take place, due to, for instance, the movement of the speech participants and/or other entities in the immediate situation.

Situational information also plays a role when it comes to locating events in time. Here too, the dynamic nature of the contextual information is crucial, as it allows speech participants to keep track of the passage of time. This kind of information obviously forms the basis of time deixis, which is relevant for the expression of tense (past, present, future). Consider the following simple dialogue:

(3)   A: Look! A deer!
      B: Where?
      A: There—it's hiding behind those bushes. Now it's gone. Did you see it?
      B: No, I'm afraid I missed it. But I'm sure we'll see another one.

During this brief conversation, tense shifts from the present (indicating that the event described—the deer hiding behind the bushes—coincides with the time of speaking) to the past (referring to the same event at a later moment in time), to the future (making a prediction about what will happen at some point after the moment of speaking). These different ways of coding the time of occurrence of the events described show that Speakers must keep track of the passage of time and, more specifically, of when events took place (in relation to the moment of speaking or other events).

Dynamic situational knowledge also plays an important role in the identification of entities. Thus, the presence of a uniquely identifiable entity in the immediate discourse context will lead the Speaker to use a definite noun phrase (e.g. *Can you pass me **the salt**?*). Note, however, that the use of a definite article can also be triggered by long-term information, as apparent from the fact that the definite article can be used in cases where the referent is uniquely identifiable on the basis of long-term information, but not present in the immediate situation (*Have you ever met* **the Queen**?).

The dynamic nature of the Contextual Component is also crucial when it comes to textual information, which forms the basis for the appropriate use of (definite and indefinite) **anaphoric** pronouns. Note in this respect the use of *it* and *one* in example (3), which can only be used appropriately if the textual information required for successful reference can be retrieved from the preceding discourse. This means that for a correct use (and interpretation) of such pronouns this (short-term) textual information must be continually kept up to date: with each new contribution to a discourse, new antecedents are added to the Contextual Component, while old ones may either be reactivated or gradually cease to be available. What also needs to be stressed is that potential antecedents are fed into the Contextual Component at each level of representation in the Grammatical Component (as indicated by the arrows in Figure 2.1). We will come back to this point when we discuss the four levels of analysis that make up the Grammatical Component (Section 2.3).

What is not included in the Contextual Component are such factors as style, genre, and register. This may come as a surprise, as it could be argued that in these cases the context does influence the form of a linguistic utterance. We all know that stylistically the language of academic texts differs considerably from that of an informal letter, even when they deal with the same topic: not only will we find different kinds of words (*to perform an experiment* vs. *to run a test*), but in addition there will be differences in the type and complexity of the grammatical constructions used (passive vs. active constructions, complete clauses vs. clause fragments etc.), as well as differences in intonation and punctuation, etc. The reason that these differences are not seen as grammatical markers of a particular style is that they are unsystematic and unpredictable. Thus, although in academic writing we typically find more passives than in any informal kind of writing, active sentences do occur in academic writing, while passives can also be found in informal texts. Moreover, the choice between an active and a passive sentence is not determined by stylistic factors only. It is for this reason that FDG does not consider these factors as grammatically relevant; therefore they are not included in the Contextual Component. (See Hengeveld and Mackenzie 2008: 10; 2014: 205.)

2.2.3. The Output Component

Once the operations of Formulation and Encoding have taken place, the work of the Grammatical Component is done: at this point, the output of the Grammatical Component is fed into the Output Component, where the operation of Articulation converts the grammatical information into acoustic, orthographic, or signed form (for spoken, written, and signed languages, respectively). The operation of Articulation takes place outside the grammar of a language. The outcome may be affected by contextual factors, both short-term: (a cold, for instance, may affect the acoustic form of the output) and long-term (e.g. pitch differences between individual Speakers due to differences in the length of the vocal folds). Being outside the control of the language user, these factors do not, however, serve a communicative function, and are therefore not regarded as forms of grammatical encoding.

2.3. The Grammatical Component

Since it is the Grammatical Component that makes up the FDG of a language, it is this component that will be the focus of interest in the rest of this book. In this chapter, we will begin by briefly describing the internal organization of this component, taking Figure 2.1 as our point of departure. Here we see that the Grammatical Component (the grey area) is made up of a number of interrelated parts: there are operations (represented by means of ovals), primitives (given in boxes), and levels of analysis (given in rectangles). This section will provide general characterizations of these different parts; more detailed discussions will follow in Chapters 3–6.

2.3.1. Operations

Operations are those parts of the model where the rules of a specific language are applied and linguistic utterances are gradually constructed. Operations can be compared to black boxes in the sense that we do not know exactly what takes place during these operations. What we do know is that they take a certain input and yield a certain output. As shown in Figure 2.1, the Grammatical Component contains two types of operation:

Formulation and **Encoding**. In what follows we will specify for each of these operations the kind of input it takes and the kind of output it produces.

In the top-down approach of FDG, the first operation is that of Formulation. This operation takes three types of input (see Figure 2.1):

- The first type of input comes from the Conceptual Component: the main task of the operation of Formulation is to translate the conceptual representations from this component into the appropriate language-specific pragmatic and semantic representations (Hengeveld and Mackenzie 2008: 13).
- In order to perform this task, the operation of Formulation draws on different types of primitives available in the language in question: frames, lexemes, and operators (for more details see Section 2.3.2).
- Meanwhile, information from the Contextual Component feeds into the operation of Formulation, making available those elements from the discourse setting (e.g. potential referents and their properties) that may influence the form of the output (Hengeveld and Mackenzie 2008: 14).

After the operation of Formulation has been completed, the operation of Encoding takes place. This operation consists of two stages: Morphosyntactic Encoding and Phonological Encoding. We will discuss these two stages together.

Each operation of Encoding has, again, three forms of input:

- First of all, the output of the operation of Formulation, that is, the pragmatic and semantic representations of a linguistic expression, feeds into the Morphosyntactic Encoder, which subsequently converts these representations into morphosyntactic ones. The output of Morphosyntactic Encoding, in turn, feeds into the Phonological Encoder, except in those cases where an utterance lacks morphosyntactic structure; in that case, the Phonological Encoder takes as its input the output of Formulation. The Phonological Encoder converts this information into phonological representations. These form the final output of the Grammatical Component, which subsequently form the input of the Output Component.
- The Encoder makes use of its own set of primitives: **templates**, **morphemes** (for the Morphological Encoder), **suppletive forms**, and phonological operators (for the Phonological Encoder).
- Both encoders receive information from the Contextual Component (for instance where the morphosyntactic or phonological form of an earlier expression, now stored in the Contextual Component as short-term information, may affect the formal properties of the utterance under construction).

It is important to realize that the rules applied in each of these operations are language specific. This means that FDG does not assume the existence of absolute language universals. This is one of the reasons for strictly separating the Conceptual Component and the Grammatical Component: Speakers of different languages may have the same communicative intention (the same prelinguistic conceptual representation), but this conceptual information will trigger different pragmatic and semantic configurations; these, in turn, will result in different morphosyntactic and phonological encodings. A good example is the coding of so-called **Prohibitives**, that is, expressions forbidding an Addressee to carry out a certain action; they are, in fact, the exact opposite of Imperatives. In some languages, like Tauya (MacDonald 1990), Prohibitives take a special form, whereas in other languages, such as English, they take the form of a negated **Imperative** (e.g. *Don't wait for me!*). This means that although the Speakers of these languages have the same intention (namely ordering someone not to do something), different linguistic configurations are used to convey this intention (Hengeveld and Mackenzie 2008: 12; for a more detailed discussion, see Section 3.5).

2.3.2. Primitives

As we have just seen, the different operations taking place during the construction of a linguistic utterance make use of different sets of primitives. Primitives can best be seen as the building blocks needed for the construction of an utterance: they are ready-for-use elements that together make up the long-term linguistic knowledge of the Speaker of a language (Hengeveld and Mackenzie 2008: 19). Primitives come in three kinds. First of all, there are structuring primitives (frames, templates), which define the possible combinations of elements at each level. During Formulation, Speakers make use of frames, specifying the possible combinations of pragmatic or semantic units. In Encoding we find templates: Morphosyntactic templates, which specify the order in which elements appear within a Clause or Phrase, and Phonological templates, which represent the possible intonation and stress patterns of a language.

The second set of primitives consists of the relevant linguistic elements at each level. In Formulation these take the form of lexemes, that is, all the meaningful elements that the Speakers of a language have at their disposal to provide the descriptive information needed for successful communication.

These lexemes are drawn from the lexicon and subsequently inserted into the selected frames. In Morphological Encoding, we find Grammatical Morphemes, that is, elements used to express grammatical (rather than lexical) information (e.g. auxiliaries, particles, and affixes), while Phonological Encoding provides us with suppletive forms (e.g. irregular forms of the plural or past tense).

The third set of primitives contains operators, which represent grammatical information at each of the levels. In Formulation, for instance, use is made of pragmatic operators (e.g. providing interpersonal grammatically expressed information, such as the identifiability of a referent) and semantic operators (indicating such 'real-world' grammatically expressed information as number or tense). In Phonological Encoding, phonological operators are used to represent the prosodic features of the various units (e.g. rising or falling tone).

2.3.3. Levels of representation

We have now come to what may be considered one of the most important features of the theory of FDG: the distinction, within the Grammatical Component, of four levels of analysis. Each of these levels will be described in detail in Chapters 3–6. In this section, we will concentrate on (i) the correspondences between the four levels in terms of their general structure and (ii) the kind of information represented at each of these levels.

2.3.3.1. General structure of the four levels

Each of the four levels of representation is hierarchically organized, consisting of several layers. Each of these layers is provided with its own variable, which is restricted by a **head**, and specified by one or more operators, representing grammatically expressed information about the layer as a whole. These layers, in turn, typically consist of different units, which may be supplied with a **function**, representing grammatically expressed information about the relation between this unit and other units within the same layer. At the Interpersonal and Representational Levels, each layer further contains a position for **modifiers**, which provide optional lexical information. The general structure of each layer can be represented as follows (Hengeveld and Mackenzie 2008: 14):

(4) $(\pi\ \alpha_1:\ [\text{head}]:\ \sigma)_\varphi$

      where α_1 = variable at the relevant layer

                π = one or more operators

                σ = one or more modifiers

                φ = the function of the linguistic unit

A simple instantiation of this schema at the Representational Level is given in example (5b), which provides the semantic representation of the phrase *that big dog* in the sentence in (5a):

(5)   a. *That big dog* chased our cat.

      b. $(\text{dis}\ x_1:\ \text{dog}:\ \text{big})_A$

          where x_1 = variable at the layer of the Individual

                  dis = operator indicating distance (*that*)

                  dog = lexical head of the layer

                  big = modifier of the head

                  A   = the semantic function Actor

Since FDG only represents information that is linguistically coded, not all layers need to be present in every act of verbal communication.

2.3.3.2. The Interpersonal Level

The Interpersonal Level (IL) deals with 'all the formal aspects of a linguistic unit that reflect its role in the interaction between the Speaker and the Addressee' (Hengeveld and Mackenzie 2008: 46). In keeping with the overall architecture of FDG, the units of discourse relevant at this level are organized hierarchically. Each layer is provided with its own variable, representing the type of entity evoked:

(6)

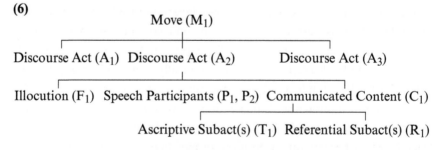

At the top of the hierarchy, we find the **Move** (M_1), which describes the entire segment of discourse relevant at this level. The Move consists of one or more (temporally ordered) **Discourse Acts** ($A_1, A_2 \ldots A_n$), which together form its (complex) head. Each Act in turn consists of an **Illocution** (F_1), the

Speech Participants (P_1 and P_2) and a **Communicated Content** (C_1). Finally, within the Communicated Content, one or more **Subacts of Reference** (R_1) and **Ascription** (T_1) are evoked by the Speaker.

In the previous section, we saw that the production of a linguistic utterance requires, first of all, the selection of the appropriate frame(s), defining the possible combinations of elements at each layer. A possible frame at the layer of the Communicated Content would be the following (the relevant frame is given in bold):[1]

(7) $(\Pi\ C_1: [(T_1)_{FOC}\ (R_1)_{TOP}]: \Sigma\ ^C)_\Phi$

     where Π = one or more operators

               Σ = one or more modifiers (at the layer of C)

               Φ = the function of the linguistic unit

Here the Communicated Content (C_1) consists of two subacts, each with a pragmatic function: a Subact of Ascription (T_1) which is assigned Focus function and a Subact of Reference (R_1), functioning as the Topic. This would be the frame selected for an utterance like *John is ill* in answer to a question like *What's wrong with John?*, that is, in those cases where *John* is the subject of discussion (($R_1)_{TOP}$) and his being ill forms the new information (($T_1)_{FOC}$).

The next step consists in selecting the modifiers (lexemes; Σ) and operators (grammatical elements; Π) needed to further specify the message. Again, these can be found at each of the layers. At the layer of the Move, for instance, modifiers may take the form of discourse-structuring devices, such as *to sum up, to keep things short*, etc.; at the layer of the Discourse Act, modifiers may express stylistic properties of the Act (e.g. *briefly, finally*); at the layer of the Illocution modifiers may function to modify the illocutionary manner (e.g. *honestly, frankly*), etc. Similarly, grammatically expressed information can be specified at each of the layers. At the layer of the Illocution, for instance, operators may be used to reinforce or mitigate the Illocution, while at the layer of the Speech Participants operators may be used to represent honorifics (expressions of politeness).

---

[1] The superscripts preceding the closing bracket (C in example (7)) are added here (and throughout the book) to enhance the readability of the representations by indicating the end of a complex layer. These superscripts are not part of the standard theory (Hengeveld and Mackenzie 2008), which uses closing variables instead; in the case of (7), this would yield $(\Pi\ C_1: [(T_1)_{FOC}\ (R_1)_{TOP}]: \Sigma\ (C_1))_\Phi$.

As pointed out by Hengeveld and Mackenzie (2008: 4–5), one of the reasons for distinguishing a separate Interpersonal Level is that anaphoric reference to units at this level is possible. In the following example, for instance, the expression *like that* refers back to the communicative strategy (as reflected in the use of an Imperative Illocution). This is taken as evidence that a level of interpersonal organization is relevant in the analysis of linguistic utterances.

(8)   A: Get out of here!
      B: Don't talk to me *like that*!

The Interpersonal Level will be discussed in more detail in Chapter 3.

2.3.3.3. The Representational Level

The Representational Level deals with the semantic aspects of a linguistic unit. The term 'semantics' is used in a very specific way in FDG, in that it is restricted to the ways in which language relates to (represents) the real or imagined world it describes. This means that at the Representational Level we find all the information about real or imagined entities that is required for a successful communication and that does not depend on the identity of or relation between the speech participants, that is, all the information needed to describe (or 'designate') those entities (or sets of entities) that play a role in the message that the Speaker wishes to convey. Thus, where units at the Interpersonal Level can be described as being 'evoked' and speaker-bound, representational units can be described as being 'designated' and non-speaker-bound (Hengeveld and Mackenzie 2008: 130).

At the Representational Level the utterance is filled in with semantic content, that is, with descriptions of entities as they occur in some non-linguistic world. Since these entities are of different types (or 'order'), the linguistic units at this level differ with respect to the ontological category they designate. At the highest level we find the **Propositional Content**, which can be assigned a truth value. The Propositional Content consists of one or more **Episodes**, that is, thematically coherent sets of **States-of-Affairs**. Each state-of-affairs is, in turn, characterized by a **Property** (i.e. a predicate), one or more **Individuals**, and, possibly, expressions designating a **Location** or a **Time**. The hierarchical structure of the Representational Level is given in (9) (cf. Hengeveld and Mackenzie 2008: 140, 142; more information about the different layers will be given in Chapter 4):[2]

(9)

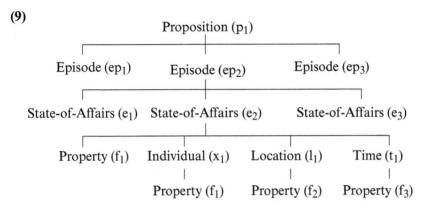

Like the Interpersonal Level, the Representational Level has access to three kinds of primitives: frames, lexemes, and operators. Again, the first step is the selection of the relevant frames. An example of such a frame can be found in (10) (given in bold print):

(10) $(\pi\ p_1: (\pi\ ep_1: (\pi\ e_1: [(f_1: \blacklozenge)\ (x_1)_A\ (x_2)_U]: \sigma^e): \sigma^{ep}): \sigma^P)_\phi$

where π =   one or more operators

σ =   one or more modifiers (at the layer of e, ep, and p, respectively)

$\blacklozenge$ =   lexical primitive functioning as the head

ϕ =   the function of the linguistic unit

This would be the frame used for an utterance like *That big dog chased our cat*, which designates an action (as a special kind of State-of-Affairs) involving a

---

[2] Hengeveld and Mackenzie (2008) distinguish a few more layers at the Representational Level, which, for practical reasons, will not be included here. Most importantly, they have added a layer between the State-of-Affairs and the Property, Individual, etc. This layer, called the Configurational Property (i.e. a Property consisting of more than one unit), thus functions as the head of the State-of-Affairs, and is in turn headed by a combination of a Property, one or more Individual(s), and, where relevant a Time and a Location. If we add the Configurational Property, the representation in (9) would look as follows:

(i) $(\pi\ p_1: (\pi\ ep_1: (\pi\ e_1: (f_1: [(f_2: \blacklozenge)\ (x_1)_A\ (x_2)_U]: \sigma^f): \sigma^e): \sigma^{ep}): \sigma^P)$

In addition, a number of minor categories have been added, in analogy with Time and Location: Manner, Reason, and Quantity. Although two of these (Manner and Reason) are relevant for English, they will not be discussed in this book.

verbal Property (f_1) (*chase*) describing the action in question and two Individuals (x_1) and (x_2), with the semantic functions of Actor (A) (*that big dog*) and Undergoer (U) (*our cat*).

Modifiers and operators are selected next. Each layer takes its own kind of modifier: modal adverbs like *probably* or *certainly*, for instance, apply at the layer of the Propositional Content, manner adverbs (*quickly*, *secretly*) at the layer of the Property, and narrative-organizing adverbs (*first*, *next*) at the layer of the Episode. Similarly, operators can be found at each layer: Number (singular/plural), for instance, is represented as an operator specifying Individuals, Aspect is expressed as an operator at the layer of either the State-of-Affairs or the Property, while Modality operators can be found at the layer of the Propositional Content or the State-of-Affairs.

It will be clear that the Representational Level is the level at which lexemes are selected. These lexemes typically function as heads of f-variables, describing the Properties assigned to the various entity types. Thus, the Lexical Properties 'red' and 'car' are typically assigned to Individuals, the Property 'recent' to a State-of-Affairs, and the Property 'undeniable' to a Propositional Content.

Finally, anaphoric reference to units of this level is possible (Hengeveld and Mackenzie 2008: 5), as shown in (11B), where *that* refers back to the situation in the external world (the State-of-Affairs) that is described within (11A).

(11) A: There are lots of traffic lights in this town.
B: I didn't notice *that*.

The Representational Level will be discussed in more detail in Chapter 4.

2.3.3.4. The Morphosyntactic Level

The Morphosyntactic Level accounts for all the linear properties of a linguistic unit, both with respect to the structure of sentences, clauses, and phrases and with respect to the internal structure of complex words.

The set of primitives used at this level includes, first of all, the templates on the basis of which the Morphosyntactic Level is structured. These templates specify the basic ordering patterns of a language at each of the relevant layers (sentence, clause, phrase, and word). Among the functions assigned at this level are, where relevant, the syntactic functions Subject and Object. Furthermore, it is at this level that Grammatical Morphemes (e.g. auxiliaries) and so-called secondary operators are introduced; the latter can be seen as 'placeholders' for bound morphemes expressing, for instance, past tense or plurality (the exact form of which depends on the stem with which they combine). The major units of analysis at the Morphological Level are **Linguistic Expressions, Clauses, Phrases**, and **Words**; a possible internal structure of a Linguistic expression is given in (12) (where X stands for the type of Phrase or Word—verbal, nominal, adjectival, etc.; Hengeveld and Mackenzie 2008: 291):

(12)

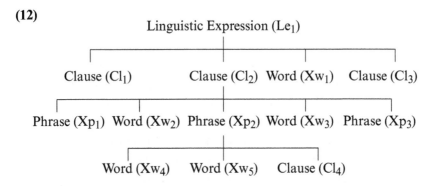

Like the other levels, the Morphological Level is hierarchically organized. The largest unit of analysis at this level is that of the Linguistic Expression, which typically contains one or more Clauses, but may also contain or consist of lower-level units (Phrases or Words). Clauses, in turn, may consist of one or more Phrases and Words. Phrases may contain one or more Words, as well as other Phrases or Clauses. The different possible combinations lead to a large number of templates, which can be reduced to a limited number of macrotemplates. A sentence like (13a), for instance, would satisfy the macro-template in (13b) (Hengeveld and Mackenzie 2008: 295):

(13) a. I saw him in London on Thursday with his mother in a car on several occasions.

b. $(Cl_1: [(Np_1) (Vp_1) (Np_2) (Adpp_{1+N})]^{Cl})$

Just like units at the Interpersonal and Representational Levels, units at the Morphosyntactic Level can be anaphorically referred to. In (14B), for instance, *that* does not refer to the individual referred to by the pronoun *me* in (14A) (i.e. Speaker A); instead it refers (metalinguistically) to the morphosyntactic form chosen (the non-subject form *me*).

(14) A: Jack and me got married very quietly yesterday afternoon (BNC-BYU, written, fiction prose)

B: Shouldn't *that* be 'Jack and I'?

The Morphological Level has a transitional character: it forms the outcome of an interplay between interpersonal and representational considerations and functions as input to the Phonological Level, where the various lexical and grammatical elements receive their phonological representation.

The Morphosyntactic Level will be discussed in more detail in Chapter 5.

2.3.3.5. The Phonological Level

The Phonological Level receives its input from the other three levels, though not necessarily from all three; distinctions made at the Interpersonal Level, for instance, may be directly expressed at the Phonological Level (as, for instance, in the case of Interjections, which are regarded as lacking semantic content and morphosyntactic structure). The first set of primitives relevant at the Phonological Level consists of phonological templates, which organize the phonological information coming in from higher levels into coherent blocks. The second set of primitives consists of suppletive forms (irregular forms of verbs, nouns, or adjectives) expressing grammatical information triggered by operators at the higher levels of organization (e.g. tense, number, or comparative). The third set of primitives that is relevant at this level consists of tertiary operators, which will have their ultimate effect (e.g. rising or falling intonation) in the Output Component.

Like the higher levels of representation, the Phonological Level is hierarchically organized: at the top we find the **Utterance** (u), which consists of one or more **Intonational Phrases** (IP), which in turn consist of one or more **Phonological Phrases** (PP). Each Phonological Phrase consists (typically) of one or more **Phonological Words** (PW), which can be further analysed in **Feet** (F) and **Syllables** (S). The most important layers of the Phonological Level can be represented as follows (cf. Hengeveld and Mackenzie 2008: 428 for greater detail):

(15)

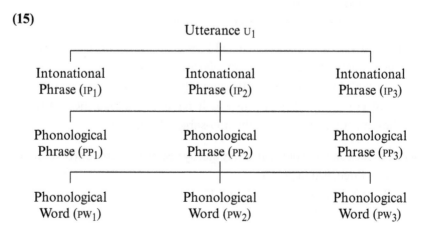

Utterance u_1

Intonational Phrase (IP_1)	Intonational Phrase (IP_2)	Intonational Phrase (IP_3)
Phonological Phrase (PP_1)	Phonological Phrase (PP_2)	Phonological Phrase (PP_3)
Phonological Word (PW_1)	Phonological Word (PW_2)	Phonological Word (PW_3)

An example of a simplified phonological representation of a declarative sentence can be found in (16), with the operator 'f' indicating a falling intonation at the layer of the Intonational Phrase.

(16)   a. The students complained.
       b. (f IP$_1$: [(PP$_1$: / ðə'stjudnts / ^{PP}) (PP$_2$: / kəm'pleɪnd / ^{PP})] ^{IP})

As at the other levels, at the Phonological Level, too, anaphoric reference can be made to the different units. An example is *that* in (17B), which has as its antecedent the phonological unit /tʃu'letasdekor'dero /:

(17)   A: Peter had /tʃu'letasdekor'dero/ yesterday.
       B: Shouldn't *that* be '/tʃu'letasdeθor'dero /'?

The Phonological Level will be discussed in more detail in Chapter 6.

Finally, it is important to realize that the top-down organization of the FDG model, as represented in Figure 2.1, does not mean that all elements are inserted at the highest level and are then passed on to the next levels. Instead, as indicated in this section, constructions are gradually filled in, as at each of the subsequent levels primitives belonging to that level are inserted. Thus, in a sentence like *Peter ate all the cookies yesterday*, the proper name *Peter*, as a referential unit without descriptive contents, is inserted at the Interpersonal Level, the lexemes *cookie* and *yesterday* are inserted at the Representational Level, the quantifier *all* (expressing a representational operator) and the definite article *the* (expressing an interpersonal operator) are inserted at the Morphosyntactic Level, while the suppletive form *ate*, as well as the plural allophone *-s* in *cookies* only appear at the Phonological Level. Each of these phenomena, and many more, will be discussed in detail in the following four chapters. In working your way through these chapters, it is, however, important to keep the overall organization of the model, as outlined in this section, in mind.

2.4. Summary

This chapter has provided a description of the most important distinctive features of the theory of FDG and of the overall organization of the model. The main points can be summarized as follows:

- FDG differs from other functional theories in that it has a top-down approach taking the Discourse Act as the basic unit of analysis. Furthermore, FDG analyses linguistic utterances in terms of four different levels (a pragmatic, a semantic, a morphosyntactic, and a phonological level). These levels make up the Grammatical Component (i.e. the FDG of a language), which interacts with a Conceptual, a Contextual, and an Output Component.
- In the Grammatical Component, two major operations take place. First of all, there is the operation of Formulation, which turns conceptual information into pragmatic and semantic representations. These representations contain all the linguistically relevant elements selected by the Speaker to convey the contents of the intended message. These representations form the input to the operation of Encoding, which turns them into morphosyntactic and phonological representations. Together these representations contain all the formal elements needed to trigger the correct output.
- Each of the four levels that make up the Grammatical Component consists of a number of hierarchically organized layers, representing the linguistic units relevant at each level. Each layer is furnished with a specific variable and draws for its construction on a specific set of primitives.
- Although the model as a whole has universal validity, the primitives available at each level, and the representations resulting from the operations of Formulation and Encoding, are language specific. Each language can therefore be said to have its own FDG.

Exercises

1. The Interpersonal Level is described as a strategic level, representing the interpersonal aspects of the Speaker's communicative intention. Try to describe, in your own words, the communicative intention of the italicized elements in the following examples and explain why these elements could be argued to have an interpersonal function.

(i)   a. I thought if people would feel sorry for me, then I wouldn't be able to cope with this thing, *like*. (BYU-BNC, written, academic)
   b. But with a *sort of* lovely *sort of* shortbready *kind of* taste to it. (ICE-GB, spoken, direct conversation)
   c. His life was a series of secret missions, full of risks and rewards. *Or so he said*. (COCA, spoken, NBC)
   d. He is also a disturbed person, and *frankly*, you don't want to agitate him. (COCA, spoken, CBS)

e. *Perhaps* you would get in touch with us on or after 12 September about undertaking the investigations. (ICE-GB, written, business letters)

f. I wanted to make three points *really*. (BNC, spoken, interview)

2. Go back to the list in Exercise 5, Chapter 1. Read it again and try to assign the different concepts mentioned to the Conceptual Component, Contextual Component, Output Component, or the Grammatical Component. Also think of arguments to justify your classification.

3. During the operation of Formulation, prelinguistic conceptual information (from the Conceptual Component) is converted into pragmatic and semantic representations using the linguistic means available in a particular language (i.e. become part of the Grammatical Component). For each of the following sentences:

a. determine the Speaker's intention;
b. bearing in mind the Principle of Formal Encoding, decide whether this intention is represented in the grammar.

   (i)   Do you have the time?
   (ii) Have a nice weekend!
   (iii) Have a chair.

4. In this chapter, it has been shown that anaphoric pronouns can refer to units at different levels of representation (see examples (8), (11), (14), and (17)). In the following examples, the pronoun *that* is used to refer to different types of entity. Try to establish to which level of representation (interpersonal, representational, morphosyntactic, or phonological) the entity referred to belongs.

(i)   a. *That* was wrong. It's supposed to be stressed on the first syllable if it's a noun.
   b. I've never heard it said like *that*, almost Scottish.
   c. "*That* was really delicious," said Melissa, laying down her knife and fork. (BYU-BNC, written, fiction)
   d. Is *that* how they taught you to start a presentation?
   e. Is *that* really true?
   f. *That's* not allowed here. Go outside.
   g. *That* is only one of the ways to talk about past events in Russian.
   h. Is *that* a dangling participle?
   i. Is *that* how you address your mother?!
   j. *That's* wrong. The "told" is supposed to come before the "him".
   k. A: I've lived here for 16 years. B: *That's* a long time.

5*.

a. In Section 2.2.2, it was argued that, although style plays a role in the choice between an active and a passive sentence, it is not the only factor involved. Collect a sample of 50 passive sentences and identify other possible factors that may favour the use of a passive sentence.

b. Decide which of the factors you have identified should be represented in the grammar.

Suggestions for further reading

Since everything mentioned in this chapter will be discussed in more detail in the chapters to follow, the suggestions for further reading will at this stage be restricted to publications providing brief overviews of (parts) of the theory of FDG. For general outlines of the theory as a whole, students are referred to Hengeveld and Mackenzie (2010) and Mackenzie and Olbertz (2013). An introduction to the Interpersonal Level can be found in Keizer and Van Staden (2009); an overview of the Morphosyntactic Level is provided in García Velasco and Wanders (2012). A general discussion of the role of context in FDG can be found in Alturo et al. (2014b).

3

The Interpersonal Level

3.1. Introduction	44	3.7. Communicated Content	72
3.2. The organization of the Interpersonal Level	45	3.8. Ascriptive Subacts	83
		3.9. Referential Subacts	90
3.3. The Move	48	3.10. Summary	96
3.4. The Discourse Act	52	Exercises	97
3.5. The Illocution	60	Suggestions for further reading	101
3.6. The Speech Participants	68		

The present chapter will be devoted to the first (highest) of the four levels of representation that make up the Grammatical Component of a language, the Interpersonal Level. After a brief general characterization of the Interpersonal Level, we will turn to the various hierarchically organized units (layers) to be found at this level. Each of these layers will be described in terms of the kind of unit (or linguistic act) it represents and the primitives that are available for its formation (i.e. lexemes, frames, and operators). Here, as in the chapters to follow, the focus will be on English; in other words, what will be presented in these chapters is an FDG of English. Every now and then examples from other languages will be used to illustrate important distinctions which are not formally expressed in English, as well as alternative forms of expression of a particular notion. Apart from making the description of the model more complete, this approach serves the purpose of illustrating (and emphasizing) FDG's strong typological orientation.

3.1. Introduction

The Interpersonal Level is meant to capture all the linguistically coded aspects of an utterance that relate to the interaction between a Speaker and an Addressee. What is represented is not the contents of the message but the sequence of actions performed by the Speaker in building up a linguistic utterance. It is, in other words, a strategic level, representing the steps taken by the Speaker to realize his/her communicative intention.

   As pointed out in the previous chapter, the communicative intention itself is not part of the grammar but of the Conceptual Component. It is this component which activates the Grammatical Component, which in turn transforms this intention into one or more linguistic utterances. In line with the functional, top-down orientation of the model, the first steps taken by the Speaker in this process concern the rhetorical and pragmatic aspects of the interaction. Rhetorical considerations, for instance, play a role in the way utterances (Discourse Acts) are ordered, as well as with the way in which the relations between different Discourse Acts are expressed. A sentence like *My brother, he lives in London*, for instance, can be seen as consisting of two Discourse Acts, the first of which (*my brother*) sets the scene for the second (*he lives in London*). The relation between these two Discourse Acts is captured by the assignment of a **rhetorical function** to the first (dependent) Discourse Act. Pragmatic considerations influence the choices made by a Speaker to ensure that a linguistic utterance has the intended effect on the Addressee's current state of mind. They serve to indicate, for instance, whether certain information is presented as salient (as opposed to given) or as identifiable (vs. unidentifiable), or whether a linguistic unit is presented as an instruction to the Addressee to add infor-mation to his/her knowledge base (i.e. as a statement) or to carry out some kind of action (i.e. as a command).

   From these few examples it will be clear that these strategic actions pertain to different parts (different layers) of a linguistic utterance, that they serve a wide range of functions, and that they may be expressed in many ways. The topics and constructions to be dealt with in this chapter are therefore highly diverse and will include the analysis and representation of the basic illocutions in English, irony, politeness strategies, reported speech, information packaging, identifiability and specificity, and approximation strategies.

In the following section we will look at the overall organization of the Interpersonal Level. The remainder of the chapter will then deal with the various linguistic units (layers) that make up the Interpersonal Level and the linguistic choices made at each of these layers.

3.2. The organization of the Interpersonal Level

The Interpersonal Level consists of the following eight layers, each of which represents a particular linguistic unit (or action), symbolized by a variable:

- Move (M)
- Discourse Act (A)
- Illocution (F)
- Speaker (P_S)
- Addressee (P_A)
- Communicated Content (C)
- Ascriptive Subact (T)
- Referential Subact (R)

Although 'complete' utterances (e.g. full clauses) typically require the presence and specification of all eight layers, there are many instances where one or more layers are not present in the interpersonal representation of an utterance. After all, Discourse Acts need not be realized by complete clauses: they may consist of a single word or phrase. In that case, only those layers will be present that are needed to trigger the word or phrase in question. Thus, as we will see below, the Addressee slot need not always be present in the representation of a Discourse Act. The same is true for the Communicated Content, as well as for the Subacts of Ascription and Reference. This is one of the ways in which the model attains cognitive economy: representations contain only those elements that are linguistically coded or which somehow affect the form of the linguistic utterance.

Each layer has a similar kind of internal structure. The only obligatory element at each level is the variable. In most cases, however, other elements are present:

1. a head
2. operators (Π)
3. modifiers (Σ)
4. functions (Φ)

This can best be illustrated by means of a simple example. Consider the following short exchange:

(1)   A. Did you buy anything?
       B. Yes, *a really expensive tie*.

Let us concentrate on the phrase *a really expensive tie*. As we will see later, this phrase will be analysed at the Interpersonal Level as a Referential Subact (R_1), that is, it represents the Speaker's attempt to evoke a referent. This Referential Subact has a complex head consisting of two Ascriptive Subacts, ultimately expressed as *expensive* and *tie*. One of the Subacts of Ascription, *expensive*, contains a modifier: *really*. Unlike most modifiers, this modifier is analysed at the Interpersonal Level because it is regarded as providing pragmatic information (emphatic commitment on the part of the Speaker) rather than descriptive information (see Hengeveld and Mackenzie 2008: 111). Furthermore, the Speaker presents the evoked referent as unidentifiable for the Addressee. This is captured by the operator [–identifiable], which triggers the use of the indefinite article. Finally, since the information provided in this phrase is assumed to be new to the Addressee, filling a gap in her knowledge base, it will be analysed as salient information. As such it will be provided with the **pragmatic function** of Focus. This simple phrase thus contains all the possible ingredients of a layer at the Interpersonal Level: a head, a modifier, an operator, and a function. The exact interpersonal representation of this phrase will be given in Section 3.8.3.

> The element *really* in (1) is described as having an interpersonal function, indicating the Speaker's attitude towards the ascribed property (*expensive*). Now replace *really* by *very*; how would you characterize the difference between the two modifiers? (Note that the two modifiers can also co-occur: *a really very expensive tie*.)

In the previous chapter we saw that each of the four levels of representation making up the Grammatical Component is organized hierarchically. A simplified representation of the internal structure of the Interpersonal Level was given in Section 2.3.3.2. There we saw that the highest layer, the Move, consists of one or more Discourse Acts (A_{1-N}). Discourse Acts consist of an Illocution (F_1), the two Speech Participants (P_1, P_2) and a Communicated Content (C_1). The Communicated Content, in turn, consists of one or more Ascriptive or Referential Subacts (T_{1-N}, R_{1-N}). A more sophisticated representation of the overall organization of the Interpersonal Level is given in (2) (adapted from Hengeveld and Mackenzie 2008: 49; note that, in accordance with the convention, capitals are used to represent variables at this level):

(2) (Π M_1: [   ]: Σ ^{M}) Move

         (Π A_{1-N}: [   ]: Σ ^{A})   Discourse Act

              (Π F_1: ILL: Σ ^{F})   Illocution

              (Π P_1: [...]: Σ ^{P1})   Speaker

              (Π P_1: [...]: Σ ^{P2})   Addressee

              (Π C_1: [   ]: Σ ^{C})   Communicated Content

                  (Π T_{1-N} [...]: Σ ^{T})   Ascriptive Subact

                  (Π R_{1-N} [...]: Σ ^{R})   Referential Subact

In (2) we find the eight different layers and the hierarchical relations between them. Each layer has a head (given between square brackets) as well as slots for operators (Π) and modifiers (Σ). Operators always immediately precede the variable of the layer at which they apply; modifiers follow the head of the layer. When discussing specific examples, representations will typically be given in a linear form; in that case the (simplified) general schema for the Move will look as follows:

(3) (M_1: (A_1: [(F_1: ILL) (P_1)$_S$ (P_2)$_A$ (C_1: [...(T_1) (R_1)...] ^{C})] ^{A}) ^{M})

The rest of this chapter will be devoted to a detailed description of each of the layers represented in (2). We will look in turn at the kind of linguistic action these layers represent and the kind of primitives (lexemes, frames, operators) relevant for each of them. Examples will be used to illustrate all aspects of analysis and representations will be provided for each of the layers involved. In keeping with the top-down approach of the model, we will start our discussion with the highest layer (i.e. the Move) and work our way down to the lowest layers (the Referential and Ascriptive Subacts).

3.3. The Move

3.3.1. General characterization

In FDG the Move is regarded as 'the largest unit of interaction relevant to grammatical analysis' (Hengeveld and Mackenzie 2008: 50). Within a communicative situation, it functions as 'an autonomous contribution to an ongoing interaction' (Hengeveld and Mackenzie 2008: 50), a description based on Kroon's (1995: 66) definition of the Move as 'a minimal free unit of discourse'. An important characteristic of Moves is that they are used by a Speaker to start an interaction, that is, to provoke some reaction from the Addressee, or that they themselves form such a reaction (e.g. an answer to a question, an indication of agreement to some statement, etc.).

The clearest examples of Moves and the reactions they provoke (which themselves constitute Moves) can be found in conversation, where a Move typically corresponds with a Speaker's turn. This is what we find in example (4):

(4)   A: Where's the first aid kit?
       B: It's in the top drawer on the left.

That Moves need not always correspond to a complete turn is clear from the following example, where B's turn consists of two separate Moves:

(5)   A: Where's the first aid kit?
       B: It's in the top drawer on the left. Why?
       A: I just cut my finger.

In spoken language Moves are typically coded intonationally: information from the Interpersonal Level is in this case directly fed into the Phonological Level. In conversation, Speakers tend to indicate the end of a Move by a falling intonation; a rising tone is typically used to indicate that the Move has not yet ended. An example is (6), where B gives a number of instructions, which form part of one, complex Move:

(6)   A: Can you tell me the way to Covent Garden?   Move A1
B: Sure, you follow this road for about 300 yards,   ⌣   Move B1
    then you turn left,   ⌣
    then you take the second or third street on your right ⌣
    (to his dog) Sh, quiet—sit   ⌐   Move B2
    then you walk for about 100 yards   ⌣   Move B1
    and you'll find Covent Garden at the end.   ⌐
A: Thank you!   ⌐   Move A2

Note that B's first complex Move (Move B1) is interrupted by a short second Move (Move B2), after which Move B1 continues.

In written language Moves may be more difficult to recognize. On the whole, however, it may be assumed that the start of a new paragraph coincides with the start of a new Move. Here, too, however, Moves may be interrupted by other Moves (elaborations, digressions, etc.). Often such interrupting Moves are given in parentheses, or indicated lexically by such phrases as *by the way*; or, indeed, by both, as in the following passage (see also Sections 3.3.3 and 3.3.4):

(7)   So if you know that the owners of a site don't want you linking inside, and you do it anyway just so people can get around their rules, then I think that if their rules are upheld as valid (unknown) then you could be held liable for contributory infringement. You aren't doing any copying, but you are taking actions solely to cause other people to make allegedly illicit copies for themselves. *(This, by the way, is part of what Napster was sued for.)* Generally this 'deep linking' would need to be costing them money to make a case out of it. (Internet)

> Can you think of other expressions that can be used to indicate the beginning or end of a Move in English?

3.3.2. The head

The head of a Move consists of one or more Discourse Acts. Consider once again example (5):

(5)   A: Where's the first aid kit?
B: It's in the top drawer on the left. Why?
A: I just cut my finger.

Here each Move (four in all) consists of one Discourse Act only. In example (8), on the other hand, there is reason to assume that we are dealing with one Move consisting of two Discourse Acts (Hengeveld and Mackenzie 2008: 53–4):

(8)   Watch out, because there will be trick questions in the exam.

The Speaker's intention here is to warn the Addressee. In order to do this he uses two Discourse Acts, each with its own intonation contour and its own Illocution (Imperative and Declarative, respectively).

3.3.3. Modifiers

Modifiers at the layer of the Move provide additional (optional) information about the role of the Move in the ongoing discourse (Hengeveld and Mackenzie 2008: 58–9). Examples are such expressions as *to cut a long story short*, *to conclude*, or *to sum up*. An attested example is given in (9), where the modifier *to sum up* clearly has scope over a number of Discourse Acts:

(9)   *To sum up*, in 1922 the Soviet government found itself in a situation similar to that of the late Tsarist regime, which in its final years had grasped the connection between literacy and modernization and between formal schoolwork and social control. Neither political system could rely with confidence on those to whom it entrusted the task of educating the peasants. (BYU-BNC, written, academic)

A highly simplified representation of this Move is given in (10), where *to sum up* takes the position of the Move Modifier (Σ):

(10) $(M_1: [(A_1) (A_2) (A_3)]: \textbf{to-sum-up}^M)$

Although we seem to be dealing with relatively fixed phrases, we still regard them as lexical expressions, as they can be expanded and modified, as illustrated in (11):

(11)   a. So, *to sum up the main points so far*: the scriptible as a value and the commentary as a form of reading both imply an approach which is largely incompatible with the chief principles of classical structuralism ... (BYU-BNC)
        b. *To sum up briefly*, I hope I have shown that Edward Albee tailors his dramatic language to the specific play. (Internet)

Modifiers of the Move can also serve to indicate a digression from or return to the main storyline, that is, as a kind of 'push' and 'pop' markers (Polanyi and Scha 1983). Some examples of the latter are given in (12):

(12) a. But ... But inside the great doors of the colleges there is often a small notice. It reads: 'This college is closed to visitors'. And indeed it is. These beautiful buildings, along with a whole realm of cultivated human intellect, are closed to the vast majority of humankind. And this is not because humanity isn't up to it. The only belief I'll never recant is that every single undamaged baby is born with fabulous, infinite intellectual potential. And that, of all the terrible wastage of resources in the world, it is the wasting of that intellectual potential that is the worst. *Anyway, to come back to Oxford:* ... (BYU-BNC, written, non-academic)

b. And of course another thing and and my Uncle Jonathan was a very great liberal and a great believer in free trade, but I think his faith in free trade started to take a a bashing because he was inundated by French and Belgian sl er er not slate er Tile. Tile. Mm. Was coming i Yes. in other words, there were very n very little new building Mm. going on with with with the specifications of of of of slates. I remember for example having to to to send reams of letters to architects Mm. and I found that you do not address an architect as Mr Jones, it must be Edward T Jones Esquire. Yeah. And er because they were professional men you see. Yeah. Yeah. Yeah. *To come back to* Jonathan for a moment, you say he was a great liberal, he was an admirer of Lloyd George? (BYU-BNC, spoken, interview)

3.3.4. Operators

Operators at the layer of the Move fulfil the same functions as modifiers but are grammatical in nature. Thus, unlike modifiers, they are no longer modifiable and do not allow for expansion. Examples of expressions triggered by operators are *in-sum* or *in-conclusion*:

(13) *In sum*, the domain specific dictionaries are less reliable, lack sufficient coverage and are based on optimistic assumptions about domain identification. (BYU-BNC, written, academic)

Likewise, a discourse marker like *anyway* can be used to indicate a return to the main topic of discussion (example (14a), see also example (12a)), while the discourse marker *well now* can be used to indicate a change in direction (example (14b)):

(14)   a. I know this is a true story, because when my Aunt Peg was a little girl she used to live next door to Mrs Sugar, who was a witch. Mrs Sugar used to curl her hair with rags and take snuff, and every Saturday she had a bet on the horses. Everybody in the street knew she was a witch. She used to give you silverweed for freckles and camomile for bellyache. *Anyway*, Mrs Sugar died, and she was buried in the cemetery, and had an angel on her grave. Soon after a story started going round that Mrs Sugar was still taking her usual walk out on Saturday evenings. I don't know how the story got started. (BYU-BNC, spoken)

   b. Morning Mrs. Good morning Doctor. *Well now*, what can I do for you today? (BYU-BNC, spoken)

Each of these discourse markers will be represented by means of an operator, the exact form of which will depend on the specific function of the discourse marker. Example (14a), for instance, could be given the (highly simplified) representation in (15), where the 'pop' operator triggers the discourse marker *anyway*:

(15)   (**pop** M_1: [(A_1) (A_2) (A_3)] ^{M})

> Can you think of other elements or expressions that can serve as 'push' and 'pop' markers in English?

3.4. The Discourse Act

3.4.1. General characterization

FDG adopts Kroon's definition of Discourse Acts as 'the smallest identifiable units of communicative behaviour. In contrast to the higher order units called Moves, they do not necessarily further the communication in terms of approaching a conversational goal' (Kroon 1995: 65). Like Moves, Discourse Acts do not have a specific formal (morphosyntactic) equivalent. The default correlation is with the clause, but Discourse Acts may consist of less than a clause (e.g. a single phrase, as in example (1)) or more than a clause (see Section 3.4.3).

As mentioned in the previous section, one Discourse Act can be a complete Move. In that case, the distinction between Move and Discourse Acts is not always easy to make. There are, however, some clues that may help to tell the difference between them. Consider the following short dialogue:

(16)   A: What happened at Wimbledon yesterday? $(M_1: (A_1))$
      B: Murray won. And Federer lost. $(M_1: [(A_1) (A_2)]^M)$

Moves either provoke or constitute a reaction from the Addressee; a clear example can be found in (16A), which elicits an answer from B. Discourse Acts do not do this: they may provoke a backchannel from the Addressee, but these are merely intended to encourage the Speaker to continue, and do not 'further the communication in terms of approaching a conversational goal'. Thus, in (16B), no answer is expected from A after the first Discourse Act (*Murray won*), although a cooperative Addressee may show interest by uttering an expression like *oh* or *mm*. It is only after the second Discourse Act (*And Federer lost*) that the Addressee is invited to respond.

Secondly, Moves and Discourse Acts have different phonological features. As we will see in Chapter 6, Moves by default correspond to the largest grammatically relevant phonological unit, the Utterance; these Utterances are characterized by a specific overall intonation pattern, as well as by the fact that they are separated from each other by relatively long pauses. Discourse Acts, on the other hand, correspond to a smaller phonological unit, the Intonational Phrase, which is characterized, among other things, by a specific pitch movement, which correlates to the Illocution. In (16B), for instance, both Discourse Acts have the falling intonation associated with the Declarative Illocution. This falling tone, however, is stronger in the second Discourse Act, which, together with the presence of a pause, indicates the end of the Move (see Chapter 6 for more details).

If a Move contains more than one Discourse Act, the relation between these Acts can be either one of **equipollence**, in which case both Acts have the same communicative status, or one of **dependence**, in which case one Act depends on, or is subsidiary to, the other (Hengeveld and Mackenzie 2008: 53). An example of two equipollent Discourse Acts is given in (16B), where the two Discourse Acts are of equal communicative importance, as indicated by the fact that they both have their own intonation contour (corresponding to a Declarative Illocution) and that both could form a complete Move by themselves.

In example (8) above (repeated below as (17)), on the other hand, the relation between the two Discourse Acts is one of dependence. Here the first

Discourse Act is communicatively more important, expressing the Speaker's main intention; therefore, this Discourse Act forms the Nucleus. The second Discourse Act serves the subsidiary communicative function of indicating the Speaker's motivation for uttering the first Discourse Act. In the case of dependence, the subsidiary Discourse Act will be assigned a rhetorical function (in this case **Motivation**) expressing its relation to the Nucleus.

(17)   Watch out, because there will be trick questions in the exam.

The difference between the two examples can be represented as follows:

(18)   a. Equipollence:
           $(M_1: [(A_1: - \text{Murray won} - ^A) (A_2: - \text{Federer lost} - ^A)] ^M)$
       b. Dependence:
           $(M_1: [(A_1: - \text{Watch out} - ^A) (A_2: - \text{there will be trick questions in}$
           $\text{the exam} - ^A)_{\text{Motiv}}] ^M)$

The order in which the Discourse Acts are given in these representations reflects the order in which they appear in the discourse. This is particularly important in the case of (18b), where the order in which the two Discourse Acts appear determines the form of the conjunction. This is illustrated in (19a), where we find the same two Discourse Acts, with the same relation between them, but in the reverse order. As we see, use of *because* is now impossible; instead the conjunction *so* has to be used. In other words, whereas *because* introduces the dependent Discourse Act, *so* is used to introduce the nuclear Discourse Act (Hengeveld and Mackenzie 2008: 54).

(19)   a. $M_1: [(A_1: - \text{there will be trick questions in the exam} - ^A)_{\text{Motiv}}$
           $(A_2: - \text{Watch out} - ^A)] ^M)$
       b. *Because there will be trick questions in the exam, watch out.
       b'. There will be trick questions in the exam, so watch out.

It is important to realize that the rhetorical function of Motivation is different from the semantic function of Cause. Motivation is an interpersonal concept: it is a communicative strategy on the part of the Speaker, intended to indicate the relation between two linguistic actions. The semantic function Cause, on the other hand, reflects the relation between two (extra-linguistic, real-world) events. In example (20), for instance, the Speaker uses the subordinator *because* to indicate that it was the presence of trick questions in the exam that caused John to warn the Speaker; it does not indicate the Speaker's motivation for providing this information. That the element *because* fulfils a different function in this sentence becomes clear from the fact that here it can appear at the beginning of a sentence. The sentences in (20a) and (20b) will be analysed as a single Discourse Act; the causal relation will be represented at the Representational Level (Chapter 4, Section 4.5.6).

(20) a. John warned me because there were trick questions in the exam.
      b. Because there were trick questions in the exam, John warned me.

Apart from Motivation, we can distinguish a number of other rhetorical functions, including **Orientation, Correction, Concession,** and **Aside**. Discourse Acts with the rhetorical function of Orientation serve to prepare the Addressee for the (nuclear) Discourse Act that follows by drawing attention to part of the following Discourse Act; an example is given in (21a). Subsidiary Discourse Acts of this kind can also follow the Nucleus, as in (21b). In that case, their function is not to orient the Addressee towards (part of) the following Discourse Act, but to clarify (part of) the preceding Discourse Act.

(21) a. It was because the Communist Party fed me, that my learning stood me in good stead and I know at least this much and I live like this. But *my sister*, she has forgotten everything and it's all just wasted. (BYU-BNC, written, non-academic)
      b. In that same first year of the war, Constanza met Simon, *my father* (BYU-BNC, written, fiction)

That the dependent expressions (*my sister, my father*) do indeed constitute Discourse Acts is clear from the fact that they form separate intonation units. Furthermore, as shown in the examples in (22), they can have their own Illocution: in (22a) the subsidiary act is an Interrogative, while the Nucleus is a Declarative; in (22b), the subsidiary is a Declarative and the Nucleus an Imperative. Since every Discourse Act can have only one Illocution, we must be dealing with two different Discourse Acts (see also Section 3.5).

(22) a. My sister? She had forgotten all about it.
      b. Ask Simon, my father.

When the relation between two Discourse Acts is one of Concession, the Speaker uses the subsidiary act to admit that he/she is aware of the fact that the content of the preceding Discourse Act may not have been expected. It is for this reason that subsidiary Acts of Concession often (but not necessarily) contain such phrases as *I must admit that* or *I concede that*. That these utterances are indeed separate Discourse Acts is confirmed by the fact that they are often added as a separate unit, as a kind of afterthought. Some examples are given in (23):

(23)   a.   What's done is done. And it was done for the best, *although I must admit it didn't turn out like that*. (BYU-BNC, written, fiction)
       b.   We come here most days. *Although I must admit that to begin with I was a bit twitchy about taking the kids to a park*—even here in London. (BYU-BNC, written, fiction)

As in the case of Motivation, the order of the Acts is important. If we are indeed dealing with a subsidiary concessive Discourse Act, it can only follow the Nucleus. What the Speaker communicates in that case is that he/she expresses the nuclear Act even though he/she knows that its content may come as a surprise to the Addressee. Note that this is different from the use of the concessive clauses in (24), where the Speaker communicates that a certain proposition is true, despite indications to the contrary. In that case, the concessive clause may precede the main clause, while adding a phrase like *I must admit* is not possible. The relation between the two clauses will not be represented at the Interpersonal Level but at the Representational Level (Hengeveld and Mackenzie 2008: 55):

(24)   a.   Although it didn't turn out very well, it was done for the best.
       b.   *Although I must admit it didn't turn out very well, it was done for the best.

Finally, there is the rhetorical function of Aside, which is assigned to dependent Discourse Acts providing background information about one of the entities evoked within the Nuclear Discourse Act. Asides are typically expressed as non-restrictive relative clauses or appositive elements (Hengeveld and Mackenzie 2008: 58, see also Hannay and Keizer 2005); examples are given in (25a) and (25b), respectively:

(25)   a.   The couple, *who dumped the car and fled*, were being hunted last night. (BYU-BNC, written, newspaper)
       b.   Edinburgh, *the capital of Scotland*, is one of Europe's most handsome cities. (BYU-BNC, written, miscellaneous)

Note that once again, the non-restrictive expressions have their own intonation contour. In addition, they have their own Illocution, as shown in (26), where the main clause is Interrogative, while the relative clause is Declarative:

(26)   ...when and why did the Democrats, *who had been the party of limited federal government*, begin to favor expanding Washington's power? (Internet)

Consider the sentence *I didn't steal them, just in case you're wondering.* (COCA, written, magazine). What would you say is the relation between the two Discourse Acts in the sentence? Is it a relationship of equipollence or of dependence? If the latter, what is the rhetorical function of the dependent Act?

3.4.2. The head

Discourse Acts have a **configurational head**, consisting of a maximum of four elements that are not in a hierarchical relation: the Illocution, the two participants (Speaker and Addressee), and the Communicated Content. In the large majority of cases, all four elements are present; in that case we are dealing with a Contentive Communicative Discourse Act, that is, a Discourse Act that is used by a Speaker to communicate some content to an Addressee. Their general structure is represented in (27):

(27)   CONTENTIVE COMMUNICATIVE DISCOURSE ACTS:
$$(\Pi \ A_1: [(F_1) \ (P_1)_S \ (P_2)_A \ (C_1)]: \Sigma \ ^A)$$

In some cases, Discourse Acts contain only three elements. In that case, a Speaker does perform a communicative action, but the utterance is a phatic one: the linguistic utterance serves a social or discourse function, but no content is transferred. Such utterances typically consist of some conventionalized, invariable expression, such as *Congratulations*, *Thank you*, or *Hello*. As we will see in Section 3.5, these expressions will be analysed as direct expressions of the illocutionary force of an expression. These Discourse Acts will be referred to as Interactive Communicative Discourse Acts and can be represented as follows:

(28)   INTERACTIVE COMMUNICATIVE DISCOURSE ACTS:
$$(\Pi \ A_1: [(F_1) \ (P_1)_S \ (P_2)_A]: \Sigma \ ^A)$$

Finally, there are the Expressive Discourse Acts. These are direct expressions of a Speaker's feelings and are not intended to communicate any content. Such expressive Discourse Acts often take the form of an interjection, which, like the invariable expression in Interactive Discourse Acts, are regarded as direct expressions of the Illocution. These Expressive Discourse Acts therefore lack both a Communicated Content and an Addressee:

(29)   EXPRESSIVE DISCOURSE ACTS:

$(\Pi \ A_1: [(F_1) \ (P_1)_S]: \Sigma^A)$

A more detailed description of each of these subtypes of Discourse Act will be provided in Section 3.5, which will deal with the Illocution. Sections 3.6 and 3.7 will be devoted to the Speech Participants and the Communicated Content, respectively.

3.4.3. Modifiers

Modifiers at the layer of the Discourse Act can fulfil a number of functions. What they have in common is that they allow the Speaker to comment on the Discourse Act. In many cases, the modifier is used to indicate the stylistic properties of a Discourse Act (e.g. *briefly*), or its role within the Move (e.g. *in addition*, *finally*). In other cases, they indicate a Speaker's emotional state while uttering the Discourse Act, such as sadness or surprise (examples (30a) and (30b), respectively).

(30)   a. *Sadly*, we have to report the death of Mr. Jim Parker, no. 112 (BYU-BNC, written, miscellaneous)

b. I remember being at primary school and the boys went to play football and you sat in the corner playing talking or the boys played football and the girls, *would you believe it*, got sex education! (BYU-BNC, spoken, broadcast discussion)

Once it has been established that a modifier (e.g. *briefly*) is firmly associated with a particular layer, it can serve as a criterion for distinguishing such a layer. Consider once more the example in (16):

(16)   A: What happened at Wimbledon yesterday?

B: Murray won. And Federer lost.

B's answer was analysed as consisting of two separate Discourse Acts, each with its own intonation contour and separated by a pause. Note, however, the same content could also be expressed in a single Discourse Act:

(31)   A: What happened at Wimbledon yesterday?

B: Murray won and Federer lost.

In (31), there is no pause between the two clauses in B's answer; moreover, B's entire answer is characterized by a single (rise-fall) intonation contour. That we are indeed dealing with a single Discourse Act here is confirmed by the fact that if we add the modifier *briefly*, it can take the entire utterance in its scope:

(32)   *Briefly*, Murray won and Federer lost.

Conversely, the fact that we can add *briefly* to the second part of example (16) shows that we are indeed dealing with two separate Discourse Acts:

(33)   Watch out, because—*very briefly*—there will be trick questions in the exam.

Modifiers of the Discourse Act are expressed directly at the Interpersonal Level and have no correlate at the Representational Level. We thus find the lexeme or lexical expression in question filling the modifier position (Σ). The single discourse Act in (31), for instance, will be represented as in (34):

(34)   (A_1: [- Murray won and Federer lost -]: **briefly** ^{A})

3.4.4. Operators

At the layer of the Discourse Act we find operators representing (grammatically coded instances of) Irony and Emphasis. In English, Irony is typically indicated by a special intonation contour (e.g. Bryant and Fox Tree 2002). The sentence in (35), for instance, may be pronounced with a rather flat intonation contour with stress on a non-focal element (the copula). In that case, the Speaker wishes to communicate that he is not having fun (Hengeveld and Mackenzie 2008: 65).

(35)   This IS fun.

Another operator at this layer is Emphasis, which, as we will see, may apply at different layers, including that of the Illocution. It will be analysed as a Discourse Act operator in those cases where it has scope over the entire Discourse Act and applies irrespective of the Illocution of the Discourse Act. Since in English, Declarative, Interrogative, and Imperative can all be uttered with an emphatic intonation pattern, the operator will be represented at the layer of the Discourse Act (Hengeveld and Mackenzie 2008: 66):

(36)   a. She has grown!
       b. Did you say you were pregnant?!
       c. Hurry up!

Constructions with an Emphatic operator working at this layer will therefore be represented as follows:

(37)   **(emph** A_1: [(F_1) $(P_1)_S$ $(P_2)_A$ (C_1)] ^{A})

3.5. The Illocution

3.5.1. General characterization

The Illocution forms one of the four units that make up the head of a Discourse Act. In FDG Illocutions are defined as the formally expressed conventionalized means available in a language to indicate the Speaker's communicative intentions. English, for instance, has three main types of Illocution (Declarative, Interrogative, and Imperative), as well as a number of minor types (which will be discussed below). As the 'smallest identifiable unit of communicative behavior' (Kroon 1995: 65), Discourse Acts contain only one Illocution; the presence of an Illocution, in other words, can be used as a diagnostic for identifying Discourse Acts. In example (38), for instance, the Illocution of the non-restrictive relative clause (Declarative) differs from that of the main clause (Interrogative). Consequently, non-restrictive relative clauses (in general) will be analysed as separate (dependent) Discourse Acts (Asides, see Section 3.4.1).

(38)   Is her brother, who lives in Brazil, also coming to the wedding?

It is important to realize that FDG assumes that there is no one-to-one relationship between the Illocutions of a language and the actual communicative intentions a Speaker may wish to convey. First of all, the number of Illocutions (as conventionalized indications of Speaker intention) of a language is much more restricted than the number of intentions Speakers of that language may have (e.g. requesting, promising, warning, calling attention, encouraging or discouraging the Addressee to do something). Secondly, languages differ in which indications of Speaker intention have become conventionalized, as well as in the way in which these conventionalized intentions are formally distinguished. We will come back to this issue in the next section.

3.5.2. The head

Illocutions have simplex heads, which may be either abstract or lexical. Since most Illocutions are abstract, we will consider these first.

3.5.2.1. Abstract heads

In the case of an abstract head, Speakers make use of one of the ready-made illocutionary devices available in a language, often referred to as 'sentence types'. These abstract heads represent broad conventionalized intentions, like 'informing the Addressee of the contents evoked in the Discourse Act' (**Declarative**) or 'directing an Addressee to carry out the action evoked in the Discourse Act' (**Imperative**), and trigger the appropriate morphosyntactic and/ or phonological form. This means that, in accordance with the Principle of Formal Encoding, there are only as many Illocutions in each language as there are specific grammatical forms for expressing them. English, for instance, has only seven abstract Illocutions (Hengeveld and Mackenzie 2008: 73):

(**39**) a. Declarative:
             Barbara went to London.
         b. Interrogative
             Yes–No: Did Barbara go to London?
             Wh: Where did Barbara go?
         c. Imperative:
             Go to London!
         d. Optative:
             Let her rest in peace. (BYU-BNC, written, fiction)
             May she rest in peace. (BYU-BNC, written, miscellaneous)
         e. Hortative:
             Let us go to London.
         f. Exclamative:[1]
             How easily she'd tricked him! (BYU-BNC, written. fiction)
         g. Interpellative:
             Peter!

---

[1] Hengeveld and Mackenzie (2008: 72) use the term Mirative for sentences of this type. Hengeveld and Olbertz (2012), however, regard mirativity as a representational category, 'characteriz[ing] a proposition as newsworthy, unexpected, or surprising' (Hengeveld and Olbertz 2012: 501; see also Olbertz 2012). To avoid confusion, the more traditional term **Exclamative** will here be used to refer to the kind of Illocution illustrated in example (39f).

In (39a), the Speaker informs the Addressee of the fact that Barbara went to London. The form chosen is that of a declarative sentence, which is characterized by a falling intonation and by the fact that the element in first position is neither a verb nor a *wh*-word. In (39b), the Speaker uses an **Interrogative** Illocution, which is used to ask for information from the Addressee, either in the form of a (dis)confirmation, or in the form of specific information (e.g. place, time, reason, or the identity of a participant in some State-of-Affairs). Each of these forms is again characterized by the fact that they have a specific intonation pattern and a distinctive element in first position (verb, *wh*-word). Example (39c) serves as an instruction (or command) to the Addressee to carry out some action. Once again, it is characterized by a specific intonation pattern, as well as by the absence of a subject and the placement of the verb in first position. Examples (39d)–(39g) illustrate some less frequently used English Illocutions, each of which is clearly characterized by a distinctive combination of intonation, word order, and/or internal structure: in (39d) we find an **Optative**, meant to express a wish; in (39e) we find a **Hortative**, meant to encourage the Speaker and Addressee to perform some action; (39f) provides an example of an **Exclamative**, expressing the Speaker's strong feelings about something or someone (delight, anger, surprise, excitement, etc.); and in (39e) we find an **Interpellative**, used to attract an Addressee's attention (see also Section 3.5.2.2).

English, then, is regarded as having seven illocutionary primitives: DECLarative, INTERrogative, IMPerative, OPTative, HORTative, EXCLamative, and INTERPellative. These Illocutions are represented by means of abstract predicates taking the ILL position (see also (2) and (3) above):

(40)   a. Barbara went to London
       b. $(A_1: [(F_1: \text{DECL}) (P_1) (P_2) (C_1)]^A)$

Abstract Illocutions in other languages

As pointed out above, languages differ with regard to which communicative intentions have become conventionalized and how these conventionalized intentions are coded (Hengeveld and Mackenzie 2008: 70ff.). Mandarin Chinese, for instance has a special particle (*ou*) to code Admonitives (or warnings), i.e. Discourse Acts intended to advise

Addressees to carry out an action for their own benefit, as illustrated in (41) (from Li and Thompson 1981: 311). Note that English lacks a special device to code warnings, typically using (as suggested by the translation) an Imperative instead.

(41) Xiǎoxīn   *ou!*
      careful   ADMON
      'Be careful!'

Other languages have explicit grammatical means of coding a promise. An example from Jamul Tiipay is given in (42) (from Miller 2001: 191); here the affix *ma* indicates that the Speaker wishes to communicate that he/she commits him/herself to performing the action evoked at some future time. In this case, English speakers typically use a declarative Discourse Act.

(42) Xiikay   ny-iny-*ma*.
      some   1/2-give-COMM
      'I'll give you some.'

Another interesting difference concerns the possibility in some languages to code not only positive actions—positive wishes, encouragements, affirmative imperatives—but also negative actions—negative wishes (*May he rot in hell!*), discouragements (*Let's not go to London*) or negative imperatives (*Do not go to London*). An example of a language which codes negative imperatives (orders-not-to) is Scottish Gaelic; an example can be found in (43) (from Mackenzie 2009: 901):

(43) *Na*   pòg   mi.
      PROH   kiss me
      'Don't kiss me!'

Note that English does not make this distinction, but instead uses a negated (affirmative) imperative to express an order not to perform an action.

It will be clear that the FDG analysis of Illocutions has important consequences for the treatment of indirect speech acts (Searle 1969). As we can see from the examples above, English often codes intentions indirectly, using an Imperative to code a warning, or an Interrogative to indicate a request, as illustrated in examples (44a) and (44b), respectively.

(44)   a. Mind your head!
      b. Could you pass the salt?

Thus we see, once again, that FDG only represents what is explicitly coded (e.g. Imperative), not what may actually be intended (e.g. warning). The actual intention will be part of the Conceptual Component, but will not be present in the Grammatical Component, which requires a Speaker to select one of the ready-made Illocutions. In doing so, a (cooperative) Speaker will act on the assumption that the Contextual Component will provide the Addressee with the information needed to arrive at the intended interpretation (in accordance with Grice's Cooperative Principle).

Alternatively, a Speaker may choose to make the communicative intention explicit by using lexical rather than abstract means. Such lexically expressed Illocutions may take various forms, depending on their function. These different forms will be described in the next section.

3.5.2.2. Lexical heads

One lexical strategy available to speakers of English to express their communicative intentions is the use of **performative verbs**. As pointed out by Austin (1962), performative verbs behave differently from non-performative verbs. Consider, for instance, the examples in (45). Although the verbs *pronounce*, *promise*, and *confirm* here seem to behave like regular (complement-taking) main verbs, they differ semantically, syntactically, and pragmatically from regular main verbs. Semantically, these verbs do not describe events in the real world, as these events do not, as yet, exist; rather, by using these verbs, the Speaker performs the action designated (hence the term 'performative verb'). As a result, the sentences cannot be checked against any non-linguistic world, and cannot be given a truth value (i.e. they cannot be denied). Instead, constructions of this kind are evaluated pragmatically, in terms of felicitousness: they are only felicitous (appropriate) when uttered by certain people, under certain circumstances. Finally, in terms of form, performative constructions are characterized by the fact that they take first person subjects only (*I, we*) and always appear in the present tense.

(45)   a. I hereby pronounce you man and wife.
      b. I promise I'll be home by eight.
      c. I hereby confirm that your request for 5 days paternity leave has been granted. (BYU-BNC, written, non-academic)

To capture these specific features of performative verbs, FDG analyses them not as main predicates, but as direct instantiations of the Illocution (Hengeveld and Mackenzie 2008: 69), that is, as lexical indications of the Speaker's communicative intention. As such, they are represented as lexical heads of the Illocution. This means that FDG distinguishes between performatives and non-performatives in a principled manner: the former are analysed as abstract Illocutions (as described in the previous section), the latter as lexical ones:

(46)   NON-PERFORMATIVE (ABSTRACT) ILLOCUTIONS:
      a. I'll be home by eight.
      b. $(A_1: [(F_1: \text{DECL}) (P_1)_S (P_2)_A (C_1)]^A)$

(47)   PERFORMATIVE (LEXICAL) ILLOCUTIONS:
      a. I promise I'll be home by eight.
      b. $(A_1: [(F_1: \textbf{promise}) (P_1)_S (P_2)_A (C_1)]^A)$

> Think of two more performative verbs in English and find authentic examples of a performative use and a non-performative use.

Apart from performative constructions, there are a number of other constructions that are analysed as lexical Illocutions in FDG. In what follows we will discuss two of these constructions: **interjections** and **vocatives**.

Interjections are represented in FDG as Expressive Discourse Acts (Hengeveld and Mackenzie 2008: 76). As we have seen above, such Discourse Acts are not intended to communicate any information (referential, ascriptive, or otherwise) and, as such, do not contain an Addressee slot, nor a slot for a Communicated Content; they consist of an Illocution and a Speaker only. In the case of interjections, the head of the Illocution is a lexeme, namely the interjection itself. An expression like *Ouch!* in (48a) is thus given the interpersonal representation in (48b):

(48)   a. Ouch!
      b. $(A_1: [(F_1: \textbf{ouch}) (P_1)_S]^A)$

> It might be argued that if an utterance does not express a communicative intention, it should not be part of the grammar (i.e. it should not be analysed as a Discourse Act). Can you think of a reason why a purely expressive Discourse Act (e.g. *Ouch!*) should nevertheless be considered part of the Grammatical Component?

Vocatives differ from interjections in that they do fulfil a communicative function: they are a special subclass of Interactive Discourse Acts, used to gain the Addressee's attention (Hengeveld and Mackenzie 2008: 78). If a language has a lexical item used specifically for this purpose, such as English *Hey*, this item will be analysed as the lexical head of the Illocution: the sole function of this item is to indicate that the communicative intention of the Speaker is to draw the Addressee's attention:

(49) a. Hey!

b. $(A_1: [(F_1: \textbf{hey}) (P_1)_S (P_2)_A]^A)$

In many cases, such vocatives can be expanded with a second person pronoun or proper name, as in example (50). In addition, vocatives can take the form of one or more descriptive elements, as in (51); in that case the Illocution has an abstract head (Interpellative; Hengeveld and Mackenzie 2008: 78–9), while the descriptive elements are analysed as the head of the Addressee (P_2):

(50) a. Hey you/Peter!

b. $(A_1: [(F_1: \textbf{hey}) (P_1)_S (P_2: \textbf{you/Peter})_A]^A)$

(51) a. Ladies and gentlemen!

b. $(A_1: [(F_1: \text{INTERP}) (P_1)_S (P_2 - \text{ladies and gentlemen }^{P2})]^A)$

3.5.3. Modifiers

Modifying expressions at the layer of the Illocution are lexical elements that affect the illocutionary force of the Discourse Act. An example is the adverb *frankly* when used to describe the way in which the Illocution is carried out. Consider, for instance, (52a). What the adverb *frankly* does in this example is indicate that the Speaker is being frank in conveying his/her communicative intention; it could therefore be paraphrased as 'I am telling you frankly that...' (compare also *sincerely, honestly, in all honesty, to tell you the truth,* etc.). For this reason, the adverb is analysed as modifying the Illocution, leading to the representation given in (52b):

(52)   a. *Frankly*, I didn't have a clue.
  b. $(A_1: [(F_1: \text{DECL}: \textbf{frankly}^{\ F}) (P_1)_S (P_2)_A (C_1: \text{- I didn't have a clue -}^{\ C})]^{\ A})$

Note that, despite the similarity in form, this use of *frankly* differs from its use as a manner adverb describing the way in which some action is carried out, as in example (53):

(53)   Peter told me *frankly* he made a big mistake.

One clear difference between the two uses of *frankly* is that in example (53) the property assigned by the adverb can be denied: a response like *No, that is not true* can be interpreted as meaning that Peter did not tell me this in a frank manner. In the case of (52a) such a response is not possible: since the adverb is a performative one, its application cannot be denied. Further evidence that the two uses of *frankly* are indeed different can be found in the fact that a sentence like *Frankly, I lied to you* is perfectly acceptable, whereas *I frankly lied to you* would clearly be contradictory.

Manner adverbs vs. Illocution modifiers in other languages

Whereas in English manner adverbs and Illocution modifiers often take the same form (e.g. *frankly*), in other languages the two forms are formally distinguished. An example is Dutch:

(54)   a. Peter heeft mij alles *eerlijk* verteld. (Manner)
    Peter has me everything honestly told
    'Peter honestly told me everything.'
  b. *Eerlijkgezegd* ken ik hem helemaal niet. (Illocution)
    frankly know I him wholly not
    'Frankly, I don't know him at all.'

What English and Dutch have in common, however, is that the two kinds of modifier typically appear in different positions, reflecting the scope relations between them (with the higher, interpersonal, modifier (Illocution) appearing at the periphery of the clause, indicating wider scope than the representational modifier (Manner); for more details, see Chapter 5).

3.5.4. Operators

Operators at the layer of the Illocution typically serve to **mitigate** (weaken) or **reinforce** (strengthen) the illocutionary force of an expression. Mitigating elements are often used to express tentativity or politeness. Examples are given in (55). Note that whereas the expression *please* in (55a) is typically used in this function, *perhaps* in (55b) is used in a non-prototypical manner: whereas its usual function is to express the possibility that an event takes place, here it is clearly used to turn a rather strong statement into a more tentative suggestion (note also the use of *okay*).

(55) a. *Please*, leave me alone.
      b. so *perhaps* we can change that, okay? (BYU-BNC, spoken, meeting)

An example of reinforcement would be the use of *do* in Imperatives, as illustrated in example (56). Note that the effect of adding *do* is to strengthen the Speaker's intention, irrespective of whether this is a negative one (resulting in rudeness, as in (56a)) or a positive one (expressing politeness, as in (56b)):

(56) a. Oh, *do* shut up!
      b. (Please,) *do* sit down.

> Can you think of other lexical or grammatical means of indicating mitigation in English?

3.6. The Speech Participants

3.6.1. General characterization

The two Speech Participants P_1 and P_2 alternate as Speaker and Addressee; S(peaker) and A(ddressee) therefore are functions indicating the interactive role of the unit in the Discourse Act (Hengeveld and Mackenzie 2008: 84). As such they need to be distinguished from referring expressions, which, as we will see below, are part of the Communicated Content. We can clarify the distinction by looking at the difference between Discourse Acts with non-performative verbs and with performative verbs, as illustrated in examples (46) and (47), repeated here for convenience:

(46)   NON-PERFORMATIVE (ABSTRACT) ILLOCUTIONS:
  a. I'll be home by eight.
  b. $(A_1: [(F_1: DECL) (P_1)_S (P_2)_A (C_1)]^A)$

(47)   PERFORMATIVE (LEXICAL) ILLOCUTIONS:
  a. I promise I'll be home by eight.
  b. $(A_1: [(F_1: \textbf{promise}) (P_1)_S (P_2)_A(C_1)]^A)$

The sentences in (46a) and (47a) both communicate the same contents (*I'll be home by eight*), the only difference being that in (47a) the Illocution is expressed explicitly (by the lexical item *promise*), whereas in (46a) the Illocution is expressed implicitly (through grammatical means, i.e. word order and intonation.). Within this shared Communicated Content, one Individual (the Speaker) is referred to by means of the pronoun *I* (for more details see Section 3.9.2). In the performative Discourse Act in (47a) example, however, we find another occurrence of the pronoun *I*, this time as part of the phrase *I promise*. As shown in the previous section, this phrase does not describe a situation in the non-linguistic (real or imaginary) world; instead the Speaker, by using this phrase, performs an action. The phrase *I promise* is therefore not analysed as part of the Communicated Content. Instead, the verb, as we have seen before, is analysed as a direct instantiation of the Illocution; the presence of a special slot for the Speaker allows us to use this slot to represent the pronoun *I*. This is illustrated in the slightly expanded representation of (47b) given in (47c):

(47)   c. $(A_1: [(F_1: promise) (P_1: I)_S (P_2)_A (C_1: - I'll \ be \ home \ by \ eight -^C)]^A)$

This neatly captures the fact that the subject of a performative verb can indeed only represent the Speaker. The representation further suggests that an Addressee can be present in a performative Discourse Act. As shown in example (57), this is indeed the case:

(57)   a. I promise you that I'll be home by eight.
  b. $(A_1: [(F_1: promise) (P_1: I)_S (P_2: \textbf{you})_A (C_1: - I'll \ be \ home \ by \ eight -^C)]^A)$

Also in other respects, the presence of separate slots for the two Speech Participants turns out to be useful. Thus, as we have already seen, they allow us to distinguish between Expressive Discourse Acts (which contain a slot for Speaker, but not for Addressee) and Communicative Discourse Acts (with slots for both Speaker and Addressee). Moreover, as with all other layers at the Interpersonal Level, additional information about Speaker and Addressee that is formally encoded in the linguistic utterance can be provided in the form of operators and modifiers, specifying, for instance, number, social status, or gender (see Section 3.6.4). Finally, the presence of a Speaker and Addressee slot proves useful to indicate shifts in the deictic centre, as in the case of direct speech (see Section 3.7.3).

3.6.2. The head

In the large majority of cases, the heads of the Speaker and Addressee slots remain empty. In those cases where a head is present, it may be either abstract or lexical. Abstract heads are found in those cases where the Speaker or Addressee is evoked by means of a pronoun, as in the performative Discourse Acts in (47a) and (57a). Since pronouns lack descriptive information, they are not represented as lexical items, but rather as combinations of the features [±Speaker] and [±Addressee]. A more accurate representation of example (57a) would therefore be the following:

(58)   a. I promise you that I'll be home by eight.
       b. $(A_1: [(F_1: promise) (P_1: [+S, -A])_S (P_2: [-S, +A])_A (C_1: - I'll be home by eight - ^C)] ^A)$

Similarly, a vocative construction like *Hey you!* would contain an Addressee slot with an abstract head (see example (50) above):

(59)   a. Hey you!
       b. $(A_1: [(F_1: hey) (P_1)_S (P_2: [-S, +A])_A] ^A)$

Occasionally, the Speaker unit has a lexically specified head, as in the following example, which is taken from a peace agreement drawn up by the Salvadoran government:

(60)   a. (With regard to those lands illegally taken over after the agreement,) *the Salvadoran Government* hereby states that it has reserved the right to apply the law to guarantee the existence of the state of law. (COCA, written)
       b. $(A_1: [(F_1: state) (P_1: - the Salvadoran Government - ^{P1})_S (P_2)_A (C_1: - it has reserved . . . state of law - ^C)] ^A)$

Here the italicized phrase obviously represents the Speaker (or in this case Writer) of the Discourse Act, actually meaning *we, the Salvadoran Government*, and is as such represented as the lexical head of the Speaker unit (Hengeveld and Mackenzie 2008: 84–5).

3.6.3. Modifiers

Speech Participants are rarely modified, which is not surprising given that they are typically headless. However, when the head is specified, as in the case of a performative Discourse Act, modifiers can be used. An example can be found in (61a), where the phrase *your little buddies* provides an optional further specification of the Speaker and will therefore be analysed as a modifier at the layer of the Speech Participants (see also Hengeveld and Mackenzie 2008: 85):

(61)   a.   Marshal, here are we before you, O savior of France. *We your little buddies* swear to follow where you advance (COCA, written)

   b. $(A_1: [(F_1: swear) (P_1: [+S, -A]: \textbf{your-little-buddies}^{P1})_S (P_2)_A (C_1: -$ to follow where you advance $-^C)]^A)$

Modifiers can also be found in vocatives with explicit Addressees, as illustrated in example (62) (compare example (59) above):

(62)   a.   You fool!

   b. $(A_1: [(F_1: \text{INTERP}) (P_1)_S (P_2: [-S, +A]: \textbf{fool}^{P2})_A])$

3.6.4. Operators

Like modifiers, operators at the layer of the Speech Participants are rare, at least in English. Once again, we tend to find such operators only in those cases where a Speech Participant is expressed. In the case of a performative Discourse Act, for instance, the Speaker is typically marked for number (*I* vs. *we*). The information needed to trigger the right form of the pronoun is provided by an operator specifying singularity (1) or plurality (m):

(63)   a.   I promise you-guys that I'll be home by eight.

   b. $(A_1: [(F_1: promise) (1 P_1: [+S, -A])_S (m P_2: [-S, +A])_A (C_1: - I'll be$ home by eight $-^C)]^A)$

> **Operators of the Speech Participants in other languages**
>
> Operators at the layer of the Speech Participants can also be used to indicate the social status attributed to the Addressee by the Speaker in languages which possess systematic means of indicating (relative) social status. In example (64) from peninsular Spanish, for instance, the
>
> *(continued)*

Speaker uses the polite form of the copula (*están* rather than *estáis*) to indicate that he/she thinks the Addressee deserves respect (indicated by the operator 'h'; Hengeveld and Mackenzie 2008: 86):

(64)   a. ¿*Están*   *despiertas?*

2.PL.FORMALCOP.PROG   awake.PL.FEM

'Are you awake?'

b. $(A_1: [(F_1: \text{INTER}) (P_1)_S (h P_2)_A (C_1)]^A)$

In languages like French, German, and Dutch, the presence of the 'h' operator triggers the polite form of a pronoun (*vous*, *Sie*, *u*), while in languages with elaborate systems of expressing social rank and politeness, such as Japanese and Javanese, it may result in the presence of specialized affixes and/or particles, as well as in the selection of a special vocabulary. The analysis of such languages may require a larger set of politeness operators.

English does not possess such specialized devices for expressing politeness or formality. One could, however, argue that some uses of the modal verbs *can* and *may* could be seen as rough equivalents. In that case, the use of the modal form in example (65) can be seen as resulting from the presence of a politeness marker in the Addressee slot:

(65)   *Might* I go to the toilet mam (COCA, spoken).

3.7. Communicated Content

3.7.1. General characterization

The Communicated Content is that part of the Discourse Act that contains everything the Speaker wishes to evoke in his/her communication (Hengeveld and Mackenzie 2008: 87). Generally speaking, every Communicated Content contains one or more Subacts, used either to evoke a property (**Subact of Ascription**) or a referent (**Subact of Reference**). Consider, for instance, the sentence in (66):

(66)   That big dog chased our cat.

In (66) the Speaker evokes two entities, described as *that big dog* and *our cat*, represented within the Communicated Content as two Subacts of

Reference, (R_1) and (R_2). In addition, the Communicated Content contains a Subact of Ascription (T_1), specifying the relation between these two entities (*chase*). Furthermore, in order for the Subacts of Reference to be successful, the Speaker ascribes a number of properties to these entities: the properties 'dog' and 'big' to one entity, the property 'cat' to the other. The Communicated Content thus reflects the intention of the Speaker to refer to certain entities and to say something about these entities, before he/she selects the actual lexical means to do so (this happens at the Representational Level). The Discourse Act in (66) can therefore be given the following simplified interpersonal representation:

(67) $(A_1: [(F_1: \text{DECL}) (P_1)_S (P_2)_A (C_1: [(T_1) (R_1) (R_2)]^C)]^A)$

For a Communicated Content to be informative, it must contain information that is 'new' (or 'salient') for the Addressee in the given discourse situation. In many cases, the Communicated Content also contains information that is 'given' (or familiar), but it may also consist of new information only. To indicate the informational status of the Subacts contained in the Communicated Content—or of the Communicated Content as a whole—the different units are assigned pragmatic functions, like Topic and Focus. These will be discussed in more detail in the next section.

Like all other interpersonal units, the Communicated Content also contains slots for modifiers and operators, specifying, for instance, a Speaker's subjective attitude towards the Communicated Content (conveyed by such expressions as *unfortunately, luckily*, or *understandably*) or the source of the Communicated Content (expressed by such expressions as *reportedly, allegedly*, or *supposedly*). These will be dealt with in Sections 3.7.3 and 3.7.4.

3.7.2. The head

As can be seen from example (2), the head of a Communicated Content consists of one or more Subacts; in other words, like Discourse Acts, Communicated Contents have a configurational (complex) head. One way of inventorizing the possible heads of a Communicated Content is by describing these heads in terms of the different combinations of pragmatic functions they allow. These pragmatic functions reflect the communicative status of a linguistic unit (i.e. of a Subact or the Communicated Content as a whole) in terms of saliency in and/or relevance to the ongoing discourse.

FDG distinguishes the following three major pragmatic functions (or rather: dimensions of pragmatic functions) (Hengeveld and Mackenzie 2008: 89–99):

- *Focus* (*vs. Background*): **Focus** function is assigned to Subacts presenting new information, either to fill a gap in the Addressee's knowledge (New-Foc) or to correct the Addressee's knowledge (CorFoc).
- *Topic* (*vs. Comment*): **Topic** function is assigned to Subacts which signal how the Communicated Content relates to the gradually constructed record in the Contextual Component. In most cases Topics contain information that is given in (or inferable from) the Contextual Component.
- *Contrast* (*vs. Overlap*): **Contrast** function signals the Speaker's desire to bring out certain differences between two or more Communicated Contents or between a Communicated Content and other contextually available information.

What needs to be stressed is that, in accordance with the Principle of Formal Encoding, pragmatic functions will only be assigned to units that are singled out for special treatment. In English, for instance, special treatment of Focus constituents may take the following forms (Hengeveld and Mackenzie 2008: 90):

(a) a special prosodic contour (e.g. tonic accentuation);
(b) a special Focus construction (e.g. a cleft construction);
(c) unusual position in the sequence of constituents (e.g. initial position of direct objects);
(d) the presence of a Focus marker (e.g. use of emphatic *do*).

In many cases a combination of two or more Focus devices is used. In example (68), for instance, the most salient information, *in Scotland*, not only occurs in a special focus construction (an *it*-cleft), but is also marked by prosodic prominence:

(68)   Mr P R Field of the Oldbury Steam Live Railway Museum (Bridg-north) was our guest speaker on 2 February 1990 when he gave his views on Britain's railways over the years, first explaining that *it was in Scotland that* he began to take an interest in them and then he become 'hooked'! (BYU-BNC, spoken, miscellaneous)

The requirement that the pragmatic function be explicitly coded means that not all languages make use of the Topic function: if a language lacks the means of explicitly marking Topic function, such a language simply does not have Topics (Hengeveld and Mackenzie 2008: 92). All languages, on the other hand, appear to have at least one way of coding Focus information. In addition, it will be clear that it is typically only one of the two values of each dimension that is explicitly marked (i.e. Focus rather than Background, Topic rather than Comment, Contrast rather than Overlap); the other dimensions either lack any marking or are left out altogether.

Let us consider some more examples. It will be clear that the assignment of pragmatic functions depends entirely on the context (including previous discourse, immediate situation, shared background knowledge) in which it occurs: the pragmatic function indicates how the Speaker wishes the Addressee to incorporate the information presented in a particular linguistic unit in his/her mental representation of the discourse. Consider, for instance, the following passage:

(69)   A: You told me to think of this as a second honeymoon.
        B: No, I did not say that.
        A: You did, too.
        B: No, I did not. (COCA, spoken, talk show)

As it is clearly beyond the scope of this section to analyse the information status of each element in detail, we will only look at B's first reaction and A's response to that reaction. In the short sentence *I did not say that*, Focus is assigned to the element *not*, as it provides the only new as well as the most salient information; it is also the element that is given focal stress. The rest of the sentence functions as Background; however, since this function is not explicitly coded, there is no need to assign it. Within this background information, the element *I* may be regarded as having Topic function; its occurrence in initial position in the form of a non-emphatic pronoun seems to support such an analysis. The rest of the sentence serves as the Comment (providing information about the Topic). Note that the Comment as a whole is not marked; it is only the focal element *not* within the Comment that is singled out for special treatment. A's response *You did (, too)* does not seem to provide any new information at all; instead it serves to emphasize the contrast between the two situations evoked. This contrastive function is expressed by placing means of contrastive stress on the element *did*.

Comment on the function of *too* in A's second turn in (69). How would you represent this element in FDG?

Consider finally the passage in (70):

(70)   On my way through town I met *Mr Wopsle*, and together we started
the long walk home to the village. *It was a dark, wet, misty night*, and
we could only just see someone ahead of us. 'Hello!' we called. 'Is that
Orlick?' 'Yes!' he answered. 'I'll walk home with you. Been in town all
afternoon, I have. Did you hear the big gun firing, from the prison-
ships? *Must be some prisoners who've escaped.*' (BYU-BNC, written;
from Charles Dickens, *Great Expectations*)

In the first sentence of this passage the element *Mr Wopsle* is assigned Focus
function, as it contains the most salient information. This clearly shows that
a Focus element need not provide information that is entirely new to the
Addressee: in (70), for instance, the reader can be assumed to know who
Mr Wopsle is. This explains why Focus elements need not be indefinite, and
why, consequently, Focus and (in)definiteness are represented separately.

   In the second sentence we find a special type of sentence, often referred to
as a **thetic sentence** (Cornish 2004). Thetic sentences provide all new information: none of the elements they contain is coded as being related to the
current discourse. This is indeed the case in the sentence *It was a dark, wet,
misty night*, which simply evokes a new, temporal entity (*night*) and a
number of properties (*dark, wet, misty*); the element *it* being regarded as
non-referential (a 'dummy' subject, see Chapter 5, Sections 5.3 and 5.5.5).
Thetic sentences are thus different from **categorical sentences**: whereas a
Thetic sentence consists of a Comment only, categorical sentences (the large
majority of sentences) contain a Topic and a Comment. Note finally that
sentences can be categorical even when the Topic element remains unex-
pressed, as in the last italicized sentence in the passage in (70). Although the
subject of this sentence, being retrievable from the context, has been left out,
the remainder of the sentence will still be interpreted as a Comment on the
referent of the implicit subject (and as such as related to the ongoing
discourse).

   What is special about the FDG approach to pragmatic function assignment is that the definitions of Focus and Topic given allow constituents to
carry both functions at the same time. Focus and Topic, in other words, are
not seen as being in complementary distribution, but as belonging to different dimensions in the domain of information structure. Likewise, Contrast
can be combined with both Focus and Topic. An example of the combination Topic/Contrast is given in (71a), where the element *I* in B's response

functions both as the Focus (providing the new, most salient information) and as the Topic (linking the Communicated Content to information already contained in the Contextual Component). This combination of Topic and Contrast of pragmatic functions can also be found in contrastively used cleft-constructions, as illustrated in (71b):

(71)   a. A: Who said that? B: *I* did. (BYU-BNC, spoken, conversation)
       b. Philip speared his peas. Lee hadn't seemed violent to him. *It was him, Philip, that had been violent. It was Lee that had the bleeding nose, not him.* (BYU-BNC, written, fiction)

Both *it*-clefts in (71b) express a contrast between two Communicated Contents: the first, *It was him, Philip, that had been violent*, expresses a contrast between a presupposed (contextually given) piece if knowledge ('Lee had been violent') and a newly evoked contrasting piece of knowledge ('Philip had been violent'); in the second two different situations ('Lee had the bleeding nose' vs. 'Philip had the bleeding nose') are contrasted. At the same time both Individuals, Philip and Lee, function as Topics, relating the Communicated Content in which they occur to the Addressee's gradually constructed representation of the discourse.

In English, as well as in many other languages, the combination of Focus and Topic is typically coded by a special type of construction, the **presentative construction**, which serves to introduce a new Topic into the discourse (but see also Mackenzie and Keizer 1991: 208). An example is given in (72), where the newly introduced expert systems become the new discourse topic:

(72)   Now *there is a class of systems, so-called expert systems*, which have come out of artificial intelligence research, which can do much more than that, are much more intelligent. Internally, they mirror the structure of an expert's thought, in this case of a doctor's thoughts, which tends to be much more. (BYU-BNY, spoken, broadcast discussion)

Pragmatic functions in other languages

Other languages may use other means to mark the communicative status of (parts of) the Communicated Content. Tariana, for instance, uses a specific suffix (*-nhe/-ne*) to mark Subjects in Focus (for more details see Aikhenvald 2003: 139), while Wambon makes use of a Focus particle (*-nde*) (de Vries 1985: 172). In other languages Focus elements are placed

(continued)

in a special position; in Aghem, for instance, a Focus element is placed immediately after the verb (Watters 1979: 144), while in Hungarian Focus elements immediately precede the verb (Kenesei et al. 1998: 166; Lotti Viola, personal communication). Some examples are given in (73) and (74):

(73) WAMBON:

    A: Jakhove   kenonop-**nde**   takhim-gende?
       3.PL   what-**FOC**   buy-3PL.PRS.FINAL
       'What do they buy?'
    B: Ndu-**nde**   takhim-gende.
       Sago-**FOC** buy-3PL.PRS.FINAL
       'They buy sago.'

(74) HUNGARIAN:

    a. A vendégek **tegnap**   érkeztek a szállodá-ba
       the guests   yesterday arrived   into the hotel
       'It was yesterday that the guests arrived at the hotel.'

    b. A vendégek **a szállodá-ba** érkeztek tegnap
       the guests   into the hotel arrived   yesterday
       'It was at the hotel that the guests arrived yesterday.'

As pointed out before, not all languages have specific means of marking Topics. Some languages, however, do have specific means for indicating Topic function. An example is Tidore, which marks Topic elements through a combination of formal properties: (i) the Topic occurs in initial position, (ii) the Topic is followed by a locative marker, and (iii) there is an intonation break between Topic and clause. It is this combination of features that in the following sentence singles out the referent of the element *una* 'he/him' as the Topic (van Staden 2000: 273):

(75) turus **una=ge**,   mina   mo-sango una
      then   he=there she   answered   him
      'Then she answered him (Topic).'

Finally, there are languages that have specialized markers for Contrast. Kham, for instance, uses the particle *te* (Watters 2002: 183):

(76) Ao   po:-lə   **te**   tam   jaːh-si-u   li-zya.
      this   place-in CONTR   wheat   put   has been
      'In this place, as opposed to others, wheat has been sown.'

We started this subsection by saying that one way of inventorizing the possible heads of a Communicated Content is by giving the different combinations of pragmatic functions. Now that we know which pragmatic functions are distinguished in FDG, we can list the most typical combinations of these functions (also called **content frames**) for English (cf. Hengeveld and Mackenzie 2008: 101):

(77) TYPICAL CONTENT FRAMES FOR ENGLISH (NB: SA stands for any Subact, i.e. T or R, which are given in arbitrary order)

    a. Thetic: $(C_1: [(SA_1) \dots (SA_N)]_{FOC})$
                    e.g. It was a dark, wet, misty night (example (70))

    b. Categorical: $(C_1: [(SA_1)_{TOP} \dots (SA_N)_{FOC}])$
                    e.g. I met Mr Wopsle (example (70))

    c. Presentative: $(C_1: [(SA_1) \dots (SA_N)_{TOPFOC}])$
                    e.g. there is a class of systems, so-called expert systems (example (72))

3.7.3. Modifiers

Generally speaking, modifiers of the Communicated Content provide additional information concerning the information contained in this layer, such as the source of this information or the Speaker's subjective attitude towards this information. Examples of the latter category would be adverbs such as *(un)fortunately*, *luckily*, *sadly*, and *understandably*, when used to express the Speaker's attitude towards, or evaluation of, the Communicated Content as a whole. As in the case of Illocution modifiers, these adverbs may take the same form as regular manner adverbs (see Section 3.5.3). Consider in this respect the examples in (78). In (78a) the Speaker uses the adverb *sadly* to describe the manner in which an action (in the real world) was performed by some Individual (in this case not the Speaker). In example (78b), on the other hand, the adverb *sadly* can only be interpreted as expressing the Speaker's attitude towards the Communicated Content.

(78)   a. He smiled *sadly*, as if remembering something too personal to be shared. (BYU-BNC, written, fiction)

        b. And now, *sadly*, much of that global resource is contaminated by mercury. (BYU-BNC, spoken, documentary)

Speaker attitude modifiers in other languages

As pointed out above, in English modifiers at the Layer of the Communicated Content can take the same form as manner adverbs, although they typically occupy a different position in the sentence (see examples (78a) and (78b)). There are also languages, like Dutch, which formally distinguish Communicated Content modifiers from manner adverbs

(79) a. Hij sprak *begrijpelijk*   tot het volk.   (Manner)
     he   spoke understandably to   the   people
     'He spoke to the people in comprehensible language'

    b. Hij sprak *begrijpelijkerwijs* tot het volk.(Communicated Content)
     he   spoke understandably   to   the people
     'Understandably, he spoke to the people'

That the two adverbs do indeed perform different functions also becomes clear from the fact that they can be combined in one sentence, without leading to redundancy or semantic anomaly. Note that in that case the position of the two modifiers is fixed, with the interpersonal modifier appearing in the more peripheral position, reflecting its scope over the manner modifier:

(80) a. *Begrijpelijkerwijze*, sprak hij *begrijpelijk*   tot het volk.
     understandably   spoke he understandably to the people
     'Understandably, he spoke to the people in comprehensible language'

    b. **Begrijpelijk*, sprak hij *begrijpelijkerwijze* tot het volk

---

Modifiers at the layer of the Communicated Content can also serve to indicate the source of the information contained in the Communicated Content. In many cases, such modifiers serve to indicate that the Speaker is merely passing on ('reporting') information expressed by others. Use of such **reportatives** thus allows Speakers to distance themselves from the relayed information. Some examples are given in (81):

(81)   a. On May 18 a Byelorussian policeman was shot dead by Lithuanian personnel at a customs post on the Byelorussia-Lithuania border. *Reportedly*, the victim's car had been stopped at the post as it was leaving Lithuania, and an exchange of shots had followed, although reports from Lithuania and Byelorussia offered conflicting versions of events. (BYU-BNC, written, non-academic)

b. You must have heard how Charles died? *Supposedly*, he wandered into a darkened room and banged his head on a cupboard. I know different. He was murdered. (BYU-BNC, written, fiction)

Also belonging to this class of modifier is the (almost entirely) fixed expression *I hear (that)*, as exemplified in examples (82) and (83), where the italicized phrases do not describe (real world) events of hearing, but simply indicate that the Speaker has received the information in question from a third party (and may, in fact, be looking for confirmation). Such an analysis is further confirmed by the fact that in both examples A's utterance is clearly intended as a question:

(82)   A: *I hear* you are planning to take your entire family to Ireland.
B: Yep. (COCA, written, newspaper)

(83)   *I hear that* you have accepted Rs 5,000 for this appointment. Is it true? (BYU-BNC, written, biography)

Finally, the class of reportative modifiers may also be taken to include certain **quotatives**. Consider in this respect the following example (from Reinhart 1975: 140):

(84)   John would be late, *or so he said.*

Note that the exact form of the quotative is important here: first of all there is the presence of the elements *or so*; secondly, the modifying phrase has to follow the Communicated Content; thirdly, the phrase has a very distinctive intonation pattern; and lastly, a truly reportative reading is only available when the modifying phrase includes an anaphoric pronoun. Together these formal properties code the phrase as a reportative modifier (and can in fact be replaced by, for instance, the adverb *reportedly*). Note that in all other cases, use of such phrases is either inappropriate or does not have the required distancing effect (see also Reinhart 1975; Vandelanotte 2004; Keizer 2009b):

(85)   a. *Or so he said, John will be late.
b. *?He would be late, or so John said.
c. John said he will be late. (objective indication of indirect speech)
d. He will be late, said John. (objective indication of indirect speech)

In terms of representation, all these modifiers simply take the modifier position at the layer of the Communicated Content. Some examples are provided in (86) and (87):

(86) a. *sadly*, much of that global resource is contaminated by mercury

   b. $(C_1: [(T_1) (T_2) (R_1)]: \textbf{sadly}^C)$

(87) a. *Supposedly*, he wandered into a darkened room and banged his head on a cupboard

   b. $(C_1: [(T_1) (R_1) \ldots]: \textbf{supposedly}^C)$

3.7.4. Operators

It seems that English tends to use modifiers (i.e. lexical elements) rather than operators (i.e. grammatical means) to provide additional information concerning the source or evaluation of the Communicated Content.

Communicated Content operators in other languages

Many languages use grammatical means to indicate the relayed status of a Communicated Content. In Shipibo, for instance, the suffix *-ronqui* is used to indicate that the Speaker is passing on information expressed by others (Faust 1973):

(88) Cai-**ronqui** reocoocainyantanque.
going-REP   he.turned.over
'Reportedly, while he was going (in the boat), he turned over.'

German, too, uses a special construction type for relayed speech. In (89), for instance, the use of the modal auxiliary *sollen* ('have to') indicates that the Speaker is speaking on behalf of someone else (example (89a)). In the case of a direct order, the Speaker would use an imperative (example (89b); Hella Olbertz, personal communication).

(89) a.

Sie	sollen	sofort	zum	Chef kommen
you-FORMAL	should	immediately	to-the	boss come

'You must immediately go to the boss!'

   b.

Kommen	Sie	sofort	zum	Chef!
come	you-formal	immediately	to-the	boss

'Go immediately to the boss!'

In both these cases the reportative form will be triggered by an operator at the layer of the Communicate Content:

(90) $(\textbf{rep } C_1: [\ldots (T_1) (R_1) \ldots]^C)$

3.8. Ascriptive Subacts

As pointed out before, the Interpersonal Level is a level of actions. First of all, there is the Move, which may either constitute the start of an interaction or a reaction to part of an ongoing interaction. Secondly, there are the Discourse Acts, the smaller units of communicative behaviour that allow the Speaker to achieve his/her communicative goal. Thirdly, there are the Subacts, the smallest interpersonal units, which together 'evoke' the totality of the message the Speaker wishes to convey. These Subacts come in two kinds: Subacts of Reference and Subacts of Ascription.

Reference is often regarded as a semantic concept, in which case it is a linguistic element, typically a noun, that, on the basis of its meaning (or **'designation'**), establishes a relation with an entity in some extra-linguistic world. Functional approaches, on the other hand, see reference as an interactional, or pragmatic notion: it is an action performed by a Speaker as part of some verbal interaction. The act of reference is thus seen as separate from both the entity referred to and the linguistic means used. In FDG, the act of reference belongs to the Interpersonal Level, the referent evoked to the Contextual Component, and the linguistic (descriptive) means selected to the Representational Level.

A novel feature of FDG is that it also considers ascription to be actional in the same way: where Acts of Reference evoke some entity (typically with the intention of saying something about this entity), Acts of Ascription evoke some property (typically with the intention of ascribing it to some entity). We will now discuss these two types of Subact in some more detail. In this section we will discuss Subacts of Ascription; Subacts of Reference will be dealt with in Section 3.9.

3.8.1. General characterization

Ascriptive Subacts serve to evoke a property, that is, anything that can be ascribed to some entity. Thus Speakers can evoke a property like 'sleep' and ascribe it to a referent (*the lazy dog*), as in (91):

(91)   a. The lazy dog was sleeping.
      b. $(C_1: [(T_1) (R_1)]^C)$
     where: (T_1) = 'sleep'
                 (R_1) = 'the lazy dog'

Ascription also takes place, however, within the Referential Subact *the lazy dog*, as two properties, 'dog' and 'lazy' are evoked and ascribed to the referent of the Referential Act:

(92)   a. the lazy dog
       b. $(R_1: [(T_2) (T_3)]^C)$
       where: (T_2) = 'dog'
                (T_3) = 'lazy'

Similarly, the sentence in (93a) can be represented as in (93b):

(93)   a. The meeting was boring.
       b. $(C_1: [(T_1) (R_1: (T_2))]^C)$
       where: (T_1) = 'boring'
                (T_2) = 'meeting'
                (R_1) = 'the meeting'

Although the representations in (91b), (92b), and (93b) are obviously simplified, we can nevertheless learn a number of things from them. First of all, it will be clear that in (91b) and (93b) the element *was* is missing. The reason for this is that the verb *be* is not regarded as evoking and/or ascribing any property. In (91a), *was* functions as an **auxiliary verb**, providing information about the internal temporal structure of the SoA described by the sentence. In FDG such auxiliaries are analysed as grammatical elements, represented as operators at the Representational Level (see Chapter 4, Section 4.5.7). In (93a), the element *was* is a **copular verb**. Like auxiliaries, copular verbs are not regarded as ascribing a property; instead they are seen as grammatical devices used for the expression of tense and number (both representational features). The status and analysis of the verb *be* will be discussed in more detail in Chapters 4 and 5.

   Secondly, we find that the element *the* is also not present in the representations in (91b), (92b), and (93b). Like *be*, *the* is seen as a grammatical element: it does not ascribe a property (we cannot say that something has the property 'the'). In this case, however, we are dealing with a grammatical element with an interpersonal function; as such it is analysed at the Interpersonal Level, as an operator at the layer of the Referential Subact (see Section 3.8.2).

   Thirdly, the representations in (92b) and (93b) show that Ascriptive Subacts may occur within Referential Acts: in (92b) for instance, the Ascriptive Subacts *dog* and *lazy* are analysed as the head of the Referential Subact *the lazy dog*. Ascriptive Subacts themselves, on the other hand, are usually headless: their function is to evoke a property, not to specify this property. The Ascriptive Subact (T_1), for instance, can be said to evoke the property 'dogness', which may eventually be expressed by means of the noun *dog*, but also by means of the noun *canine*, depending on various contextual factors. This decision, however, is seen as a matter of semantics rather than pragmatics, and will therefore be taken at the Representational Level. The same would hold for the choice between the verb *sleep* and the adjective *asleep*—at the Interpersonal Level the sentences *The lazy dog was sleeping* and *The lazy dog was asleep* would be given the same interpersonal structure, the choice between them being determined by semantic, morpho-syntactic, and phonological factors rather than pragmatic ones.

So far we have defined Ascriptive Subacts as acts evoking a property which can be ascribed to some entity, and this is indeed what happens in the large majority of cases (including examples (91) to (93)). The essential part of this definition, however, is the **Evocation** of a property, not its ascription to some entity. The reason for this is that there are Ascriptive Subacts that evoke properties without ascribing them to a referent. In English, for instance, there is a special class of verbs, the so-called 'weather' verbs, that evoke a property without ascribing it to any entity. Thus, in a sentence like (94), the verb *rain* evokes a property at the Interpersonal Level, without, however, ascribing this property to any entity:

(94)   It is raining.

In FDG, the element *it* is not analysed as a Referential Subact, since it does not evoke a referent; instead it is regarded as non-referential, a 'dummy' subject, inserted simply to fill the (obligatory) subject slot (see also Chapter 4, Section 4.5.3.1, and Chapter 5, Section 5.3). This means that in utterances like those in (94) the Communicated Content consists only of a single Subact of Ascription, as represented in (95):

(95)   (C_1: (T_1))

3.8.2. The head

As we have seen, the head of an Ascriptive Subact is generally empty: the selection of specific lexical items takes place at the Representational Level, which deals with all semantic aspects of an utterance. Nevertheless, in some cases it might be argued that Ascriptive Subacts do have a head. This is, for instance, the case when the Speaker selects a semantically empty 'dummy' head, either because he/she cannot find the appropriate lexical item, or because he/she chooses to use an uninformative item (Hengeveld and Keizer 2011). Some examples are given in (96) and (97):

(96)　a. The beauty, symmetry and delight of all things mathematical passed me by, though I was very fond of the gadgets, the set square and the *thingummy* you drew the circles with. (Internet)

　　　b. Couldn't believe it! Honestly! Miserable *so and so*! Isn't she? (BYU-BNC, spoken, conversation)

(97)　... and am now at home reading the forum whilst marinating pork and frying tofu, to be *thingummied* with tomatoes and spring onions. (Internet)

In (96a) the Speaker cannot find the right expression to describe the property he/she wishes to evoke, while in (96b) the dummy *so-and-so* can be seen as having a mitigating effect: the Speaker wishes to imply rather than to explicitly mention an offensive term. Example (97) shows that this kind of strategy can also be used for Ascriptive Subacts corresponding to verbs. In all these cases, we may regard the use of a dummy expression as a communicative strategy on the part of the Speaker, to indicate to the Addressee either his/her incapacity or his/her unwillingness to evoke the relevant property; as such, dummy expressions are seen as belonging to the Interpersonal Level, where they will be analysed as the head of the Ascriptive Subact in question:

(98)　a. that thingummy

　　　b. $(R_1: (T_1: thingummy))$

Another exception to the general tendency for Ascriptive Subacts to be headless may be certain uses of proper names. Normally, proper names fulfil a referring function: a Speaker wishes to evoke a specific entity and uses a proper name to do so (see also Section 3.9.2):

(99)　a. I saw Peter.

　　　b. $(C_1: [(T_1) (R_1) (R_2)]^C)$

　　　where　(T_1) = see

　　　　　　(R_1) = Peter

　　　　　　(R_2) = I

There are, however, situations where proper names are not used to refer to a specific Individual, but rather to attach a label to this Individual. Consider in this respect the following short passage:

(100)   A man came towards them as they pulled up, and Robert said, 'This is *George*—the head keeper.' (BYU-BNC, written, fiction)

Here it is unlikely that the proper name *George* is used to refer to a person— the subsequent noun phrase strongly suggests that the Addressee was not aware of the existence of anyone named George (in the specific discourse context). Instead the label 'George' is attached to a person. Since this label is non-descriptive and typically serves to facilitate future reference to a particular entity, it seems justified to represent proper names in such introductory situations as the head of an Ascriptive Subact:

(101)   a. This is *George*.
        b. $(C_1: [(T_1: George) (R_1)] ^C)$

3.8.3. Modifiers

One function of modifiers at the layer of the Ascriptive Subact is that of Emphasis (Hengeveld and Mackenzie 2008: 111). You may recall the example we used at the beginning of this chapter, repeated here for convenience:

(102)   a really expensive tie

Here the modifier *really* is analysed at the Interpersonal Level because it is regarded as indicating emphatic commitment on the part of the Speaker rather than providing descriptive information (the tie's expensiveness is not described as being real).

Other modifiers found at this layer are the same adverbs we found at the layer of the Communicated Content, such as *fortunately* and *allegedly*. When used as modifiers of an Ascriptive Subact, these adverbs serve to indicate the Speaker's attitude towards the ascription of the property in question (e.g. *sadly* in (103a)), or the source of the ascription (e.g. *supposedly* and *allegedly* in (103b) and (103c)):

(103)   a. Great stuff but a half star has been deducted for the *sadly* inconsistent sound quality between the three sessions. (BYU-BNC, written, popular)

b. More than 1,500 lives were lost in the accident, which occurred when the *supposedly* unsinkable ship hit an iceberg. (BYU-BNC, written, newspaper)

c. All this imposes a powerful constraint on language acquisition from the *allegedly* scanty data available to any child. (BYU-BNC, written, academic)

Modifiers of the Ascriptive Subacts may also serve to indicate that the property evoked can only be ascribed approximately to the referent in question. Although in English **approximators** are often grammatical in nature (see Section 3.8.4), lexical approximators can also be found (see Hengeveld and Keizer 2011). Some examples are given in (104):

(104)   a. 'light hair is to be regarded as a "subdued orange," which is *more or less* yellow, red, or brown' (Internet)

b. Anger is 'drained off', *so to speak*, by 'living through' (in imagination) or 'acting out' these situations. (BYU-BNC, written, academic)

It may be argued that English also has the means to express the opposite of approximation—namely that the property evoked applies exactly to the referent (Hengeveld and Keizer 2011: 1969). In English **exactness** at the layer of the Ascriptive Subact can be expressed by the adverb *very*, in which case it is (non-prototypically) followed by a noun:

(105)   Just north of Bordeaux, at *the very centre* of the wine-making country, the team time trial takes place on the roads around the ancient citadel-town of Libourne. (BYU-BNC, written, miscellaneous)

In most cases, however, English makes use of such modifiers as *real, true, right*, and *proper*. Examples are given in (106):

(106)   a. 'Nothing will change my commitment to the idea that a *truly* liberal education is much more than an examination syllabus,' she says. (BYU-BNC, written, newspaper)

b. I always feel tempted to say that I can be a *right* bastard as well (BYU-BNC, written, popular)

Once again, these adjectives are analysed at the Interpersonal Level because they serve to indicate to the Addressee how (to which extent) the property evoked is ascribed to some entity, rather than to describe that entity. To understand the difference, compare the expression *a right bastard* in (106b) to the superficially similar expression *a right answer*:

(107)   a right answer   a right bastard
            the answer is right   *the bastard is right

a wrong answer   *a wrong bastard

an almost right answer   *an almost right bastard

To account for these differences, FDG assumes that the two uses of *right* perform different functions. In *a right answer*, *right* functions as a descriptive adjective; as such it will, as we will see, be analysed as a modifier at the Representational Level. In *a right bastard*, on the other hand, *right* is used to indicate that the property 'bastard' applies exactly to the entity in question; as such it is analysed as a modifier at the Interpersonal Level.

> Try to think of more adjectives that can function as exactness markers and apply the tests in (107).

All modifiers of the Ascriptive Subact will appear in the same position in the general schema, as illustrated in (108) and (109). Note that in most cases the head of the Subact will be empty (being specified at the Representational Level):

(108)   a. *supposedly* unsinkable
       b. $(T_1: [...]: \textbf{supposedly}^{\ T})$

(109)   a. *more or less* yellow
       b. $(T_1: [...]: \textbf{more-or-less}^{\ T})$

3.8.4. Operators

Approximation can in English also be indicated through grammatical means, for instance by the affix *-ish*, or by such invariable (grammaticalized) forms as *sort of* (*sorda*), *kind of* (*kinda*), and *like* (see Keizer 2007a; Hengeveld and Mackenzie 2008: 112; Hengeveld and Keizer 2011). In each of the examples in (110) the approximating element serves to indicate that the property evoked does not quite apply to the entity in question, but that this property somehow provides the best possible characterization:

(110)   a. The color of my eye is *yellowish*. (Internet)
       b. In her amiable presence, it almost all made sense, her contention that she was a professional adventurer on an expedition, a *sort of* ambassador of fun. (COCA, written, magazine)
       c. ...even comedy movies will have scenes of people running people off the road or running pedestrians down, and it's *sort of*, you know, *like* laughed at. (COCA)

These grammatical(ized) markers of approximation are all represented as operators at the layer of the Ascriptive Subact:

(111)   (approx T$_1$)

Operators of the Ascriptive Subact in other languages

In cases where English uses lexical means to further specify the property evoked by an Ascriptive Subact, other languages may use grammatical means. Leti, for instance, has a grammatical exactness marker, indicating that the property evoked definitely applies to the referent. In (112), for instance, the element *e* indicates that the Speaker definitely considers the entity referred to to be a big mountain. Omission of this marker automatically results in an approximate reading: the entity need not be a big mountain, but may merely look like one (van Engelenhoven 2004: 160). The element *e* can thus be seen as expressing an exactness operator:

(112) a. vuar=lalavn=**e**
         big=mountain=EXACT
         'big mountain'
       b. **(exact T$_1$)**

Kham has a special particle (*zə*) indicating Emphasis at the layer of the Ascriptive Subact (Watters 2002: 185):

(113) a. Ma-che:-də **zə**   ge-li-ke.
         unafraid   EMPH   we-remained
         'We remained (totally) unafraid.'
       b. **(emph T$_1$)**

3.9. Referential Subacts

3.9.1. General characterization

Referential Subacts perform the function of evoking an entity, either to introduce this entity into the discourse (referent construction) or to add information about an entity already available from earlier discourse (referent identification). Although Referential Subacts are often expressed as noun phrases, this need not be the case; similarly, not all noun phrases express Referential Subacts. Consider, for instance, the examples in (114):

(114)   a. We saw a lovely cottage yesterday. We are thinking of buying *it*.
        b. I took the car to work yesterday, but *it* broke down.
        c. I went to Amsterdam by bike, *?but *it* broke down yesterday.
        d. I went to Amsterdam by bike, because *it* is cheaper.
        e. How did you go to Amsterdam? By bike.

In (114a) a new entity is being introduced into the discourse (*a lovely cottage*), which is presented as unidentifiable for the Addressee (indefinite). As soon as the entity has been introduced, it becomes identifiable and available for future reference (*it*). In (114b), the entity *the car* is introduced into the discourse, but is nevertheless presented as identifiable on the basis of long-term knowledge. Once it has been introduced, it can be anaphorically referred to by means of a pronoun. In (114c) the noun *bike* is used; it does not, however, introduce an entity into the discourse. Therefore, anaphoric reference by means of *it* is not possible (unless in the case of 'sloppy' reference). As shown in (114d), the pronoun *it* can felicitously be used after this sentence, but only to refer to the event of going to Amsterdam by bike. This means that whereas the noun phrases *a lovely cottage* and *the car* in (114a) and (114b) constitute Referential Subacts, the noun *bike* in (114c) and (114d) does not. Example (114e) shows that the phrase *by bike* does express a Referential Subact, as shown by the fact that it can be questioned.

What the examples in (114) also show is that the entities evoked by Referential Subacts can be of different semantic types: whereas *a lovely cottage* and *the car* introduce Individuals, the pronoun *it* in (114d) refers back to a State-of-Affairs, while the referent of the phrase *by bike* is a Manner (as shown by the use of the question word *how*). Information concerning the type of entity evoked is, however, not represented at the Interpersonal Level: this is regarded as semantic information, specifying properties of entities as they occur in the real (or some imagined) world. As such, this information is represented at the Representational Level (see Chapter 4). The Interpersonal Level, on the other hand, reflects the inter-personal properties of the entities evoked, such as their identifiability, specificity, and availability for (anaphoric or deictic) reference.

3.9.2. The head

In our discussion of other interpersonal layers, we have seen that there are three types of head:

(i) Abstract heads:
     Most heads at the Interpersonal Level are abstract: they consist either of a combination of other units (e.g. a Move consisting of one or more Discourse Acts, a Discourse Act consisting of an Illocution, the Speech Participants and a Communicated Content) or of one or more features (e.g. the head of an Illocution may take the form of an abstract predicate like DECL or INTER, while the Speech Participants can be headed by combinations of features indicating Speaker and Addressee ($\pm$S, $\pm$A)).

(ii) Lexical heads:
     Although most lexemes are selected at the Representational Level, we have seen that certain (semantically (nearly) empty, non-descriptive) lexemes can function as heads at the Interpersonal Level. Illocutions, for instance, can have a lexical head (e.g. in the case of vocatives and interjections); Ascriptive Subacts, too, sometimes have a lexical head, as in the case of dummy expressions like *thingummy*.

(iii) Empty heads:
     Both Speech Participants and Ascriptive Subacts are typically headless. In that case the expressions used to realize these units are selected at lower levels of representation.

Referential Subacts are rather special in that they can take any of these types of head:

3.9.2.1. Abstract heads

In many cases the head of a Referential Subact consists of one or more Ascriptive Acts, and possibly one or more other Referential Subacts. A simple Referential Subact like *the car* in (115b) will be analysed as having a single Ascriptive Subact as its head (representing the property 'car'), while a more complex phrase like *a lovely cottage* will have a head consisting of two Ascriptive Subacts (representing the properties 'lovely' and 'cottage') (Note that, just like the Subacts within a Communicated Content, these Ascriptive Subacts are given in arbitrary order.)

(115)   a. the car
        b. $(R_1: (T_1))$

(116)   a. a lovely cottage
     b. $(R_1: [(T_1) (T_2)]^R)$

The head of a Referential Subact may also contain another Referential Subact, as in the case of genitive constructions like *Sue's car*, which will be given the representation in (117), where R_2 represents *Sue*:

(117)   a. Sue's car
     b. $(R_1: [(T_1) (R_2)]^R)$

When a Referential Subact is expressed as a **deictic pronoun**, its head consists of a combination of features, specifying Speaker, Addressee, or other participants. A combination like [+S, −A], for instance, indicates that reference is made to the Speaker only, the combination [−S, +A] that reference is made to the Addressee only, and the combination [−S, −A] that some third party present in the immediate situation is referred to. Apart from these three basic distinctions, a further distinction can be made between inclusive reference (*we* including the Addressee) and exclusive reference (*we* excluding the Addressee). This leads to the following possible combinations of features for deictic pronouns in English:

(118)   first person singular: $(R_1: [+S, -A])$ I/me
     first person singular exclusive: $(R_1: [+S, -A])$ we/us (−you)
     first person plural inclusive: $(R_1: [+S, +A])$ we/us (+you)
     second person: $(R_1: [-S, +A])$ you, you-all, you-guys
     third person: $(R_1: [-S, -A])$ he/she/they

Although number distinctions (singular vs. plural) are obviously important to trigger the right form of the pronoun, they are not represented here; they are regarded as being semantic in nature and are as such represented at the Representational Level. The difference between the subject and the object form of the pronoun (e.g. *I* vs. *me*) is also not reflected at the Interpersonal Level; these forms are seen as expressing a morphosyntactic distinction and are therefore captured at the Morphosyntactic Level. Pronouns are therefore a good example of how the different levels interact to produce the correct linguistic form:

(119)   IL: $(R_1: [+S, -A])$
     RL: singular
     ML: subject
     →   I

3.9.2.2. Lexical heads

As in the case of Ascriptive Subacts, Referential Subacts can take a proper name as their head. Since proper names do not (normally) have an ascriptive function, the proper name functions as the immediate head of the Referential Subact. This kind of analysis will be given to all prototypically used (i.e. referential) proper names.

(120)   a. Sue
b. (R_1: Sue)

Dummy expressions can also be used as proper names, in which case they function as the head of a Referential Subact (Hengeveld and Keizer 2011: 1970). Some examples are given in (121):

(121)   a. It was a wonderful night. *Thingummy* was there—you hadn't seen him for years. And *what's-his-name* was looking better than ever. (Internet)
b. He just had his picture taken by that famous photographer. *Whosis*. The guy who did Churchill (Internet)

3.9.2.3. Empty heads

Some Referential Subacts do not have a head at all. This kind of analysis is reserved for **anaphoric pronouns**. Such pronouns, like *it* in example (122), will be represented by the Referential Subact variable only. The use of an anaphoric pronoun can thus best be seen as an instruction of the Speaker to the Addressee to find the intended referent by looking at referents present from his/her mental representation of the ongoing discourse (see Keizer 2012). We will return to the analysis of pronouns in Chapters 4 and 5.

(122)   a. We saw a lovely cottage yesterday. We are thinking of buying *it*.
b. it
(R_1)

3.9.3. Modifiers

Referential Subacts are typically unmodified. The only modifiers we find at this layer are those expressing the subjective attitude of the Speaker (see Butler 2008; Hengeveld 2008: 49; Hengeveld and Mackenzie 2008: 121):

(123)   a. Likewise, from small, insignificant incidents, a tragedy can emerge. And this was to be *poor Mary*'s destiny. (BYU-BNC, written, fiction)

b. '... She doesn't complain, but you can see she feels the tension.'
   '*Poor her*,' said Lydia (BYU-BNC, written, fiction)

c. Where was Clive? *Good old Clive*? Clive the dealer. Clive the healer.
   Where was Clive? (BYU-BNC, written, fiction)

When an adjective, like *lovely* in *a lovely cottage*, is used to ascribe a
property to some entity, it is, as we have seen, analysed as an Ascriptive
Subact. The modifiers *poor*, *good*, and *old* in the examples in (123), however,
do not (objectively) ascribe the property in question to the entities evoked:
Mary may, but need not be poor, nor does Clive need to be old or even
good. Instead, these modifiers seem to express some kind of sympathy for or
empathy with the persons referred to. That they are different from other
adjectives is also clear from the fact that (i) only a few adjectives allow for
this kind of use; (ii) they cannot be replaced by their antonyms (*rich*, *bad*,
and *young*); (iii) they typically combine with proper names and pronouns.
Rather than analysing these adjectives as Ascriptive Subacts, they are
therefore analysed as modifiers of the Referential Subact:

(124)   a. good old Clive
   b. $(R_1$: Clive: **good-old** $^R)$

3.9.4. Operators

Operators applying at the layer of the Referential Subact are primarily concerned with the identifiability of the referent, as assessed by the Speaker. The
operator '–id', for instance, is used to indicate that the Speaker assumes that the
referent is not identifiable for the Addressee, and triggers the use of the indefinite
article *a*, as illustrated in (125a). In (126a), the use of the definite article in the
phrase *the car* indicates that the Speaker assumes that the Addressee can
identify the entity in question. This is captured by the operator '+id'.

(125)   a. We saw *a lovely cottage* yesterday.
   b. $(\text{–}\textbf{id}\ R_1$: $[(T_1)\ (T_2)]\ ^R)$

(126)   a. I took *the car* to work yesterday.
   b. $(\textbf{+id}\ R_1$: $(T_1)\ ^R)$

A related operator is the one representing the specificity of the entity evoked
by a Referential Subact. In FDG, the operator +s is used to indicate that the

Speaker has a specific entity in mind. Compare, for instance, examples (127) and (128). In (127) the Speaker, in using the Referential Subact *a lovely cottage*, has a specific entity in mind, one he/she can identify for the Addressee; in (128) on the other hand, the Speaker evokes an entity (any entity) with the property *cottage*, without, however, singling out a specific entity.

(127)   a. We saw *a lovely cottage* yesterday.
　　　 b. $(-id +s R_1: [(T_1) (T_2)]^R)$

(128)   a. We are looking for *a cottage*, preferably in the Lake District.
　　　 b. $(-id -s R_1: [(T_1) (T_2)]^R)$

In both these examples, the entity evoked is presented as unidentifiable for the Addressee. The operator ±s can, however, also co-occur with the operator '+id'. In (129), for instance, the entity referred to as *the car* is presented as identifiable for both Addressee ('+id') and Speaker ('+s'). In (130), on the other hand, the question word *who* is used to indicate that the Speaker cannot identify the entity in question ('−s'), but does expect the Addressee to be able to do so ('+id').

(129)   a. I took *the car* to work yesterday.
　　　 b. $(+id +s R_1: (T_1)^R)$

(130)   a. *Who* took the car this morning?
　　　 b. $(+id -s R_1)$

Suppose someone has been murdered in a particularly gruesome manner. The conclusion of the investigating officer is 'The murderer must be insane'. How would you represent (in terms of identifiability and specificity) the noun phrase *the murderer*? (example based on Donnellan 1966).

3.10. Summary

- In this chapter we have discussed the internal organization of the Interpersonal Level. After a brief introduction to the nature of the various units at this level and the (hierarchical) relation between them, we have focused on the individual units (layers).
- Each of these units was described in terms of (i) the kind of interpersonal entities they evoke (Moves, Discourse Acts, Illocutions, Speech Participants, Communicated Contents, and Ascriptive and Referential Subacts);

(ii) the frames available for their construction (the variable representing the entity evoked and its head); (ii) the operators, functions, and modifiers relevant for each layer.

• Using English examples (where possible authentic), a large number of interpersonal phenomena were discussed, including rhetorical and pragmatic functions, different illocutionary forces, vocatives and explicit performatives, reportatives and quotatives, irony, emphasis, reinforcement and mitigation, pronominal (anaphoric, deictic, and cataphoric) reference, exactness and approximation, and identifiability and specificity. Examples from other languages were used where the phenomenon in question could not be illustrated on the basis of English, or where a comparison between different languages was thought to provide extra insight into the distinctions made and the reasons for making them.

• In addition, the chapter has provided a systematic discussion of more general theoretical notions such as the distinction between grammatical and lexical elements and the presence of scope relations (e.g. between modifiers at the different layers).

Exercises

1. In Chapter 1, FDG was described as 'form-oriented in providing, for each of the languages analysed, an account of only those interpersonal and representational phenomena which are reflected in morphosyntactic or phonological form' (Hengeveld and Mackenzie 2008: 39). In this chapter, we saw that English has seven basic Illocutions: Declarative, Interrogative, Imperative, Optative, Hortative, Exclamative, and Interpellative.

a. Bearing in mind these properties of FDG, which Illocution would you give the following expressions:

   (i)   Have fun!
   (ii)   Come in!
   (iii) Beware of the dog.
   (iv)   Much joy may she have of him. (BNC, written, fiction)
   (v)   You can't take your bag into the museum.
   (vi)   I will be there at eight.
   (vii) Can't you read?
   (viii) What has he ever done for you?

b. Provide each of these examples with a representation at the Interpersonal Level.

2.* In Section 3.4.2 interjections are analysed as expressive Discourse Acts, that is, as direct expressions of some emotion (pain, surprise, disgust) without any communicative intention. Now consider the use of interjections in the following examples:

(i)   Hold on a sec ... *Ouch!* Just pinching myself to check I'm not dreaming! (BYU-BNC, written, popular lore)

(ii) A: What do you want me to say?
      B: I want you to say *ouch*. (BYU-BNC, written, fiction)

(iii) 'Marriage calls for a certain degree of maturity. Some people never achieve it.' *Ouch*, she thought. A sore subject.

(iv) Would you believe that numerous banks have as many as 49 possible fees for checking accounts? And many have raised monthly fees to an average that's creeping close to $15—*ouch!* (COCA, written, magazine)

(v)   She ends up digging her two-inch heel into my foot. '*Ouch!*' I yell, hopping up and down on my good foot. (COCA, written, fiction)

a. What kind of Discourse Act do you think we are dealing with here (expressive or interactive)?

b. How would you analyse these interjections at the Interpersonal Level?

3. Consider the following sentence:

(i)   I *sincerely* promise that I will *sincerely* consider the proposal.

a. How would you characterize the two uses of *sincerely* in this sentence? How do they differ?

b. How would you represent the first use of *sincerely* in FDG?

c. Any thoughts about the representation of the second occurrence of *sincerely*?

4.* Reflect on the use of the *if*-clauses in the following examples, in particular on their relation to the main clause. Which of the two *if*-clauses would you say belongs to the Interpersonal Level? Why?

(i)   There's a good poster up there *if you are interested*. (BYU-BNC, spoken, conversation)

(ii) I'll give you a pound *if you pass*, (BYU-BNC, written, academic)

5. Identify all Referential and Ascriptive Subacts in the following examples and provide them with a representation (including, where relevant, operators and modifiers):

(i)   They promised me a new computer.
(ii)   Who has eaten all the chocolates?
(iii) John came by car this morning.
(iv)   Whatsisname is looking for you.

6.* Provide an interpersonal representation for each of the following sentences (Subacts can be represented simply as R and T, without internal structure):

(i)   Seriously, we've got no money. (COCA, written, fiction)
(ii)   Damn! I deleted your files!
(iii) I promised myself a nice quiet evening.
(iv)   I'm begging you to stay.
(v)   What a mess!
(vi)   Poor you!

7. Consider the use of the adverb *really* in the following examples. Which uses would you classify as interpersonal? Why?

(i)   Well it's not that wonderful a film *really* (ICE-GB, spoken, direct conversation)
(ii)   I mean I'm too lazy *really* for that I think (ICE-GB, spoken, direct conversation)
(iii) It's all I mean it's all very exciting *really* (ICE-GB, spoken, direct conversation)
(iv)   He's uhm he was a *really* nice guy (ICE-GB, spoken, direct conversation)
(v)   The Newly Industrialising countries (NIC's) are *really* made up of 2 groups—the commonly termed 'Gang of Four'; and the higher income Latin-American countries of Brazil, Mexico and Argentina. (ICE-GB, written, students' examination scripts)

8. One characteristic of performative Discourse Acts is that they often contain the adverb *hereby*. Given the example in (60a) and its representation in (60b) (repeated here as (ia) and (ib)), how would you represent the element *hereby*?

(i)   a. (With regard to those lands illegally taken over after the agreement,) *the Salvadoran Government* hereby states that it has reserved the right to apply the law to guarantee the existence of the state of law. (COCA, written)

   b. $(A_1: [(F_1: state) (P_1: - the Salvadoran Government - {}^{P1})_S (P_2)_A (C_1: - it has reserved ... state of law - {}^{C})] {}^{A})$

9.* For each of the italicized elements in the following sentences, decide

a. which communicative function they perform
b. to which interpersonal layer they belong

   (i)   The prosecution has put together a case that suggests to you that O. J. Simpson is an *utter* fop, a *complete* fool. (COCA, spoken, CBS)
   (ii) In the first place the scheme *literally* drowned in its own success. (BYU-BNC, written, academic)
   (iii) First of all, I'm still married to Tommy. Plus, I am *so* not interested in men now. (COCA, written, magazine)
   (iv) You might remember I've been pressing for this for about eighteen *bloody* months. (BYU-BNC, spoken, meeting)

10.** In Section 3.7.2, cleft constructions are described as a focalizing device (example (60)), which can also be used to highlight contrastive elements (example (71b)). Hannay (1985: 76), however, provides the following example of a cleft construction:

(i)   A: What makes you suspect John?
      B: Well, it was John who, years ago when you were just small, so you won't remember, came up to me one day and said ...

a. What is the focal information in (iB)?
b. Would you still consider the cleft construction in (i) to be a focalizing device?
c. Can you think of a characterization of cleft constructions that would cover all these different uses?

11.** In Section 3.5.2.1 it is argued that English does not have Prohibitive Illocutions, since prohibitive expressions simply take the form of a negative Imperative, that is, an Imperative with the negator *not* and a form of dummy *do* (e.g. *Don't fidget!*). One could claim, however, that the following examples provide evidence of a Prohibitive Illocution in English:

(i)   Don't be a spoilsport!
(ii) Don't be so sensitive!

Explain why these sentences cannot simply be regarded as negated Imperatives.[2]

Suggestions for further reading

An account of pragmatic aspects dealt with in FDG is provided in Hannay and Hengeveld (2009). A collection of papers dealing with the interpersonal aspects of a variety of constructions in a range of languages can be found in Van Staden and Keizer (2009). Butler (2008) and García Velasco (2008) both discuss specific interpersonal features of English noun phrases. Smit (2010) provides a detailed discussion of pragmatic functions and content frames from a cross-linguistic perspective. A discussion of dummy elements like *thingummy*, approximators like *sort of* and exactness markers like *true* (in English as well as in other languages) can be found in Hengeveld and Keizer (2011). Hannay and Keizer (2005) offer a classification and FDG analysis of non-restrictive appositions (e.g. *my brother, John*). Keizer (2014) presents an alternative account of the active–passive alternation in FDG.

---

[2] I am grateful to Tamás Biró for bringing this to my attention.

4

The Representational Level

4.1. Introduction	103	4.6. The Property	146
4.2. The organization of the Representational Level	104	4.7. The Individual	152
		4.8. Locations and Times	159
4.3. The Propositional Content	108	4.9. Summary	166
4.4. The Episode	117	Exercises	167
4.5. The State-of-Affairs	124	Suggestions for further reading	171

The present chapter is devoted to the second of the four levels of representation that make up the Grammatical Component of a language: the Representational Level. After a brief general characterization of the Representational Level, we will turn to the various hierarchically organized units (layers) to be found at this level. These layers will be described in terms of the kind of unit (or semantic category) they represent and the primitives that are available for their formation (i.e. lexemes, frames, and operators). Of the four levels, the Representational Level has the largest number of layers. Some of these layers (representing minor semantic categories) will not be discussed here, either because they are of little relevance to English or simply for reasons of simplification. A detailed discussion of all representational layers can be found in Hengeveld and Mackenzie (2008: ch. 3). Where relevant, representations at the Representational Level will be compared to those at the Interpersonal Level to show how the two levels interact with and complement each other. For the sake of clarity, these comparisons will be presented separately (in boxes).

4.1. Introduction

At the Representational Level, the input received from the Interpersonal Level is filled in with semantic content, that is, with descriptions of entities as they occur in some non-linguistic world. The Representational Level deals with those aspects of meaning that can be described independently from the communicative intention of the Speaker. It thus complements the information represented at the Interpersonal Level: where the nature of the units at the Interpersonal Level can best be described in terms of Evocation, the nature of representational units can be described in terms of **Designation** (Hengeveld and Mackenzie 2008: 130). Together these two levels capture the complete pragmatic and semantic contents (intention and meaning) of the utterance.

Let us look at some simple examples to illustrate the division of labour between the Interpersonal and Representational Levels.

(1)   a. We bought a lovely cottage.
   b. $(A_1: [(F_1: \text{DECL}) (P_1) (P_2) (C_1: [(T_1) (R_1: [+S, -A]^R)$
   $(-\text{id } R_2: [(T_2) (T_3)]^R)_{\text{FOC}}]^C)]^A)$

(2)   a. Hey you!
   b. $(A_1: [(F_1: \text{hey}) (P_1)_S (P_2: [-S, +A]^{P_1})_A]^A)$

The representations given in examples (1b) and (2b) specify those elements of the utterances in (1a) and (2a) that belong to the Interpersonal Level. Example (1a), for instance, is represented as an Interactive Communicative Discourse Act with an abstract Illocution (DECL) and a Communicated Content (C_1) consisting of an Ascriptive Subact (T_1) and two Referential Subacts $(R_1$ and $R_2)$; one of these Referential Subacts is specified by the abstract features $[+S, -A]$, while the other consists of two Ascriptive Subacts $(T_2$ and $T_3)$ and is assigned the pragmatic function Focus. The representation in (1b) thus accounts for all the formally expressed pragmatic aspects of the utterance in (1a): it indicates (i) how the Addressee is intended to interpret the Discourse Act (as a declarative, i.e. as providing information); (ii) that one of the referents (or referent sets) (R_1) is (or includes) the Speaker, but not the Addressee; (iii) that the other referent (set) (R_2), provides the most salient information (Foc), is ascribed two Properties $(T_2$ and $T_3)$, and is assumed to be unidentifiable for the Addressee (–id); and (iv) that there is another Property (T_1) relating these referents. What the interpersonal representation in (1b) does not tell us, however, is what kind of entity R_2 refers to, and which properties are being ascribed. Nor are we provided with any other semantic information about the entities or entities evoked (tense, aspect, number, etc.). It is this semantic (representational) information that is provided at the Representational Level.

It is important to realize that not all utterances contain representational information. In example (2), for instance, there is no Communicated Content; in that case, there is no semantic content either, which means that the Representational Level is skipped and information goes directly from the Interpersonal Level to (morphosyntactic and/or phonological) Encoding.

Like the Interpersonal Level, the Representational Level consists of a number of hierarchically organized layers, representing different types of non-linguistic (real or fictional) entities. In the following section (4.2) we will look at the overall organization of the Representational Level. Subsequently, we will discuss various aspects of the different layers: the kind of entity they symbolize, their internal structure, and their individual features (Sections 4.3–4.8). As in the previous chapter, linguistic evidence will be supplied to justify the distinctions made. In addition, representations at the Representational Level will, where relevant, be related to those at the Interpersonal Level to show how the two levels interact with each other and to emphasize the difference between them.

4.2. The organization of the Representational Level

As pointed out in Section 4.1, the Representational Level deals with descriptions ('designations') of entities as they occur in some non-linguistic world. These entities belong to different ontological categories: objects (e.g. *chair*) are different from events (e.g. *John met Peter*) and these are again different from properties (e.g. *big*), places (e.g. *seashore*), and times (e.g. *today*). Within these broad ontological categories, further subdivisions can be made. Objects, for instance, can be divided into countable objects (*chair*) and substances (*water*), while events can be subdivided into actions (*John ran away*) and states (*John stayed at home*). And we can go on: within the category of countable objects, chairs are different from tables, and kitchen chairs are different from desk chairs. However, whereas the difference between objects and events and between actions and states is linguistically relevant (i.e. reflected in the form and behaviour of the linguistic units used to describe them), the difference between chairs and tables is not. This is important, since in FDG only those ontological categories that are linguistically relevant are represented in in the grammar, where they correspond to the different **semantic categories** that form the basic units of analysis at the Representational Level.

Four of these semantic categories are regarded as basic in the sense that the differences between them is reflected in the majority of languages, including English. These basic semantic categories are given in Table 4.1 (note that, in accordance with the convention, lower case symbols are used to represent variables at this level):

Table 4.1. Basic semantic categories

Semantic category	Variable	Example
Property	f	*colour, size*
Individual	x	*chair, dog*
State-of-Affairs	e	*meeting, concert*
Propositional Content	p	*idea, news*

Three of these semantic entity types reflect the three different 'orders of entities' distinguished by Lyons (1977: 442–7). **Individuals**, symbolized by the variable x, are what Lyons referred to as 'first-order entities'. These can be seen as the most straightforward type of entity, as they are concrete, can be seen and touched, can be located in time and space, and can be evaluated in terms of their existence. **States-of-Affairs** (SoAs, symbolized by the variable e) are second-order entities. They can be located in space and time, and evaluated in terms of their reality. **Propositional Contents**, symbolized by the variable p, are third-order entities. They are mental constructs which cannot be located in time or space, but whose contents can be evaluated in terms of their truth. The fourth basic semantic category is that of the **Property** (sometimes referred to as zero-order entities; see Hengeveld 1992; Keizer 1992; Dik 1997a, 1997b), which do not have independent existence but can only be evaluated in terms of their applicability. The following examples demonstrate the difference between these entities:

(3) a. My dog is black/*at ten/*false.
     b. The meeting is at ten/*black/*false.
     c. The news turned out to be false/*black/*at ten.

The Property *black* can (when used literally) only be used to describe Individuals, not SoAs or Propositional Contents, while a Property like *at ten* can only be assigned to SoAs, and a Property like *false* only to Propositional Contents.

> To which semantic category does the phrase *our lunch* belong in the following sentences: *We ate our lunch in the park* and *Our lunch took two hours?*

In addition to these four basic semantic categories, a number of minor categories have proved to be relevant; three of these will be discussed here (see Table 4.2; cf. Hengeveld and Mackenzie 2008: 132–5).

Table 4.2. Further semantic categories

Semantic category	Variable	Example
Location	l	*home*
Time	t	*week*
Episode	ep	*incident*

Both conceptually and linguistically, **Locations** and **Times** are different from other categories. That Locations are different from Individuals, for instance, is clear from the fact that the Individuals are necessarily situated at a Location. Similarly, SoAs take place at a particular time and place; this clearly shows that Times and Locations cannot be reduced to other entity types, but must be regarded as separate semantic categories (cf. Mackenzie 2005 for Location and Olbertz 1998 for Time).

Finally, there is linguistic evidence for a separate category of **Episodes**, which may be defined as a semantically coherent set of SoAs. An example of an Episode is given in (4) (for further details see Section 4.4):

(4)   He opened the door and slipped into the kitchen. (BYU-BNC, written, fiction)

As indicated in Tables 4.1 and 4.2, each layer at the Representational Level (i.e. each semantic category) contains a variable symbolizing the kind of entity designated. In addition, each layer typically contains a head, while modifiers, operators, and functions may provide further information about the designated entity. Heads may take four different forms. In the sections to follow, these different types of head will be discussed in detail for each semantic category; here a brief illustration of the different heads (at the layer the Individual) will suffice:

(5) a. The burglar smashed the window and Ø entered   absent
        the house
     b. The burglar took an expensive watch but left *a*   empty
        cheap one.
     c. *The burglar* left the house through the front door   lexical
     d. *The burglar's brother* was waiting in the car.   configurational

In (5a) the subject of the second clause is left implicit: there is an agent (*the burglar*), but this agent is not expressed. In such cases, the entity in question will be represented as a variable (x) without a head. In (5b), the phrase *a cheap one* does have a head (the Property 'watch'), but this head is not lexically expressed: instead the pronoun *one* is used to instruct the Addressee to retrieve the relevant Property from the previous discourse. In that case, the expression has a head (f), but this head is itself headless. In (5c), the expression *the burglar* has a simple, lexical head (the lexically expressed Property 'burglar'). In (5d), the phrase *the burglar's brother* has a configurational (i.e. a complex) head, consisting of more than one element (the Property 'brother' and the Individual 'the burglar'). The differences between the four types of head can be represented as shown in Table 4.3.

Table 4.3. Different types of representational head (layer of the Individual)

Type of head	Representation
Absent	(x_1)
Empty	$(x_1: (f_1))$
Lexical	$(x_1: (f_1: \text{LEX}))$
Configurational	$(x_1: [(f_1) (x_2)]^x)$

Finally, for reasons that will become apparent in the course of this chapter, the different representational layers are hierarchically organized as in example (6):

(6)   (π p$_1$: [   ]: σ P) Propositional Contents

      (π ep$_{1-n}$: [   ]: σ ^{ep})   Episode

          (π e$_1$: [   ]: σ ^{e})   State-of-Affairs

             (π f$_1$: [...]: σ ^{f})   Property

             (π x$_{1-n}$: [...]: σ ^{x})   Individual

             (π l$_1$: [...]: σ ^{l})   Location

             (π t$_1$: [...]: σ ^{t})   Time

The highest representational layer is that of the Propositional Content (p$_1$), which contains one or more Episodes (ep$_{1-n}$). Each Episode consists of one or more States-of-Affairs (e$_1$), which, in turn, consist of a Property (f$_1$) and one or more Individuals (x$_{1-n}$), and which may contain a Location (l$_1$) and a Time (t$_1$). Each layer has its own operator slot (symbolized by the variable π), as well as a slot for modifiers (symbolized by the variable σ) (cf. Hengeveld and Mackenzie 2008: 140). In the analysis of specific examples representations will typically be given in a linear form; in that case the (simplified) general schema for the Propositional Content will look as follows:

(7)   (p$_1$: (ep$_1$: (e$_1$: [(f$_1$) (x$_1$) (l$_1$) (t$_1$)...] ^{e}) ^{ep}) ^{P})

The remainder of this chapter will be devoted to a detailed description of each of the layers represented in (6). We will have a closer look at the nature of the entities these layers represent, starting with the Propositional Content and working our way down to Properties, Individuals, Locations, and Times. We will describe the distinctive linguistic behaviour of the units at each layer and will analyse and represent these units using the relevant primitives (lexemes, frames, and operators).

4.3. The Propositional Content

4.3.1. General characterization

Propositional Contents are mental constructs that do not exist in space or time but only in people's minds. They are not physical objects, and as such cannot be seen, heard, or touched; nor are they events that can happen. Instead they are 'contents', that is, information that can be known, believed, claimed, questioned, hoped, or wished for. These contents may be factual, as in the case of generally accepted pieces of knowledge or reasonable beliefs about the actual world, or non-factual, as in the case of questions, hopes, or wishes. Consider the following examples:

(8) a. But . . . we knew that *it was probably inevitable.* (BYU-BNC, spoken, interview)
     b. We hoped that *a local MP who was a leading sportsman would identify with our cause* (BYU-BNC, written interview)
     c. It is our hope that *these articles will pave the way for even more research on this subject.* (COCA, written, academic)

The italicized parts in (8) are all Propositional Contents, either factual (example (8a)) or non-factual ((8b) and (8c)). This is clear from the fact that they are introduced by lexical items such as *know* and *hope* (either verb or noun), which explicitly indicate their status as Propositional Contents. Propositional Contents can also be recognized by the fact that they can be asserted or denied: note that each of the sentences in (8) can be followed by expressions like *I don't believe that* or *That's not true*. Note also that in all three cases, such a response would be ambiguous: in (8a), for instance, the pronoun *that* in a reaction like *I don't believe that* may be taken to refer either to the whole sentence (*we knew that . . .*) or the embedded Propositional Content (*it was probably inevitable*). This tells us that not only the italicized part but also the utterance as a whole forms a Propositional Content. In addition, Propositional Contents may be 'qualified in terms of propositional attitudes' (Hengeveld and Mackenzie 2008: 144), that is, they may be qualified in terms of how certain a person is that the contents of the proposition are true. An example can be found in (8a), where the adverb *probably* expresses some degree of doubt on the part of the Speaker about the truth of the statement (see also Section 4.3.3).

> Explain why, in response to the utterance *I promise I will be there*, it is possible to say *No, you won't*, but not *No, you don't* (see also Chapter 3, Section 3.5.2.2).

4.3.2. The head

The head of a Propositional Content may be absent, empty, lexical, or configurational (see Table 4.4). We will discuss each type of head separately.

4.3.2.1. Absent heads

When an anaphoric pronoun is used to refer back to an earlier introduced Propositional Content, this pronoun will be represented without a head, that is, simply as a variable. In (9a) for instance, the first main clause introduces a factual Propositional Content (*I'm a marked man*), which, in the second main clause, is referred to by the anaphoric pronoun *that*. The representation of this pronoun is given in (9b), which does not itself contain any lexical content, but instead functions as a signalling device, inviting the Speaker to retrieve this content from elsewhere (by identifying the antecedent). The anaphoric relation is captured by means of co-indexing of the two variables representing antecedent and anaphor (i.e. both Propositional Contents, *I'm a marked man* and *that* are represented by the same variable, p_1).

(9)   a. 'People are starting to tell me [I'm a marked man] but I don't believe *that*,' he said. (**BYU-BNC**, written, newspaper)
     b. that
        (p_1)

4.3.2.2. Empty heads

Empty heads, too, are used when there is an anaphoric relation between two Propositional Contents. In this case, however, the anaphoric expression does not refer to the entire previously mentioned Propositional Content, but only to its head. An example is given in (10a), where the indefinite pronoun *one* designates the Property *idea* that functions as the head of the previous Propositional Content. In those cases, the Propositional Content does have a head (the Property 'idea'), but since the lexical content is not expressed, it is an empty head. The empty head is represented as a simple f-variable (f_1 in example (10b)). The anaphoric relation between the two expressions is once again indicated by co-indexation, but in this case of the two heads (*idea* and *one*, both represented by the same f-variable). Because a head is present, modification (here by means of the Property *simple*) is possible.

(10)   a. The [idea] behind budgetary accounting is, therefore, a simple *one*.
        (**BYU-BNC**, written, commerce)
     b. a simple one
        $(p_1: (f_1): (f_2: simple)^P)$

4.3.2.3. Lexical heads

Lexical heads of Propositional Contents come in two kinds. In most cases, lexical heads consist of a Property (f) consisting of a single lexical item, for instance *idea* in example (11a). Propositional Contents with this type of head can—and often are—modified by means of (premodifiying) adjectives or (postmodifying) clauses or phrases:

(11) a. Well, somebody gets *a weird idea* into their head, and they start to carry it out . . . (BYU-BNC, written, academic)

      b. a weird idea

        (p_1: (f_1: idea): (f_2: weird) ^{P})

The second type of lexical head is unusual in that it consists in its entirety of a single word that by itself forms the full Propositional Content of the utterance. In English, this type of Propositional Content typically takes the form of *yes* or *no* when used to answer a question:

(12) a. Teacher: . . . What did you decide to do in the end? Did you become a sportsman eventually? Michael: *Yes.* (BYU-BNC, written, academic, social sciences)

      b. Child: Were you still at school in the war? Mrs Glews: *No.* (BYU-BNC, written, academic)

The words *yes* and *no* in in these examples stand for a complete Propositional Content (they are, as it were, pro-Propositional Contents), assigning this Propositional Content either a positive ('yes') or a negative ('no') truth value. When used this way, the words *yes* and *no*, will be represented as follows (Hengeveld and Mackenzie 2008: 146).

(13) a. (p_1: yes)

      b. (p_1: no)

How would you analyse the element *one* in the following example; what kind of head does this expression have?

A: I just had an idea
B: I just had *one* too

'Yes' and 'no' in other languages

Evidence for the full propositional (or pro-propositional) status of the words *yes* and *no* can be found in such languages as Portuguese where these words can occur as the argument of a verb like *think* or *believe*, which take a propositional argument:

(14) Creio   que   sim/não
     I think that yes/no
     'I think so/I don't think so'

Other languages, like Scottish Gaelic, have no words for (propositional) *yes* and *no*; in answering a *yes–no* question, part of the Propositional Content has to be repeated (Hengeveld and Mackenzie 2008: 147):

(15) A: An tàinig Seumas?
         Q   come   Seumas
         'Did Seamas come?'
     B: Cha tàinig.
         not   come
         'No.' (Lit. 'He didn't come.')

4.3.2.4. Configurational heads

The head of a Propositional Content is configurational when it consists of one or more Episodes. An example of a Propositional Content headed by a single Episode is given in (16a), where the clause *it was probably inevitable* (whether used independently or as an argument of some verb) designates a single Episode. In (16b), the configurational head of the italicized Propositional Content consists of two Episodes (located at different points in time; see Sections 4.4.3 and 4.4.4). That these two Episodes (can) form one Propositional Content is clear from the fact that a propositional modifier like *possibly* can have scope over both Episodes (example (16b′).

(16)   a. (we knew that) *it was probably inevitable.* (adapted version of (8a))
       b. For all he knows, *the food was poisoned and will kill him instantly.*
          (Internet)
       b′. Possibly, *the food was poisoned and will kill him instantly.*

Simplified representations of (16a) and (16b) are given in (17a) and (17b) respectively:

(17) a. $(p_1: (ep_1))$
  b. $(p_1: [(ep_1) (ep_2)]$ $^P)$

Summing up, the head of a Propositional Content can have the following forms:

Table 4.4. Different types of head: Propositional Contents

Type of head	Representation
Absent	(p_1)
Empty	$(p_1: (f_1))$
Lexical	$(p_1: (f_1: \text{LEX}))$
	$(p_1: \text{LEX})$
Configurational	$(p_1: [(ep_1) (ep_2)]$ $^P)$

4.3.3. Modifiers

Modifiers of the Propositional Content take different forms, partly depending on the type of head of the Propositional Content. When the head is lexical, modifiers can take the form of a premodifying adjective (f_2 in (18b)) or a postmodifying clause or phrase (e.g. (e_1 in (19b)); in each case the modifier provides additional information about the designated entity.

(18) a. a weird idea
  b. $(\pi\ p_1: (f_1: \text{idea}): (\textbf{f}_2\textbf{: weird})$ $^P)$

(19) a. an idea that not everyone agrees with (BYU-BNC, written, academic)
  b. $(\pi\ p_1: [(f_1: \text{idea}): (\textbf{e}_1\textbf{: – that not everyone agrees with – })]$ $^P)$

When the head is configurational, modifiers serve as lexical specifications of propositional attitude; examples are modifiers that specify 'the kind and degree of commitment of a rational being to the Propositional Content' (Hengeveld and Mackenzie 2008: 151). Included in this category are modifiers expressing what is often referred to as **subjective epistemic modality**, like *probably* in (16a) and *possibly* in (16b'); that is, modifiers which indicate the extent to which the Speaker (or some other participant) is committed to the truth of a proposition (ranging from complete certainty to strong doubt). Some more examples are given in (20):

(20) a. He *certainly* was a contributor and a key supporter, no question about it. (COCA, written, newspaper)

b. If there are only two specimens in the aquarium *in all likelihood* the weaker specimen will be bullied to death. (BYU-BNC, written, popular lore)

c. *Perhaps* the human race is beset by problems which it lacks the moral capital to resolve. (BYU-BNC, written, advert)

Also to be found in the category of modifiers expressing propositional attitude are adverbs like *hopefully* (indicating that the Speaker wishes the (non-factual) proposition to be or become true), and *arguably* (indicating the Speaker's awareness that there may be disagreement concerning the truth of the proposition):

(21) a. I think he made a great decision. *Hopefully* we can prove him right and *hopefully* we can win a lot of games here. (COCA, written, newspaper)

b. Dylan is *arguably* the least accessible artist in rock 'n roll (COCA, written, newspaper)

A different set of propositional modifiers consists of expressions specifying the (non-verbal) source of the Propositional Content (**evidential modality**). One such source is the Speaker's own experience (**experiential evidentiality**); an example of such an experiential modifier is given in (22). In other cases, the Speaker has inferred the proposition from external (e.g. visual) evidence (**inferential evidentiality**); some examples are given in (23). Note that in (23b), the modifier is not an adverb, but the expression *I see*. Although this expression looks like a clause, it will not be analysed as such. The reason for this is that the Speaker does not actually see the purchasing event—what he/she sees is the necklace, from which he/she infers that the Addressee must have purchased it. This means that the expression *I see* as a whole functions as an inferential modifier.

(22) *In my experience*, if you slice fruit into small pieces and make it fun, no kid is going to refuse it. (COCA, written, magazine)

(23) a. In the Auvergne, where 656,000 hectares (26% of the land) is wooded, ... local farmers and Communes have a traditional involvement in woodland management, if only to provide firewood. In France it is *apparently* illegal to graze livestock in woodland. (BYU-BNC, written, miscellaneous)

b. *I see* you purchased a necklace. (COCA, written, fiction)

The general schema for modified Propositional Contents with configurational heads is given in (24), where the position of the modifier is given in bold:

(24) $(p_1: [(ep_1) \dots (ep_{1+n})]: \boldsymbol{\sigma}^{\,P})$

Comparison: Propositional Contents and Communicated Contents

The Propositional Content is the representational counterpart of the Communicated Content: the former supplies the latter with semantic information. At first sight, however, they may seem very similar, especially since the modifiers used at the two layers (e.g. *allegedly* and *reportatively* at the layer of the Communicated Content and *probably* and *evidently* at the layer of the Propositional Content) are often grouped together as expressing subjective epistemic modality. What distinguishes Communicated Contents from Propositional Contents, however, is that the former are necessarily Speaker-bound, whereas the latter need not be. Thus, in example (25a), the modifier *probably* does not reflect the Speaker's degree of commitment to the truth of the embedded proposition, but that of the subject of the main clause, Mr Tanner. This explains why an adverb like *reportedly* cannot occur in this position: being Speaker-bound (indicating that the Speaker has obtained the Communicated Content from someone else), it cannot be attributed to some other participant (example (25b)).

(25)   a. Mr Tanner believes that AEI is *probably* at the forefront of its particular industry in trading electronically with both its customers and the airlines. (BYU-BNC, written, commerce)

b. *Mr Tanner believes that AEI is *reportedly* at the forefront of its particular industry in trading electronically with both its customers and the airlines.

Likewise, there is a difference between reportatives (e.g. *allegedly* and *reportedly*) and evidentials (experientials like *in my experience* and inferentials like *evidently*) in that the former indicate that the Speaker relays information obtained from someone else (and are as such necessarily Speaker-bound), while the latter serve to indicate the (non-verbal)

(continued)

source of the information, that is, the 'evidence' that the person present-ing a proposition (not necessarily the Speaker) has for its validity.

That we are dealing with two sets of modifiers operating at different levels is also clear from the fact that they can be combined in one utterance without causing contradictions or redundancies. Note that once again, the Communicated Content modifier must have the Propositional Content modifier in its scope (from Hengeveld and Mackenzie 2008: 152):

(26)   a. *Allegedly* the area stimulated for the upper plexus would *pre-sumably* include C7 (Internet).
       b. Even some of C.'s friends *reportedly* are suggesting *maybe* he ought to cut back. (Internet).

4.3.4. Operators

Operators at the layer of the Propositional Content trigger the grammatical specification of propositional attitude. Since in English propositional atti-tude (subjective epistemic modality, evidential modality) is typically expressed lexically, propositional operators hardly occur. One example, however, is the expression of **hypothetical modality** (a subtype of subjective epistemic modality), for which English uses the subordinator *if*, as in examples (27a) and (27b) (Hengeveld and Mackenzie 2008: 154):

(27)   a. If he comes, (I'll leave)
       b. If he came, (I would leave)

In both these examples, the subordinator *if* introduces a non-factual, hypo-thetical Propositional Content, creating as it were a possible world in which other Propositional Contents may be true. Both *if*-clauses can be represented by the following general structure (where 'hyp' stands for hypothetical):

(28)   (**hyp** p_1: [...])

> ## Propositional Content operators in other languages
>
> Cross-linguistically, a wide range of propositional operators can be found. Some of these express subjective modality, like the dubitative marker (*kur*) in the following example from Pawnee (Parks 1976, cited in Bybee 1985; see also Hengeveld and Mackenzie 2008: 155)
>
> **(29) Kur**-rau   pi:ta   a   ku   capat.
>   DUB-was   man   or   a   woman
>   'It was either a man or a woman.'
>
> Pawnee also uses grammatical means to indicate inferential modality, as in (30), where the prefix *tir* indicates that the Speaker has inferred the Propositional Content presented (Parks 1976):
>
> **(30) Tirraku:tik**   ku:ruks.
>   INF-has-killed   bear
>   'He must have killed a bear.'

4.4. The Episode

4.4.1. General characterization

The second highest layer at the Representational Level is that of the Episode, which is defined as a thematically coherent combination of States-of-Affairs characterized by unity of Time (t), Location (l), and Individuals (x). By way of illustration, consider the following passage:

(31) ['Did you say what I thought you said?' Mr Trotter fumed. 'How dare you,' he continued, 'Get yourself into the headmasters office, now.']$_{ep1}$ ['Yes Sir,' David calmly answered, rising from his seat and walking across the cold classroom.]$_{ep2}$ [When he had left the room, Mr Trotter sat down, trembling.]$_{ep3}$ (BYU-BNC, written, school essay)

Although the entire passage takes place at one location at some time in the past, we can clearly distinguish three separate Episodes. The first describes Mr Trotter talking to David. Although the two main clauses (Mr Trotter fumed, he continued) obviously do not occur at the same time, they nevertheless show continuity of time, forming one unit in the course of events described. The next Episode describes David's reaction, which consists of a number of partly overlapping SoAs (answering, rising, walking), which once again form one temporal unit. The final Episode in this passage takes place after David has left, and describes two simultaneous SoAs, both involving Mr Trotter (sitting down and trembling).

Episodes can be also be explicitly introduced into a story, for instance by certain verbs. In English, for example, new Episodes often appear as (extraposed) subjects of the verb *happen* (Hengeveld and Mackenzie 2008: 133). An example can be found in (32), where the verb *happen* introduces a complex series of SoAs which together describe a single Episode showing unity of Time (as indicated by the Episode modifier *several times*, indicating that each sequence of events described took place at a particular time), Location (Marakesh (Valley)), and Individuals (all relating to weather conditions):

(32)   The people were convinced that the sounding of the bells would ward off any kind of calamity. Several times it happened that [mighty black clouds had threatened Marakesh, thunder had rumbled, it had started hailing, but as soon as someone passing by began ringing the bells, the dark clouds broke as if by a miracle, skirting the entire Marakesh Valley.] (COCA, written, fiction)

Where different Times, Locations, and Individuals are involved, Episodes are, of course, easier to recognize. Thus, in the following short dialogue, A's second turn consists of two Episodes:

(33)   A: The district council has no objections and of course the county's granted themselves planning permission on it
       B: Yes.
       A: and [that actually came through this morning]$_{ep1}$. [So so they will now be getting on with it fairly quickly.]$_{ep2}$

Episodes in other languages

In many languages, Episodes are quite explicitly coded in the grammar. A good example is Tidore (van Staden 2000: 14), which uses tail–head linkage (indicated in bold) to show that several SoAs are connected, forming one Episode:

(34) Turus jafa cahi   saloi   enage turus paka   **ine**.
then   Jafa carry.on.the.back basket there   then   ascend go.upward
Ine   una **oka** **koi**   enage. **Oka** **koi**   ngge
go.upwards   he   pick banana   there   pick   banana   there
kam-kam tora   oma   salo   ngge   madoya
fill   downwards   LOC   basket   there   inside
'Then Jafa, carrying the basket, went up; he picked the bananas and
filled the basket with them.'
'Then Jafa carried the basket and went upwards. Went upwards he
picked the bananas. Picked the bananas and filled (downwards) the
inside of the basket.'

In other languages, like Tauya (McDonald 1990: 218), coherence within
an Episode is achieved by the use of 'same subject' and 'different subject'
markers, as well as by the use of tense markers that apply to a sequence of
clauses. In Koryak (Bógoras 1917: 43–5), a particle-like element is used
to indicate a change of scene.

4.4.2. The head

The head of an Episode may be absent, empty, lexical, or configurational
(see Table 4.5). We will discuss each type of head separately.

4.4.2.1. Absent heads

Episodes can be referred to by means of an anaphoric pronoun, as in
example (35). In that case the pronoun, lacking descriptive information,
will be represented as a variable without a head. The anaphoric relation
between antecedent and anaphoric pronoun is captured by means of co-
indexing of the two variables at the Representational Level (both the
antecedent and the anaphoric expression are represented by the same variable, ep_1).

(35)   a. And on every page, you'll find warmth, humour and lively illustration making [the educational process] as joyful as *it* is instruct-
ive. (BYU-BNC, written, advert)
b. it
(ep_1)

4.4.2.2. Empty heads

In the case of an empty head English makes use of the indefinite pronoun *one*, which is anaphorically related to a previously mentioned (retrievable) lexical head. An example can be found in (36a), where the pronoun *one* functions as an instruction to the Addressee to look for a plausible lexical head in the preceding discourse.

(36)   a. Maybe your plot is a ticking-bomb story—the protagonist has to accomplish something before a terrible thing happens. Perhaps there is a smaller [plot] disguising a larger *one*. (COCA, written, academic)

      b. a larger one

      $(ep_1: (f_1): (f_2: larger)^{ep})$

4.4.2.3. Lexical heads

Lexical heads, like *incident, process, plot,* and *procedure,* describe a property of the designated Episode. Some examples are given in example (37a) and (38a): the semantic representations of these units are given in (37b) and (38b), respectively:

(37)   a. Maybe your plot is a ticking-bomb story—the protagonist has to accomplish something before a terrible thing happens. Perhaps there is *a smaller plot* disguising a larger one. (COCA, written, academic)

      b. a smaller plot

      $(ep_1: (f_1: plot): (f_2: smaller)^{ep})$

(38)   a. *The process* begins with a practical question and ends with positive outcomes for students. (COCA, academic)

      b. the process

      $(ep_1: (f_1: process))$

4.4.2.4. Configurational heads

The head of an Episode is configurational when it consists of one or more SoAs. The sentence in example (39a) consists of two Episodes (taking place at different times), each consisting of a single SoA. Example (40a), on the other hand consists of one Episode (displaying unity of Time, Location, and Individuals), consisting of three SoAs. The difference is reflected in the representations given in (39b) and (40b):

(39)   a. She married Joey Le Beau, Jr. in 1990, and the couple has three children (COCA, written, fiction)

      b. $(ep_1: (e_1: -$ She married Joey Le Beau, Jr. in 1990 $-))$ $(ep_2: (e_2: -$ the couple has three children $-))$

(40) a. I heard a car coming, and I dropped the book and craned out the front window to see if it was the Mighty UnButt Crack's truck (COCA, written, fiction)

      b. $(ep_1: [(e_1: - I heard the car coming -) (e_2: - I dropped my book -) (e_3: - I craned out the front window \ldots -)]^{ep})$

In summary, the head of an Episode can have the forms outlined in Table 4.5:

Table 4.5. Different types of head: Episodes

Type of head	Representation
Absent	(ep_1)
Empty	$(ep_1: (f_1))$
Lexical	$(ep_1: (f_1: \text{LEX}))$
Configurational	$(ep_1: [(e_1) (e_2)]^{ep})$

4.4.3. Modifiers

Modifiers of the Episode are typically used to specify **absolute time**, that is, to specify the fixed moment in time at which the Episode took place. There are various ways in which absolute time can be designated. First of all, Speakers can do so deictically, in which case they anchor an Episode in the moment of speaking, as in the following example:

(41) *Now* he supervises the production end of the business\ldots(COCA, written, fiction)

Speakers can also choose to specify the moment of occurrence of an Episode non-deictically. In that case, they either relate the Episode to the occurrence of some other event or they specify the moment of occurrence of the Episode calendrically (in terms of a culturally determined fixed unit of time). An example of the latter was given in (39a), where *in 1990* indicates the calendrically fixed time at which the Episode took place.

Several examples of Episode modifiers referring to other events can be found in the following passage:

(42) [He was a rather ordinary boy *until he went away to college*]$_{ep1}$. [He got involved with a radical environmentalist group and dropped out of school to save whales and hug trees.]$_{ep2}$ [*When his parents died in a car crash*, he showed up with long, greasy hair and grubby clothes and a contemptuous smirk. I noticed that he spent a lot of time talking to his uncle, Charles Finnelly.]$_{ep3}$ [*Six weeks after that*, Ethan arrived with Pandora and they moved into what had been his parents' house]$_{ep4}$. [That was seven years ago]$_{ep5}$. [*Now* he supervises the production end of the business . . .]$_{ep6}$ (COCA, written, fiction)

In this passage, each of the italicized expressions functions as a modifier of an Episode, specifying the absolute time of occurrence of the Episode. Thus, the non-deictic expression *until he went away to college* refers to a specific time in the past, say 1992. The Speaker, however, chooses to provide a non-calendrical specification, either because he/she does not know the exact year, or because it is not the exact time that is relevant, but rather the relation between the Episode and some other event (in this case, his going away to college). The time of occurrence of the second Episode is not given, but implied (while he was at college). The third Episode does contain a time modifier (*when his parents died in a car crash*), once again providing a specific time in the past. The fourth Episode also contains a time modifier, relating the Episode to the previous one; the time specification, however, is once again an absolute one. Finally, the sixth Episode contains the deictic time modifier *now* (= example (41)). What is important is that in all these cases the point of view is that of the Speaker at the moment of speaking; hence the change from past to present tense in the last Episode.

The absolute time modifiers in examples (41)–(42), irrespective of their internal structure, all occupy the same slot in the general schema for the Episode (given in bold):

(43)   (ep$_1$: [(e$_1$) . . . (e$_{1+n}$)]: $\boldsymbol{\sigma}$ ^{ep})

Let us finally look at some examples which not only justify the distinction between the Propositional Contents and Episodes, but which, in addition, can explain some of the restrictions on the placement of certain types of adverbs. As mentioned before, the extraposed subject of the verb *happen* takes the form of an Episode. This means that such subjects do not include a Propositional Contents, as these are higher up in the representational hierarchy. Consequently, the prediction is that modifiers belonging to the layer of the Propositional Contents cannot occur after the verb *happen*. This is confirmed by the example in (44b), where the addition of the attitudinal adverb *probably* seems to yield a questionable result. Example (44c) shows that with a verb like *believe*, which takes a propositional complement, the attitudinal adverb *probably* is fully acceptable:

(44) a. *It so happened that* the summer was an exceptionally hot one
(BYU-BNC, written, miscellaneous)

b. *[?]*It so happened that* probably the summer was an exceptionally
hot one (BYU-BNC, written, miscellaneous)

c. *He believed that* probably the summer was an exceptionally hot
one (BYU-BNC, written, miscellaneous)

4.4.4. Operators

The most important operator at the layer of the Episode is that of **absolute
tense**. In English, this operator can have three values: past, present, and
future. Since these operators have scope over the Episode as a whole, all the
SoAs within the Episode must share the feature for absolute tense. By way
of illustration, consider once more example (40), here repeated as (45):

(45) a. I *heard* a car coming, and I *dropped* the book and *craned* out the
front window to see if it was the Mighty UnButt Crack's truck
(COCA, written, fiction)

b. (**past** ep_1: [(e_1: – I heard the car coming –) (e_2: – I dropped my book –)
(e_3: – I craned out the front window . . . –)] ^{ep})

The entire episode is situated in the past, indicated in (45b) by the presence
of the operator 'past'. This operator is formally expressed on the verb of
each of the three SoAs contained within the Episode.

Tense operators in other languages

English has a relatively simple tense system, consisting of three tenses:
present, past, and future. Some languages have more subtle tense systems, with different types of past or future indicating different degrees of
remoteness. In Garo, for instance, a distinction is made between non-
imminent future (46a) and imminent future (46b) (Burling 2004: 122–3):

(46) a. Ang-na   i-ko   nang-noa
I-DAT   DEM-ACC   need-FUT
'I will need this'

b. Cha·-ja-ni   gimin   okri-najok
eat-NEG-GEN   because   hungry-IMM-FUT
'Because of not eating, I will soon be hungry.'

4.5. The State-of-Affairs

4.5.1. General characterization

States-of-Affairs are entities that are located in place and (relative) time, and which may be real or non-real. They may, in other words, happen (or not happen) at a particular time and place. Some examples are given in (47), where the italicized expressions designate different kinds of SoA: action (*meeting*, *bombing attacks*), event (*party*), process (*arrival*), and state (*illness*).

(47) a. The play-reading group are currently reading An Inspector Calls and *the next meeting* is on Thursday at 14 Candleford Gate at 10 a.m. (BYU-BNC, written, newspaper)

b. She had timed *her arrival* for half an hour after *the party* was due to commence. (BYU-BNC, written, fiction)

c. *Immediate bombing attacks* were expected, and when these did not take place the evacuees began to trickle back. (BYU-BNC, written, non-academic)

d. *Mozart's final illness* lasted 15 days (BYU-BNC, written, biography)

That SoAs are to be distinguished from, for instance, Propositional Contents and Individuals is clear from the following examples (see also example (3) earlier in the chapter):

(48) a. *The next house/belief is on Thursday.

b. *She had timed her house/belief.

c. *The house/belief did not take place.

The distinction between SoAs and Episodes is less straightforward; the difference between these two semantic categories will be discussed in Sections 4.5.6 and 4.5.7.

In example (47), the italicized expressions are all noun phrases. Note, however, that each of the clauses in these examples also designate SoAs. The difference between these two types of SoA designating unit is that in the case of a noun phrase the head of the unit is lexical, while in the case of a clause, the head is configurational. Some further examples are given in (49):

(49) a. The enemy withdrew.

a'. The enemy's withdrawal

b. The enemy attacked the city.

b'. The enemy's attack on the city.

The sentence in (49a) describes an event that involves a verbal Property (*withdrew*) and one participant (*the enemy*). Using a different terminology, we say that the SoA designated by this sentence consists of a **predicate** (the verb *withdraw*), which predicates over (assigns a Property to) its **argument** (the participant). Together, these elements form the configurational head of the SoA. As shown in (49a'), the same event can also be described by means of a noun phrase. In that case the SoA has a lexical head (*withdrawal*). The event described in (49b) contains two participants (*the enemy* and *the city*). Here the Property *attack* indicates a relation between these participants. In (49b) we thus have a predicate (in this case a verb) with two arguments. The combination of predicate and arguments (i.e. the configurational head of an SoA) is often referred to as a **predication**. This term is used to describe both SoAs with configurational heads (like the ones in (49a) and (49b)) and those with lexical heads (such as *withdrawal* and *attack* in (49a') and (49b')).

The rest of this section is organized as follows. The different types of head an SoA may have are described in Section 4.5.2. Subsequently, Section 4.5.3 discusses some specific aspects of SoAs with configurational heads. Section 4.5.4 deals with a special group of SoAs, traditionally referred to as copular constructions. Section 4.5.5 is concerned with complex SoAs, that is, SoAs containing more than one predication. Finally, Sections 4.5.6 and 4.5.7 are devoted to a discussion of the most important SoA modifiers and operators.

4.5.2. The head

As with the previously discussed layers, the head of an SoA may be absent, empty, lexical, or configurational (Table 4.6). This section will briefly describe the four types of head; subsequently, Section 4.5.3 will focus on some specific aspects of SoAs with configurational heads.

4.5.2.1. Absent heads

In (50a), the pronoun *it* is used to refer anaphorically to the SoA designated by the noun phrase *the accident* in the previous clause. Since it does not contain any descriptive information, the pronoun *it* will be represented as an SoA denoting a unit without a head, that is, simply as a variable (e_1). The anaphoric relation is captured by means of co-indexing of the variables symbolizing the two units (*the accident* and *it*).

(50) a. I was there at [the accident] just after *it* happened (BYU-BNC, written, newspaper)

   b. it

   (e_1)

4.5.2.2. Empty heads

Empty heads are used when there is an anaphoric relation between the heads of two SoAs. An example is given in (51a), where the indefinite pronoun *one* designates the Property *visit* (f_1) that functions as the head of the SoA designated by the expression *this visit*. Since this Property is predicated but not expressed, the variable symbolizing this Property is present, but does not have a head, as illustrated in example (51b). The presence of a head explains why modification (in this case by the adjective *previous*) is possible.

(51) a. Despite the general chaos, this [visit] was much more relaxed than the previous *one*. (BYU-BNC, written, prose)

   b. the previous one

   $(e_1: (f_1): (f_2: previous)^e)$

4.5.2.3. Lexical heads

The italicized expressions in example (47) above are all examples of SoA-designating units with a lexical head. In (47a), for instance, repeated here as (52a), the noun *meeting* functions as the head of the expression *the next meeting*, with the element *next* functioning as a modifier.

(52) a. ... *the next meeting* is on Thursday at 14 Candleford Gate at 10 a.m.

   b. $(e_1: (f_1: meeting): (f_2: next)^e)$

4.5.2.4. Configurational heads

Configurational heads of SoAs consist of a combination of a Property (f) and one or more obligatory participants (Individuals or Locations) functioning as its arguments. Configurational heads are the default way of designating SoAs. Some examples are provided in (53) (for the sake of simplicity, higher layers—Episodes, Propositional Contents—have been ignored here):

(53) [We saw numerous examples [where people bought equipment]$_{e2}$]$_{e1}$. For example [Amina has bought a sewing machine]$_{e3}$. [This will give her financial independence and a steady income]$_{e4}$. (BYU-BNC, spoken, meeting)

Example (53) contains four SoAs with configurational heads. The first, e_1, consists of a Property (*see*) and two participants (*we* and *numerous examples... equipment*). The second participant contains a relative clause designating another SoA, e_2, consisting of the Property *buy* and the participants *people* and *equipment*. The third SoA, e_3, contains the same Property (*buy*), but different participants (*Amina* and *a sewing machine*). The fourth SoA, e_4, consists of a Property (*give*) and three participants (*this*, *her*, and *financial independence and a steady income*). The number of participants depends on the kind of Property selected: two-place properties (like *see* and *buy* in example (53)) require the presence of two participants, whereas a three-place predicate (like *give*) requires the presence of three participants. In the next section, the internal structure of configurational heads will be discussed in closer detail.

We will end this section with Table 4.6, which gives a brief summary of the possible heads of SoAs.

Table 4.6. Different types of head: States-of-Affairs

Type of head	Representation
Absent	(e_1)
Empty	$(e_1: (f_1))$
Lexical	$(e_1: (f_1: \text{LEX}))$
Configurational	$(e_1: [(f_1) (x_1) (x_2) \ldots]^e)$

4.5.3. Configurational heads: number and roles of the participants

As we have seen, the configurational heads of SoAs consist of a Property designating the action, process, or state in question and the arguments of this Property, that is, the participants that are obligatorily involved in this action, process, or state. It will be clear that SoAs differ both with regard to the number of participants (their quantificational valency) and with regard to the role these participants play in the SoA (their qualificational valency). In this section we will consider both of these aspects in more detail.

4.5.3.1. Number of participants (quantificational valency)

Languages differ with regard to the number of participants they allow in an SoA; that is, different languages allow different minimum and maximum **valencies**. Some languages require the presence of at least one participant, whereas other languages, like English, accept SoAs without any participants (see example (59)). Likewise, whereas many languages, again including English, allow for three participants, other languages have a maximum valency of two.

In English, most SoAs contain one or two participants, the result being an intransitive or monotransitive clause, respectively; as pointed out, however, SoAs with zero or three participants are also possible. This means that English has frames (**predication frames**) for SoAs with one, two, three, or no arguments. Depending on the situation the Speaker wishes to describe and the vantage point from which he/she wishes to describe it, he/she selects the appropriate Property and predication frame. Consider, for instance, the sentences in example (54):

(54)   a. Matthew preceded Mary into the room.
      b. Mary followed Matthew into the room.

The sentences in (54a) and (54b) may be used to describe the exact same event; the difference is that in (54a) *Matthew* is taken as the vantage point and in (54b) *Mary* (Dik 1997a: 249–50). To bring out the difference, the Speaker selects different Properties (*precede* and *follow*, respectively), but selects the same predication frame; that is to say, the internal structure of the predication in terms of number of participants and their roles in the designated SoA is the same in the two sentences (see Section 4.5.3.2).

Now consider the sentences in examples (55a) and (56a), which, despite the obvious difference in meaning, can be used to describe the same event:

(55)   a. The ship sank.
      b. $(e_1: [(f_1: sink) (x_1: ship)]^e)$

(56)   a. The enemy sank the ship.
      b. $(e_1: [(f_1: sink) (x_1: enemy) (x_2: ship)]^e)$

Once again, the two sentences reflect different vantage points. In this case, however, the Speaker selects the same verb, but with two different predication frames: in example (55a) the verb *sink* is combined with a one-place predication frame, in (56b) with a two-place predication frame. This example shows that although most Properties (in this case verbs) are typically combined with a certain predication frame (e.g. *laugh* with a one-place predication frame, *buy* with a two-place predication frame, *give* with a three-place predication frame), the system is in fact a very flexible one, in which verbs can be combined with different predication frames, according to the communicative needs of the Speaker (see García Velasco and Hengeveld 2002). Thus, verbs can quite easily be combined with non-prototypical predication frames, as long as the Addressee can be expected to reconstruct the Speaker's intention. This explains why it is perfectly acceptable for a verb like *laugh* to appear in a two-place predication (example (57a)), for a verb like *buy* to combine with a one-place predication (example 57b)), and for a verb like *cough* to appear in a three-place predication (example (57c)).

(57) a. Kwame didn't think the joke was that funny, but *when Biddy Owens laughed that high little laugh of his*, Kwame couldn't help but laugh himself. (COCA, written, fiction)
  b. *Annie Wozzie bought and bought*, picking out nearly a hundred dollars worth of what Uncle Abe, shaking his head, called 'useless tchotchkes': pottery birds, silk flowers, cache-pots, throw pillows, candlesticks. (COCA, written, fiction)
  c. The second interview closed as *the landlady gracefully coughed us into the passage*, and so into the healthy, silent streets. (Rudyard Kipling, *From Sea to Sea*, Chapter 8)

So far, we have looked at SoAs whose Property takes the form of a verb. There are, however, also SoAs without a verbal Property. An example is the copular sentence in (58):

(58) a. She is clever.
  b. $(e_1: [(f_1: clever) (x_1)] ^e)$

In FDG, the verb *be* is analysed as a semantically empty element, introduced only at the Morphosyntactic Level as a carrier of number and tense distinctions (in this case third person singular, present tense). In other words, the verb *be* does not add to the meaning of the sentence in (58); the only descriptive element in (58a) is, in fact, the adjectival Property *clever*, which is asserted to apply to the person referred to by the subject *she*. In sentences like these, it is therefore the adjective that is analysed as the lexical Property: in (58) the adjective *clever* functions as a non-verbal predicate, predicating over a single argument (*she*). The sentence in (58a) is therefore based on a one-place predication frame. The only semantic (representational) difference between a sentence like *She laughed* and a sentence like *She is clever* is the type of Property it contains (verbal vs. adjectival). Because in English such grammatical information as number and tense cannot be expressed on the adjective, the verb *be* is introduced. This, however, does not have an effect on the semantics of the sentence; it is simply the result of a morphosyntactic feature of English (see also Chapter 5, Section 5.6.3).

Finally, English also has a small set of verbs that occur without any arguments. These so-called weather verbs (*rain, snow, hail*, etc.) designate SoAs that implicitly involve a participant (the rain, snow, and hail in question), but where grammatically this participant does not function as an argument of the verb. Consider the examples in (59):

(59)   a. it rained, hailed, blew, and we got home soaked to the skin (BYU-BNC, spoken, interview)
   b. *?the rain rained
   c. *the rain/hail/wind rained, hailed, blew, and we got home soaked to the skin (BYU-BNC, spoken, interview)
   d. $(e_1: (f_1: rain))$

The pronoun *it*, functioning as the subject in (59a), does not refer to a participant in the SoA designated: there is no participant who performs that action or undergoes the process of raining. Consequently, replacing *it* by the noun phrase *the rain* yields an unacceptable (or at least highly questionable) result. Moreover, in (59a) the pronoun *it* functions as the subject not only of *rain*, but also of *hail* and *blow*; nevertheless, it will be clear that one and the same pronoun cannot have three different referents (example (59c)). In FDG it is therefore assumed that verbs like *rain, hail*, and *blow* do not take an argument; the predication frame in question consists only of a (zero-place) verbal Property (example (59d)). The presence of *it* can be explained by the fact that English, as a fairly strict SVO language, requires the presence of a subject. In those cases where there are no arguments to function as the subject, a 'dummy' subject is added to fill the subject position (we will come back to this issue in Section 5.3).

Table 4.7 lists the four basic predication frames relevant for English.

Table 4.7. Predication frames in English

Valency	Example	Representation
Zero-place	It rains	$(e_1: (f_1))$
One-place	She laughed; She is clever	$(e_1: [(f_1) (x_1)]^e)$
Two-place properties	The enemy sank the ship	$(e_1: [(f_1) (x_1) (x_2)]^e)$
Three-place properties	This will give her financial independence	$(e_1: [(f_1) (x_1) (x_2) (e_3)]^e)$

How many arguments does the sentence *It is six o'clock* have? And what about *I bet you 10 pounds that he won't show up*?

Number of participants in other languages

As mentioned above, languages differ with regard to the number of participants an SoA allows. In English the minimum number of arguments is zero, the maximum number three. Mandarin Chinese, however, does not allow more than two arguments. Thus, whereas in English a verb like *pour* can combine either with a two-place predication frame (*I poured the tea*) or with a three-place predication frame (*I poured him some tea*), in Mandarin Chinese *pour* can only be used with a two-place predicate. If a third argument is added, a serial construction is used, consisting of two verbal Properties (*pour* and *give* in example (60)); in that case the serial construction as a whole involves three participants, while the individual verbs have only two arguments (Li and Thompson 1981: 366):

(60) Wǒ   gěi   nǐ   dào   chá.
      1   give   you   pour   tea
      'I'll pour you some tea.' (lit. 'I pour tea give you.')

Four-place predication frames seem to be rare; a possible example may be the Turkish causative construction (Kornfilt 1997: 332). In (61), for instance, the verb *koy* 'put' could be argued to take four arguments (*I*, *Hasan*, *the pitcher*, and *the cupboard*).

(continued)

(61) Ben Hasan-a   sürahi-yi   dolab-a   koy-dur-du-m
    I   Hasan-DAT pitcher-ACC cupboard-DAT put-CAUS-PST-1.SG
    'I made Hasan put the pitcher into the cupboard.'

Finally, there are languages which do not allow for zero-place predications. In those languages, sentences describing the weather have a fully referential subject that functions as an argument of the verb. An example is Saramaccan, where sentences describing weather conditions contain a referential subject functioning as the argument of a one-place verbal Property (Haabo 2002):

(62) a. Tyúɓá   tá   kai.
          rain   PROG   fall
          'It's raining.' (lit. 'Rain is falling.')
    b. Véntú   tá   ko.
          wind   PROG   come
          'It's blowing.' (lit. 'Wind is coming.')
    c. Gaángádű   tá   ɓái.
          great-god PROG   shouting
          'It's thundery (weather).' (lit. 'God is shouting.')

4.5.3.2 Semantic roles of the participants: qualificational valency

Predication frames, we have seen, consist of a Property and one or more (and occasionally zero) arguments, representing the participants involved in the SoA designated. Depending on the type of SoA, these participants play distinct roles. To indicate these roles, a **semantic function** is attached to each participant. In the literature, a great many semantic functions have been distinguished, including agent, experiencer, force, patient, theme, recipient, beneficiary, instrument, possessor, location, direction, source, and path. Although all of these functions may indeed be needed to account for the formal aspects of certain languages, FDG does not assume all of these functions to be relevant for all languages; that is, specific semantic functions are not universally valid. Instead it is assumed that three universally relevant clusters of semantic functions (or macro-roles) can be distinguished (cf. Foley and Van Valin 1984; Dowty 1991):

(i) *Actor (including agent, force)*: The participant playing an active role in the designated SoA.

(ii) *Undergoer (including patient, theme, experiencer)*: The participant playing a passive role in the designated SoA.

(iii) *Locative (including recipient, beneficiary, direction, source, path, possessor)*: The location (in the most general sense) where the designated SoA takes place.

Individual languages differ with regard to the specific subcategories distinguished. Here we see once again the Principle of Formal Encoding at work, in the sense that additional semantic functions will only be included in the grammar of a language if they are systematically reflected in form (Hengeveld and Mackenzie 2008: 194). Thus, if in a language recipients and beneficiaries exhibit the same formal behaviour, there is no need to include two different semantic functions, even if intuitively the difference between them will be perfectly clear. In this way, an unnecessary proliferation of semantic functions can be avoided.

Find some sentences with recipients and beneficiaries in English. Would you say English needs two semantic roles to account for the data?

The difference between Actor and Undergoer is clearest in the case of **dynamic** two-place SoAs like (63a) and (63b):

(63)   a. My sister (A) burnt the letter (U).

b. The cat (A) chased the mouse (U).

In both these SoAs one participant plays a more active role than the other: in (63a) it is my sister who is doing something to the letter, while in (63b) it is the cat who takes the initiative in the hunt. Both SoAs contain a prototypical Actor, since both my sister and the cat are volitionally involved in the SoA. Example (63a) also contains a prototypical Undergoer, since the letter is clearly affected by the SoA. Note, however, that the notions Actor and Undergoer are relative notions, with the Actor playing a more active role than the Undergoer. This also means that when an SoA is not volitionally performed, one participant may still be the Actor. An example is given in (64), where the fire, although not volitionally performing the action of destroying, will still be assigned the semantic function of Actor, since it plays a more active role than the other participant, the school, which, being passive and affected, is a prototypical Undergoer.

(64)   The fire (A) destroyed the school (U).

In the assignment of semantic functions, the distinction between dynamic and **non-dynamic** SoAs is a crucial one. Dynamic SoAs are those that require the input of energy (Hengeveld and Mackenzie 2008: 196), such as actions and processes. Clear examples are (63a) and (63b), where the energy can be said to flow from the Actor to the Undergoer, causing some kind of change (e.g. a change of state, as in (63a), or a change of location, as in (63b)). The SoA in (64) is also dynamic, since the destruction of the school required the input of energy, irrespective of who or what the source of that energy is. Some further examples of dynamic SoAs are given in (65):

(65)   a. The girl (A) smiled.
      b. The girl (U) fell.
      c. The girl (A) jumped from the fence (L).
      d. The girl (U) fell from the fence (L).
      e. The girl (A) threw the ball (U) into the pond (L).
      f. The wind (A) blew the leaves (U) into the pond (L).

The SoAs in (65a) and (65b) have only one participant. As the source of energy, the participant in (65a) is actively involved in the SoA; this participant will therefore be assigned the semantic function of Actor. In (65b) on the other hand, the single participant plays a passive role. Although the SoA requires the input of energy, the participant is not the source of this energy; it will therefore be assigned the role of Undergoer. In (65c) and (65d) we find two participants. In both SoAs one of these participants (*from the fence*) is the Location where the SoA takes place (more specifically, the source of the movement); this participant is therefore assigned the semantic function of Locative. However, whereas in (65c) the second participant (the girl) is a prototypical Actor, in (65d) the second participant is the Undergoer. Finally, in (65e) and (65f), we find all three macro-roles combined. The only difference between these two SoAs is the degree of prototypicality of the Actor: (65e) contains a prototypical Actor, volitionally performing the action designated, whereas in (65f) the Actor is the non-volitional source of energy.

    Let us now turn to non-dynamic SoAs. These, as may be expected, do not require the input of energy; they are stative. Since in non-dynamic SoAs there is no energy flow, they cannot contain an Actor (since Actors are— whether or not volitionally—always the source of energy). This leaves us with the following possibilities:

(66) a. Kure Island (U) lies in the Pacific Ocean (L).
    b. Kure Island is beautiful (U).

In (66a), Kure Island can, rather non-prototypically, be regarded as the Undergoer in the sense that it is being located in space. In (66b), too, Kure Island is assigned the function of Undergoer, as it is being assigned the Property 'beautiful'.

Table 4.8. Possible combinations of basic semantic functions in English

Dynamic SoAs		
Valency	**Semantic functions**	**Example**
one-place	A	The girl (A) smiled.
	U	The girl (U) fell.
two-place	A + U	My sister (A) burnt the letter (U).
	A + L	The girl (A) jumped from the fence (L).
	U + L	The girl (U) fell from the fence (L).
three-place	A + U + L	The girl (A) threw the ball (U) into the pond (L).
Non-Dynamic SoAs		
Valency	**Semantic functions**	**Example**
one-place	U	Kure Island is beautiful (U).
two-place	U + L	Kure Island (U) lies in the Pacific Ocean (L).

Combinations of semantic functions in other languages

As can be seen from Table 4.8, English does not allow Locatives to act as the sole participant of an SoA. Other languages, like German, allow for such constellations in non-dynamic SoAs (example (67)), while in Icelandic the sole participant of a dynamic SoA can have the semantic function of Locative (example (68); Barðdal 2001; cf. Hengeveld and Mackenzie 2008: 198). In both cases the only participant appears in the dative.

(67) Mir   ist   kalt.
    1.SG.DAT is   cold
    'I am cold.'

(68) Honum   sárnaði.
    3.SG.M.DAT became.hurt
    'He became hurt.'

4.5.4. Copular and existential constructions

The classification of SoAs proposed in the previous section is based on two different features of the SoA: (i) the number of participants involved in the SoA (quantificational valency) and (ii) the semantic functions of the participants, expressing the relation between these participants and the Property (qualificational valency). There is, however, a special group of SoAs, typically involving the verb *be*, which cannot be classified on the basis of the quantificational or qualificational valency of the Property they contain. The reason is that these constructions, traditionally referred to as copular sentences, are regarded as lacking a lexical Property. As pointed out above, the verb *be* is analysed in FDG as a grammatical element, introduced at the Morphosyntactic Level as a carrier of tense and number distinctions; as such, it does not appear at the Representational Level. We have also seen that in copular sentences with an adjective, such as *Peter is intelligent*, it is the adjective that functions as the non-verbal predicate, with *Peter* as its argument. In some cases, however, copular sentences do not contain a lexical Property at all. In the sentences in (69), for instance, what is predicated of the subject is expressed in the form of a prepositional phrase (examples (69a)–(69c)) or a noun phrase (examples (69d)–(69e)):

(69)   a. The dog is in the garden.
       b. This poem is by Keats.
       c. The letter was from a friend.
       d. Robert is a teacher.
       e. Violet is the winner.

The copular sentences in (69) can be divided into three different types. In examples (69a)–(69c), a prepositional phrase is used to describe the Property assigned to the sole participant of the SoA. These sentences are therefore based on one-place predication frames, with the prepositional phrase functioning as a non-verbal predicate. Since the preposition introducing the prepositional phrase specifies the semantic relation between the predicate and its argument (location, agency, source), these sentences are referred to as **relational sentences**. In (69c), for instance, the prepositional phrase *from a friend* functions as a one-place non-verbal predicate, assigning a Property to the argument *the letter*. The preposition *from* identifies the relation between predicate and argument as one of source. This analysis leads to the semantic representation in (69c′):

(69)   c. The letter was from a friend

      c'. $(e_1: [(f_1: (x_1: friend)_{So}) (x_2: letter)_U]\ ^e)$

The configurational head of the SoA in (69c') consists of the Property (f_1) and its argument (x_2). The Property consists of the Individual *a friend* (x_1), which has the semantic function Source (So), yielding the prepositional phrase *from a friend*. The argument position is taken by the Individual *the letter* (x_2). Since the SoA designated is non-dynamic (describing the result of an action rather than the action itself), the argument is assigned the semantic function Undergoer.

> Taking (69c') as an example, provide representations for the sentences in (69a) and (69b).

The second type of copular sentence, illustrated in (69d), consists of two noun phrases, the second of which is indefinite. Since the purpose of sentences of this type is to classify the entity referred to by the subject, they are called **classificational sentences**. In (69d), for instance, the Individual *Robert* is asserted to belong to the class of teachers. The second (indefinite) noun phrase is thus not used to refer to a specific entity, but to designate a class. Since, however, the entities belonging to this class are Individuals, the unit in question is still represented by means of the variable x. The entity undergoing classification (*Robert*, x_2), is assigned the semantic function Undergoer. Note that in classificational sentences the two elements must always be of the same semantic category. The representation of example (69d) is given in (69d'); some further examples are given in (70).

(69)   d. Robert is a teacher.

      d'. $(e_1: [(x_1: teacher) (x_2)_U]\ ^e)$

(70)   a. The 1989 flooding of Lake Torrens was a rare event (COCA, written, magazine)

      a'. $(e_1: [(ep_1: -rare\ event -) (ep_2: - 1989\ flooding\ of\ Lake\ Torrens)_U]\ ^e)$

     b. Patience is a virtue.

      b'. $(e_1: [(f_1: virtue) (f_2: patience)_U]\ ^e)$

The third type of copular sentence is the so-called **identificational sentence**. An example can be found in (69e). Like classificational sentences, identificational sentences consist (typically) of two noun phrases. In this case, however, both these noun phrases are used to refer to an entity. Since these two entities are equated, there is no dependency relation between them—neither is therefore assigned a semantic role. As in the case of classificational sentences, the two entities have to belong to the same semantic category. In addition, the two entities are represented by co-indexed variables, reflecting the fact that both units designate the same entity. Note finally that the analysis proposed can also account for the fact that, unlike classificational sentences, identificational sentences allow for the two noun phrases to be reversed. An example of an identificational sentence is given in (69e); its semantic representation is given in (69e').

(69)   e. Violet is the winner.

   e'. $(e_1: [(x_1: winner) (x_1)]^e)$

The final type of SoA to be discussed in this section is that expressed by what are commonly referred to as **existential sentences**; an example is given in (71):

(71)   a. There was only one candidate.

   a'. $(e_1: (x_1))$

Just as in copular constructions, in sentences like (71) the verb *be* is regarded as a dummy verb and as such is not analysed at the Representational Level. Similarly, the element *there* is seen as lacking any semantic contents; like the element *it* in sentences like *it rains*, the element *there* simply serves to fill the subject position. This means that sentences like (71) consist, at the Representational Level, of only a single element, in this case the phrase *only one candidate*. The sentence in (71a) is therefore given the semantic representation in (71a').

Table 4.9 provides a brief overview of the different kinds of sentences with the verb *be* discussed in this section:

Table 4.9. Further types of SoA in English

Type of SoA	Example	Semantic representation
Relational	The letter was from a friend	$(e_1: [(f_1: (x_1)_{So}) (x_2)_U]^e)$
Classificational	Robert is a teacher	$(e_1: [(x_1) (x_2)_U]^e)$
Identificational	The winner is Violet	$(e_1: [(x_1) (x_1)]^e)$
Existential	There was only one candidate	$(e_1: (x_1))$

Comparison: interpersonal and representational units

At this point it may be useful to look at the relation between units at the Representational Level and the Interpersonal Level. As mentioned in the introduction to this chapter, the Representational Level provides the semantic content of the Speaker's message; as such it provides a semantic elaboration of the interpersonal layer of the Communicated Content. Although (as we will see later), there is no one-to-one relationship between the units at both levels, we can recognize a default relation between the units contained within the Communicated Content and those making up the head of an SoA. Thus, in most cases, there is a relation between Ascriptive Acts (T) at the Interpersonal Level and Properties (f) at the Representational Level, and likewise between Referential Acts (R) at the Interpersonal Level and the arguments of the Properties at the Representational Level (typically x). This reflects the general assumption that Properties are used to ascribe properties and that arguments designate the referents to which these properties are ascribed. The following example illustrates these default relationships:

(72)   My sister burnt the letter.
RL: $(e_1: [\ (f_1: burn)\ (x_1: sister)_A\ (x_2: letter)_U]\ ^e)$
IL: $\qquad\quad T_1 \qquad\quad R_1 \qquad\quad R_2$

In some cases, however, the relationship between the two levels is less straightforward—which is, of course, a compelling reason for distinguishing separate levels. Consider once more the analyses suggested for copular constructions. In a relational construction like (73), the Property (expressed as a prepositional phrase) is headed by an Individual. At the Interpersonal Level, the Property corresponds to an Ascriptive Act, while the Individual corresponds to an Act of Reference:

(73)   The letter was from a friend
IL: $(e_1: [\ (f_1:\ (x_1\ friend)_{So})\ (x_2: letter\ )_U]\ ^e)$
RL: $\qquad T_1\ R_1 \qquad\qquad R_2$

Of particular interest in this respect are classificational and identificational sentences. At the Representational Level these two types of sentence are distinguished by (i) the presence of the semantic function Undergoer on the argument in classificational sentences, and (ii) the co-indexing of the two units in identificational sentences (see examples

(continued)

(74a) and (74b)). The pragmatic difference (i.e. the difference in what the Speaker intends in uttering these sentences) is reflected at the Interpersonal Level. Since in classificational sentences one of the two elements is used to predicate a Property of the other, these sentences consist of an Ascriptive and a Referential Act. In identificational sentences, on the other hand, two entities are equated; as such they are analysed at the Interpersonal Level as consisting of two Referential Acts.

(74) a. Robert is a teacher
$$\text{RL:} \quad (e_1: [\quad (x_1) \quad (x_2)_U]^e)$$
$$\text{IL:} \qquad\qquad T_1 \quad R_1$$
  b. The winner is Violet
$$\text{RL:} \quad (e_1: [\quad (x_1) \quad (x_1)]^e)$$
$$\text{IL} \qquad\qquad R_1 \quad R_2$$

Note finally that although the two x-variables in (74b) are co-indexed, the two R-variables are not, reflecting the fact that one and the same entity is referred to twice.

> Can you think of other examples of noun phrases that designate Individuals at the Representational Level, but which function as Ascriptive Acts at the Interpersonal Level?

4.5.5. Complex SoAs

Complex SoAs are SoAs that contain more than one predication frame. So far we have seen various instances where an SoA functions as an argument within another SoA; some of these examples are repeated in (75) for convenience:

(75) a. She had timed *her arrival* for half an hour after *the party* was due to commence. (BYU-BNC, written, fiction)
  b. *Mozart's final illness* lasted 15 days (BYU-BNC, written, biography)

The SoAs in these examples have lexical heads (*arrival, party, illness*). It is, however, also possible for SoAs with configurational heads to function as arguments within a larger SoA; in that case we speak of **embedding**. As can be seen from the examples in (76), the embedded SoA can be assigned different semantic functions (Actor vs. Undergoer):

(76)   a. *That she passed the exam* surprised me.

   (e$_1$: [(f$_1$: surprise) (e$_2$: [(f$_2$: pass) (x$_1$)$_A$ (e$_3$: exam)$_U$] ^{e})$_A$ (x$_2$)$_U$] ^{e})

   b. I saw *her steal the exam papers.*

   (e$_1$: [(f$_1$: see) (x$_1$)$_A$ (e$_2$: [(f$_2$: steal) (x$_2$)$_A$ (x$_3$: exam papers)$_U$] ^{e})$_U$] ^{e})

Now consider the sentence in (77):

(77)   The student persuaded his girlfriend to steal the exam papers.

Here, too, we have two predication frames, one with the verb *persuade*, the other with the verb *steal*. The sentence differs, however, from the one in (76b) in that the string *his girlfriend to steal the exam papers* is not the Undergoer argument of the verb *persuade*: it is not the event of the girlfriend stealing the exam papers that is persuaded, but the girlfriend. A simple substitution test shows that the string *his girlfriend to steal the exam papers* is not even one unit (*The student persuaded it*). This suggests that *his girlfriend* functions as a separate argument of *persuade*. At the same time, however, *the girlfriend* clearly functions as the Actor within the embedded predication frame. This complex situation can be represented as follows:

(78)   (e$_1$: [(f$_1$: persuade) (x$_1$: student)$_A$ (x$_2$: girlfriend)$_U$ (e$_2$: [(f$_2$: steal) (x$_2$)$_A$ (x$_3$: exam papers)$_U$] ^{e})$_{Res}$] ^{e})

The first SoA (e$_1$) is based on a three-place predication frame: the first argument of *persuade*, *the student*, has the semantic role of Actor; the second argument, *the girlfriend*, functions as the Undergoer; and the third argument, the embedded SoA e$_2$, is assigned the semantic function of Resultative. The fact that *the girlfriend* also functions as the Actor argument in the embedded SoA is captured by the co-indexation of these two arguments (both are represented as x$_2$). Note that on its second appearance, this variable does not have a head, resulting in its non-expression in the final utterance.

Yet another form of embedding can be found in sentences with the verb *consider*. These are, in fact, very similar to the sentence in (77): here, too, the Undergoer of the verb *consider* takes the form of an SoA (*she is a friend*). The difference between the two complex SoAs is, of course, that in constructions with *consider* the embedded SoA contains a non-verbal predicate (as indicated by the fact that the copular *be* can be added). In a sentence like (79), for instance, the embedded SoA (e$_2$) is a classificational sentence, consisting of the non-verbal Property *friend* (f$_2$) and its sole argument *her* (x$_2$):

(79) a. I consider *her (to be) a friend.*

　　　b. $(e_1: [(f_1: \text{consider}) (x_1)_A \ (e_2: [(f_2: \text{friend}) (x_2)_U] \ ^e)_U] \ ^e)$

4.5.6. Modifiers

Modifiers at the layer of the SoA provide additional information concerning the occurrence of the SoA. Some major types of SoA modification are listed in (80) (cf. Hengeveld and Mackenzie 2008: 171–80, 208–10):

(80) a. Place of occurrence:

　　　The book first appeared *in Vienna* in 1937. (COCA, spoken, talk show)

　　　b. Relative time of occurrence:

　　　One night in June I went for a bike ride *after dinner*. (COCA, spoken, talk show)

　　　c. Frequency of occurrence:

　　　We used to text *frequently, all the time*. (COCA, spoken, talk show)

　　　d. Duration:

　　　For weeks he'd been thinking of proposing to her. (COCA, written, fiction)

　　　e. Reality status:

　　　In reality, few new technologies are subjected to rigorous evaluation. (COCA, written, magazine)

　　　f. Cause:

　　　I only took her to the doctor *because she had a bad nose bleed at playgroup*. (BYU-BNC, written, newspaper)

　　　g. Purpose:

　　　Armed with a lamp, Dyson set off *to check the connection*. (BYU-BNC, written, miscellaneous)

As expected, all these modifiers can be combined with and fall within the scope of episodical absolute time modifiers; examples can be found in (80a) and (80b) above, where the absolute temporal expressions *in 1937* and *one night in June* take scope over the SoA modifiers indicating place (*in Vienna*) and relative time of occurrence (*after dinner*). Thus, in (80b), the time designated by the phrase *after dinner* can only be determined in relation to the absolute time indicated by the phrase *one night in June*. We will return to the difference between absolute and relative time in Section 4.5.7.

Another kind of modifier found at the layer of the SoA is that used to introduce additional participants (Hengeveld and Mackenzie 2008: 208). Some examples are given in (81a) and (81b):

(81)   a. Beneficiary:
Can you sing that song *for me*? (COCA, spoken, talk show)
   b. Instrument:
Martha reportedly struck her makeup artist *with a brush*. (COCA, spoken, talk show)

Finally, SoAs with lexical heads, being expressed as noun phrases, accept modifiers that are normally allowed within the noun phrase, such as restrictive relative clauses, adjectival modifiers, and genitival modifiers:

(82)   a. The meeting *that took place yesterday* was boring.
   b. It was *a boring meeting*.
   c. *Yesterday's* meeting was boring.

In the general schema of the SoA, these modifiers take the position given in bold in (83):

(83) $(e_1: [(f_1) \ldots (x_{1+n})]: \boldsymbol{\sigma}^{\,e})$

4.5.7. Operators

Cross-linguistically, SoAs can be specified by a large number of operators (Hengeveld and Mackenzie 2008: 172–80), many of which are also relevant for English. One of these is the relative tense operator. The relevance of this operator for English becomes clear in the following passage (example (32), repeated here for convenience):

(84)   The people were convinced that the sounding of the bells would ward off any kind of calamity. Several times it happened that $[_{ep1}$ $[_{e1}$ mighty black clouds had threatened Marakesh], $[_{e2}$ thunder had rumbled], $[_{e3}$ it had started hailing], but $[_{e4}$ as soon as someone passing by began ringing the bells], $[_{e5}$ the dark clouds broke as if by a miracle], $[_{e6}$ skirting the entire Marakesh Valley)]]. (COCA, written, fiction)

As pointed out in Section 4.4.4, the verb *happen* takes an Episode as its only argument (ep$_1$). The entire Episode is indicated to have taken place at an absolute time in the past (the reference time), as evidenced by the past tense ending on the verb *happen*. The Episode consists of six SoAs, whose time of occurrence is specified in relation to the time of occurrence of the entire Episode (ep$_1$). Thus, the first three SoAs are indicated as having taken place before the ep$_1$. As such, each of these SoAs will be analysed as containing an anterior operator (ant), which, in combination with the episodical past tense operator triggers the past perfect forms *had threatened, had rumbled,* and *had started.* The last three SoAs are indicated to take place at the reference time; these will contain the simultaneous operator (sim), which in combination with the episodical past tense operator yields the simple past tense. The entire Episode will thus be given the simplified representation in (85):

(85)   (past ep$_1$: [(**ant** e$_1$) (**ant** e$_2$) (**ant** e$_3$) (**sim** e$_4$) (**sim** e$_5$) (**sim** e$_6$)] ^{ep})

Another important set of operators at the layer of the SoA is responsible for the specification of **phasal aspect**. In English, different kinds of phasal aspect can be distinguished. The most important of these for English are **progressive aspect** (indicating that an SoA is in progress) and **perfect aspect** (indicating the result or relevance of an SoA that started in the past). In addition, English has a number of minor types of aspect, such as **habitual aspect** (indicating a past or present habit), **ingressive aspect** (indicating the start of a new SoA), and **prospective aspect** (indicating that an SoA is about to happen). Each of these operators ('prog', 'perf', 'hab', 'ingr' and 'pros') triggers its own grammatical form, as illustrated in examples (86a)–(86d):

(86)   a. I *was calling* the office to say I was ill when the doorbell rang. (Progressive)
      b. I *have called* the office to say I am ill. (Perfect)
      c. I *used to call* them every day. (Habitual)
      d. I *got to know* them very well. (Ingressive)
      e. I *was about to* leave when John called. (Prospective)

SoA operators are also used to specify certain types of modality. As we saw in Section 4.3.3, adverbs like *certainly, probably,* and *possibly,* expressing subjective epistemic modality, apply at the layer of the Proposition. As shown in (87) these modal adverbs can combine with other modal elements, even if the two modal expressions seem to be contradictory:

(87)   a. There *certainly may* be an element of self-protection in this type of reasoning (COCA, written, academic)

b. If you want to have a decent social safety net, you *probably have to* raise some taxes to pay for it. (COCA, spoken, talk show)

The reason that these combinations do not result in a semantic anomaly is that the two modal expressions operate at different layers, where they perform different functions. In (87a), for instance, we find a combination of a propositional modifier (*certainly*) and a modal auxiliary (*may*) expressing the SoA operator probability ('prob'). Whereas the former expresses subjective epistemic modality, indicating the extent to which the Speaker is committed to the truth of a proposition, the latter expresses **objective epistemic modality**, simply indicating the existence of a logical possibility, without involving any judgement by the Speaker (Hengeveld and Mackenzie 2008: 174). In (87b), we find a combination of a propositional modifier indicating subjective epistemic modality (*probably*) and a **deontic modal auxiliary** (*have to*), indicating what is obligatory or permitted according to a certain moral code or legal system. The latter type of modality, specifying general rules of conduct, is represented by the SoA operator obligation ('obl') (Hengeveld and Mackenzie 2008: 176).

Both objective epistemic modality and deontic modality are **event-oriented**, indicating the likelihood or desirability of the SoA's taking place. Another type of modality, also specified at the layer of the SoA, is that of **participant-oriented modality**. This kind of modality also describes the possibility or desirability of an SoA, but now from the point of view of one of the participants (Hengeveld and Mackenzie 2008: 212). **Facultative participant-oriented modality**, for instance, is used to indicate that a participant has the ability to participate in the designated SoA, while **deontic participant-oriented modality** is used to indicate that a participant has permission to participate in the SoA. Examples are given in (88a) and (88b), respectively:

(88)   a. Medical researchers *are* now *able* to take adult stem cells and coax them back into an embryonic state. (COCA, written, academic)
     b. You *may* now kiss the bride.

Note that different event-oriented and participant-oriented modal expressions may also be combined:

(89)   You *might have to be able* to convert watt-hours to calories though. (Internet)

    where *might*   = objective epistemic modality (event-oriented)
           have to   = deontic modality (event-oriented)
           be able to = facultative modality (participant-oriented)

Finally, SoAs can be specified by the polarity operator negation ('neg'), indicating the non-occurrence of the SoA designated; note that in English (as in most languages) only the negation of an SoA is explicitly marked:

(90)   You know, I have *not* decided what I'm going to do.

4.6. The Property

4.6.1. General characterization

As will have become clear from the previous sections, Properties are a basic unit of analysis at the Representational Level, providing the descriptive information needed to designate (sets of) entities. This descriptive informa- tion is given in the form of primitives: the lexemes that—in the default case—function as the head of a Property. Different classes of lexemes can be distinguished, depending on the function they perform at the Represen- tational and Interpersonal Levels. The three major classes of lexemes (or **parts-of-speech**) are given in Table 4.10.

Table 4.10. Different semantic classes (parts-of-speech)

Property expression	Type of lexical head
$(f_1: buy_V)$	verbal lexeme (verb)
$(f_1: house_N)$	nominal lexeme (noun)
$(f_1: old_A)$	adjectival lexeme (adjective)

Let us first consider the differences between the various types of lexemes in terms of their function at the Representational Level. Property expres- sions with verbal heads typically function as the lexical Property (the predicate) of a predication frame (e.g. *buy* in (91b)), while Property expres- sions with nominal heads typically function as the head of a unit that fills an argument position (e.g. *man* and *house* in (91b)).

(91)   a.   The man bought a house.
         b. $(e_1: [(f_1: \mathbf{buy_V}) (x_1: (f_2: \mathbf{man_N}))_A (x_2: (f_3: \mathbf{house_N}))_U] \,^e)$

Adjectival lexemes typically function as the head of an expression that functions as a modifier. An example is given in (92b), where the adjective *old* is represented as the head of a unit that modifies the Individual represented as x_1:

(92)   a. The man bought *an old house*.
      b. RL: $(e_1: [(f_1: buy_V) (x_1: (f_2: man_N))_A (x_2: (f_3: house_N): (f_4: \textbf{old}_A)^{\,x})_U]^e)$
      c. IL: T_1 $(R_1: (T_2))$ $(R_2: [(T_3)$ $(T_4)])$

The adjectival Property *old* itself can also be modified, as illustrated in example (93). Here, the adjectival Property contains a modifier headed by another adjective (*extreme*); this adjective is then morphosyntactically expressed as an adverb (see also Section 4.6.3 and Chapter 5, Sections 5.3 and 5.7.2):

(93)   a. The man bought *an extremely old house*.
      b. $(x_1: (f_1: house_N): ((f_2: old_A): (f_3: \textbf{extreme}_A)^{\,f})^{\,x})_U$

Given the analysis in (93b), how do you think the adverb *soundly* in *He slept soundly* will be analysed at the Representational Level?

Comparison: relation between Properties and Subacts

The different types of lexemes are not only associated with different functions at the Representational Level, but also at the Interpersonal Level. Consider once more example (92).

(92)   The man bought an old house.
    RL: $(e_1: [(f_1: buy_V) (x_1: (f_2: man_N))_A (x_2: (f_3: house_N): (f_4: old_A)^{\,x})_U]^e)$
    IL: T_1 $(R_1: (T_2))$ $(R_2: [(T_3)$ $(T_4)])$

As can be seen from the IL-analysis, Property expressions with verbal heads correspond to independent Ascriptive Acts at the Interpersonal Level (T_1). Property expressions with nominal heads also correspond to Ascriptive Subacts $(T_2$ and $T_3)$, but these Ascriptive Subacts function in turn as the head of a Referential Act $(R_1$ and R_2, respectively). Property expressions with adjectival heads also correspond to Ascriptive Subacts that are part of a Referential Subact $(T_4$ as part of $R_2)$; in this case, however, the head of the Referential Act must be configurational, with the adjectival Property functioning as an additional Ascriptive Subact.

4.6.2. The head

The head of a Property may be absent or lexical. Lexical heads, in turn, can be either simple or compositional.

4.6.2.1. Absent heads

In (94a), the pronoun *it* is used to refer anaphorically to the Property designated by the noun phrase *the colour* in the previous clause. Since it does not contain any descriptive information, the pronoun *it* will be represented as a Property-designating unit without a head, that is, simply as a variable (f_1). The anaphoric relation is captured by means of co-indexing of the variables symbolizing the two units (*the colour* and *it*).

(94) a. A: But do you like *the colour*? B: Yes, *it*'s gorgeous that isn't it eh?
          (BYU-BNC, written, newspaper)
      b. it
          (f_1)

The anaphoric pronoun *one* can also be used to refer back to an earlier introduced Property with a nominal head. In that case, the pronoun will again be represented as a Property expression without a head. In (95a) for instance, the pronoun *one* picks up the previously mentioned nominal lexeme *building*. Lacking any descriptive content, the pronoun is represented as a Property (f_1) without a head. The anaphoric relation is captured by means of co-indexing of the two f-variables. Note that Properties with an absent head typically function as the empty heads of other units (in this case x_1).

(95) a. In the building trade it is well known that the cost of building a
          new building may be less than the cost of modifying an old *one*.
          (BYU-BNC, written, miscellaneous)
      b. an old one
          (x_1: (f_1): (f_2: old) ^{x})

4.6.2.2. Simple lexical heads

In the large majority of cases, the head of a Property takes the form of a lexeme. Numerous examples have already been given, for example in Table 4.10 and in example (92), here repeated as (96). In this example, all four Properties have a lexical head.

(96)   a. The man bought an old house.

   b. $(e_1: [(f_1: \textbf{buy}_V) (x_1: (f_2: \textbf{man}_N))_A (x_2: (f_3: \textbf{house}_N): (f_4: \textbf{old})^{x})_U]^{e})$

4.6.2.3. Compositional lexical heads

Compositional lexical heads consist of two lexical elements which together designate a single concept and are typically expressed as compounds. Compounds are often divided into different types: **endocentric**, **exocentric**, and **copulative**. Endocentric compounds are by far the most common. They consist of a head (the rightmost component), indicating the entity designated, and a modifier, specifying some additional property of this entity. Some examples can be found in (97):

(97)   a. file name, memory stick
   b. hard disk, software
   c. flash drive, playstation

The complex heads of the lexical Properties in (97) are analysed as consisting of two separate lexemes. These lexemes may belong to the same semantic class (like the noun–noun compounds in (97a)), but may also belong to different classes (examples (97b) and (97c)). In either case, the two lexemes together form one complex Property. Compounds of this type are given the general structure in (98a), where f_1 represents the Property as a whole, f_2 the head within this Property and f_3 the modifier. The specific representation of the compound *file name* is given in (98b).

(98)   a. $(f_1: (f_2: \text{LEX}: (f_3: \text{LEX})^{f})^{f})$
   b. $(f_1: (f_2: \text{name}_N: (f_3: \text{file}_N)^{f})^{f})$

Occasionally, compounds are exocentric. In terms of internal structure, they follow the pattern of endocentric compounds; in terms of meaning, however, they differ from endocentric compounds in that the rightmost element does not indicate the entity designated. Examples are *skinhead* and *farmhand*. These compounds clearly involve metonymy (in this case pars-pro-toto), which, as a figure of style, is not accounted for within the grammar (see Chapter 2).

   Finally, there are the copulative compounds, which consist of two lexemes with equal status, both applying directly to the entity designated. Consequently, the two lexemes have to belong to the same semantic class. Examples are *sofa-bed*, *bittersweet*, and *sleepwalk*. To reflect the equal status of the two lexemes, these compounds are provided with a configurational head in which the two lexemes have equal status:

(99)   a. $(f_1: [(f_2: \text{LEX}) (f_3: \text{LEX})]^f)$
b. $(f_1: [(f_2: \text{bitter}_A) (f_3: \text{sweet}_A)]^f)$

Table 4.11. Different types of head: Properties

Type of head	Representation
Absent	(f_1)
Simple lexical	$(f_1: \text{LEX})$
Compositional, endocentric/ exocentric	$(f_1: (f_2: \text{LEX}: (f_3: \text{LEX})^f)^f)$
Compositional, copulative	$(f_1: [(f_2: \text{LEX}) (f_3: \text{LEX})]^f)$ where both lexemes must belong to the same class

4.6.3. Modifiers

Modifiers at the layer of the Property fulfil a variety of functions, depending on the semantic class of the lexeme functioning as the head of the Property. In (100a), for instance, the adverb *viciously* describes the manner in which the Property designated by the verbal head is performed, in (100b) *extremely* specifies the degree to which the Property designated by the adjective *old* applies, while in (100c) the adjective *former* serves to indicate that the Property 'president' no longer applies.

(100)   a. smile *viciously*
b. *extremely* old
c. *former* president

It is important to realize that not all manner adverbs apply at the layer of the Property. Compare in this respect the two sentences in (101) (cf. Hengeveld and Mackenzie 2008: 209):

(101)   a. The boy answered the question *stupidly*.
b. The boy *stupidly* answered the question (intelligently).

In (101a) *stupidly* describes the manner in which the boy answered the question; *stupidly* is therefore analysed as a modifier of the verbal Property *answer*. In (101b) on the other hand, the adverb *stupidly* indicates that it was stupid of the boy to answer the question (even if the answer itself was given intelligently). It is therefore not the Property *answer* that is being modified, but the SoA as a whole. The difference between the two sentences is reflected in the representations in (102):

(102) a. (e_1: [(f_1: answer$_V$: (**f_2: stupid$_A$**) ^{f}) (x_1: (f_3: boy$_N$))$_A$ (p_2: (f_4: question$_N$))$_U$] ^{e})

      b. (e_1: [(f_1: answer$_V$:) (x_1: (f_2: boy$_N$))$_A$ (p_2: (f_3: question$_N$))$_U$]: (**f_4: stupid$_A$**) ^{e})

Finally, notice that in these representations the adverb *stupidly* is represented in adjectival form. The reason for this is that regularly formed adverbs are not seen as independent lexemes: unlike lexical primitives, which are listed in the lexicon and have to be learned, these adverbs are formed on the basis of a rule of grammar, applying at the interface between the Representational and the Morphosyntactic Level (we will come back to this in Chapter 5, Sections 5.3 and 5.7.2).

4.6.4. Operators

English does not seem to have operators that apply at the layer of the Property.

Property operators in other languages

Property operators can be found in languages that have set nouns, like Georgian or Oromo. Set nouns are nouns that do not intrinsically designate a singular object, but rather a set of objects, which may consist of one or more members. In order to make clear whether the designated set consists of one object (a singleton set) or more objects (a collection), specific markers are used. In the absence of such a marker, the noun is unspecified for number. The following examples from Oromo illustrate this process (Stroomer 1987: 77, cited in Rijkhoff 2002: 102–3):

(103) a. c'irreesa
        'doctor/doctors'
     b. c'irr-oota
        doctor-COLL
        'doctors'

(*continued*)

> c. c'irree-ttii
>   doctor-SGLTV
>   'doctor'
>
> Rijkhoff analyses the collective and singulative suffixes in (103b) and (103c) as nominal aspect markers, applying at the layer of the (nominal) Property. These Property expressions would then have the following abstract representation:
>
> (104)   (coll/sgltv f_1: LEX$_N$)

4.7. The Individual

4.7.1. General characterization

Individuals are concrete, tangible entities that occupy a (unique) portion of space (Lyons's (1977: 442) first-order entities). Cross-linguistically, Individuals come in (at least) six different types (or 'Seinsarten'), depending on their countability and internal composition. Three of these are relevant to English; they correspond to the traditional distinction between **count**, **mass**, and **collective** nouns. Count nouns are used to designate Individuals that are countable and heterogeneous. Take for instance the noun *bike*. This noun clearly designates a countable Individual: we can have one bike (singular) or a set of more than one bike (plural). As for their internal composition, bikes are heterogeneous: they consist of different parts, which means that a part of a bike is not a bike. Mass nouns, like *water*, are non-countable: they do not describe well-delineated, separate objects, but undifferentiated masses. These masses are homogeneous: if we take a portion of water, we still have water. Collective nouns share properties with both count and mass nouns. In the singular, collective nouns, like *cattle* or *police*, designate sets of Individuals. This means that, although as sets they are not countable, they have an inherent plurality. In terms of internal composition, they are homogeneous: a portion of cattle is still cattle. As shown in the following examples, these different subclasses of Individuals exhibit different morpho-syntactic behaviour with regard to, for instance, pluralization, quantification, and the form and presence of an article:

(105) a. The bike was / *were stolen.

  b. Some / many two bikes were stolen. (*little / *much bike)

  c. A bike /*bike was standing in front of the house.

(106) a. The water was / *were pumped into the tank.

  b. Some / much water was pumped into the tank. (*few / *many waters)

  c. Water / *a water was pumped into the tank.

(107) a. The cattle were / *was driven along the streets.

  b. Some / many cattle were driven along the streets. (*little / *much cattle; *few / *many cattles)

  c. Cattle / *a cattle were driven along the streets.

To account for these differences in formal behaviour, the distinction between the different types of Individual needs to be reflected in their semantic representation. This is done by adding a superscript to the x-variable indicating the subclass of Individual designated:

(108) a. $(^{c}x_1: (f_1: bike_N))$

  b. $(^{m}x_1: (f_1: water_N))$

  c. $(^{coll}x_1: (f_1: cattle_N))$

Note finally that English is quite flexible in the sense that conversion from one category to another is often possible. Thus, mass nouns like *gas* and *water* can be used to designate countable objects (example (109)); similarly a count noun like *bike* can be used to designate a mass, as in (110). It is for this reason that it is not the lexeme that is subclassified, but rather the variable in the frame: this means that, according to a Speaker's needs, one and the same lexeme may be combined with different frames.

(109) a. All of the *gases* present in the atmosphere are also present in surface *waters*. (BYU-BNC, spoken, lecture)

  b. The waitress stepped into their shadows, brought Evelyn *a water* and a menu, giggled at her sunglasses. (COCA, written, fiction)

(110) a. You really do get a hell of *a lot of bike for* your money. (Internet)

  b. Did you find it to be *too much bike?* (Internet)

4.7.2. The head

The head of an Individual may be absent, empty, lexical, or configurational.

4.7.2.1. Absent heads

In many cases Individuals are designated by means of expressions that do not contain any semantic content, such as proper names or personal pronouns. In some cases, the designating expression may even remain implicit. Since in these cases no Property is being ascribed to the designated Individual, such expressions will be represented without a head, that is, simply as an x-variable. In (112a), for instance, the proper name *George* is specified at the Interpersonal Level (see Sections 3.8.2 and 3.9.2.2). All that remains to be done at the Representational Level is to indicate that we are dealing with an Individual. In the case of an anaphoric pronoun (as in (111a)) or zero-realization of an argument (as in (111b)), the Addressee is instructed to identify the entity referred to by looking at the preceding discourse (or rather by searching his/her short-term representation of the preceding discourse). In such cases, the relation with the antecedent is captured by means of co-indexing of the two variables.

(111)   a. *The child* was born on 10 May 1977 and *he/Ø* was adopted two years later. (BYU-BNC, written, newspaper)
   b. the child: $(x_1: (f_1: child_N))$
   c. he/Ø: (x_1)

The absence of a head suggests that modification is not possible. By and large, this is indeed what we find: neither proper names nor pronouns allow, for instance, modification by means of descriptive adjectives (112a). As can be seen from example (112b), they do allow for modifiers expressing the subjective attitude of the Speaker. As explained in Section 3.9.3, however, these are interpersonal modifiers, applying to the layer of the Referential Subact.

(112)   a. *rich George; *rich you
   b. poor George; poor you

Proper names can sometimes be modified, as in *a regular Al Capone* or *a triumphant Tony Blair*. Would you regard these phrases as counterexamples?

4.7.2.2. Empty heads

In some cases the Property that is ascribed to an Individual is not explicitly mentioned. In that case the indefinite pronoun *one* may be used to instruct the Addressee to retrieve this Property from the preceding discourse. In such cases, the Individual is represented as an x-variable with an empty head (i.e. a Property (f) with an absent head, see Section 4.6.2):

(113) a. At least it's a white [cloud], not a black *one* (BYU-BNC, spoken, conversation)
  b. a black one
    $(x_1: (f_1): (f_2: black)^x)$

4.7.2.3. Lexical heads

Individuals with lexical heads are the default case. An example is the expression *a white cloud* in example (114a), which has the semantic representation in (114b):

(114) a. a white cloud
  b. $(x_1: (f_1: cloud): (f_2: white)^x)$

4.7.2.4. Configurational heads

The head of an Individual is configurational when it consists of more than one unit. Examples are expressions headed by a kinship or body part noun like *father, cousin, head,* or *leg*. What is special about these nouns is that the entities they designate do not exist independently but are always possessed by (or related to) some other entity: a father is always someone's father, a head is always someone's head. Semantically, this means that such nouns (sometimes called relational nouns) require the presence of an argument. This is illustrated in example (115), which shows that in unmarked (i.e. non-generic, non-existential) expressions, the use of such nouns without an argument yields a degraded result. It is for this reason that the relation between the predicate and its argument is often described as one of **inalienable possession**.

(115) a. I met *the boy's sister* / $^{??}$*a sister* yesterday.
  b. He kicked *the boy's leg* / $^{??}$*a leg*.

Since the nominal heads in these examples require the presence of an argument, they typically combine with a one-place predication frame. For the expression *the boy's sister*, this leads to the semantic structure in (116b), where the Individual designating expression *the boy* (x_2) is represented as the argument of the one-place nominal Property *sister* (f_2). The relation of inalienable possession is expressed by the presence of the semantic function Ref(erence) on the argument (as the entity with reference to which the Property applies).

(116)   a. the boy's sister
       b. $(x_1: [(f_1: sister_N) (x_2: (f_2: boy_N))_{Ref}]^x)$

Another instance of an Individual designating expression with a configurational head can be found in (117), where the Property assigned to the Individual takes the form of a headless relative clause (*what you read*) (Hengeveld and Mackenzie 2008: 241). In constructions like these, the head of the Individual takes the form of an SoA (e_1). Note that the Undergoer argument of the SoA is co-indexed with the Individual as a whole (both are represented as x_1), reflecting the fact that the entity designated by the headless relative clause is at the same time the Undergoer argument of the verb *read*.

(117)   a. I will read *what you read*.
       b. $(x_1: (e_1: [(f_1: read) (x_2)_A (x_1)_U])^e)$

Summing up, the head of an Individual can have the following forms:

Table 4.12. Different types of head: Individuals

Type of head	Representation
Absent	(x_1)
Empty	$(x_1: (f_1))$
Lexical	$(x_1: (f_1: \text{LEX}))$
Configurational	$(x_1: (f_1/e_1: [(f_2: \text{LEX})\ldots])^x)$

4.7.3. Modifiers

Modifiers at the layer of the Individual can take a variety of forms: adjectival, possessive, prepositional, and clausal. A few examples of each kind of modifier will suffice to demonstrate how they are analysed.

Adjectival modifiers provide additional (optional) information about the designated Individual. In (118a), for instance, the Individual symbolized by the variable x_1 is first assigned the Property *president* (f_1). The additional Property *popular* (f_2) provides extra information: it serves to further restrict the set of Individuals designated by the expression, but does not change the kind of entity designated.

(118)   a. a popular president
   b. $(x_1: (f_1: \text{president}): (f_2: \text{popular})^x)$

Remember that in Section 4.6.3 the adjective *former* was analysed as a modifier at the layer of the Property. One of the reasons for doing so is that *former* does not ascribe a Property to the designated Individual (**The president is former*), but instead serves to indicate that the Property *president* no longer applies to this Individual. When we combine the two modifiers, the order in which they appear reflects the scope relation between them: the adjective *former*, which has scope over the Property *president* only, takes the innermost position, while the adjective *popular*, which has scope over the combination of *former* and *president*, appears in the outermost position.

(119)   a. popular former president
   b. $(x_1: (f_1: \text{president}_N: (f_2: \text{former}_A)^f): (f_3: \text{popular}_A)^x)$

How would you analyse the phrase *a formerly popular president*?

Modifiers can also take the form of a possessive phrase, in which case the modifier designates the possessor (in a very broad sense) of the entity designated by the phrase as a whole. That the notion of possession is indeed a very broad one is clear from the examples in (120): whereas in (120a) the relation between the bike and the boy is (or at least can be) one of possession, the relation in (120b) is not; instead the boy and his school are linked through some unspecified, culturally determined association. Since, however, both relations are coded in exactly the same way, the two constructions are given the same semantic representation: in both cases, the modifier, analysed as a Property (f_2) consisting of an Individual (x_2), is assigned the semantic function Associative (cf. Li and Thompson 1981; Hengeveld and Mackenzie 2008: 243).

(120)   a. the boy's bike.
   a'. $(x_1: (f_1: \text{bike}_N): (f_2: (x_2: (f_3: \text{boy}_N)))_{Ass}^x)$
   b. the boy's school
   b'. $(x_1: (f_1: \text{school}_N): (f_2: (x_2: (f_3: \text{boy}_N)))_{Ass}^x)$

Note that expressions like those in (120), expressing **alienable possession**, are analysed quite differently from those expressing inalienable possession, which were analysed as predicate–argument constructions (see example (116) above, repeated here for convenience), thus doing justice to the fact that, despite the superficial similarity in form, these constructions differ both semantically and morphosyntactically.

(121)   a. the boy's sister
        b. $(x_1: [(f_1: sister_N) (x_2: (f_2: boy_N))_{Ref}] {}^x)$

Another type of modifier occurring at the layer of the Individual can be found in example (122), where the modifier takes the form of a prepositional phrase. For the time being, we will represent this modifier in a simplified form; more details on the analysis of prepositional phrases will be provided in Section 4.8.

(122)   a. the boy on the bike
        b. $(x_1: (f_1: boy_N): (l_1: - on the bike -) {}^x)$

Finally, modifiers at this layer may take the form of a restrictive relative clause. As shown in (123b), such modifiers are represented as SoAs. Note that the link between the relative clause and its antecedent is established by the co-indexation of one of the arguments of the SoA with the variable symbolizing the entity designated by the expression as a whole (x_1 in example (123)) (Hengeveld and Mackenzie 2008: 243):

(123)   a. the boy riding the bike
        b'. $(x_1: (f_1: boy_N): (prog e_1: [(f_2: ride) (x_1)_A (x_3: bike)_U] {}^e) {}^x)$

4.7.4. Operators

The most important operators at the layer of the Individual are those indicating number (singular vs. plural), quantity (*many, all, every*, etc.) and distance (*this, that, these, those*). Number distinctions are indicated by the operators '1' (for singular) and 'm' (for plural):

(124)   a. a bike $(1 x_1: (f_1: bike_N))$
        b. bikes $(m x_1: (f_1: bike_N))$

Some examples of noun phrases containing quantifiers and numerals are given in (125). Note that in the case of an indefinite pronoun (*someone, everyone, no one*), these pronouns are represented without a head:

(125)   a. all bikes   ($\forall$ x_1: (f_1: bike$_N$))
     b. some bikes   ($\exists$ x_1: (f_1: bike$_N$))
        someone/something ($\exists$ x_1)
     c. every bike   (distr x_1: (f_1: bike$_N$))
        everyone   (distr x_1)
     d. no bikes   (Ø x_1: (f_1: bike$_N$))
        no one   (Ø x_1)
     c. three bikes   ($3x_1$: (f_1: bike$_N$))

Finally, operators at the layer of the Individual are used to indicate the relative distance between the Speaker and the designated entity. English has a binary system, consisting of two pairs of demonstrative determiners: *this* and *these* to indicate proximity and *that* and *those* to indicate distance). As shown in example (126), it is through the combination of the operators for number ('1'/'m') and the operators for distance ('prox'/'dis') that we arrive at the correct form of the demonstrative determiner:

(126)   a. this bike   (1 prox x_1: (f_1: bike$_N$))
     b. that bike   (1 dis x_1: (f_1: bike$_N$))
     c. these bikes   (m prox x_1: (f_1: bike$_N$))
     d. those bikes   (m dis x_1: (f_1: bike$_N$))

As can be seen from example (127), other semantically compatible combinations of operators are also possible:

(127)   a. I think the answer to *all those three questions* is 'No.' (COCA, spoken, talk show)
     b. (all dis 3 p_1: (f_1: question$_N$))

4.8. Locations and Times

4.8.1. General characterization

As argued by Hengeveld and Mackenzie (2008: 135, 248–75), there is cross-linguistic evidence for the existence of a number of other (minor) semantic categories: Location, Time, Manner, Reason, and Quantity. Although the first four of these can be shown to be relevant for English, the discussion here will be confined to only two: Location (l) and Time (t). Since these two categories have (both conceptually and linguistically) much in common, they will be discussed together.

Locations, or places, can best be defined as 'portions of space', where physical entities (Individuals) can be located. This clearly shows that we are dealing with two semantic categories: if an Individual is, by definition, located in place, then Locations cannot be Individuals (as this would mean that they would again be located in place) (Mackenzie 2005: 142–3). Conceptually, we therefore make a distinction between Individuals, such as 'Sam', 'student', or 'water', and places, like 'area', 'London', or 'country'. Linguistically, too, it seems plausible to assume that some lexemes are inherently Individual designating, for example *thing, object, water, student,* whereas other lexemes are inherently place designating, for example *place, north, area, country.* Formal evidence for this distinction can be found in the fact that Individuals and Locations trigger different anaphoric, relative, or interrogative pronouns: *who, which, that, what,* or *it* for Individuals versus *where* and *there* for Locations:

(128) a. And, you know, this is *the thing that* affects a lot of people. (COCA, spoken)

b. They have been able to track that to exactly *the place where* these chimpanzees lived. (COCA, spoken)

At the same time, however, it turns out that we can often use one and the same lexeme to designate either an Individual or a Location. Consider, for instance, the following examples with the word *station*:

(129) a. One buys the Sintra tickets right in *the station which* is conveniently located on Praca Dom
Joao da Camara right off the big square that bears the same name. (Internet)

b. From 2018 Farringdon station will be *the only station where* Thameslink, Crossrail and Underground services meet. (Internet)

In example (129a), the entity designated by the phrase *the station* is conceptualized as an Individual, as can be seen from the use of the relative pronoun *which*. As shown in example (129a), however, the noun *station* can also be used to designate a place. The difference between these constructions is reflected in their semantic representation. The noun phrase *the station* in (129a) is analysed as designating an Individual, represented by the variable

x_1 (example (130a)). The noun phrase in (129b), on the other hand, is analysed as designating a Location, represented by the variable l_1 (example (130b)):

(130)   a. (1 x_1: (f_1: station$_N$))
   b. (1 l_1: (f_1: station$_N$))

> Can you think of other lexemes that can used to designate either a location or an Individual?

The most typical way to designate a Location in English, however, is by using a preposition. In example (131), for instance, the prepositional phrase used in answer to the *where*-question clearly designates a Location. In this case, the designation of the phrase as a whole is determined by the element *in*, which takes an Individual as its argument. Thus, in the semantic representation given in (131b), the (configurational) head of the Location (l_1) consists of the locative Property *in* (f_1) and an Individual, *the station* (x_2), functioning as its argument. Like the arguments in constructions expressing inalienable possession (Section 4.7.2), this argument is assigned the semantic function Reference.

(131)   a. Where can one buy the Sinta tickets? *In the station.*
   b. (l_1: [(f_1: in$_{Adp}$) (1 x_1: (f_2: station$_N$))$_{Ref}$])

Time-designating expressions can be dealt with in a similar way. Here, too, we find specialized lexemes, like *day, today, Monday, August 25th*, etc.

(132)   That was *the day when* his life as he knew it changed forever. (COCA, written, fiction)

As can be seen from example (133b), however, it is not only specialized temporal lexemes that can be used to designate Times; occasionally an SoA-designating lexeme can be used for this purpose. Again the form of the pronoun can be taken as an indication of the kind of entity designated, with *when* and *then* functioning as specialized temporal pronouns:

(133)   a. Was that—was that *the scene that* was cut out of 'Brokeback Mountain' (COCA, spoken, talk show)
   a'. (1 e_1: (f_1: scene$_N$))
   b. This annunciation is *the scene when* Gabriel informs Mary that she will be the mother of God. (COCA, written, academic)
   b'. (1 t_1: (f_1: scene$_N$))

Finally, as in the case of Locations, Times are often designated by means of prepositional phrases. As is well-known, in English many spatial prepositions can also be used temporally (*in a week*, *at that moment*, *on Monday*, *through the day*, etc.). Some prepositions, however, can only be used to designate Times (*during*, *before*, *after*):

(134)   a. I cried seven or eight times *during the movie*. (COCA, written, magazine)

        b. $(t_1: [(f_1: during_{Adp}) (1\ e_1: (f_2: movie_N))_{Ref}]\ ^t)$

4.8.2. The head

The head of a Location or a Time can be absent, empty, lexical, or configurational.

4.8.2.1. Absent heads

When an anaphoric pronoun is used to refer back to an earlier introduced Location or Time, the pronoun will be represented without a head, that is, simply as a variable:

(135)   a. He lived in [one of the most affluent neighborhoods of suburban New York]. Most of the people who live *there* are millionaires. (COCA, spoken, talk show)

        b. there

          (l_1)

(136)   a. This video was first posted on YouTube [in 2008]. Since *then* it has racked up over 100 million views and resulted in countless parodies (COCA, spoken, talk show)

        b. then

          (t_1)

4.8.2.2. Empty heads

In some cases the Property that is ascribed to a Location or Time is not explicitly mentioned. In that case the indefinite pronoun *one* may be used to instruct the Addressee to retrieve this Property from the preceding discourse. In such cases, the Location or Time is represented as a variable with an empty head.

(137)   a. That [space] is, once again, a desolate *one*, (COCA, written, academic)

   b. a desolate one
      $(l_1: (f_1): (f_2: desolate_A)^1)$

(138)   a. Today promised to be a lovely [day]—and a long *one*, she realized with an inner sigh. (COCA, written, fiction)

   b. a long one
      $(t_1: (f_1): (f_2: long_A)^t)$

4.8.2.3. Lexical heads

Locations and Times with lexical heads will be given the following representation:

(139)   a. this area
      a'. $(1 prox\ l_1: (f_1: area_N))$
   b. this week
      b'. $(1 prox\ t_1: (f_1: week_N))$

4.8.2.4. Configurational heads

The head of a Location or Time is configurational when it consists of more than one unit. In most cases, these units are a (prepositional) Property and its argument. Examples can be found in (131) and (134) above, repeated here for convenience:

(140)   a. in the station
      a'. $(l_1: [(f_1: in_{Adp}) (1\ x_1: (f_2: station_N))]_{Ref}\ ^1)$
   b. during the movie
      b'. $(t_1: [(f_1: during_{Adp}) (1\ e_1: (f_2: movie_N))]_{Ref}\ ^t)$

In sum, the head of a Location or Time designating expression can take the forms shown in Table 4.13.

Table 4.13. Different types of head: Locations and Times

Type of head	Representation: Location	Representation: Time
Absent	(l_1)	(t_1)
Empty	$(l_1: (f_1))$	$(t_1: (f_1))$
Lexical	$(l_1: (f_1: LEX))$	$(t_1: (f_1: LEX))$
Configurational	$(l_1: [(f_1) (x_2)]^1)$	$(t_1: [(f_1) (x_2)]^t)$

4.8.3. Modifiers

As in the case of Individuals, modifiers of Locations and Times can take a whole range of forms:

(141)   Locations:
  a. Adjectival: a *large* area
  b. Adverbial: *dangerously* close
  c. Phrasal: the area *to the north of Paris*
  d. Clausal: the place *where I work*

(142)   Times:
  a. Adjectival: a *long* day
  b. Adverbial: *incredibly* soon
  c. Phrasal: the day *after the wedding*
  d. Clausal: the moment *when I met my first love* (Internet)

An interesting feature of Times is that the relative pronoun *when* in (142d) can be replaced by the element *that*, as illustrated in (143):

(143)   the rules have been very, very strict from the moment *that they went into that school* (BYU-BNC, spoken, conversation)

In FDG, the difference between (142d) and (143) can be explained in terms of the difference between modifiers and arguments. Thus, in (142d), the *when*-clause is analysed as a relative clause, with the element *when* functioning as a relative pronoun, taking the preceding temporal nouns as its antecedent. The function of this modifier is to provide additional information about the moment in question, enabling the Addressee to identify it. The relative clause in example (142d) will thus be represented as in (144b), where the Time designated by the phrase as a whole (t_1) is modified by an SoA (e_1), which contains a temporal modifier designating the same Time ($_1$) as the phrase as a whole. This co-indexation triggers the use of the relative pronoun *when*:

(144)   a. the moment when I met my first love
  b. $(1\ t_1: (f_1: moment_N): (e_1: [(f_2: met_V)\ (x_1)_A\ (x_2)_U]: (t_1)^e)^t)$

In (143), on the other hand, the clause introduced by *that* does not provide extra information about the Time specified by the temporal noun *moment*; instead it designates a moment in time, and this moment IS the moment designated by the entire phrase. To reflect the difference with the construction in (142d), the *that*-clause is not analysed as a modifier but as an argument of the temporal head of the phrase. The relation of identity between the head and the *that*-clause is captured by co-indexation of the phrase as a whole and the *that*-clause, both of which are analysed as designating Times. The *that*-element functions as a linking element between the two co-designating units and only appears at the Morphosyntactic Level:

(145)   a. the moment that I met my first love
        b. (1 t_1: [(f_1: moment$_N$) (t_1: – **I met my first love** –)$_{Ref}$] ^{t})

An interesting parallel can be found at the layer of the Propositional Content. Here, too, a distinction needs to be made between Propositional Contents modified by a relative clause (example 146a) and those containing a content-clause (example (147b)):

(146)   a. It was *an idea that persisted.* (BYU-BNC, written, non-academic)
        b. (1 p_1: (f_1: idea$_N$): (**e_1: [(f_2: persist$_V$) (p_1)$_U$]**) ^{P})

(147)   a. Even *the idea that people have a split personality* isn't strictly true.
            (BYU-BNC, spoken, broadcast discussion)
        b. (1 p_1: [(f_1: idea$_N$) (**p_1: – people have a split personality** –)$_{Ref}$] ^{P})

Here, too, there is a crucial difference between the italicized units in examples (146a) and (147a): whereas in (146a) the clause introduced by *that* is a relative clause functioning as a modifier, in (147a) the *that*-clause, specifying the contents of the idea designated by the noun phrase as a whole, functions as an argument. Thus, in (146b) the element *that* functions as a relative pronoun (replaceable by *which*), which takes the noun *idea* as its antecedent and occupies an argument position in the modifying clause (where it functions as the argument of the verb *persist*). In (147b), on the other hand, the element *that* is not a relative pronoun: it does not have an antecedent, does not fill an argument position in the following clause (which is complete without the element *that*) and cannot be replaced by *which*. Instead it simply functions as a link between the propositional noun and a clause specifying its contents: that people have a split personality IS the idea designated by the noun phrase as a whole. The differences between the two constructions are reflected in their semantic representation in the same way as in (144) and (145) above. In (146b), the *that*-clause is analysed as a modifier of p_1; this modifier takes the form of an SoA (e_1) containing an Undergoer argument that is co-indexed with the variable of the phrase as a whole, thus triggering the relative pronoun *that* (or *which*). In (147b), on the other hand, the *that*-clause is analysed as an argument of the Property f_1; this argument designates the same Proposition as the phrase as a whole, as indicated by co-indexation. The *that*-element simply functions as a linking element between the two co-designating units.

4.8.4. Operators

Finally, the parallelism between Locations and Times (and Individuals) is also demonstrated by the fact that they can be specified by the same operators:

(148)   a. all places $(\forall\ l_1: (f_1: place_N))$
           b. somewhere $(\exists\ l_1)$
           c. everywhere $(distr\ l_1)$
           d. nowhere $(\emptyset\ l_1)$
           e. three places $(3\ l_1: (f_1: places_N))$

(149)   a. always $(\forall\ t_1)$
           b. some time $(\exists\ t_1)$
           c. every time $(distr\ t_1)$
           d. never $(\emptyset\ t_1)$
           e. twice $(2\ t_1)$

4.9. Summary

- In this chapter we have looked at the kind of units that can be found at the Representational Level, the relations between these units, and the primitives available for their formation (lexemes, frames, and operators).
- We saw that entities at this level belong to different semantic categories, depending on the kind of real world (or extra-linguistic) entity they designate. As for the relations between these entities, we saw that these can be hierarchical (between the Episodes within a Propositional Content, between different States-of-Affairs within an Episode), or non-hierarchical (or configurational), as in the case of the units that make up a State-of-Affairs (a predicate and its arguments).
- Each unit (layer) was then discussed in detail in terms of the kind of entity designated, the kinds of head and possible modifiers and operators. Here, as in the previous chapter, the difference between lexical and grammatical

elements, as well as scope differences between the layers, turned out to be important.

- In the course of the chapter, a number of important representational concepts and phenomena were discussed and provided with an FDG analysis, such as different kinds of anaphoric pronoun, the distinction between relative and absolute tense, the distinction between different types of aspect and (subjective and objective) modality, the distinction between predicates and arguments, the notions of qualitative and quantitative valency, the difference between verbal and non-verbal predicates, different kinds of States-of-Affairs, the different parts-of-speech, copular and existential sentences, embedding, compounding, and the difference between alienable and inalienable possession.
- Finally, at various places a comparison was made between certain units at the Interpersonal Level and units at the Representational Level to show the differences between them, and thus to justify the presence of two different levels.

Exercises

1. For each of the following compounds (a) determine which type it belongs to and (b) provide the appropriate representation.

(i)   low-life
(ii) pickpocket
(iii) gardener-caretaker
(iv) paperclip
(v)   paperback
(vi) tax-free

2. Give a complete representation (at the Interpersonal and Representational Level) of the following phrases:

(i)   an extremely successful actor
(ii) Peter's cat
(iii) the guy holding the torch
(iv) a poor liar

3. Determine the semantic category of the entities designated by the phrase *the school* in the following examples:

(i)   They met, by arrangement, outside the entrance to *the school* where his evening class was held (BYU-BNC, written, fiction)

(ii) They linked up in a silent demonstration of support for *the school* which is threatened with closure (BYU-BNC, written, scripted news)

(iii) *The school* was built in 1877 and is now the village hall. (BYU-BNC, written, non-academic)

4. What is indicated by the co-indexing of units at the Representational Level? Mention at least two situations in which co-indexation occurs.

5.* The following sentences all contain a form of the dummy verb *be*. For each of these sentences decide:

a. what type of construction it is (copular or existential, if the former: relational, classificational, identificational);

b. how to represent them at the Representational Level;

c. how to represent them at the Interpersonal Level.

Example: Robert is a teacher

    a. classificational

    b. RL: $(e_1: [\quad (x_1) \quad (x_2)_U])$

    c. IL: $T_1 \quad R_1$

(i)   Dr Jekyll is Mr Hyde.
(ii) There are no unicorns.
(iii) The winner was Roger Federer.
(iv) This present is for Jane.
(v)   His parents are actors.
(vi) It was a cold day.
(vii) His girlfriend is from Amsterdam.

6. Determine for each of the following sentences:

a. the quantitative valency (number of arguments)
b. the qualitative valency (semantic functions of the arguments)

(i)   We gave the presents to the children
(ii) My parents live in Utrecht.

(iii)   My little brother is very clever.
(iv)   The drought ruined the harvest.
 (v)   It was Mark who wrecked the car.
(vi)   The driver ran into a lamppost.
(vii)   The bus approached the station.
(viii)   The car had broken down.

7. Consider the following sentence:

My brother was upset by the news that his old school had burnt down.

Are the following statements true or false? Explain your answer.

 (i)   *my brother* has the semantic function of Undergoer
(ii)   *that* is a relative pronoun
(iii)   *my* functions as the argument of *brother*
(iv)   *old* modifies the Individual *his school*
 (v)   the auxiliary *had* is triggered by a past tense operator

8. The following examples (from COCA) all include a form of the verb *see*. Determine the meaning/function of this element in each example and think about a way of representing it at the Interpersonal and/or Representational Level:

 (i)   I see you took my advice.
(ii)   I see you drive by sometimes, see you slow down when you do.
(iii)   'Uh, yeah, OK. See you,' I said.
(iv)   A: One's bartending and the other delivers food.
       B: I thought they were both actors.
       A: They are.
       B: I see. What are their names again?
 (v)   On the beach the next morning, Ronnie sees a raccoon pawing at the sand.
(vi)   But as he sees it, there are few obstacles that cannot be overcome with solid organization and some planning.

9.
a. Consider the following examples (from the Internet) and decide which type of Individual (count or collective) is designated by the phrase *the Government*. Explain your answer.

(i)   This worries *the Government*, which has placed great importance on blocking the internet to exert ideological control.

(ii)   The head of government—usually the leader of the majority party or coalition—forms *the government*, which is answerable to parliament

(ii)   it's not *the government* who are to blame.

(iv)   The red shirts, loyal to the previous Prime Minister, Thaksin Shinawatra, are protesting against the *government* who are in power despite losing the last election.

b. In view of these examples, explain why it is an advantage to distinguish different types of Individual rather than different types of noun (see Section 4.7.1).

10. For each of the italicized phrases in following examples, decide:

a. the semantic category

b. the type of head (absent, empty, lexical or configurational)

(i)   Shocking—*Gloria Allred* is her attorney? I can't believe *it*. (COCA, spoken, CNN)

(ii)   *Sadie's heart* sank. Why could *she* never meet anyone of her own class? (BYU-BNC, written, miscellaneous)

(iii)   *The sheriff* is now operating on *the assumption that these two cases are actually one case*. (COCA, spoken, ABC)

(vi)   Wow! Does this mean I get *a wish*? I forgot to make *one* while you were falling. (COCA, written, fiction)

(v)   My dogs were frantic, and *so* was I. (BYU-BNC, written, miscellaneous)

11.** In Section 4.5.3.2, it is stated that non-dynamic (stative) SoAs do not contain an Actor. As the following examples show, this claim is somewhat oversimplified:

(i)   John resembles his father.

(ii) Parents love their children.

a. What kind of SoA are we dealing with in these sentences?

b. What is the semantic function of the first argument?

c. Why could these sentences be regarded as problematic?

d. Can you think of a reason for not regarding these sentences as counterexamples? (see Hengeveld and Mackenzie 2008: 202)

Suggestions for further reading

The idea of regarding predicates and frames as separate primitives, and of storing them separately, was first introduced in García Velasco and Hengeveld (2002). Hengeveld and Smit (2009) show how the hierarchical organization FDG can be made dynamic by the introduction of two procedural rules (top-down and depth-first). Some problems with the FDG analysis of copular constructions are discussed in Keizer (2008a). A detailed discussion of the representation of different kinds of pronouns is presented in Keizer (2012). García Velasco (2013a) offers an FDG account of English degree words. The difference and interaction between absolute and relative tense in English indirect speech is discussed in Leufkens (2013). Mackenzie (2013a) deals with secondary predications, while resultatives are discussed in Taverniers and Kelepouris (2013). The representation of resultatives is also discussed in Keizer (2009a), which deals with verb–preposition constructions. Other papers dealing with (spatial) prepositions (or adpositions) are Keizer (2008b) (on English prepositions) and Mackenzie (2013b) (a typological approach).

5

The Morphosyntactic Level

5.1. Introduction   173
5.2. The organization of the
     Morphosyntactic Level   175
5.3. Transparency and synthesis   178
5.4. Linguistic Expressions   181
5.5. Clauses   184

5.6. Phrases   218
5.7. Words   231
5.8. Summary   246
     Exercises   247
     Suggestions for further
     reading   250

The present chapter is devoted to the third of the four levels of representation that together form the Grammatical Component of a language, the
Morphosyntactic Level. This means that we move from the operation of
Formulation, concerned with all the pragmatic and semantic aspects of an
utterance as represented at the Interpersonal and Representational Levels,
to the operation of Encoding, concerned with the way in which interpersonal and representational information is formally expressed. In this
chapter we will concentrate on how interpersonal and representational
information is coded morphosyntactically, that is, in the form and order
of constituents. It will be shown that FDG allows for a unified approach to
morphosyntactic coding, in that the same underlying principles apply to
Clauses, Phrases, and Words alike. The chapter is structured in much the
same way as the previous chapters: after a brief introduction, we will look at
the overall organization of the Morphosyntactic Level (Section 5.2), before
moving on the some specific issues (Section 5.3) and a discussion of the
various layers (Clauses, Phrases, and Words; Sections 5.4–5.6). Finally,
since the Morphosyntactic form of an utterance is regarded as being

triggered by information represented at the Interpersonal and Representational Levels, reference will often be made to these latter levels, to demonstrate the way in which the pragmatic, semantic, and morphosyntactic properties of an utterance interact.

5.1. Introduction

In the previous chapters we have been concerned with the analysis and representation of the functional, that is, (discourse-)pragmatic and semantic, aspects of an utterance—those aspects of an utterance that relate to the communicative intention of the Speaker. These functional aspects of an utterance result from the operation of Formulation and are represented at the Interpersonal and Representational Levels. In order to express his/her communicative intentions, however, the Speaker has to encode these intentions in a particular form, an operation referred to as Encoding. As we have seen in Chapter 2, the FDG model distinguishes two suboperations of Encoding. First of all, there is Morphosyntactic Encoding, which is concerned with the way in which interpersonal and representational information is expressed in linear form, as well as with such matters as Subject and Object assignment, agreement, and subordination. Next the operation of Phonological Encoding (discussed in Chapter 6) deals with the phonological form of utterances.

Since the function of the Morphosyntactic Level is to encode the communicative intentions of the Speaker, it receives its input from the two higher levels of representation. Although there is no one-to-one relationship between the units at the different levels (see also Section 5.3), languages around the world seem to be governed by a number of general principles that maximize the parallelism between the levels by establishing a direct relation between function (Formulation) and form (Encoding). The first of these principles is that of **iconicity**, which results in a direct relation between the order in which interpersonal and representational units appear at the formulation levels and the linear order in which these units are expressed. Thus, Discourse Acts (at the Interpersonal Level) and Propositional Contents (at the Representational Level), are typically represented in the order in which they appear in the actual utterance. An example is given in (1), where the two Discourse Acts A_1 and A_2 correspond to two Clauses, appearing in the same order:

(1) The students worked very hard and they all passed the exam
   IL: (A$_1$)   (A$_2$)
   ML: (Cl$_1$)   (Cl$_2$)

The second principle is that of **domain integrity**. According to this principle, units of information that belong together at the Interpersonal and Representational Levels are also placed next to each other at the Morphological Level. Thus in example (2), the restrictive relative Clause is placed immediately after its antecedent, since antecedent and relative Clause form one semantic unit (an Individual, x_1). At the Morphosyntactic Level this semantic unit is expressed as one (complex) Noun Phrase (Np$_1$):

(2) *The students who worked very hard* all passed the exam.
   RL: (x_1)
   ML: (Np$_1$)

A final principle governing the relation between the Interpersonal and Representational Levels on the one hand and the Morphosyntactic Level on the other is that of **functional stability**. This principle states that units with a certain interpersonal or representational specification tend to be placed in the same position with regard to each other. In English, for instance, place adverbs typically precede time adverbs (when they apply to the same layer, as in example (3)), while adjectives describing size, colour, and provenance also have a preferred order of occurrence (example (4)).

(3) a. I saw Jane in London last Monday.
    b. $^?$I saw Jane last Monday in London.

(4) a. a big blue American car
    b. $^{*?}$an American blue big car

Although there is strong evidence that cross-linguistically these three principles play an important role, it is not difficult to find counterexamples. If, for instance, an utterance contains a non-restrictive relative Clause, the principle of iconicity can be overruled. As we saw in Chapter 3 (Section 3.4.1), non-restrictive relative Clauses are analysed as separate (dependent) Discourse Acts with the rhetorical function Aside. This means that a sentence like (5) contains two Discourse Acts, corresponding to two Clauses at the Morphosyntactic Level. Unlike in example (1), however, the Interpersonal and Morphosyntactic units now no longer appear in the same order: whereas at the Interpersonal Level the nuclear Discourse Act (as a whole) precedes the dependent Discourse Act, at the Morphosyntactic

Level the relative Clause (corresponding to the dependent Discourse Act) interrupts the main Clause (corresponding to the nuclear Discourse Act):

(5)   The students, who worked hard, all passed the exam.
   IL: $(A_1:$ –the students all passed the exam–$)$ $(A_2:$ –they all worked hard–$)_{Aside}$
   ML: $(Cl_1:$ – the students– $(Cl_2:$ –who worked hard–$)$ –passed the exam–$)$

Similarly, the principle of domain integrity can be overruled, for instance if the Speaker prefers to place complex and/or salient information at the end of the sentence. In example (6), for instance, the relative Clause and its antecedent are no longer juxtaposed, although at the Representational Level they are still one unit:

(6)   The indications are that Europe will once again become the priority because slowly and awkwardly, *a treaty* is taking shape *which will most likely emerge by the end of this year as a new European union* (ICE-GB, spoken, broadcast discussion)

For the same reasons, the principle of functional stability can be violated, as demonstrated in example (7), where the (long and complex) place modifier follows the (much shorter) time modifier:

(7)   The first Denver-area 1-2-3 Fit opened *last month in a Safeway-anchored shopping center at 64th Avenue and Ward Road in Arvada.* (COCA, written, newspaper)

These examples clearly show that the relation between Formulation and (Morphosyntactic) Encoding is far from straightforward—which is, of course, exactly why a separate level needs to be distinguished. We will return to this issue in Section 5.3, where we will discuss some more mismatches between units relevant during Formulation and those relevant for Morphosyntactic Encoding. Before we do so, however, we first need to introduce the different units (layers) distinguished at the Morphosyntactic Level.

5.2. The organization of the Morphosyntactic Level

At the Morphosyntactic Level four basic units are distinguished (note that, in accordance with convention, variables at this level are represented as a combination of upper and lower case symbols):

- The Linguistic Expression (Le)
- The Clause (Cl)

- The Phrase (Xp), where X represents the head of the Phrase
- The Word (Xw), where X represents the head of the Phrase, i.e. noun, verb, adjective, adverb or adposition.

Both Phrases and Words come in various types, depending on the type of head. At the layer of the Phrase a distinction is thus made between Noun Phrases (Np), Verb Phrases (Vp), Adjectival Phrases (Ap), Adverbial Phrases (Advp), and Adpositional Phrases (Adpp). These Phrases differ in the kind of head Word they contain: Nominal Words (Nw), Verbal Words (Vw), Adjectival Words (Aw), Adverbial Words (Advw), and Adpositional Words (Adpw), respectively. In addition, there is a class of Grammatical Words (Gw), consisting of function Words (articles, auxiliaries, conjunctions, etc.). These Grammatical Words do not head Phrases; they are either part of a Phrase (e.g. articles) or of a Clause (e.g. conjunctions).

At the Morphosyntactic Level many elements (Words) receive their final phonemic form, which is supplied along with the selected primitive. When the primitive is a lexeme, the phonological information is stored in the lexicon along with the lexeme and inserted at the Interpersonal or Representational Level—although for the sake of simplicity, this information has been given in orthographic form. This information is then simply transferred to the Morphosyntactic Level. If the primitive takes the form of an Affix or a Grammatical Morpheme, it is inserted at the Morphosyntactic Level; this information also appears in phonemic form, provided that this form is not 'sensitive to further phonological adaptation' (Hengeveld and Mackenzie 2008: 418). In a Noun Phrase like *the best students*, for instance, only the Nominal Word *student* appears in its phonological form at the Morphosyntactic Level; this is illustrated in (8b):

(8)   a. the best students
   b. (Np$_1$: (Gw$_1$: the) (Ap$_1$: (Aw$_1$: good-sup)) (Nw$_1$: stju:dənt.pl) ^{Np})

The determiner *the* is not given in phonological form since it has two allomorphs (/ ðə / and / ði: /); which allomorph is chosen is determined at the Phonological Level (on the basis of the first phoneme of the following word). The adjective *best* is not given in its phonological form either. Since *good* has suppletive forms for the comparative (*better*) and the superlative (*best*), the correct phonological form is not predictable from the combination of the basic form (*good*) and the regular superlative ending (*-est*). Here, too, the decision over which form to use is taken at the Phonological

Level. In the case of the plural ending, we are dealing with a regular form, but one which has three different allomorphs. Since the form of allomorph depends on the final sound of the preceding noun, its exact realization can only be determined after all the elements have been placed in linear order. This linear ordering takes place at the Morphological Level; on the basis of the outcome of this ordering process, the correct form of the plural suffix is triggered at the Phonological Level. For the sake of readability, however, Words will still be represented in their orthographic form in this chapter; in the next chapter, all units will be represented in their phonological form.

> Which elements in the sentence *The students bought many books* receive their phonological form at the Phonological Level?

Just like the Interpersonal and the Representational Levels, the Morpho-syntactic Level is hierarchically organized, in that **Linguistic Expressions**, as the highest units of analysis, contain one or more **Clauses**, Clauses contain one or more **Phrases**, and Phrases contain one or more **Words**. A sentence like (9a) could thus be represented by means of the general schema in (9b):

(9) a. John put the money in the safe.

b. $(Le_1: (Cl_1: [$ $(Np_1:$ $(Nw_1: John))$
    $(Vp_1:$ $(Vw_1: put))$
    $(Np_2:$ $(Gw_1: the)$
            $(Nw_2: money)$ $^{Np})$
    $(Adpp_1:$ $[$ $(Adpw_1: in)$
            $(Np_3: [$ $(Gw_2: the)$
                $(Nw_3: safe)]$ $^{Np})]$ $^{Adpp})]$ $^{Cl})$ $^{Le})$

As shown in examples (10) and (11), however, not every layer has to be present. Thus, Linguistic Expressions need not contain a Clause: they may also consist of a combination of Phrases or Words, or even of a single Phrase or Word:

(10) a. (What did you buy?) Two books, one DVD.

b. $(Le_1: [(Np_1) (Np_2)]$ $^{Le})$

(11) a. (How many books did you buy?) Two.

b. $(Le_1: (Gw_1))$

These examples show that representations at the Morphosyntactic Level only contain information that is actually expressed: there is no need to assume the presence of a complete Clause if, as in examples (10) and (11), no complete Clause is uttered. In this sense morphosyntactic representations in FDG are quite minimalistic. At the same time, however, it will be clear that, in principle, each unit can contain an endless number of other units, which may be added either through **stacking** (adding units at the same layer; example (12)) or **nesting** (embedding units within other units; example (13)):

(12)   John bought [two apples, three bananas, two pears, six kiwis, some strawberries ...]

(13)   John took the money from [the safe [in a room [at the end [of a corridor [on the first floor [of the building [on the corner [of our street ....]]]]]]]]

This means that each language has an infinite number of morphosyntactic templates (linearly ordered sequences of morphosyntactic units). For reasons of simplification and generalization, these **microtemplates** will, where possible, be reduced to a limited number of **macrotemplates**. Thus the unlimited number of Noun Phrases that can be added to the expression in (12) can be represented by the general schema in (14a), while the infinite number of Adpositional Phrases that can be added to example (13) can be achieved by recursively applying the two general schemas in (14b) (for Nominal and Adpositional Phrases, respectively):

(14)   a. $[...(Np_{1+n})...]$ (where $n \geq 0$)
   b. $(Np_1: [...(Adpp_1)...])$
      $(Adpp_1: [...(Np_1)...])$

In Sections 5.4–5.7 each of the morphosyntactic layers will be discussed in more detail. Before we embark on this enterprise, however, let us return to the relationship between the units introduced during Formulation and those used in morphosyntactic Encoding.

5.3. Transparency and synthesis

Now that the various morphosyntactic units have been introduced, we can briefly return to the question of how units represented at the Interpersonal and Representational Levels are mapped onto the units distinguished at the Morphosyntactic Level. As pointed out in Section 5.1, this mapping is, to a considerable extent, governed by the principles of iconicity, domain integrity and functional stability. If these principles were applied without exception, we would in all likelihood end up with a one-to-one relationship between interpersonal, representational, and morphosyntactic units. In that case, a Referential Subact with the pragmatic function Topic at the Interpersonal Level would always correspond to an Individual with the semantic function Actor at the Representational Level and would at the Morphosyntactic Level take the form of a Noun Phrase with the **syntactic function** of Subject, which would invariably appear in first position. As can be seen from example (15), such a one-to-one correspondence is indeed possible, and may even be regarded as a default relation between the three levels:

(15)   (What did John buy?)

          John   bought   two books.

   IL: $(R_1)_{TOP}$ (T_1) $(R_2)_{FOC}$

   RL: $(x_1)_A$ (f_1) $(x_2)_U$

   ML: $(Np_1)_{Subj}$ (Vp_1) $(Np_2)_{Obj}$

Such a straightforward (or **transparent**) relation between the various levels clearly has its advantages: it makes utterances easier to interpret and languages easier to learn. In fact, if the correspondence between units at the various levels were consistently one-to-one, there would be no need to distinguish different levels of analysis: one level, with one set of units, operators and functions, would suffice for the description of such a language.

However, as we already saw in Section 5.2, in many cases the relation between the different levels of analysis is not one-to-one; in fact, although languages may exhibit different degrees of transparency, there are no languages that are fully transparent. The reason for this seems to be that a fully transparent language is either communicatively too restricted (the Speaker may, for instance, have good communicative reasons for not expressing the Actor as the Subject of a Clause) or, from the point of view of language processing, too user unfriendly (it is, for instance, easier, for both Speaker and Addressee, to place long and complex units towards the end of the Clause, irrespective of their semantic or syntactic function). Languages are, therefore, cross-linguistically characterized by 'mismatches' between interpersonal, representational, and morphosyntactic units, although languages differ both in the number and in the kind of mismatches they exhibit. In this section we will look at some examples in English of mismatches between the Interpersonal and Representational Levels on the one hand and the Morphosyntactic Level on the other.

One important, and very systematic, mismatch between the Representational Level and the Morphosyntactic Level concerns the expression of manner adverbs, for example *ferociously* in example (16):

(16)   The dog barked *ferociously*.

At the Representational Level, the adverb *ferociously* is analysed as an adjective modifying the verb *bark* (see example (17a)). The normal, unmarked function of adjectives is, however, to modify nouns (as in *a ferocious dog*). The mismatch between the noun-modifying function of adjectives and the verb-modifying function of manner adverbs is resolved at the Morphosyntactic Level by the addition of the affix *-ly*, which explicitly codes the representational function of the modifier (see example (17b)) (Hengeveld and Mackenzie 2008: 218, 295–6; see also discussion in Section 5.7.2).

(17)   a. $(p_1: (past\ ep_1: (e_1: [(f_1: bark_V: (\mathbf{f_2: ferocious_A})^f)\ (1x_1: (f_3: dog))_A]^e)^{ep})^P)$
    b. $(Le_1: (Cl_1: (Np_1: (Gw_1: the)\ (Nw_1: dog)^{Np})\ (Vp_1: (Vw_1: barked))$
     $(Advp_1: (\mathbf{Advw_1: ferociously}))^{Cl})^{Le})$

Another example of non-transparency between Formulation and Morphosyntactic Encoding is the existence of so-called **dummy elements**, that is, morphosyntactic elements which do not correspond to any specific unit at the Interpersonal or Representational Level. Remember that Functional Discourse Grammar is a functional model in that it assumes that the form of linguistic utterances (as represented in Encoding) encodes their pragmatic and semantic function (that is, the Speaker's communicative intention). At the same time, however, it is acknowledged that languages also contain a-functional elements, that is, elements which do not (or no longer) fulfil a specific pragmatic or semantic function. In some cases these dummy elements seem to be a result of language internal pressures. For instance, in a fairly rigid SVO language like English, there is a strong tendency (i) for the Subject position to be filled; and (ii) for the Subject to precede the verb. If there is no pragmatic or semantic unit available for the Subject position, or if, for some reason, a Speaker prefers to place the Subject in a post-verbal position, a dummy element may be used to fill the (obligatory) Subject position. An example of such a dummy element is weather-*it* (example (18)). As argued in Chapter 4 (Section 4.5.3.1), weather verbs like *rain*, *snow*, and *hail* do not have any arguments (are zero-place predicates). In the absence of any argument to function as the Subject, the dummy element *it* is placed in the Subject position. Other dummy elements are presentative *there* and provisional *it*, as well as such verbal forms as the copula *be* and dummy *do*, all of which are required for morphosyntactic reasons, but lack a pragmatic or semantic counterpart.

(18)   **It** rained.

> IL: $(A_1: - (C_1: (T_1)) -)$
> RL: $(p_1: - (e_1: (f_1: rain_V)) -)$
> ML: $(Le_1: (Cl_1: [(Np_1: (Nw_1: \textbf{it}))_{Subj} (Vp_1: (Vw_1: rained))]^{Cl)}{}^{Le})$

Non-transparency between the Interpersonal/Representational Levels and the Morphosyntactic Level may also result from a process referred to as **synthesis**. In the case of synthesis the lack of a one-to-one relation between units at different levels is caused by the fact that two or more pragmatic/semantic units are fused into one morphosyntactic unit. Examples of this process are personal, possessive, and demonstrative pronouns. Take for instance the deictic demonstrative pronoun *those* in a sentence like (19):

(19)   I want *those*!

> IL: $(A_1: -- (C_1: [(T_1) (R_1) (+id R_2: [\textbf{-S, -A}])_{FOC}]^{C)}-- {}^{A})$

> RL: $(p_1: -- (e_1: [(f_1: want_V) (1x_1)A (\textbf{dis m } x_2)_U]^{e})-- {}^{P})$

> ML: $(Le_1: (Cl_1: [(Np_1: (Nw_1: I))_{Subj} (Vp_1: (Vw_1: want)) (Np_2: (Nw_2: \textbf{those}))_{Obj}]^{Cl)}{}^{Le})$

Here the appropriate morphosyntactic form is triggered by a combination of interpersonal information (identifiability, deictic reference, third person) and representational information (distal, plural).

As we will see, there are many more cases where there is no one-to-one correspondence between interpersonal and representational units on the one hand and morphosyntactic units on the other. These, however, will be described when we discuss the relevant morphosyntactic layer.

5.4. Linguistic Expressions

Linguistic Expressions form the highest layer at the Morphosyntactic Level. They typically consist of a number of lower-layer morphosyntactic units (Clauses, Phrases, or Words), but may also contain just one of these units, provided it can be used independently. Examples of Linguistic Expression consisting of one, two, and three units were given in examples (11), (18), and (19), respectively (here repeated for convenience):

(11)   a.   (How many books did you buy?) Two.
>   b. $(Le_1: (Gw_1))$

(18) a. It rained.

b. (Le$_1$: (Cl$_1$: [(Np$_1$: (Nw$_1$: it))$_{Subj}$ (Vp$_1$: (Vw$_1$: rained))] ^{Cl}) ^{Le})

(19) a. I want those!

b. (Le$_1$: (Cl$_1$: [(Np$_1$: (Nw$_1$: I))$_{Subj}$ (Vp$_1$: (Vw$_1$: want)) (Np$_2$: (Nw$_2$: those))] ^{Cl}) ^{Le})

Note that in order to qualify as a unit at the layer of the Linguistic Expression, an expression must not be part of another unit. Thus, in (20a), we find a Linguistic Expression consisting of two Clauses and a coordinator, none of which is part of either of the other parts; the Linguistic Expression in (20b), on the other hand, consists of just one Clause, which in turn contains another Clause:

(20) a. Matthew bought two books and Mary bought a DVD.

(Le$_1$: [(Cl$_1$) (Gw$_1$) (Cl$_2$)] ^{Le})

b. Matthew thought that Mary bought two DVDs.

(Le$_1$: (Cl$_1$: [– (Cl$_2$)]))

When we look at the possible combinations of units within the Linguistic Expression, it turns out that a limited number of macrotemplates can be distinguished, which differ with regard to the types of units they contain and the relation between these units.

First of all, Linguistic Expressions may consist of two or more Clauses, each of which can be used independently. An example of such a configuration, referred to as **coordination**, was given in example (20a). A more general schema for such constructions is provided in (21):

(21) (Le$_1$: [(Cl$_1$) (Cl$_{n-1}$) (Gw$_1$) (Cl$_n$)] ^{Le})   Coordination

A similar construction, but now containing a number of coordinated Phrases, is illustrated in (22a); the general schema for such constructions is given in (22b) (where Xp stands for any type of Phrase). This particular configuration is referred to as **Listing**:

(22) a. (What did Matthew buy?) A book, two DVDs and some magazines.

b. (Le$_1$: [(Xp$_1$) (Xpl$_{n-1}$) (Gw$_1$) (Xp$_n$)] ^{Le})   Listing

What these two configurations have in common is that the individual parts are not dependent on each other: each constituent part can be used by itself. There are, however, also Linguistic Expressions which contain one unit that can be used independently and one or more units that cannot (but which are not part of the independent unit). Some examples are given in (23) and (24). In example (23a) we find an example of what is referred to as **cosubordination**: a combination of two Clauses (neither part of the other), such that one

Clause can, and the other cannot, be used independently. Example (24a) illustrates a similar phenomenon referred to as **extra-clausality**: a combination of a Noun Phrase and a Clause, such that the Clause, but not the Noun Phrase, could be used independently (see Van der Auwera 1997; Hengeveld and Mackenzie 2008: 308).

(23) a. As for the Beatles being boring, you should read Lennon's biography ... (Internet)

     b. $(Le_1: [^{dep}(Cl_1) (Cl_2)]^{Le})$ Cosubordination

(24) a. As for the Beatles, I think they are rather boring.

     b. $(Le_1: [(Xp_1) (Cl_1)]^{Le})$ Extra-clausality

Finally, it seems to be possible for a Linguistic Expression to consist of two units of the same type (Clause or Phrase), which are mutually dependent on each other. For this phenomenon, illustrated in (25a), the term (clausal or phrasal) **equiordination** is used:

(25) a. The longer it went on, the worse it got.

     a'. $(Le_1: [^{dep}(Cl_1)\ ^{dep}(Cl_2)]^{Le})$ Clausal Equiordination

     b. the bigger, the better

     b'. $(Le_1: [(Xp_1) (Xp)]^{Le})$ Phrasal Equiordination

Summing up, Linguistic Expressions can have the configurations of units shown in Table 5.1.

Table 5.1. Possible configurations of Linguistic Expressions

Configuration	Template	Example(s)
Coordination	$(Le_1: [(Cl_1) (Cl_{n-1}) (Gw_1) (Cl_n)]^{Le})$	(20a), (21)
Listing	$(Le_1: [(Xp_1) (Xpl_{n-1}) (Gw_1) (Xp_n)]^{Le})$	(22)
Cosubordination	$(Le_1: [^{dep}(Cl_1) (Cl_2)]^{Le})$	(23)
Extra-clausality	$(Le_1: [^{dep}(Xp_1) (Cl_1)]^{Le})$	(24)
Equiordination	$(Le_1: [^{dep}(Cl_1)\ ^{dep}(Cl_2)]^{Le})$	(25a)
	$(Le_1: [(Xp_1) (Xp_2)]^{Le})$	(25b)

Decide which of the configurations in Table 5.1 applies to each of the following Linguistic Expressions: *Between you and me, I don't really like the Beatles; the more the merrier; I wouldn't go, if I were you.*

5.5. Clauses

5.5.1. Introduction

The second layer at the Morphosyntactic Level is that of the Clause. Clauses consist of a sequenced combination of Words (Xw), Phrases (Xp) and other (embedded) Clauses, all of which may occur more than once within a single Clause. Some possible combinations are given in example (26):

(26) a.   John   put   the money   into the safe
     (Cl$_1$: [(Np$_1$)$_{Subj}$ (Vp$_1$)   (Np$_2$)$_{Obj}$ (Adpp$_1$)]^{Cl})
    b.   Do   you   know   where Sue is?
     (Cl$_1$: [(Gw$_1$)   (Np$_1$)$_{Subj}$ (Vp$_1$)   (Cl$_2$)$_{Obj}$]^{Cl})

The Clause in (26a) consists of four constituents: two Noun Phrases, a Verb Phrase and an Adpositional Phrase. Note that the Verb Phrase consists of the verb *put* only, and not, as in many other models, of the verb and its complements (in this case *the money* and *into the safe*). The reason for this is the absence of clear evidence for the relevance of such groupings of verbs and their complements (direct object, indirect object, prepositional object) for all languages (Van Valin 2001: 212; see Hengeveld and Mackenzie 2008: 299); FDG therefore does not recognize a layer in between the Phrase and the Clause. This means that in FDG Verb Phrases contain only verbal elements, that is, main verbs and possible (adjacent) auxiliaries (on the absence of this intermediate layer in FDG, see also Keizer 2012). The Clause in (26b) also consists of four elements: a Word, a Noun Phrase, a Verb Phrase, and an embedded Clause. Note that the Word is a Grammatical Word (the dummy element *do*): as we saw in Section 5.2, lexical Words (Nominal Words, Verbal Words, etc.) are always the head of a Phrase, which means that single Words at the Clause layer can only be Grammatical Words (conjunctions, particles, dummy elements, etc.).

As we can see from the representations in (26), the Clause is the layer at which syntactic functions are assigned. For English, two morphosyntactic functions are relevant: **Subject** and **Object**. We will return to the assignment of syntactic function in Section 5.5.3.

Finally, it will be clear from the examples in (26) that the units in the representation are linearly ordered. This is indeed a distinctive feature of the Morphosyntactic Level: it is at this level that elements are placed in the order in which they are expressed. The ordering of elements takes place in two stages: first the non-core units at the Interpersonal and Representational

Levels are given a position in the Clause, then the core units. Let us consider this distinction in some more detail. Remember that both the Interpersonal and the Representational Level have a hierarchical, multi-layered organization. At the Interpersonal Level, the highest layer, the Move, consists of one or more Discourse Acts, which in turn consist of an Illocution, the Speech Participants and the Communicated Content, with the Communicated Content consisting of one or more Subacts of Ascription and/or Reference. Similarly, the outer layer at the Representational Level, the Propositional Content, consists of one or more Episodes, which in turn contain States-of-Affairs, which consist of a Property (the predicate) and its arguments. Now, it could be argued that at both levels there is one unit that forms the core of that level in that it contains information that is absolutely essential at that level. At the Interpersonal Level, this would be the configurational head of the Communicated Content, that is, the Subacts of Reference and Ascription that make up the message communicated by the Speaker (the content frame). At the Representational Level, this special unit would be the configurational head of the State-of-Affairs, that is, the predicate and its arguments, as the basic components of the extra-linguistic situation designated (the predication frame). These central parts of the Interpersonal and Representational Level are indicated in examples (27) and (28):

(27) $(M_1: (A_1: [(F_1) (P_1)_S (P_2)_A (C_1: [... (T_1) (R_1) ...]^C)]^A)^M)$

⟵————————⟶

Content Frame
(core unit)

(28) $(p_1: (ep_1: (e_1: [(f_1) (x_1) (x_2) ...]^e)^{ep})^p)$

⟵————————⟶

Predication Frame
(core unit)

The distinction between the core and non-core parts in (27) and (28) is crucial when it comes to the ordering of constituents at the Morphosyntactic Level, not only because the placement of non-core units precedes the placement of core units, but also because different ordering principles apply to the two sets of units.[1]

---

[1] Hengeveld and Mackenzie (2008) do not use the terms core and non-core, distinguishing instead between hierarchically related (non-core) and non-hierarchically related (core) elements instead. This, however, is confusing since part of the non-core unit (e.g. the Illocution) is in fact a non-hierarchically related unit.

The rest of this section will be devoted to the principles underlying the linear placement of elements and some related morphosyntactic phenomena. First, in Section 5.5.2, the ordering of non-core units will be discussed. The following section (5.5.3) discusses the assignment of the syntactic functions Subject and Object, introducing the notion of alignment. Subsequently, Section 5.5.4 is concerned with the ordering of core elements. The last three sections deal with a number of specific morphosyntactic phenomena: the insertion of dummy elements (Section 5.5.5), the application of agreement rules (Section 5.5.6), and the form and placement of subordinate Clauses (Section 5.5.7).

5.5.2. The ordering of non-core units

As pointed out in the previous section, the ordering of elements at the Morphosyntactic Level starts with the non-core elements at the Interpersonal and Representational Levels. It is further assumed that this ordering takes place in a top-down manner, starting with the highest layer at the Interpersonal Level and ending with the lowest non-core layer at the Representational Level. Furthermore, within each layer, the ordering proceeds in an inward manner, starting with the function of the layer as a whole, followed by the expression of operators and modifiers. These ordering principles can thus be represented as follows:

(29) $\pi^M / \Sigma^M \quad \to \quad \Phi^A / \pi^A / \Sigma^A \quad \to \quad \pi^F / \Sigma^F \quad \to \quad \Phi^C / \pi^C / \Sigma^C / \quad \to$
$\Phi^P / \pi^P / \sigma^P \quad \to \quad \Phi^{ep} / \pi^{ep} / \sigma^{ep} \quad \to \quad \Phi^e / \pi^e / \sigma^e$

According to (29), the first elements to be placed in an appropriate (clausal or extra-clausal) position are operators and modifiers of the Move, followed by functions, operators, and modifiers of the Discourse Act, etc. Functions, modifiers, and operators of the State-of-Affairs are the last units to be put in their respective positions.

The next question to be answered is where these elements are placed. For English, three absolute positions are available at the start of the ordering process: the Clause-initial position (P^I), the Clause-medial position (P^M), and the Clause-final position (P^F):

(30) $P^I \quad P^M \quad P^F$

In addition, there may be a number of relative positions, which become available as soon as one of the absolute positions is filled. Thus, as soon as the initial position is filled, a post-initial position (P^{I+1}) will become available. The same is true for the position before the final position and those surrounding the medial positions. As soon as these additional positions are filled, new relative positions become available. In this way the infinite length and complexity of Clauses can be dealt with. A number of possible Clause patterns, of increasing complexity, are given in (31):

(31) P^I P^{I+1} $\qquad$ P^M $\qquad\qquad\qquad\qquad$ P^F

$\qquad$ P^I P^{I+1} $\qquad$ P^M $\qquad\qquad\qquad$ P^{F-1} P^F

$\qquad$ P^I P^{I+1} $\qquad$ P^M P^{M+1} $\quad$ P^{F-1} P^F

$\qquad$ P^I P^{I+1} P^{I+2} P^M P^{M+1} $\quad$ P^{F-1} P^F

Since Clauses can also combine with extra-clausal elements, we need further positions outside the Clause, but still within the Linguistic Expression. In other words, within the Linguistic Expression, clausal elements appear in the middle, surrounded by two extra-clausal constituents, the preclausal position (P^{pre}) and the postclausal position (P^{post}). This provides us with the overall pattern represented in (32) (where bars (|) indicate clause boundaries):

(32) Le: P^{pre} | $\qquad\qquad$ Clause $\qquad\qquad$ | P^{post}

$\qquad$ Cl: $\qquad\qquad$ | P^I P^M $\qquad$ P^F |

The best way to illustrate how the ordering of non-core clausal elements works for English is by looking at the modifiers that can occur at each of the interpersonal and representational layers. Starting with the Interpersonal Level, consider the following sentences:

(33) a. Finally (Σ^A), he frankly (Σ^F) knows very little about international politics.

$\qquad$ b. Frankly (Σ^F), he unfortunately (Σ^C) knows very little about international politics.

$\qquad$ c. Unfortunately (Σ^C), he knows very little about international politics.

In (33a), we find two interpersonal modifiers, one occurring at the layer of the Discourse Act (*finally*), the other at the layer of the Illocution (*frankly*). According to the ordering principles in (29), the placement of modifiers of the Discourse Acts precedes the placement of Illocution modifiers. Moreover, from the examples in (33), as well as from further evidence, we can tell that modifiers tend to be ordered in a centripetal manner, starting from the outside and then gradually moving inwards. This means that as the relatively highest modifier, *finally* will be placed in the outermost non-clausal position (P^{pre}). The next element to be put in its appropriate position is the Illocution modifier *frankly*. This element will be placed in one of the other absolute positions, in this case P^M. (Note that P_1 is reserved for the Subject (Hengeveld 2013: 3).) We thus end up with the following pattern:

(34) P^{pre} | P^I P^M P^F | P^{post}
         $^{\Sigma A}$finally $^{\Sigma F}$frankly

In example (33b), we find the same Illocution modifier, *frankly*, but now in combination with a lower-layer modifier, *unfortunately*, which occurs at the layer of the Communicated Content. In this case, the first element to be assigned a position is therefore *frankly*. Since, in the absence of a higher-layer modifier, the outermost position is available, this is where this modifier is placed.

(35) P^{pre} | P^I P^M P^F | P^{post}
         $^{\Sigma F}$frankly $^{\Sigma C}$unfortunately

If, as in example (33c), the highest interpersonal modifier occurs at the layer of the Communicated Content, this modifier ends up in the pre-clausal position:

(36) P^{pre} | P^I P^M P^F | P^{post}
         $^{\Sigma C}$unfortunately

Theoretically, it is, of course, possible for all three modifiers to occur in the same sentence, although such combinations very rarely occur. In the case of the three modifiers used in example (33), the highest modifier, *finally*, would again go in the pre-clausal position, and the next highest, *frankly*, into the medial position. The third modifier, *unfortunately*, could then be placed in the post-medial position, which has now become available. This would result in the pattern in (37a). Note, however, that in such cases one of the modifiers is more likely to end up in the post-clausal position, as illustrated in (37b):

(37)   a. Finally, he frankly unfortunately knows very little about international politics.

P^{pre} | P^I P^M P^{M+1} P^F
$^{\Sigma A}$finally $^{\Sigma F}$frankly $^{\Sigma C}$unfortunately

b. Finally, he frankly knows very little about international politics, unfortunately.

P^{pre} | P^I P^M P^F | P^{post}
$^{\Sigma A}$finally $^{\Sigma F}$frankly $^{\Sigma C}$unfortunately

When we apply the ordering principles in (29) to non-core elements at the Representational Level, we find the same kind of patterns. Consider, for instance, the sentences in (38):

(38) a. Presumably (σ^P), she met him again (σ^e) last week (σ^{eP}).
   b. She met him again (σ^e) last week (σ^{eP}), presumably (σ^P).
   c. Last week (σ^{eP}) she met him again (σ^e), presumably (σ^P).

Once again, the highest modifier, the Propositional Content modifier *presumably*, has to be placed first, ending up in an outermost position, that is, either in the pre-clausal position (as in (38a)) or in the post-clausal position (as in (38b) and (38c)). The second-highest modifier, the Episodic modifier *last week*, will be placed next, either in the Clause-final position (examples (38a) and (38b)), or in the pre-clausal position if this position is still available (example (38c)). As the relatively lowest-layer modifier, the SoA modifier *again* is placed last, either in the Clause-final position (when still available, as in (38c)), or, if the Clause-final position is already occupied, in the newly available prefinal position (examples (38a) and (38b)). This yields the following partial orderings:

(39)

P^{pre}		P^I P^M	P^{F-1}	P^F		P^{post}
a. $^{\sigma P}$presumably			$^{\sigma e}$again	$^{\sigma eP}$last week		
b.			$^{\sigma e}$again	$^{\sigma eP}$last week		$^{\sigma P}$presumably
c. $^{\sigma eP}$last week				$^{\sigma e}$again		$^{\sigma P}$presumably

Note that the modifier *presumably* can also go into the medial position, as illustrated in (40):

(40)

P^{pre}		P^I	P^M		P^{F-1}	P^F			P^{post}
			$^{\sigma P}$presumably		$^{\sigma e}$again	$^{\sigma eP}$last week			

Let us now consider some sentences containing both interpersonal and representational modifiers:

(41) a. Unfortunately, she presumably saw him again last week.
   b. Frankly, she unfortunately presumably saw him again last week.

In (41a), *unfortunately*, as the only interpersonal modifier, is the first element to be placed in position, ending up in the outermost position P^{pre}. As the highest representational modifier, *presumably* is the next element to be placed; since the pre-clausal position is already occupied, is placed in the medial position. Subsequently, *last week* is placed in the Clause-final position and *again* in the pre-final position.

(42) P^{pre} | P^I P^M P^{F-1} P^F | P^{post}
$^{\Sigma C}$unfortunately $^{\sigma P}$presumably $^{\sigma e}$again $^{\sigma eP}$last week

Likewise, in the highly unlikely, but theoretically possible sentence in (41b), the highest modifier, *frankly*, is placed in the pre-clausal position, after which *unfortunately* is given the medial position. Then the highest representational modifier, *presumably*, is placed in the now available post-medial position. Finally, the modifiers *last week* and *again* again end up in final and prefinal position, respectively.

(43) P^{pre} | P^I P^M P^{M+1} P^{F-1} P^F
$^{\Sigma A}$frankly $^{\Sigma C}$unfortunately $^{\sigma P}$presumably $^{\sigma e}$again $^{\sigma eP}$last week

Although the account given of the linear ordering of non-core elements in this section has been short and incomplete, some advantages of this approach will have become clear. First of all, there is no need to allocate fixed positions to specific elements, nor do elements have to occur in fixed orders. Moreover, by distinguishing between absolute and relative positions, extra positions are created only when necessary, while, at the same time, the system can generate as many relative positions as are required. As a result, the system is highly flexible: it can deal with Clauses of any length, as well as with the many different word orders found not only within a single language, but also cross-linguistically. This does not, however, mean that the system is unconstrained, as can be seen from the fact that the following (unacceptable) sentences will be excluded:

(44)   a. *Frankly, he finally knows very little about international politics.
         b. *Last week, presumably she met him again.
         c. *Presumably, she unfortunately met him again last week.

Using the ordering rules discussed in this section, explain why the sentences in (44) are not acceptable.

Ordering of non-core elements in other languages

There is considerable evidence from languages around the world that non-core elements are placed centripetally, appearing typically at the beginning or at the end of the Clause. Thus, Illocution markers tend to be placed in Clause-initial or Clause-final position (Hengeveld and

Mackenzie 2008: 314). In Mandarin Chinese, for instance, the interrogative marker *ma* occurs in Clause-final position (example (45a); Li and Thompson 1981: 550), while in Polish the (optional) interrogative marker *czy* can only appear in Clause-initial position (example (45b)):

(45) a. Nǐ   chī   píngguo   ma
       you   eat   apple   INTER
       'Do you eat apples?'

      b. (Czy)   jesz   jabłka?
       INTER   eat.2s   apples
       'Do you eat apples?'

Further support for the view that the placement of non-core elements begins at the periphery of the Clause comes from strictly verb-final languages, like Korean. Given that the final position of the Clause is necessarily occupied by the verb, it may be expected that non-core units can only appear in initial position. This prediction is indeed borne out, as illustrated in example (46) for the Communicated Content modifier *tahaynghi* 'fortunately' (Lee 2001: 58):

(46) Tahaynghi   Johni   Maryka   chaykul   ilk-key   hayessta
      fortunately, John   Mary   book   read   caused
      'Fortunately, John caused Mary to read a book.'

5.5.3. Alignment

5.5.3.1. Introduction

In the previous section, we looked at the ordering principles governing the placement of non-core elements at the Interpersonal and Representational Levels. We will now turn our attention to the morphosyntactic properties of core interpersonal and representational elements. First, in this section, we will be concerned with the way in which these core elements map onto (or are aligned with) morphosyntactic units; a process referred to in FDG as **alignment** (Hengeveld and Mackenzie 2008: 316; cf. Foley 2005: 385). Then, in Section 5.5.4, we will look at the factors determining the order in which these core elements are expressed.

In many theories, alignment is taken care of by the assignment of the syntactic functions Subject and Object. Typically, it is assumed that one of the arguments of the predicate is assigned Subject function; in the case of two- or three-place predicates another argument is assigned Object function. These elements are then morphosyntactically encoded in a particular way (e.g. by certain case endings or by agreement with the verb). Although this may work quite well for some languages, there is, as we will see, reason to believe that Subject and Object assignment is not a universal phenomenon. For this reason, FDG distinguishes three kinds of alignment: interpersonal, representational, and morphosyntactic. Before we proceed to discuss alignment in English, let us first have a brief look at these three types of alignment.

5.5.3.2. Types of alignment

Although in many languages the assignment of the syntactic functions Subject and Object is needed to explain the morphosyntactic realization of certain pragmatic or semantic elements, there are also languages that need not resort to syntactic function assignment. In some languages, for instance, the morphosyntactic behaviour of elements, such as their form and the order in which they appear, can be explained in terms of the interpersonal features of these elements. Languages of this kind are said to have a system of **interpersonal alignment**. An example of such a language is Kisi, which can be characterized as a Focus-oriented language (Hengeveld and Mackenzie 2008: 101). Thus, in example (47a), assignment of the pragmatic function Focus to the element *màalóŋ* 'rice' triggers its placement in initial position as well as the presence of the particle *ní* in final position (Childs 1995: 270–1). This means that all the morphosyntactic features of the element *màalóŋ* can be accounted for without the need for Subject or Object assignment.

(47) a. **màalóŋ**   ó   có   cùùcúúwó   **ní**
         rice   he   AUX   sow   FOC
         'It's rice he is sowing.'
      b. $(A_1: [(F_1: DECL) (P_1)_S (P_2)_A (C_1: [(T_1) (R_1)_{FOC} (R_2)])])$

In other languages it is information from the Representational Level that determines the morphosyntactic realization of elements. Such languages are said to have a **representational alignment** system. An example is the position of pronouns in Acehnese, a language in which pronouns may not only appear as free elements, but also as **clitics**, that is, as elements that behave morphosyntactically as separate words (usually function words), but which phonologically depend on (are attached to) another word; an example from English would be the element '*ll* in *We'll do it* (see also Section 6.6). In Acehnese these clitics either precede or follow the element to which they attach, depending on the semantic function of the pronoun (e.g. Actor or Undergoer) (Durie 1985: 190; Hengeveld and Mackenzie 2008: 319). In example (48a), for instance, the Actor argument (A) is expressed by the clitic pronoun *lôn* preceding the verb *jak* 'go'. In (48b), the Undergoer argument (U) is expressed both as a free pronoun (*gopnyan*) and as a clitic (*geuh*), but in this case the clitic follows the verb (examples from Durie (1985: 48, 56), given here in somewhat simplified form). In other words, the position of the clitic is directly triggered by the semantic function of the argument.

(48) a. **lôn**=jak   baroe
         I.A=go   yesterday
         'I went yesterday.'
         $(p_1: (ep_1: (e_1: [(f_1) (x_1)_A])))$

      b. **Gopyan**   galak=**geuh**   that
         he   happy=3.U   very
         'He is very happy.'
         $(p_1: (ep_1: (e_1: [(f_1) (x_1)_U])))$

There are also languages where the form of an element is determined by a combination of interpersonal and representational information (e.g. Tagalog; see Hengeveld and Mackenzie 2008: 317–19). What all these language have in common is that the morphosyntactic behaviour of clausal elements can be accounted for in terms of the pragmatic and/or semantic properties; this means that there is no need for the syntactic functions of Subject or Object.

There are, however, also languages where there is no direct relation between the pragmatic and/or semantic properties of an element and its formal properties. In such languages, the form and position of an element is sensitive to properties of the Morphosyntactic Level itself, such as the syntactic functions Subject and Object and the complexity or weight of constituents. This form of alignment is referred to as **morphosyntactic alignment**. Note that, unlike in the case of interpersonal and representational alignment, morphosyntactic alignment is a-functional (see also Section 5.3), as it does not reflect a Speaker's communicative intentions. Instead it is determined by autonomous features of the Morphosyntactic Level, which may facilitate production and comprehension without carrying any pragmatic or semantic meaning. English is an example of a language with morphosyntactic alignment. What exactly this means will be discussed in the next section.

5.5.3.3. Alignment in English

In languages with a morphosyntactic alignment system, the form and position of clausal constituents may be determined by two independent factors: (1) the assignment of syntactic functions and (2) the complexity of the constituents. Both these factors are relevant for English; they will be discussed in turn in this section.

(i) Syntactic function assignment

In English, the form and position of clausal constituents cannot be explained in terms of the pragmatic or semantic features of these constituents. This can be shown by means of the sentences in (49):

(49)   a.   *The boy* (A) ran away.   one-place predication frame
       b.   *The boy* (U) tripped over a stone.   one-place predication frame

In example (49a), the Phrase *the boy* has the semantic function Actor, while in example (49b) it has the semantic function of Undergoer. In both sentences, however, the Phrase takes the same form and appears in the same position. This clearly shows that the morphosyntactic properties of the Phrase *the boy* in these sentences cannot be triggered by its function on the Representational Level. In other cases, however, the semantic functions Actor and Undergoer may be coded explicitly. In example (50b), for instance, the Actor appears as a *by*-Phrase, while in the nominalized construction in (50c) the Undergoer is marked by the preposition *of*:

(50)   a.   *The dog* (A) chased *the boy* (U).   two-place predication
                                                                              frame
       b.   The boy (U) was chased *by the dog* (A).   two-place predication
                                                                              frame
       c.   the chasing *of the boy* (U)   nominalization

Now consider the following two examples:

(51)   a.   A: What did the boy do? B: *The boy* (Topic) ran away.
       b.   A: Who was chased by the dog? B: *The boy* (Focus) was chased by
            the dog.

In (51a), the Phrase *the boy* has the pragmatic function of Topic, while in (51b) it functions as the Focus. Nevertheless, it appears in the same form and position in both sentences. This means that the form and the position of the Phrase *the boy* in these sentences cannot be accounted for in terms of its interpersonal features.

What we witness in such examples as (49) and (51) is the '**neutralization** of semantic and pragmatic oppositions that are otherwise relevant in the language' (Hengeveld and Mackenzie 2008: 324; emphasis added). Under these circumstances languages resort to the assignment of syntactic functions to account for the morphosyntactic behaviour of clausal constituents. How exactly these syntactic functions are assigned, however, depends on the kind of morphosyntactic alignment found in a language. English makes use of the **nominative–accusative alignment** system. This means that, in active Clauses, the syntactic function Subject is assigned to the Actor or Undergoer argument in a one-place predication frame (as in examples (49a) and (49b)), as well as to the Actor argument in a two-place predication frame (example (50a)). Moreover, in passive sentences, Subject function is assigned to the Undergoer argument of a two-place predication frame (example (50b)). Arguments with Subject function appear in the nominative form. The remaining argument in a two-place predication frame, for example the Undergoer in (50a), appears in the accusative form. As can be seen from examples (49)–(51), English does not mark the nominative–accusative distinction on full Noun Phrases; in the case of pronouns, however, the distinction is still expressed:

(**52**)   a. *He* (nominative) chased the dog.
       b. The dog chased *him* (accusative).

Table 5.2 summarizes the nominative-accusative alignment in active one- and two-place predication frames (the shading reflects the distribution of nominative and accusative).

Table 5.2. Nominative–accusative alignment

	One-place predication frame	Two-place predication frame
Actor	Subject (nominative)	Subject (nominative)
Undergoer	Subject (nominative)	Undergoer (accusative)

Subject assignment in other languages

By assigning Subject function to an element, this element is selected for special (morphosyntactic) treatment. In English, we have seen, the element appears in the nominative form and in a preverbal position. Which elements are singled out for such special treatment depends, however, on the alignment system used by the language in question. Thus, whereas English has nominative–accusative alignment, other languages, including Basque, use an **absolutive–ergative alignment** system. The idea is the same as in English: since for certain elements there is neutralization of pragmatic and semantic oppositions, Subject assignment is applied to account for differences in the morphosyntactic behaviour of these elements. In the case of absolute–ergative alignment, however, Subject function is assigned to a different group of elements: here it is the Actor argument of a one-place predication frame and the Undergoer arguments of one- and two-place predications frames that receive the same morphosyntactic treatment. These elements appear in the Absolutive form, whereas the remaining argument, the Actor in a two-place predication frame, appears in the Ergative form. Some examples from Basque can be found in (53):

(53) a. Jon   etorri da   one-place predication frame
          Jon(ABS)   come   AUX
          'Jon came.' (Etxepare 2003: 365)

      b. Jon   argia   da   one-place predication frame
          Jon(ABS)   intelligent is
          'Jon is intelligent.'

      c. Jon-ek ardo-a   ekarri du   two-place predication frame
          Jon.ERG wine.DEF(ABS) bring AUX
          'Jon brought the wine.' (Etxepare 2003: 365)

In (53a) we find a one-place predication frame with an Actor argument, while the single argument of the copular construction in (53b) is an Undergoer. Both arguments, however, appear in the (zero-marked) absolutive. In the two-place predication in (53c), the Undergoer (*ardo*) again appears in the absolutive form, while the Actor argument (*Jon*) appears in the ergative form. The absolutive–ergative alignment system can therefore be summarized as in Table 5.3 (compare Table 5.2).

Table 5.3. Absolute–ergative alignment

	One-place predication frame	Two-place predication frame
Actor	Subject (absolutive)	Actor (ergative)
Undergoer	Subject (absolutive)	Subject (absolutive)

So far, we have been able to explain differences in the morphosyntactic behaviour of Actor and Undergoer arguments in English by assigning the syntactic function of Subject only: the nominative form of Actor and Undergoer arguments of one-place predications and the Actor argument of a two-place predication is triggered by assigning these elements Subject function; Undergoers of two-place predications, on the other hand, appear in the accusative. Let us now turn to three-place predications to see how the nominative–accusative system can help us to account for the form and position of the three arguments. Consider the two sentences in example (54):

(54) a. The boy gave the bone to the dog. three-place predication frame I
   b. The boy gave the dog the bone. three-place predication frame II

In (54a) the form of the three arguments can be accounted for as follows: the Actor argument (*the boy*) is assigned Subject function, triggering the nominative form, the Undergoer (*the bone*) appears in the accusative and the Recipient (*the dog*) takes the form of an Adpositional Phrase introduced by the preposition *to*. This can be represented schematically as in Table 5.4.

Table 5.4. Syntactic function assignment in three-place predication frames, Type I

	Three-place predication frame I
Actor	Subject
Undergoer	Undergoer
Recipient	Recipient

Example (54b), however, poses a problem, since here the Recipient argument is encoded in exactly the same way (in terms of form and position) as the Undergoer argument in example (54a). This means that in English neutralization can take place between Undergoers and Recipients of three-place predication frames. To resolve this neutralization, English resorts to a second syntactic function, that of Object. This function is assigned to the Undergoer argument in a two-place predication frame, as well as to the Undergoer argument in a three-place predication frame of the kind exemplified in (54a) (Type I). In a sentence like (54b), however, Object function is assigned to the Recipient, while the Undergoer receives its own coding (in terms of its position, following the Object; Type II). The assignment of the syntactic functions Subject and Object in the two types of three-place predication frames is summarized in Table 5.5.

Table 5.5. Syntactic function assignment in three-place predication frames, Types I and II

	Three-place predication frame I	Three-place predication frame II
Actor	Subject	Subject
Undergoer	Object	Undergoer
Recipient	Recipient	Object

As we can see from Tables 5.4 and 5.5, by assigning the syntactic functions Subject and Object, the morphosyntactic realization of all arguments in example (54) can be accounted for. This means that in English there is no need for a third syntactic function (indirect Object).

> Which type of alignment do we have in the sentence *Helen bought James some chocolates*? Which syntactic functions would you assign to the elements *Helen*, *James* and *some chocolates*?

(ii) Complexity
Another morphosyntactic factor that can influence the way in which core semantic and pragmatic units are mapped onto morphosyntactic units is complexity. English, for instance, is characterized by 'the tendency for long and complex elements to be placed towards the end of a clause' (Biber et al. 1999: 898; cf. Dik 1997a: 404; Quirk et al. 1985: 323, 1282ff.). This principle of **end weight** is illustrated in the following examples:

(55)   a. It is a myth *that interaction is always logical.* (BYU-BNC, written, non-academic)

  a′. *That interaction is always logical* is a myth.

  b. *The rumour* was going round *that a new tax on cattle and horse-ownership was to be introduced.* (BYU-BNC, written, academic)

  b′. *The rumour that a new tax on cattle and horse-ownership was to be introduced* was going round.

In (55a) the clausal Subject appears in final position. As can be seen from example (55a′) it is possible for this Clause to occur in the Subject position; for ease of both production and processing, however, placement in final position tends to be preferred. In example (55b), the head noun *rumour* and its complement are not juxtaposed, a clear violation of the principle of domain integrity (see Section 5.1). Adhering to this principle, however, would yield the sentence in (55b′), which is both stylistically awkward and difficult to process. This shows that the linear ordering of elements is not always functional—that is, triggered by interpersonal and representational information—but may also be determined by factors unrelated to the Speaker's communicative intentions.

5.5.4. The ordering of core units

Unlike non-core elements, whose placement proceeds in a top-down manner, the placement of core units is determined by alignment. In this process, three types of factors may play a role:

(56)   (i) Interpersonal factors: pragmatic functions

  (ii) Representational factors: semantic functions, designation

  (iii) Morphosyntactic factors: syntactic functions, complexity

In languages with interpersonal or representational alignment the form and position of core elements is determined directly by information from the Interpersonal and Representational Levels, respectively. Thus, as we saw in Section 5.5.3.2, in Kisi, a language with an interpersonal alignment system, the position of elements at the Morphosyntactic Level is determined by the presence of the pragmatic function Focus at the Interpersonal Level (see example (47)), while in Acehnese, a language with a representational alignment system, the position of the pronoun clitic is determined by the semantic function of the argument at the Representational Level (example (48)).

There are, however, also languages, like English, where the linear order-ing of core units is not determined by the interpersonal or representational properties of these units. Instead, the position of these elements is sensitive to two morphosyntactic factors: syntactic function assignment and com-plexity. Nevertheless, as we will see, there are cases where interpersonal and semantic information plays a role, overriding syntactic function assignment. This results in the following ordering principles for core units in English:

(57) a. First place elements (predicate or arguments) with a pragmatic function.

b. Next, place the predicate and those arguments whose form/pos-ition is determined by their semantic function.

c. Finally, place those elements whose pragmatic and semantic dif-ferences have been neutralized. Placement of these elements takes place on the basis of (i) their syntactic function, with elements with Subject function being placed before elements with Object func-tion; and (ii) their complexity.

However, since in English the placement of core units is in most cases determined by morphosyntactic factors, in particular syntactic function assignment, we will begin by considering the placement of elements with Subject and Object function.

In word-order typology, languages are traditionally classified on the basis of the order in which the three main clausal elements, verb, Subject, and Object, appear. Thus, although languages usually allow for more than one word order and differ in the degree to which word order is fixed, a basic word order can often be recognized; broadly speaking, languages can be classified as SVO, SOV, VSO, etc. In English, word order seems to be relatively fixed, following the SVO pattern. This clearly suggests that the placement of arguments in English is sensitive to syntactic function assignment.

In Section 5.5.2, we saw that, at the beginning of the ordering process, three absolute positions are available: the Clause-initial position (P^I), the Clause-medial position (P^M), and the Clause-final position (P^F) (example (30), here repeated as (58)):

(58) P^I P^M P^F

Now consider the sentence in (59):

(59) I visited Jane last week.

Remember that in placing elements in the appropriate positions we always start with the non-core elements. In this sentence, there are two such elements. The first of these is the absolute tense operator 'past', which belongs to the layer of the Episode. Since this operator only receives its final form at the Phonological Level (see Section 5.7.4), we put the place-holder 'past' in the appropriate position. Since tense is expressed on the finite verb, and since English is an SVO language, it follows that this placeholder is put in the Clause-medial position (PM). Next, we come to the time adverbial *last week*, which functions as a modifier at the layer of the Episode. Since non-core elements are ordered centripetally, this element is placed either in initial or, as in example (59), in final position. Then we proceed with the placement of the three core elements. First the predicate *visit* joins the past tense placeholder in P^M. Next, the Subject is placed in position P^I (Hengeveld 2013: 3). Finally, the Object is placed in the position following the verbal predicate, in this case P^{M+1}. This ordering of constituents can be represented as follows:

(60) $\quad P^I \quad\quad P^M \quad\quad\quad\quad P^{M+1} \quad\quad P^F$

$\qquad$ ^{Subj}I $\quad$ ^{vf}visit.^{œP}ed $\quad$ ^{Obj}Jane $\quad$ last week

$\qquad$ 4 $\qquad$ 3-1 $\qquad\qquad$ 5 $\qquad\quad$ 2

The reason for placing the Object, *Jane*, in P^{M+1} rather than P^{F-1} is that further elements (e.g. additional participants) can occur between the Object and the modifier *last week*, but not between the verb and the Object. This is illustrated in example (61), where the additional participant, with the semantic function Comitative (Com), is placed in the position preceding the Episodical modifier, P^{F-1}. Since the additional participant is analysed as a modifier at the layer of the SoA, it is the third element to be placed in position (after the two non-core elements 'past' (triggered by an operator at the layer of the Episode) and *last week* (modifier of the Episode)):

(61) $\quad$ I visited Jane with my brother last week.

$\qquad$ $P^I \quad\quad P^M \quad\quad\quad\quad P^{M+1} \quad\quad P^{F-1} \quad\quad\quad\quad\quad\quad P^F$

$\qquad$ ^{Subj}I $\quad$ ^{vf}visit.^{œP}past $\quad$ ^{Obj}Jane $\quad$ ^{Com}with my brother $\quad$ ^{œP}last week

$\qquad$ 5 $\qquad$ 4-1 $\qquad\qquad$ 6 $\qquad\quad$ 3 $\qquad\qquad\qquad\qquad$ 2

The same principles apply in the ordering of elements in three-place predi-cation frames. As pointed out in the previous section, three-place predica-tions have two morphosyntactic realizations. In what was referred to as Type I, the Recipient argument is realized as a *to*-PP following the Object (example (62a)). Since the form and the position of this element is deter-mined by its semantic function, the ordering principles in (57) above ensure that its placement precedes the placement of the Subject and the Object, yielding the following result:

(62) I gave the book to Jane last week.   three-place predication (Type I)

P^I	P^M	P^{M+1}	P^{F-1}	P^F
^{Subj}I	^{Vf}give.$^{\sigma ep}$past	^{Obj}the book	^{Rec}to Jane	$^{\sigma ep}$last week
5	3-1	6	4	2

In the alternative realization (Type II), it is the Recipient argument that is assigned Object function, while the Undergoer does not have a syntactic function: its position (following the Object) is triggered by its semantic function. This means that of the three arguments it is now the Undergoer that is first placed into position (going to P^{F-1}), followed by the Subject (in P^I) and the Object (in P^{M+1}).

(63) I gave Jane the book last week.   three-place predication (Type II)

P^I	P^M	P^{M+1}	P^{F-1}	P^F
^{Subj}I	^{Vf}give.$^{\sigma ep}$past	^{Obj}Jane	^{U}the book	$^{\sigma ep}$last week
5	3-1	6	4	2

The examples given so far show that the relative order of the elements in the Clause can be quite neatly explained using the ordering principles proposed in this chapter. Let us now apply these principles to a few slightly more challenging examples, containing various interpersonal and representational non-core and core elements. Consider, for instance, the sentence in (64):

(64)   Fortunately, I will presumably meet Jane next week.

Since this sentence contains one interpersonal element, the modifier *fortunately* (a subjective attitude adverb modifying the Communicated Content), this is the first element to be placed, going to P^{pre}. Next, we have three non-core representational elements (the modifier *presumably* (a subjective epistemic modality adverb at the layer of the Propositional Contents), the auxiliary *will* (expressing the future tense operator at the layer of the Episode) and the modifier *last week* (indicating absolute time at the layer of the Episode). Of these three elements, the adverb *presumably* is first placed in Clause-medial position. Then the auxiliary *will* is put into the relative position P^{M-1}. After this, the modifier *last week* is placed in Clause-final position. It is only after these elements have been placed into their appropriate positions, that placement of the core elements takes place, starting with the main verb (in P^{M+1}), followed by the Subject (in P^I) and the Object (in P^{M+2}). The placement of elements is thus as follows:

- Hierachically related elements:
  1. *fortunately* (interpersonal modifier, Communicated Contents) → P^{pre}
  2. *presumably* (representational modifier, Propositional Contents) → P^M
  3. *will* (representational operator, Episode) → P^{M-1}
  4. *next week* (representational modifier, Episode) → P^F

- core elements:
  5. *meet* (non-finite verb) → P^{M+1}
  6. *I* (Subject) → P^I
  7. *Jane* (Object) → P^{M+2}

This yields to following result:

(65) P^{pre} | P^I P^{M-1} P^M P^{M+1} P^{M+2} P^F

$^{\Sigma C}$fortunately ^{Subj}I ^{Vf}will ^{op}presumably $^{Vnon\text{-}f}$meet ^{Obj}Jane ^{oep}next week.

1   6   3   2   5   7   4

In all these examples, Subject, (finite) verb and Object appear in their canonical order, SVO. Note, however, that alternative word orders can be triggered by, for instance, the presence of a pragmatic function. Consider in this respect example (66):

(66) I like George and Paul, but *John I never liked at all.* (Internet)

In the italicized sentence, the word order is not SVO, but OSV. The basic word order is overruled here by the presence of the pragmatic function Contrast, which, as stated in (57), takes precedence over the morphosyntactic factors that normally determine the placement of the Subject and Object constituents. Due to the presence of this pragmatic function, the Clause-initial position is now filled by the Object (with the verb filling P^M and the Subject P^{M+1}).

Finally, as mentioned in Section 5.5.3.3(ii), the ordering of elements may also be sensitive to the complexity of one or more of these elements. Consider once more example (61), here repeated as (67):

(67) I visited Jane with my brother last week.

P^I P^M P^{M+1} P^{F-1} P^F

^{Subj}I ^{Vf}visited ^{Obj}Jane ^{Com}with my brother ^{oep}last week

This sentence is quite easy to process, since all of the constituents are relatively simple. In example (68), however, this is no longer the case:

(68) I visited Jane with a friend of mine from Canada who spends the summer in Vienna to do some research on Austrian German dialects last week.

This sentence clearly puts very high demands on the short-term memory of both Speaker and Addressee. This can, however, easily be remedied by placing the long Comitative element after the time modifier, in the post-clausal position:

(69) P^I P^M P^{M+1} P^F | P^{post}

^{Subj}I ^{Vf}visited ^{Obj}Jane ^{oeP}last week ^{Com}with a friend of mine from Canada . . .

The placement of clausal subjects at the end of a Clause can be explained in the same way. Thus, in a sentence like (55a), here repeated as (70), the complex Subject is placed in Clause-final position.

(70)   It is a myth *that interaction is always logical*. (BYU-BNC, written, non-academic)

Now that we have looked at the placement of all interpersonally and representationally triggered morphosyntactic units, let us briefly summarize the various stages involved in the process:

(71)   a. Placement of elements triggered by *interpersonal non-core units*, in a top-down manner, starting with functions, operators, and modifiers at the highest interpersonal layer (the Move), then moving on to functions, operators and modifiers of the Discourse Act, etc.
   b. Placement of elements triggered by *representational non-core units*, starting with the functions, operators, and modifiers at the highest representational layer (the Propositional Content) and ending with those of the State-of-Affairs.
   c. Placements of elements triggered by *core units*, that is, the predicate and its arguments, once again in a top-down fashion, considering (i) interpersonal information (pragmatic functions); (ii) representational information (semantic functions); (iii) morphosyntactic information (syntactic functions, complexity).

At the end of this process, however, some obligatory positions may still be open. In that case, we need to resort to the use of a dummy element. This last stage in the ordering process is described in the next section.

5.5.5. Dummy elements

Dummy elements, as we saw in Section 5.3, are introduced at the Morphosyntactic Level to fill an obligatory clausal position for which no interpersonal or representational material is available. The example given was that of zero-place predicates like *rain*, *hail*, and *snow*, which have no referential Subact at the Interpersonal Level, nor an argument at the Representational Level (example (18); here repeated as (72)). Since, however, English requires the presence of a Subject in preverbal position, the dummy element *it* is placed in P^I:

(72) a. **It** rained.

    IL: $(A_1: - (C_1: (T_1)) - {}^A)$

    RL: $(p_1: - (e_1: (f_1: rain_V) {}^e) - {}^P)$

   b. P^I P^M

    ^{Subj}it ^{Vf}rained

It is, however, not only with zero-place predicates like *rain*, *hail*, and *snow* that the dummy element *it* is used. It also appears in constructions like (70) above, where a complex Subject appears at the end of the Clause, leaving the Subject position empty. Nor is it only the element *it* that can function as a dummy Subject. As we saw in Chapter 4 (Section 4.5.4), existential sentences also contain a dummy Subject, which takes the form of *there*. In addition, these sentences contain the dummy verb *be*, filling the obligatory finite verb position:

(73) a. **There are** many diligent students.

    IL: $(A_1: - (C_1: (R_1)) - {}^A)$

    RL: $(p_1: - (e_1: (x_1)) - {}^P)$

   b. P^I P^M P^F

    there ^{Vf}be.pres.3.pl ^{Subj}many diligent students

Another frequently used dummy element in English is of course the dummy-verb *do*, which is used in interrogative and negative predications to express the Episodical operator tense in the absence of any other auxiliary:

(74) a. **Do** you like apples?

    IL: $(A_1: [(F_1: INTER) (P_1)_S (P_2)_A (C_1: [(T_1) (R_1) (R_2)] {}^C)] {}^A)$

    RL: $(p_1: (pres\ ep_1: (e_1: [(f_1) (x_1)_A (x_2)_U] {}^e) {}^{ep}) {}^P)$

   b. P^I P^{I+1} P^M P^{M+1}

    ^{Vf}do.pres.2.sg ^{Subj}you ${}^{Vnon-f}$like ^{Obj}apples

(75)   a. I **don't** like apples

   IL: $(A_1: [(F_1: DECL) (P_1)_S (P_2)_A (C_1: [(T_1) (R_1) (R_2)] {}^C)] {}^A)$

   RL: $(p_1: (pres ep_1: (neg e_1: [(f_1) (x_1)_A (x_2)_U] {}^e) {}^{ep}) {}^P)$

b. P^I P^M P^{M+1} P^{M+2} P^{M+3}

   ^{Subj}I ^{Vf}**do.pres.1.sg**   not ${}^{Vnon-f}$like ^{Obj}apples

In both (74) and (75), the present tense placeholder is the first element that needs to be placed in position. In (74) the Interrogative Illocution causes this placeholder to be placed in Clause-initial position; in (75), the placeholder goes into the Clause-medial position. In (75), the next element to be assigned a position is the negative element *not*, triggered by the polarity operator 'neg'. This element goes into position P^{M+1}. Subsequently, in both (74) and (75), the verbal predicate *like* is placed in position. Due to the presence of the Interrogative Illocution in (74) and the polarity operator 'neg' in (75), the verbal predicate does not join the present tense placeholder; instead it appears in infinitival form in a Clause-medial position: in (74) in the still available position P^M, in (75) in the relative position P^{M+2}. Next, in both examples, the Subject is placed in P^I, followed by the Object in the position following the main verb (P^{M+1} and P^{M+3}, respectively). This, however, means that the present tense placeholder cannot be expressed; the finite verb position, in other words, remains empty. This triggers the dummy element *do*, which joins the tense operator in the finite verb position.

It will be clear that dummy elements are always the last elements to be put in position: it is only after all other elements have been provided with a slot that the Encoder will know which obligatory slots are still open.

In analogy with example (75), give an analysis of the sentence *I DO like apples*.

Dummy elements in other languages

Apart from dummy Subjects and dummy verbs, some languages also have dummy Objects. Consider, for instance, the following examples from Dutch:

(76)   a. Peter   doet   het   goed   op school.
         Peter   does   it   well   on school
         'Peter is doing well in school'
     b. We   hebben   het   heel   goed   hier.
         we   have   it   very   good   here
         'Life is good here.'

In both (76a) and (76b) the neuter pronoun *het* 'it' fills the Object position. It does not, however, have a referent, nor does it designate any entity. This means that the element *het* does not correspond to any interpersonal or representational unit. Since, however, the verbs *doen* and *hebben* are two-place predicates, a dummy Object is used to fill the Object position.

5.5.6. Agreement

When all clausal elements, including dummy elements, have been placed in their appropriate positions, the mechanism of **agreement** becomes operational. This mechanism causes the properties of one clausal element to be copied to one or more other elements. Two kinds of agreement can be distinguished: **argument agreement** and **operator agreement**. Both types of agreement can be found in English: the agreement between the Subject and the verb is an example of argument agreement; an example of operator agreement is what is often referred to as *consecutio temporum* (or sequence of tenses). Operator agreement will be discussed in Section 5.5.7.3; in this section we will confine ourselves to argument agreement.

English is a morphologically impoverished language; over the centuries it has lost most of its inflectional endings, including almost all verb endings. One verb ending that has survived is the third person singular present tense form -*s*:

(77)   Thomas likes bananas.

The -*s* ending is triggered by the combination of the present tense operator and the number and person of the Subject. These latter features, inherited by the Subject from the Interpersonal and Representational Levels, are copied onto the verb, where they appear in the form of a placeholder (3.sg), as illustrated in (78):

(78) (Cl₁: [(Np₁: (Nw₁: Thomas)) (Vw₁: like.pres.**3.sg**) (Np₂: (Nw₂: banana.pl))] ^{Cl})

The reason that this -*s* ending takes the form of a placeholder is that its phonological form depends on the last phoneme of the verb to which it is attached. The placeholder, in other words, represents the -*s* Morpheme; the appropriate allomorph will only be specified at the Phonological Level. The same is true for the plural ending of the noun *bananas*.

5.5.7. Subordination

5.5.7.1. Introduction

As mentioned in Section 5.5.1, Clauses may contain other (embedded or subordinate) Clauses. These other Clauses come in different types, depending on the function they fulfil at the Representational Level. In the previous chapter, for instance, analyses were provided of relative Clauses and adverbial Clauses (both functioning as modifiers) and of Subject Clauses, headless relative Clauses and complement Clauses (all functioning as arguments). An example of each type of subordinate Clause is given in Table 5.6, together with their function at the Representational Level (and the relevant section in Chapter 4):

Table 5.6. Types of subordinate Clauses

Example	Type	Function at RL	Section
The book *that I wanted* was sold out.	relative	modifier (of x)	4.5.5, 4.5.6
Bill left early *because he was angry*.	adverbial	modifier (of e)	4.5.6
That they survived was a miracle.	subject	argument (A)	4.5.5
I couldn't believe *that they survived*.	complement	argument (U)	4.5.5
We heard the news *that they had survived*.	complement	argument (Ref)	4.7.3
I will read *what you read*.	headless rel.cl.	argument (U)	4.7.2

In this section we will be dealing predominantly with one type of subordinate Clause: Complement Clauses of verbs (that is, Undergoer complements). In particular we will look for evidence showing which interpersonal or representational layer the subordinate Clause belongs to (Section 5.5.7.2). This will be followed by two short sections on specific aspects of subordinate Clauses: operator agreement (*consecutio temporum*, Section 5.5.7.3) and raising (Section 5.5.7.4).

5.5.7.2. Complement Clauses

Embedded Clauses functioning as complements of a higher Clause can belong to different layers at the Interpersonal or Representational Level, depending on the type of verb in the main Clause. Consider, for instance, the examples in (79):

(79)   a. She concluded that *the man could not have stolen the money.*
       b. She said that *the man had stolen the money.*
       c. She believed that *the man had stolen the money.*
       d. She saw that *the man had stolen the money.*
       e. She saw *the man steal the money.*
       f. She wanted *(the man) to return the money.*

When we look at the meaning of the verbs used in the matrix Clauses in these examples, it will become clear that they each require a different kind of clausal complement: verbs of saying (*say/ask*) report a speech event, a verb like *see* requires some (sequence of) events that can be witnessed and a verb like *want* requires a potential event. Verbs like *believe*, *know*, or *assume*, on the other hand, take a propositional complement (something that can be true or false), while a verb like *conclude* can introduce a discourse move. In other words, the complements of these verbs differ with regard to the kind of semantic or pragmatic units they encode. A brief overview is given in Table 5.7 (note that in the case of reporting verbs (*say, ask, conclude*) we restrict ourselves, for the time being, to indirect speech only):

Table 5.7. Matrix verbs and their complements

Verb	Complement	Level
conclude	discourse move	IL
say, ask	speech event	IL
believe	proposition	RL
see	one or more events	RL
want	potential event(s)	RL

Now, intuitively this may all be very plausible, but what kind of formal evidence do we have that the complements of these verbs do indeed correspond to different interpersonal and representational units? One test (or series of tests) we can use to establish the pragmatic or semantic status of the complement is to see which modifiers and operators can be expressed within the complement. For instance, if we find that a Propositional Content modifier can occur within the complement, then we have to conclude that the complement cannot express a layer lower than the Propositional Content. If, in addition, it turns out that higher modifiers (interpersonal modifiers) are not possible, we may conclude that we are dealing with a Propositional Content. The same is true for operators: if a certain operator is expressed, the complement must at the very least express the layer at which this operator occurs (e.g. the Episode in the case of the tense operator) (see Hengeveld and Mackenzie 2008: 364–5).

Let us now apply these tests to a number of examples (see also Table 5.8). Starting with the verb *conclude*, we find that it is possible for the complement to include the Move operator *in-sum*. This confirms our idea that *conclude* takes a Move as its complement:

(80)   It can be concluded that *in sum* the requirements of magazine printing are more stringent than those for the printing of catalogues and advertisements. They differ by country, moreover. Not all printers in Europe currently offer services which match the existing specific requirements of all magazine publishers. Their current services depend on the finishing machines they use, the know-how they have concerning different distribution systems as well as the location of their printing facilities and the distance to the publisher and to the area of distribution.... (Internet: REGULATION (EC) No 139/2004 MERGER PROCEDURE)

Table 5.8. Matrix verbs and their complements: representations

Verb	Complement	Representation
conclude, say	M, A	$(f_1: conclude_V) (x_1)_A (M_1: [(A_1) (A_2) \ldots]^M)$
say, ask	C	$(f_1: say_V) (x_1)_A (C_1: [(T_1) (R_1) \ldots]^C)$
believe	p	$(f_1: believe_V) (x_1)_A (p_1: [(ep_1) (ep_2) \ldots]^P)$
see	ep	$(f_1: see_V) (x_1)_A (ep_1: [(e_1) (e_2) \ldots]^{ep})$
want	e	$(f_1: want_V) (x_1)_A (e_1: [(f_1) (x_1) \ldots]^e)$

With a verb like *say*, on the other hand, such high-layer modifiers (e.g. *in-sum* (M) or *finally* (A)) are not possible. Here the highest possible modifier is that of the Communicated Contents:

(81) Also regarding student evaluations, she said that *unfortunately* (*in sum, *finally) the few negative ones tend to stick in her memory. (Internet)

Not surprisingly, interpersonal complements (M, C) occur as complements of verbs of saying. Verbs of thinking, on the other hand, take a representational unit as their complement, more specifically a Propositional Content. Evidence for this can be found in the fact that interpersonal modifiers are not allowed, while propositional modifiers (like *possibly*) or propositional operators (e.g. for subjective epistemic modality) can be expressed in the complement:

(82) a. I. I. Krachkovsky believed that Persian cartographers *possibly* (*unfortunately) influenced Chinese mapping through Mongolia (Maqbul Ahmad, p. 1081). (Internet)
b. James was also a pluralist in that he believed that there *may* actually be multiple correct accounts of truth. (Internet, Wikipedia)

When we turn to verbs of observation (e.g. *see*, *hear*), we find that they take an Episode as their complement. Here the evidence from modifiers is less straightforward, since it is difficult to establish the scope of such time modifiers as *yesterday* in examples (83): since the event of seeing must occur at the same time as the event observed, such modifiers can be interpreted as modifying either the matrix predication or the embedded predication.

(83) I saw *him smile* yesterday. (BYU-BNC, written, fiction)

Fortunately, however, we have additional evidence that we are indeed dealing with an Episodic complement. Thus notice that in example (84a) the complement of *see* consists of two events, taking place at the same time and involving the same participants. Moreover, it is possible to express absolute tense in the complement. We can thus safely assume that the complement of *see* is, indeed, an Episode. However, since the two events (e.g. seeing and smiling in (83)) must take place at the same time, tense need not to be expressed; in that case use is made of an infinitival complement Clause (examples (83) and (84b)):

(84) a. I also saw *that he listened to the students and engaged with them in a way that made us all feel lucky*. (COCA, written, fiction)
b. Diana saw *her do it* and they both burst out into giggles just like little girls. (BYU-BNC, written, newspaper)

As to be expected, lower layer modifiers and operators can also be expressed. In (84a), for instance, a manner modifier is included in the complement Clause (*in a way*...), while in (85) the form *running* is triggered by the Progressive Aspect operator at the layer of the State-of-Affairs.

(85)   A moment later, between the nut-trees, they saw *him running off into the field*. (BNC, written, fiction)

The verb *see*, however, does not always take an Episode as its complement. As illustrated in example (86), there is another (derived) use of the verb *see* in which the two events do not take place same time (see also Chapter 4, Section 4.3.3):

(86)   a. *I see* you purchased a necklace. (COCA, written, fiction)
       b. '*I see* you've lost your sense of humor, living in Boston,' he said. (COCA, written, fiction)

Clearly, in these examples, the events designated by the complement Clause are not observed (and in (86b) cannot even be directly observed) by the Subject of the main Clause. Instead these events took place at an earlier moment: the referent of the Subject infers from what he or she perceives that these events must have happened. In these contexts the verb *see* does therefore not function as a lexical verb; instead the sequence *I see* as a whole functions as an inferential modality modifier at the layer of the Propositional Content (see Chapter 4, Section 4.3.3). In other words, although a Clause like *you purchased a necklace* in (86a) appears as a subordinate Clause at the Morphosyntactic Level; it does not function as the argument of the verb *see* at the Representational Level; instead it forms an independent State-of-Affairs. This also explains why it must be finite (note that *I saw you purchasing the necklace* cannot have the inferential meaning intended here). Further evidence that we are dealing with a Propositional Content can be found in the fact that Subjective modality modifiers are allowed:

(87)   a. We can see that confidence has *certainly* taken a hit. (COCA, spoken, CNN)
       b. Lucinda can see that this is *probably* not true. (COCA, written, newspaper)

Finally, with the verb *want* we again move down one layer. Here subjective epistemic modal modifiers and operators are not allowed; nor is it possible to express absolute tense in the embedded Clause (examples (88a) and (88b)). Lower-level modals (at least those which can appear in the infinitive, like the

State-of-Affairs modal *have to*; example (88c)) and auxiliaries (e.g. Phasal Aspect, example (88d)), however, are allowed. These observations suggest that the embedded Clause of *want* has the status of a State-of-Affairs.

(88)   a. I want to buy a book.
     b. *I want that I buy a book.
     c. He just doesn't want to *have to* deal with it again. (COCA, spoken, CBS)
     d. It's perfectly obvious he wants to *get to* know you better. (COCA, written, fiction)

Let us now briefly turn to direct speech acts. Since these involve a shift in deictic centre, they must, at least, represent a Discourse Act, since that is the layer where the roles of Speaker and Addressee are specified. In example (89a), for instance, the change in pronoun (from *she* to *I*) shows this shift in deictic centre: where it is first the narrator that fulfils the function of the Speaker, in the direct speech act this function is performed by the referent of the pronoun *she*. Example (89a) also shows that it is possible for the embedded Clause to have a different Illocution from the main Clause (Interrogative and Declarative, respectively), which again is only possible if we assume that the embedded Clause is (at least) a Discourse Act. Finally, the examples in (89b) and (89c) show that not only Discourse Act operators (the Emphatic operator expressed as *dammit* in (89b)), but also Move operators (*in-sum* in (89c)) are allowed, which means that the direct speech complements must express Moves.

(89)   a. But she laughed and said did you know that I was a good witch? (COCA, written, academic)
     b. So, when Cecil lay next to her begging she listened, like a person who is hearing for the first time. And when he said, "*Dammit* woman, you're going to marry me," she put a single finger to his mouth, shushed him, and nodded her head: Yes! (COCA, written, fiction)
     c. Similarly, in a 1983 book surveying the literature, economists Henry Grabowski and John Vernon conclude: "*In sum*, the hypothesis that the observed decline in new product introductions has largely been concentrated in marginal or ineffective drugs is not generally supported by empirical analyses." (COCA, written, magazine)

> Explain why it is possible to say *He told me that allegedly Sam had stolen the money*, but not *He feared that allegedly Sam had stolen the money*?

5.5.7.3. Operator agreement

In Section 5.5.6 we briefly discussed the notion of argument agreement and its manifestation in English in the form of Subject–verb agreement, where the properties of the Subject (number and person) are copied onto the finite verb. Agreement may, however, also obtain between operators; in that case, the presence of an operator at one layer may determine the expression of an operator at a lower layer. This is what happens in English in the case of *consecutio temporum* (sequence of tenses). Consider the following examples:

(90)   a. When he was 18 he told me he *was* gay (COCA, written, newspaper)
   b. He was not a bad looker, I thought, and shook hands as he told me his name *was* Freddy. (BNC, written, biography)
   c. Adam set the twelve sherry glasses that were cut in a Greek key pattern round their rims in the middle of the moonlight and said he *would* put them in a box *tomorrow* (BNC, written, fiction prose)

In examples (90a) and (90b), it is unlikely that the situations described in the subordinate Clause obtained only in the past, while in example (90c), it is clear that the event described in the embedded Clause is predicted to take place in the future. The presence of past tense marking of the subordinate Clauses is, therefore, not the result of any semantic information at the Representational Level, but rather of the morphosyntactic mechanism of tense operator agreement, which causes the past tense marking of the main Clause to be copied onto the subordinate Clause (see also Leufkens 2013).

As shown by the examples in (91), however, tense agreement does not always take place. In these examples, the Speaker chooses to relate the situation or event designated by the subordinate Clause to the actual moment of speaking rather than to the time of the reported situation or event:

(91)   a. However, Mr Major said he *will* retain the system of political honours. (BNC, written, newspaper)
   b. Devraux told me today he *is* going to Canton again soon (BNC, written, fiction prose)
   c. Joe Zamudio told me that he *is* convinced that he made the right call. (COCA, spoken, CNN).

5.5.7.4. Raising

Another phenomenon that involves an interaction between a main Clause and a subordinate Clause is **raising**, a process whereby a unit that semantically belongs to a subordinate Clause is 'raised' to a position in the main Clause. This alternative placement of an argument of a subordinated Clause may be triggered by interpersonal factors (e.g. pragmatic function assignment), representational factors (e.g. semantic function assignment) or morphosyntactic factors (e.g. syntactic function assignment or degree of complexity) (Hengeveld and Mackenzie 2008: 369). Interpersonal triggering of raising, for instance, can be found in Hungarian, where under certain circumstances it is possible to place the Focus constituent of a complement Clause in the Focus position of the main Clause (De Groot 1981: 51), or the Topic constituent of the complement Clause in the Topic position of the main Clause (Kenesei et al. 1998: 178). In other languages (e.g. Tuvaluan), whether or not a constituent can undergo raising depends on its semantic function (Besnier 1988: 762, 773).

In order to determine what triggers the use of a raised construction in English, let us look at some examples. Consider the sentences in (92):

(92)   a.   It seems that John has stolen the money.
        a'. John seems to have stolen the money.
                                            Subj-to-Subj raising—active
        b.   It seems that the money has been stolen by John.
        b'. The money seems to have been stolen by John.
                                            Subj-to-Subj raising—passive

In example (92), we have a one-place predicate, *seem*, which takes a clausal Subject (*that John has taken the money*). In (92a) and (92b), this embedded clausal Subject, due to both its focality and its high degree of complexity, is placed in Clause-final position, with the dummy *it* filling the Subject position. Alternatively, it is possible to 'raise' the Subject of the embedded Clause to the Subject position of the main Clause. In (92a'), it is the Actor-Subject of an active Subject Clause that is realized as the Subject of the main Clause; in (92b'), it is the Undergoer-Subject of a passive Subject Clause that is raised. In both (92a') and (92b') it is therefore the Subject of the subordinate Clause that is raised to the Subject position of the main Clause (**Subject-to-Subject raising**), irrespective of the semantic function of the Subject constituent. This clearly shows that in English the possibility of raising is not determined by the semantic function of an element.

Raising is also possible with two-place predicates that take a clausal Object, like the predicate *believe* in examples (93) and (94). In (93b) the Actor-Subject of the (active) Object Clause (*he*) is raised to the Subject position of the main Clause. In (94b) we see the same process at work, but now involving the Undergoer-Subject of a passive Object Clause (*the money*).

(93)   a. We believe that he has stolen the money.
      b. He is believed to have stolen the money.

Subj-to-Subj raising—active

(94)   a. We believe that the money has been stolen by John
      b. The money is believed to have been stolen by John.

Subj-to-Subj raising—passive

Finally, English also allows for the Object of an embedded Clause to be raised to the Subject position of the main Clause (**Object-to-Subject raising**). This form of raising can be found in constructions with a transitive verb in Subjectless, infinitival Subject Clauses:

(95)   a. It is easy to solve this problem.
      b. This problem is easy to solve

Obj-to-Subj raising.

It is important to realize that the term raising is somewhat misleading in this context. Since FDG does not allow movement of a constituent from one position to the other, it is not really correct to say that the Subject or Object of the embedded Clause is raised to the Subject position of the main Clause. The idea is rather that the choice between a raised or non-raised construction is triggered by the assignment of pragmatic functions at the Interpersonal Level (see also García Velasco 2013b). In example (92a), for instance, assignment of the pragmatic function Focus to the entire embedded Clause (or rather to the corresponding Communicated Content at the Interpersonal Level) will cause this entire Clause to be placed in Clause-final position; in that case the element *John* is straightforwardly realized as the Subject of the embedded Clause. If, on the other hand, the element *John* is assigned the pragmatic function Topic, it will be realized as the Subject of the main Clause (example (92a′)). This is represented in (96) and (97), respectively:

(96)   It seems that John has stolen the money.

$$P^I \quad P^M \qquad P^F$$

$$\qquad\qquad\qquad\qquad P^I \quad P^{I+1} \quad P^M \quad P^{M+1} \qquad P^{M+2}$$

$$^{Subj}It \; ^{Vf}seems \; ^{Subj}[that \; ^{Subj}John \; ^{Vf}has \; ^{Vnon-f}stolen \; ^{Obj}the\ money]$$

(97)   John seems to have stolen the money.

$$P^I \qquad P^M \qquad P^F$$

$$\qquad\qquad\qquad P^I \quad P^M \qquad P^{M+1} \qquad P^{M+2}$$

$$^{Subj}John \; ^{Vf}seems \; [to \; ^{Vinf}have \; ^{Vnon-f}stolen \; ^{Obj}the\ money]$$

The same mechanism can now be applied in the case of Object-to-Subject raising in (95). Let us assume that the entire Subject Clause is assigned the pragmatic function Focus. In that case, this element is the first to be placed in position. Due to its focal nature, as well as to its complexity, the Subject Clause is placed in Clause final position. The next highest element is the absolute tense operator 'present', triggering the placement of the placeholder 'pres' in P^M. Next, the adjectival predicate *easy* is placed in position P^{M+1} (note that it is possible to place an element—for example *for you*—in between the adjectival predicate and the Subject). This, however, leaves us with two unfilled positions: the finite verb position (which now only contains the placeholder 'present') and the (pre-verbal) Subject position. This means that two dummy elements need to be inserted: the dummy copula *be*, which is placed in the finite verb position, as a vehicle for the expression of tense; and the dummy element *it*, which is used to fill the Subject position, going to P^1. This results in the following ordering of constituents for the sentence in (95a):

(98)   It is easy to solve this problem.
$\quad$ P^I $\quad$ P^M $\quad$ P^{M+1} $\qquad$ P^F

$\qquad\qquad\qquad\qquad\qquad$ P^I $\quad$ P^M $\qquad\qquad$ P^{M+1}

$\quad$ It $\quad$ ^{Vf}is $\quad$ ^{Pred}easy $\quad$ ^{Subj}[to $\quad$ $^{Vnon-f}$solve $\quad$ ^{Obj}the problem]

Let us now turn to the raised construction in (95b). In this sentence, the element *the problem* functions as the Topic; as such it is the first element to be placed in position (P^I). Next, the dummy copula *be*, expressing present tense, is placed in the absolute position P^M. After that, the non-verbal predicate *easy* is placed in P^{M+1}, while the argument of *easy*, the (remainder of the) predication *to solve the problem*, is placed in the relative position p^{M+2}.

(99)   The problem is easy to solve.
$\quad$ P^I $\qquad\qquad\qquad$ P^M $\quad$ P^{M+1} $\qquad$ P^{M+2}

$\qquad\qquad\qquad\qquad\qquad\qquad\qquad$ P^I $\quad$ P^M

$\quad$ the problem $\quad$ ^{Vf}is $\quad$ ^{Pred}easy $\quad$ ^{Subj}[to $\quad$ $^{Vnon-f}$solve]

It will be clear that the raising of elements results in a mismatch between the Representational Level and the Morphosyntactic Level: what functions as a single predication at the Representational Level appears as two units at the Morphosyntactic Level. Raising, in other words, increases the degree of non-transparency of a language.

5.6. Phrases

5.6.1. Introduction

The third layer at the Morphosyntactic Level is that of the Phrase. Phrases consist of a sequenced combination of Words (Xw), Phrases (Xp), and embedded Clauses, all of which may occur more than once. Some possible combinations are given in example (100):

(100)   a. a very expensive car

$(Np_1$: $[(Gw_1$: a) $(Ap_1$: $[(Advp_1$: $(Advw_1$: very)) $(Aw_1$: expensive)] ^{Ap}) $(Nw_1$: car)] ^{Np})

b. the money in the safe

$(Np_1$: $[(Gw_1$: the) $(Nw_1$: money) $(Adpp_1$: $[(Adpw_1$: in) $(Np_2$: $[(Gw_2$: the) $(Nw_2$: safe)] ^{Np})] ^{Adpp})] ^{Np})

c. the money that he had stolen

$(Np_1$: $[(Gw_1$: the) $(Nw_1$: money) $(Cl_1$: $[(Gw_2$: that) $(Np_2$: $(Nw_2$: he)) $(Vp_i$: $[(^{fin}Vw$: had) $(^{non-f}Vw$: stolen)] ^{Vp})] ^{Cl})] ^{Np})

Example (100a) is a Noun Phrase consisting of a Grammatical Word (the determiner *a*), an Adjectival Phrase (*very expensive*) and a Nominal Word (*car*). This Nominal Word is the head of the Phrase: it is this element that determines which type of Phrase we are dealing with (Noun Phrase). The Adjectival Phrase *very expensive*, in turn, consists of an Adverbial Phrase (consisting of an Adverbial Word only) and an Adjectival Word, the head of the Adjectival Phrase. In (100b) we find another Noun Phrase, this time consisting of a Grammatical Word (*the*), a head (the Nominal Word *money*) and an Adpositional Phrase, headed by an adposition (*in*), followed by another Noun Phrase (*the safe*). Finally, in (100c), we have a Noun Phrase containing an embedded Clause, which itself contains a Grammatical Word (the conjunction *that*), a Noun Phrase (the pronoun *he*) and a Verb Phrase, consisting of a finite verb (the auxiliary *had*) and a non-finite verb (the past participle *stolen*).

In this section we will be looking at Phrases that consist of more than one element. More specifically, the aim of this section is to account for the morphosyntactic properties of these elements; that is, the form and the position in which they appear within the Phrase. As in the case of the Clause, the basic assumption is that these morphosyntactic properties are triggered by interpersonal and semantic information. We therefore need to establish which interpersonal and representational units the various constituents of Phrases correspond to. By way of example, consider the sentence in (101) and (the relevant parts of) its representation at the Interpersonal, Representational, and Morphosyntactic Levels:

(101) The cute little boy had broken a window.

IL: $(C_1: [(T_1) (+id R_1: [(T_2) (T_3) (T_4)]^R) (-id R_2: (T_5))]^C)$

RL: $(past ep_1: (perf e_1: [(f_1: break_V) (1x_1: (f_2: boy_N): (f_3: little_A)_x: (f_4: cute_A)^x)_A (1 x_2: (f_5: window_N))_U]^e)^{ep})$

ML: $(Cl_1: [(Np_1: [(Gw_1: the) (Ap_1: (Aw_1: cute)) (Ap_2: (Aw_2: little)) (Nw_1: boy)]^{Np})_{Subj} (Vp_i: [(^fVw_1: had) (^{non-f}Vw_2: broken)]^{Vp}) (Np_2: [(Gw_2: a) (Nw_2: window)]^{Np})_{Obj}]^{Cl})$

In this example, the Noun Phrase *a little boy* corresponds to a Referential Subact (R_1) at the Interpersonal Level and to the Actor argument (x_1) at the Representational Level. Within this Phrase, the definite article expresses the identifiability operator (+id), while the Nominal Word *boy* and the Adjectival Words *little* and *cute* correspond to three Ascriptive Subacts $(T_2, T_3,$ and $T_4)$. The head of the Verb Phrase, the Verbal Word *break*, corresponds to an Ascriptive Subact (T_1), while the auxiliary *had* is triggered by the combination of the operators 'past' and 'present'.

Within each of the Phrases in example (100) the order of elements is (almost entirely) fixed. This means that there must be certain ordering principles which determine the order in which constituents appear in the Phrases. As it turns out, these ordering principles are very similar to those applying at the Clausal layer, in the sense that ordering takes place in a top-down fashion and that, in order to proceed in this fashion, a distinction needs to be made between interpersonal and representational units and between non-core and core elements. In ordering constituents within the Phrase we thus have to go through the following stages:

(102) a. Placement of elements triggered by *interpersonal non-core units*, i.e. the functions, operators, and modifiers of the Referential or Ascriptive Subact in question.

   b. Placement of elements triggered by *representational non-core units*, i.e. the functions, operators, and modifiers of the Individual, followed by those of the Property.

   c. Placements of elements triggered by *core units*, i.e. the predicate and its arguments, starting with the predicate.

   d. Placement of *dummy elements*.

As for the morphosyntactic positions available for these elements, it will be assumed that, as at the layer of the Clause, there are three absolute positions: the Phrase-initial position (P^I), the Phrase-medial position (P^M), and the Phrase-final position (P^F):

(103) P^I P^M P^F

In addition, there may be a number of relative positions (P^{I+1}, P^{F-1}, etc.), which become available as soon as one of the absolute positions is filled.

From this brief discussion of certain general aspects of Phrases, it will have become clear that many of the processes and phenomena discussed in the previous section for Clauses are also relevant for Phrases. Consequently, the present section will be organized in much the same way as the previous one. In Section 5.6.2, we will discuss the ordering of elements within the Phrase, using the ordering principles given in (102). This will be followed by sections dealing with phrasal dummies (Section 5.6.3), agreement (Section 5.6.4), and subordination within the Phrase (Section 5.6.5).

5.6.2. The ordering of units within the Phrase

Let us start by applying the ordering principles given in (102) to a number of examples, starting with Phrases expressing Referential Subacts. As argued in Chapter 3 (Section 3.9.3), an adjective like *poor* can be used in (at least) two ways: to ascribe a property to some Individual (in which case that Individual is described as having little money), or to express some kind of sympathy for or empathy with the Individual referred to (in which case nothing is said about the financial status of the referent). On the former use the adjective *poor* (like most adjectives) is analysed as an Ascriptive Subact at the Interpersonal Level and as a modifier at the layer of the Individual at the Representational Level. On the latter use, however, it is analysed as a modifier of the Referential Subact at the Interpersonal Level, without a representational counterpart. In example (104), *poor* is obviously used in the latter sense, while the adjective *innocent* has an Ascriptive function at the Interpersonal Level (T_2) and a modifying function at the Representational Level (f_2):

(104)   Why do they have to be out there pestering *a poor innocent dinosaur*? (COCA, written, fiction)
   IL: (-id R_1: [(T_1) (T_2)]: poor ^{R})
   RL: ($1x_1$: (f_1: dinosaur$_N$): (f_2: innocent$_A$) ^{x})
   ML: (Np$_1$: [(Gw$_1$: a) (Ap$_1$: (Aw$_1$: poor)) (Ap$_2$: (Aw$_2$: innocent))
      (Nw$_1$: dinosaur)] ^{Np})

Now that we have the interpersonal and representational structure of the Noun Phrase *a poor innocent dinosaur*, we can use the ordering principles in

(102) to get from these representations to the ordered sequence at the Morphosyntactic Level. Starting at the Interpersonal Level, we find that there are two non-core elements: the operator '–id' and the modifier *poor*, both of which are in a hierarchical relation to the head of the Subact. In accordance with the ordering principles in (102), we start by assigning a position to the element triggered by the operator (the placeholder 'indef'), placing it in Phrase-initial position. Next, we place the modifier *poor* in position P^{I+1}. We then move on to the Representational Level, where we find two non-core elements: the operator ('1') and the modifier (*innocent*), both at the layer of the Individual. The singularity operator '1' goes into what will be the head (P^M), where it will take the form of a placeholder 'sg'. Then the modifier *innocent* is placed in P^{I+2}. Finally, the head of the Individual (*dinosaur*) joins the singularity placeholder in P^M.

(**105**)   a poor innocent (dinosaur)

P^I	P^{I+1}	P^{I+2}	P^M
$^{\pi R}$indef	$^{\Sigma R}$poor	$^{\sigma X}$innocent	dinosaur.$^{\pi X}$sg
1	2	4	5–3

Now consider the Noun Phrase in (106)

(**106**)   a famous criminal lawyer

IL: (-id R_1: [(T_1) (T_2)] ^{R})
RL: ($1x_1$: (f_1: lawyer$_N$: (f_2: criminal$_A$) ^{f}): (f_3: famous$_A$) ^{x})
ML: (Np$_1$: [(Gw$_1$: a) (Ap$_1$: (Aw$_1$: famous)) (Ap$_2$: (Aw$_2$: criminal)) (Nw$_1$: lawyer)] ^{Np})

Starting with the non-core units, the first element to be expressed is again the operator '–id', triggering placement of the placeholder 'indef' in P^I. Moving to the layer of the Individual, we first place the singularity operator 'sg' in P^M; then, the modifier *famous* is placed in P^{I+1}. The last non-core element to be placed is the modifier *criminal* (f_2). This modifier is located at the layer of the Property: it does not modify the Individual x_1, but the nominal head *lawyer* f_1 (i.e. the lawyer in question is not criminal, but is specialized in criminal law). This modifier goes to P^{I+2}. Finally, the head, *lawyer*, is placed in P^M.

(**107**)   a famous criminal lawyer

P^I	P^{I+1}	P^{I+2}	P^M
$^{\pi R}$indef	$^{\sigma X}$famous	^{of}criminal	lawyer.$^{\pi X}$sg
1	3	4	5–2

Now consider the Referential Subact in (108), evoking a Location:

(108)   from all countries

IL: $(R_1: (T_1))$

RL: $(\forall\, l_1: (f_1: country_N))_{So}$

ML: $(Adpp_1: [(Adpw_1: from) (Np_1: [(Gw_1: all) (Nw_1: countries)]$
$^{Np})]\ ^{Adpp})$

Since there are no non-core interpersonal units in this Phrase, we start with the highest layer at the Representational Level, a Location. This unit has the semantic function Source, realized as the Adposition *from*, which goes to P^I. Next the universal operator *all* is placed in P^{I+1}. Finally the head, *countries*, is placed in P^{I+2}.

(109)   from all countries

P^I	P^{I+1}	P^{I+2}
$^{\phi l}$from	$^{\pi x}$all	countries
1	2	3

Naturally, the ordering principles in (102) also apply to Phrases correspond-ing to Ascriptive Subacts at the Interpersonal Level. Consider the italicized part of example (110):

(110)   When I first saw it I *kind of laughed* (COCA, written, magazine)

IL: $(approx\ T_1)$

RL: $(f_1: laugh_V)$

ML: $(Vp_1: [(Gw_1: kind-of) (Vw_1: laughed)]\ ^{Vp})$

In (110), *kind-of* is analysed as an approximation operator at the layer of the Ascriptive Subact (see Chapter 3, Section 3.8.4). As the only non-core element in this Phrase, it is the first element to be placed, going to the Phrase-initial position. At the Representational Level, we first place the past tense place-holder in P^{I+1}, where it is subsequently joined by the predicate *laugh*.

(111)   kind of laughed

P^I	P^{I+1}
$^{\pi T}$kind-of	^{vf}laugh.$^{\pi ep}$past
1	3–2

Now apply the ordering principles in (102) to the Noun Phrases *an allegedly corrupt politician*.

So far, we have looked at examples with simple heads. As we know from Chapters 3 and 4, however, heads can also be configurational. At the Representational Level, for instance, the predicate may be a relational noun, in which case it requires an argument. In analogy with our treatment of predicates and arguments at the layer of the Clause, we regard relational nominal predicates and their arguments as core elements, forming a predication. Two examples are given in (112):

(112)   a.   the boy's sister

$(1x_1: [(f_1: sister_N) (1x_2: (f_2: boy_N))_{Ref}]^x)$ (See Section 4.7.3)

   b.   the idea that people have a split personality (BYU-BNC, spoken, broadcast discussion)

$(1p_1: [(f_1: idea_N) (p_1: – that people have a split personality –)_{Ref}]^P)$

(See Section 4.8.3)

In (112a) we find an example of inalienable possession: the relational noun *sister* requires the presence of an argument with the semantic function Reference (*the boy*). Together these two elements form a predication, functioning as the configurational head of the Individual (x_1). In example (112b) we have a Propositional Content (p_1) with a configurational head, consisting of the nominal predicate (*idea*) and its Reference argument (specifying the contents of p_1). Since we are dealing with core units, placement of the two elements is determined by the ordering principle in (102c). For the Phrase in (112a) this leads to the ordering of constituents in (113):

(113)   the boy's sister

P^I P^M

$[P^I$ $P^F]$

$[P^I$ $P^{I+1}]$

$^{\pi R}$def   boy ^{Ref}s ^{pred}sister

Of the two core elements, *the boy* and *sister*, it is the nominal predicate, *sister*, that is first placed in position, going to P^M, while the argument *the boy* is placed in P^I. Next, the semantic function Reference of the argument, expressed as the phrasal clitic *'s*, is placed in the P^F of the embedded genitival Phrase. Finally, we turn to the Noun Phrase within the genitival Phrase, where the placeholder 'def' takes the P^I position and the head, *boy*, goes to P^{I+1}.

When we look at the example in (112b), however, we see that here the elements appear in a different order: whereas in (112a) the argument precedes the predicate, in (112b) it follows the predicate, due to the fact that English does not allow clausal and phrasal modifiers in prenominal position (**the that people have a split personality idea*). This leads to the ordering of elements in (114):

(114)   the idea that people have a split personality

P^I P^{I+1} P^F

$^{\pi R}$def   idea ^{Ref}that people have a split personality

1   3   2

Now consider the example in (115), which has the same semantic representation as (112a), but a different morphosyntactic form:

(115)   the sister of the boy

In this example, the argument takes the form of an Adpositional Phrase introduced by *of*. As the expression of the semantic function Reference, the adposition *of* is the first element to be assigned a position within the Adpositional Phrase, going to P^I. Subsequently, the Noun Phrase *the boy*, as a whole, takes the P^{I+1} position. Within this Noun Phrase, the determiner *the* ('def') is first placed in P^I, after which the nominal head *boy* is placed in P^{I+1}. This quite complex placement of elements is visualized in (116) (in slightly simplified form):

(116)   the sister of the boy

P^I P^{I+1} P^F

                              [P^I P^{I+1}]

                                    [P^I P^{I+1}]

$^{\pi R}$def ^{pred}sister ^{Ref}[$^{\phi x}$of   [$^{\pi R}$the boy]]

So far, we have been able to account for the order of elements within the Clause by applying the ordering principles given in (102). There are, however, cases, where these ordering principles do not suffice. Consider, for instance the Phrase in example (117), which contains two adjectival modifiers (*cute* and *little*), both modifying the same Individual:

(117)   the cute little boy

(1x$_1$: (f$_2$: boy$_N$): (f$_3$: little$_A$): (f$_4$: cute$_A$) ^{x})

In this case the order in which these elements appear is determined by semantic factors. Thus, adjectives designating evaluative properties (such as *cute*) typically precede those designating (objective) physical properties (e.g. *little*). To obtain the linear ordering in (117), we thus need a rule stating that the placement of adjectives designating evaluative properties precedes placement of adjectives designating physical properties:

(118)   the cute little boy

P^I P^{I+1} P^{I+2} P^M

$^{\pi R}$def $^{\sigma x}$cute $^{\sigma x}$little   boy.$^{\pi x}$sg

> ### The ordering of core representational elements in other languages
>
> The order in which core units are expressed can also be determined by interpersonal factors. In French, for instance, adjectives that normally follow the nominal head (example (119a)) can appear in prenominal position when the adjectival modifier is emphasized (example (119b)) (example from Hengeveld and Mackenzie 2008: 388):
>
> (119) a. une   voiture   rouge   superbe
>   a   car   red   magnificent
>   'a magnificent red car'
>   b. une   SUPERBE   voiture   rouge
>   a   magnificent   car   red
>   'a MAGNIFICENT red car'
>
> Note that in the neutral form in (119a), the order of the two modifiers is determined by the same semantic factors governing the placement of such modifiers in English, with the adjective designating a physical property (*rouge*) being placed closest to the head (thus presenting a mirror image of English).

5.6.3. Dummy elements

Like Clauses, Phrases may contain positions that must be filled even if there is no interpersonal or representational material to fill them. In that case a dummy element will be inserted in the obligatory position. In English Noun Phrases, for instance, the head position must in most cases be filled, even in the absence of lexical information to fill it. An example is given in (120) (cf. example (113), Section 4.7.2):

(120)   At least it's *a white* **cloud**, *not a black* **one** (BYU-BNC, spoken, conversation)
       a. a white **cloud**
          IL: $(\text{-id } R_1: [(\mathbf{T_1}) \ (T_2)]^{\ R})$
          RL: $(x_1: (\mathbf{f_1}): (f_2: \text{white})^{\ x})$
          ML: $(Np_1: [(Gw_1: a) \ (Ap_1: (Aw_1: \text{white})) \ (\mathbf{Nw_1: cloud})]^{\ Np})$
       b. a black **one**
          IL: $(\text{-id } R_2: [(\mathbf{T_3}) \ (T_4)]^{\ R})$
          RL: $(x_2: (\mathbf{f_1}): (f_3: \text{black})^{\ x})$
          ML: $(Np_2: [(Gw_2: a) \ (Ap_2: (Aw_2: \text{black})) \ (\mathbf{Nw_2: one})]^{\ Np})$

In this example the head of the Noun Phrase Np$_2$ in example (120b) takes the form of the indefinite pronoun *one*, which corresponds to a headless Ascriptive Subact at the Interpersonal Level (T$_3$) and a headless property at the Representational Level (f$_1$). Since there is no lexical information to fill the head position, the dummy element *one* is inserted, instructing the Addressee to retrieve the relevant descriptive information (*cloud*) from elsewhere. Note that the anaphoric relation between the elements *cloud* and *one* is indicated at the Representational Level through co-indexing of the f-variable (f$_1$). At the Interpersonal Level, however, we still have two different Ascriptive Acts (T$_1$) and (T$_3$), since the property is evoked twice; likewise, at the Morphosyntactic Level, we have two different Nominal Words: *cloud* (Nw$_1$) and *one* (Nw$_2$).

Dummy elements may also be verbal in form, as for instance in the case of the copula *be*. As we know, main Clauses require the presence of a finite verb to express tense (present or past). Where there is no interpersonal or representational material to fill this position a dummy element is inserted. In English (and in many other languages), this is what happens in copular sentences, where the copula *be* is inserted into the finite verb position to express number and tense distinctions. An example is given in (121) (cf. example (69d), Chapter 4, Section 4.5.4). At the Interpersonal Level this sentence consists of two Subacts: a Referential Subact corresponding to the proper name *Robert* and an Ascriptive Subact evoking the Property 'teacher'. At the Representational Level, this Property functions as a non-verbal predicate, taking the Individual *Robert* as its argument. Since there is no verbal element to express tense and number distinctions, the appropriate form of the copula *be* is introduced at the Morphosyntactic Level:

(121)   Robert **is** a teacher.

   IL: (C$_1$: [(T$_1$) (R$_1$)] ^{C})

   RL: (pres ep$_1$: (e$_1$: [(x$_1$: teacher) (x$_2$)$_U$] ^{e}) ^{ep})

   ML: (Cl$_1$: [(Np$_1$: (Nw$_1$: Robert)) (Vp$_i$: [(^{fin}Vw$_1$: **be.pres.3sg**) (Np$_2$: [(Gw$_1$: a) (Nw$_2$: teacher)] ^{Np})] ^{Vp})] ^{Cl})

As it turns out, however, it is not only the position of the finite verb that needs to be filled: in most (finite and non-finite Clauses) the main verb position must also be filled. In example (122), for instance, we see that if, in a copular sentence, there is another finite verb (in this case the auxiliary *has*, expressing the operator perfect), the copula *be* still needs to be inserted to fill the obligatory main verb position.

(122)   Robert has *been* a teacher all his life.

Another verbal dummy in English is the proform *so*, which goes into the position of the non-verbal predicate if there is no interpersonal or representational material available to fill this position. As in the case of the pronoun *one*, the proform *so* invites the Addressee to look for the relevant descriptive information elsewhere. An example is given in (123), where the proform *so* has the same designation as the non-verbal predicate *a teacher* in the preceding Clause:

(123)   Robert has been a teacher all his life, and will remain *so* until he retires.

> Now consider the sentence *Robert has been teaching all his life, and will be doing so until he retires.* Which dummy element does this sentence contain? Which position does it take?

5.6.4. Agreement

In our discussion of Clauses, agreement was described as the copying of certain semantic features of one element of the Clause onto some other element of the same Clause (or, as in the case of *consecutio temporum*, onto an element of an embedded Clause) (see Sections 5.5.6 and 5.5.7.3). We also saw that English, as a morphologically impoverished language, hardly expresses any agreement at the Clausal layer. The same is true for the layer of the Phrase: since English has no grammatical gender, agreement marking within the Phrase is highly restricted. Nevertheless, number agreement is sometimes required, as shown in example (124), where there is number agreement between the determiners *this* and *those* and the head of the Noun Phrase. This kind of agreement is the result of feature copying: the number feature, expressed as a suffix on the noun, is copied onto the determiner:

(124)   a. this bike

RL: $(\mathbf{1}\ \text{prox}\ x_1\text{:}\ (f_1\text{:}\ \text{bike}_N))$

ML: $(\text{Np}_1\text{:}\ [(\text{Gw}_1\text{:}\ \text{prox}.\mathbf{sg})\ (\text{Nw}_1\text{:}\ \text{bike}.\mathbf{sg})]\ ^{\text{Np}})$

b. these bikes

RL: $(\mathbf{m}\ \text{prox}\ x_1\text{:}\ (f_1\text{:}\ \text{bike}_N))$

ML: $(\text{Np}_1\text{:}\ [(\text{Gw}_1\text{:}\ \text{prox}.\mathbf{pl})\ (\text{Nw}_1\text{:}\ \text{bike}.\mathbf{pl})]\ ^{\text{Np}})$

Another instance where feature copying could be argued to take place is illustrated in (125), where the subclass of nominal head (count or mass)

seems to determine the selection of the appropriate determiners or quantifiers; in other words, an inherent semantic feature of the head seems to be
copied onto the determiner/quantifier:

(125)   a. a bike, many bikes
           b. some water, much water

In these examples, however, it is questionable whether agreement is really
taking place. Remember that in our discussion of these kinds of expressions,
the difference in syntactic behaviour (form of the determiner/quantifier,
plural or singular form of the verb) were not so much regarded as being
triggered by different subclasses of nouns, but rather as corresponding to
different subclasses of Individuals. The examples in (125), for instance, were
analysed as in (126), where the superscripts 'c' (for count) and 'm' (for mass)
specify the Individual variable x, not the lexemes *bike* and *water*:

(126)   a. $(^{c}x_1: (f_1: bike_N))$
           b. $(^{m}x_1: (f_1: water_N))$

Given the top-down approach of FDG, this is indeed a much more attractive analysis, as it reflects the idea that Speakers first select a referent
(Interpersonal Level), which is then categorized semantically (as an Individual, either count or mass), before the lexeme used to describe this referent
(*bike*, *water*) is selected. It will be clear that on this approach there is no
feature copying from the nominal head to the determiner/quantifier; rather,
the subclass feature of the Individual (count or mass) determines both the
form of the determiner/quantifier and the selection of the nominal head.

Phrasal agreement in other languages

An example of a language where agreement is triggered by the grammatical class of the noun is Spanish. In the following examples, for
instance, the form of both the determiner and the adjective is determined
by the grammatical gender of the noun:

(127)   a. un   libro   barato
             a   book(M)   cheap
             'a cheap book'
           b. una   pluma   barata
             a   pen(F)   cheap
             'a cheap pen'

From these examples it will be clear that the gender of the nouns (masculine in (127a), feminine in (127b)) cannot be predicted on the basis of the entities they designate. This means that agreement in such Phrases is determined by an inherent feature of the noun.

5.6.5. Subordination

Subordinate Clauses within the Phrase can be divided into two groups: restrictive relative Clauses (example (128a)) and complement (or content) Clauses (128b):

(128)   a. His staff officers would be gathering by his tent, waiting to hear *the news that had come from Washington.* (COCA, written, academic)

   b. Do you remember where you were when you heard *the news that Dr. King had been assassinated*? (COCA, written, academic)

The difference between the two types of embedded Clause has already been discussed in Chapter 4 (Section 4.8.3), where relative Clauses were analysed as modifiers, while content-Clauses were analysed as arguments. In example (128a), for instance, the subordinate Clause modifies the Propositional Content designated by the expression as a whole. At the Representational Level, this expression is, therefore, analysed as in (129a), where the Propositional Content (p_1) consists of a nominal head modified by an Episode. This Episode, in turn, contains a State-of-Affairs consisting of a Property *come* and two arguments: a headless Undergoer (p_1), which shares its designation with the expression as a whole, and a Location (l_1, *from Washington*). The Undergoer argument is expressed as the relative pronoun *that* (replaceable by *which*).

(129)   a. $(p_1: (f_1: news_N): (past\ ep_1: (perf\ e_1: [(f_2: come_V)\ (p_1)_U\ (l_1)_{So}]^e)^{ep})^P)$

   b. $(p_1: [(f_1: news_N)\ (p_1: (past\ ep_1: (perf\ e_1: [(f_2: assassinate_V)\ (x_1)_A\ (x_2)_U]^e)^{ep})^P)_{Ref}]^P)$

Example (128b), on the other hand, will be given the representation in (129b) (cf. examples (112b) and (114) above). Here the element *that* is not a relative pronoun: it is not an argument of the subordinate Clause (which is complete without it) and cannot be replaced by *which*. In this case the subordinate Clause functions as the Reference argument of the relational noun *news*. This reference argument is co-indexed with the expression as a whole (both are (p_1)): after all, the contents of the expression as a whole is identical to (specified by) the contents of the subordinate Clause (the news IS that Dr King was assassinated). The element *that* in this case functions merely as a linking element.

   Due to their complexity, both relative and content-Clauses necessarily appear in postnominal position. This is illustrated for example (128a) in (130) and for example (128b) in (131):

(130)   the news that had come from Washington
$$P^I \qquad P^{I+1} \qquad P^F$$
$^{\pi R}$def   news $^{\sigma P}$[that had come from Washington]

(131)   the news that Dr. King had been assassinated
$$P^I \qquad P^{I+1} \qquad P^{I+2}$$
$^{\pi R}$def   news ^{Ref}[Dr. King had been assassinated]

In both examples the definite article is the first element to be assigned a position (P^I). In (130) this is followed by the subordinate Clause in P^F and the head in P^{I+1}. In (131), which has a configurational head, the predicate (*news*) is placed in P^{I+1}, followed by the Reference argument in P^{I+2}. When a Noun Phrase contains both a relative Clause and an argument, the ordering principles discussed earlier in this section dictate that the relative Clause (as a non-core unit) is inserted before the argument (a core unit). In example (132) the placement of elements is thus as follows: first the definite article is placed in P^I; then the subordinate Clause *who lives in Canada*, functioning as a modifier at the layer of the Individual, is placed in P^F; next the head of the expression as a whole, the nominal predicate *cousin*, is placed in P^{I+1}; and finally the Adpositional Phrase *of my wife*, functioning as an argument of *cousin*, is put in P^{F-1}:

(132)   the cousin of my wife who lives in Canada
$$P^I \qquad P^{I+1} \qquad P^{F-1} \qquad\qquad\qquad P^F$$
$^{\pi R}$the   cousin ^{Ref}[of my wife] $^{\sigma X}$[who lives in Canada]

Lastly, it needs to be mentioned that complex modifiers and arguments can also be placed outside the Noun Phrase, usually in Clause-final position. This is generally regarded as a strategy intended to make production and/or processing of the expression in question easier. Examples involving a relative Clause and content-Clause are given in (133a) and (133b), respectively:

(133) a. I've been asked out by this actor/journalist tonight *that I went to see last week*. (ICE-GB, written, social letter)

b. The rumour was going round *that a new tax on cattle and horse-ownership was to be introduced*. (BYU-BNC, written, academic)

5.7. Words

5.7.1. Introduction

This section will be concerned with the lowest of the four basic layers at the Morphosyntactic Level, that of the Word. Words can be simplex (consisting of a single **Morpheme**) or complex (consisting of more than one Morpheme). In the latter case, further distinctions can be made depending on the kind of Morphemes involved. Consider, for instance, the examples in (134):

(134) a. filename, kitchen chair, toothpaste
b. unhappy, repay, powerless
c. diver, happily, legalize
d. books, reads, reading

These examples represent only a small selection of the wide range of possible word formation processes available in English. Example (134a) gives some examples of compounds, which, at the Representational Level, were analysed as compositional heads of Properties, consisting of two lexemes (Chapter 4, Section 4.6). In (134b) we find some examples of derivations by means of bound Morphemes with lexical content (*un-*, *re-*, *-less*) adding 'an independent aspect of meaning' (Hengeveld and Mackenzie 2008: 229), the result being a new lexeme with a different, but predictable meaning ('not happy', 'pay again', 'without power'). In (134c), on the other hand, the bound Morphemes *-er*, *-ly*, and *-ize* have little or no lexical content; instead their function is to change the syntactic category of the original lexeme (*happily*, for instance, is an adverb derived from an adjective). Finally, the examples in (134d) differ from the examples in (134b) and (134c) in that they contain bound Morphemes that provide morphosyntactic information (*-s*, *ing*) instead of bringing about a change in meaning or syntactic category.

What all these complex forms have in common is that they are created through (more or less) productive word formation processes. It will be clear that any theory of grammar needs to provide an account of these processes, explaining how they take place (i.e. accounting for the form and order of the different components) and where they take place (in which part of the Grammatical Component: in the lexicon or during Formulation or Encoding). The aim of this section is to show that FDG can provide an account of the internal structure of such complex forms that is not only descriptively adequate, but which also quite elegantly brings out the difference between the complex forms illustrated in (134).

The rest of this section will be organized as follows. We will start by introducing two important distinctions: first, we will discuss the distinction between lexemes (introduced during the operation of Formulation) and Words (introduced at the Morphosyntactic Level) (Section 5.7.2); then, within the category of Words, we will make a further distinction between Lexical Words and Grammatical Words (Section 5.7.3). Subsequently, we will describe the ordering of non-core units (Section 5.7.4), alignment (Section 5.7.5), the ordering of core units (Section 5.7.6), and dummy elements (Section 5.7.7). In the course of these sections, the different word formation processes listed in (134) will be discussed in more detail. A summary of this discussion will be supplied in Section 5.7.8.

5.7.2. Words vs. lexemes

As we have seen in the previous section, the lowest layer of the Morphosyntactic Level is that of the Word: an item like *happy*, for instance, will be analysed at the Morphosyntactic Level as an Adjectival Word. At the Representational Level, however, this item is analysed as a lexeme functioning as the head of a Property:

(135) happy

      RL: (f_1: happy$_A$)

      ML: (Aw_1: happy)

So what is the difference between lexemes and Words, and why do we need this distinction?

Two reasons for making this distinction were given in Section 5.3. In that section, the term transparency was used to describe a situation in which there is a one-to-one relationship between interpersonal, representational, morphosyntactic, and phonological units. It was also argued that there are no languages that are completely transparent: although languages may be characterized by different degrees of transparency, in every language there are mismatches between at least some units belonging to different levels. A case in point are dummy elements, which are inserted for morphosyntactic reasons, but which do not have an interpersonal or representational counterpart: in such cases we have a Word without a corresponding lexeme.

Another example of a mismatch between lexemes and Words is the use of an Adverbial Word (e.g. *ferociously*) to express an Adjectival lexeme (*ferocious*). Here the addition of the suffix *-ly* is triggered by the fact that the adjective does not perform its usual function of modifier within an expression with a nominal head (such as an Individual; example (136)), but instead is used to modify an expression with a verbal head (a Property within a State-of-Affairs, example (137)) (Hengeveld and Mackenzie 2008: 218, 295–6):

(136) a *ferocious* dog   one-to-one relationship lexeme-Word

RL: $(1x_1: (f_1: dog_N): (\mathbf{f_1: ferocious_A})^x)$

ML: $(Np_1: [(Gw_1: a) (Ap_1: (\mathbf{Aw_1: ferocious})) (Nw_1: dog)]^{Np})$

(137) barked *ferociously*   mismatch lexeme-Word

RL: $(e_1: [(f_1: bark_V: (\mathbf{f_2: ferocious_A})^f)]^e)$

ML: $(Le_1: (Cl_1: [(Vp_1: (Vw_1: barked)) (Advp_1: (\mathbf{Advw_1:}$
$\mathbf{ferociously)})]^{Cl})^{Le})$

A similar example can be found in (138), where the Individual x_1 has a configurational head consisting of the one-place verbal predicate *dive* and its Actor argument. Normally, however, Individuals have a nominal head, which at the Morphosyntactic Level is expressed as the head of a Noun Phrase. In (138), the presence of a verbal predicate in the head position of an Individual thus leads to a clash at the Morphosyntactic Level. This clash is resolved by a process of **coercion**, where the class of the verbal lexeme is adapted to fit the requirements of its syntactic position: addition of the element *-er* changes the verbal lexeme *dive* into the Nominal Word *diver*, thus preparing it for its syntactic function as head of a Noun Phrase. Note also that the Actor argument of the predicate dive (x_1) is co-indexed with the expression as a whole, indicating that the two expressions designate the same Individual (a diver is a person who dives):

(138) a *diver* ('a person who dives')

RL: $(1x_1: [(f_1: \mathbf{dive_V}) (x_1)_A]^x)$

ML: $(Np_1: [(Gw_1: a) (Nw_1: \mathbf{diver})]^{Np})$

> On the basis of the analysis in (138), give the representational and morphosyntactic representations of the nouns *trainer* and *trainee*.

This process of **syntactic derivation** is not restricted to deverbal nouns (i.e. nouns formed on the basis of verbs, as in (138)) but also to other instances of word-class changing derivation. Another example of syntactic derivation is given in (139), illustrating the derivation of a deadjectival verb. In this example, the placement of the adjective *legal* in the position of a transitive verbal Property triggers the derived form *legalize*:

(139)   They have *legalized* soft drugs.

      RL: (past ep$_1$: (perf e$_1$: [(f$_1$: **legal**$_A$) (x$_1$)$_A$ (x$_2$)$_U$] ^{e}) ^{ep})

      ML: (Cl$_1$: [(Np$_1$: (Nw$_1$: they))$_{Subj}$ (Vp$_1$: [(^{f}Vw$_1$: have) (^{nonf}Vw$_2$: **legalized**)] ^{Vp}) (Np$_2$: [(Nw$_2$: soft drugs)])$_{Obj}$] ^{Cl})

Syntactic derivation is subject to a number of constraints. Thus, what the examples above all have in common is that:

(i)   the Affix has no lexical content;
(ii) the syntactic category of the lexemes is different from that of the resulting Word (word-class changing derivation);
(iii) the derivational process is productive and predictable; i.e. it can apply to a definable set of lexemes (e.g. a particular subset of verbs or adjectives) and does not introduce an unpredictable meaning aspect.

Derivational processes fulfilling these criteria are taken care of during the operation of morphosyntactic Encoding, at the interface between the Representational and Morphosyntactic Levels. When the process is not productive (e.g. the addition of the suffix -al in, for instance, *withdrawal*, *refusal*, and *approval*) or adds unpredictable meaning elements (e.g. -er in *poster*, *blusher*, or *trailer*), syntactic derivation does not apply. Instead, the lexemes in question are simply listed in the lexicon.

Note that Properties (i) and (ii) above distinguish syntactic derivation from lexical derivation, which is also predictable and productive, but which involves the use of an Affix with lexical content, and which need not change the category of the lexeme. Unlike syntactic derivation, lexical derivation takes place in the lexicon, where it is taken care of by lexeme formation rules, which derive new lexemes from existing ones. An example of such a rule can be found in (140), which turns an adjective (e.g. *happy*) into a new, semantically related (antonymous) adjective (*unhappy*):

(140)   Antonymous adjective formation:

Input: gradable lex$_A$

Output: [un-lex]$_A$

Meaning: the Property designated by [un-lex]$_A$ is the opposite of that designated by lex$_A$

It will be clear that in those cases where a derived lexeme is listed or formed in the lexicon there is a one-to-one relationship between a lexeme and the Word used to express this lexeme. In the case of syntactic derivation, on the other hand, there is a mismatch between lexeme and Word, which justifies the distinction between them.

Other examples of a mismatch between lexemes and Words are those cases where two or more lexemes are expressed as one Word, or where a single lexeme is expressed by two or more Words. Examples of the former situation are compounds such as those given in (134a) (*filename, kitchen chair, toothpaste*), which are analysed at the Representational Level as consisting of two lexemes (Chapter 4, Section 4.6), but which, morphosyntactically, behave as one Nominal Word. The reverse is true for semantically opaque multiword expressions like *to kick the bucket* (= to die). At the Representational Level such idiomatic expressions function as single, one-place verbal lexemes, listed in the lexicon with their overall (idiomatic) meaning. Since the component parts of such idiomatic expressions do not contribute to the expression's idiomatic meaning, they are not represented as separate lexemes at the Representational Level. This also explains why modification of the component parts is not possible (*John kicked the empty bucket* can only be interpreted literally). Morphosyntactically, however, this expression consists of three Words (note, for instance, that it is the verb rather than the expression as a whole that is inflected for tense: *he kicked the bucket*; **he kick the bucketed*). These examples once again show the necessity of distinguishing lexemes from Words.

Finally, there are Words that do not correspond to lexical information because they are triggered by interpersonal or representational functions or operators. These will be discussed in the next section, which will deal with a different (but related) distinction: that between Lexical and Grammatical Words.

5.7.3. Lexical and Grammatical Words

As shown in the previous sections, Words may correspond to (one or more) lexemes at the Representational Level (typically) or at the Interpersonal Level (as in the case of proper names, interpersonal modifiers or lexical heads of illocutions). Such **Lexical Words** function as the head of a Phrase, with the syntactic category of the Lexical Word determining the type of Phrase (examples (141a) and (141b)); this is true even in those cases where there is no one-to-one relationship between lexemes and Words (examples (141c) and (141d)):

(141) a. two books

　　　　RL:　$(2\ x_1: (f_1: book_N))$

　　　　ML:　$(Np_1: [(Gw_1: two) (Nw_1: book.pl)]\ ^{Np})$

　　　　b. Peter

　　　　IL:　$(R_1: Peter_N)$

　　　　ML:　$(Np_1: (Nw_1: Peter))$

　　　　c. this filename

　　　　RL:　$(1\ prox\ x_1: (f_1: (f_2: name_N: (f_3: file_N)\ ^f)\ ^f)\ ^x)$

　　　　ML:　$(Np_1: [(Gw_1: this.sg) (Nw_1: filename)]\ ^{Np})$

　　　　d. he kicked the bucket (= he died)

　　　　RL:　$(p_1: (past\ ep_1: (e_1: [(f_1: kick-the-bucket_V) (x_1)_U]\ ^e)\ ^{ep})\ ^p)$

　　　　ML:　$(Cl_1: [(Np_1: (Nw_1: Peter)) (Vp_1: (Vw_1: kick.past)) (Np_2: [(Gw_1: the) (Nw_2: bucket)]\ ^{Np})]\ ^{Cl})$

Other Words, however, are not triggered by lexical information. Such **Grammatical Words** can be divided into three classes, depending on their exact relation to information at the Interpersonal and Representational Levels:

1. Grammatical Words that do not correspond to any interpersonal or representational unit. In that case, we are dealing with dummy elements, which fill obligatory morphosyntactic slots in the absence of lexical information; e.g. dummy *it*, dummy *do*, copula *be*, the conjunction *that*; see example (142a)
2. Grammatical Words that are triggered by interpersonal or representational operators or functions; e.g. determiners, auxiliaries, the negator *not*, grammatical adpositions (e.g. *has* in example (142b))
3. Grammatical Words that correspond to interpersonal and/or representational units which do not contain a lexical head (e.g. pronouns; see example (142c)).

In some cases Grammatical Words exhibit the same syntactic behaviour as a certain class of Lexical Words, expressing, for instance, tense, aspect, number, or case distinctions. In that case they are classified and represented in analogy with the corresponding Lexical Words; in all other cases, Grammatical Words will simply be represented by the variable Gw.

(142)   a. It rained.

IL: $(C_1: (T_1))$

RL: (past ep_1: (e_1: (f_1: rain$_V$)))

ML: (Cl$_1$: [(Np$_1$: (**Nw$_1$: it**))$_{Subj}$ (Vp$_1$: (Vw$_1$: rain.past))] ^{Cl})

b. The train has arrived.

IL: $(C_1: [(T_1) (R_1)] ^C)$

RL: (pres ep_1: (**perf** e_1: [(f_1: arrive$_V$) (x_1: (f_2: train$_N$))$_U$] ^{e}) ^{ep})

ML: (Cl$_1$: [(Np$_1$: [(Gw$_1$: the) (Nw$_1$: train)] ^{Np})$_{Subj}$ (Vp$_1$: [(^{fin}**Vw$_1$: have.pres.3.sg**) (^{nonf}Vw$_2$: arrive.past-part)] ^{Vp})] ^{Cl})

c. I laughed

IL: (**R$_1$: [+S −A]**)

RL: (**x$_1$**)

ML: (Cl$_1$: [(Np$_1$: (**Nw$_1$: I**))$_{Subj}$ (Vp$_1$: (Vw$_1$: laugh.past))] ^{Cl})

Identify the Grammatical Words in the following sentence: *His letter may not have arrived yet.* Which of these Words will be represented as belonging to a lexical category?

5.7.4. The ordering of non-core units

Before we consider the ordering principles for elements within a Word, we first have to take a closer look at the kinds of elements that can make up a complex Word. For English, the crucial distinction is that between **Stems** and **Affixes**. Stems are Morphemes with lexical content that can be the sole element within a Word. They typically function as the head of a Lexical Word and can be divided into Verbal Stems (Vs), Nominal Stems (Ns), Adjectival Stems (As), Adverbial Stems (Advs), and Adpositional Stems (Adps). Affixes, on the other hand, can only be used in combination with a Stem and cannot function as the head of a Word. A Nominal Word like *dogs*, for instance, consists of a Nominal Stem *dog* and an Affix -*s*.

In English, two kinds of Affixes can be distinguished. First there is a small set of purely grammatical (inflectional) Affixes, which do not affect the meaning of the Word they attach to and do not change the class of the Word. These Affixes, which will be analysed as Grammatical Affixes (Gaff), are triggered by operators at the Representational Level. The second set of Affixes consists of those bound Morphemes that are introduced during the process of syntactic derivation (e.g. -*er*, -*ize*, -*ly*); these Affixes will be

Table 5.9. Grammatical Affixes in English

Type of Affix	Representational trigger	Example
plural	plurality operator 'm'	dogs
tense	absolute tense operators 'present' and 'past'	walked, walks
past participle	either: absolute tense operator 'past' + relative tense operator 'anterior'	had walked
	or: absolute tense operator 'present' + phasal aspect operator 'perfect'	have walked
progressive aspect	phasal aspect operator 'progressive'	is walking
comparative/ superlative	comparative' and 'superlative' operators	faster, fastest

referred to as Derivational. Since they change the class of the Word they combine with, Derivational Affixes will be categorized according to the type of Word they create (i.e. -er will be represented as a Nominal Affix, or Naff). These Affixes do not represent any representational or interpersonal information, and will be analysed as dummy elements (see Section 5.7.7).

Confining ourselves for the moment to Grammatical Affixes, we find that English has only a small number of them (Table 5.9).

Some examples of how these Affixes are represented at the Morphosyntactic Level are given in (143). In (143a), the Verbal Word *rained* consists of a Verbal Stem *rain* and the Affix 'past', triggered by the past tense operator; since this Affix is an allomorph, whose final form is determined only at the Phonological Level, it is here represented as the placeholder 'past'. In (143b), the present tense operator is expressed as a placeholder attached to the auxiliary *have* (where it combines with the agreement marker 'sg', copied from the Subject), while the perfect aspect operator triggers the placeholder 'past-part', expressed on the main verb. Similarly, in (143c), the plural Affix, triggered by the plurality operator 'm', is attached to the Nominal Stem *dog*, while in (143d) the comparative Affix -er combines with the Adjectival Stem *big*.

(143)   a. It *rained*.

RL: (**past** ep_1: (e_1: (f_1: $rain_V$)))

ML: (Vp_1: (Vw_1: [(Vs_1: rain) (Aff_1: **past**)] ^{Vw}) ^{Vp})

b. The train *has arrived*.

RL: (**pres** ep_1: (**perf** e_1: [(f_1: $arrive_V$) (x_1: (f_2: $train_N$))$_U$] ^{e}) ^{ep})

ML: (Vp_1: [($^{fin}Vw_1$: [(Vs_1: have) (Aff_1: **pres.sg**)] ^{Vw}) ($^{nonf}Vw_2$: [(Vs_2: arrive) (Aff_1: **past-part**)] ^{Vw})] ^{Vp})

c. Thomas loves *dogs*

RL: (**m** x_1: (f_1: dog_N))

ML: (Np_1: (Nw_1: [(Ns_1: dog) (Aff_1: **pl**)] ^{Nw}) ^{Np})

d. a *bigger* house

RL: (**comp** f_1: big_A)

ML: (Ap_1: (Aw_1: [(As_1: big) (Aff_1: **er**)] ^{Aw}) ^{Ap})

Since Grammatical Affixes express non-core units (functions and operators), they are the first elements within the Word to be assigned a position. Since English Words can contain only one Grammatical Affix, and since all English Affixes follow the Stem, the ordering principles for non-core units are very simple: Grammatical Affixes are always placed in Word-final position. This is illustrated for example (143a) in (144):

(144) P^I P^F

$^{\pi e}$past

The ordering of Grammatical Affixes in other languages

English Words, as we have seen, can contain at most one Grammatical Affix. There are also languages where Words can contain a combination of two or more Affixes. In those cases, the ordering principles governing the placement of these Affixes are the same as those in Phrases and Clauses: Affixes expressing the operators at the highest layer are placed first, starting with those at the Interpersonal Level, while we end with Affixes expressing the lowest-layer operators at the Representational Level. This is illustrated in example (145) for Tsafiki (Dickinson: 2002: 103; see also Hengeveld and Mackenzie 2008: 405):

(145) Manuel   ano   fi-nu-ti-e
       Manuel   food   eat-PERC-REP-DECL
       'It is said Manuel must have eaten.'

(continued)

In this example the Suffix -e expresses the Declarative Illocution, the Suffix -ti a Reportative operator (translated as *it is said*) and the Suffix -nu a Perception operator (translated as *must have*). Since the element -e expresses information belonging to the Illocution, it is placed first, in P^F. The Suffix -ti, corresponding to the Communicated Content operator Reportative, is placed next (in P^{F-1}), followed by the Suffix -nu, triggered by the State-of-Affairs operator Perception (in P^{F-2}):

(146) $(Vw_1: (Vs_1: fi) (Aff_1: \textbf{nu}) (Aff_2: \textbf{ti}) (Aff_3: \textbf{e})^{Vw})$

$\qquad P^{F-3} \quad P^{F-2} \quad P^{F-1} \quad P^F$

$\qquad fi \qquad {}^{\pi e}nu \quad {}^{\pi C}ti \quad {}^{\pi F}e$

5.7.5. Alignment

Alignment at the Word layer is relevant in those cases where a core unit (the argument of a verbal predicate at the Representational Level) is expressed as part of the Verbal Word corresponding to the verbal predicate, a process known as **incorporation**. In English, incorporation is highly constrained: there is no productive process to form such Verbal Words as *to birdwatch*, *to celloplay*, *to partygo*, or *to trainspot* (but see Feist 2013). Interestingly, however, incorporation can take place when it goes hand in hand with a process of syntactic derivation (Section 5.7.2); thus the nominalized forms *birdwatcher*, *cello player*, *partygoer*, and *trainspotting* are all perfectly acceptable. Linguists, however, have been struggling with the question of how such forms are created. Since the form *to birdwatch*, *to celloplay*, *to partygo*, or *to trainspot* do not exist, the nominalizations cannot be derived through syntactic derivation (cf. *to write—writer, to create—creator*, but not *birdwatch—birdwatcher*). Nor is it likely that these expressions are formed through a process of compounding. In that case *partygoer* would have to be analysed as a combination of *party* and *goer*; given that *goer*, although acceptable, is a very infrequent word (far less common than the nominalization *partygoer*), such an analysis is not very attractive.

FDG, however, offers an alternative way of deriving such expressions, which avoids this dilemma. Remember that in syntactic derivation a non-nominal (e.g. verbal) predicate functions as the head of an Individual. Since heads of Individuals are usually expressed as the head of a Noun Phrase, a clash occurs between the type of predicate at the Representational Level (verbal) and the type of Word at the Morphosyntactic Level (nominal). As we have seen, this clash is resolved by a process of coercion, which prepares the verbal predicate for its syntactic role by adding the Nominal Affix -er. The complete morphosyntactic representation of *diver* is given (147):

(147) a diver

RL: $(1x_1: [(f_1: dive_V) (x_1)_A]^x)$

ML: $(Np_1: [(Gw_1: a) (Nw_1: (Ns_1: [(Vs_1: dive) (Naff_1: er)]^{Ns})^{Nw})]^{Np})$

A similar process takes place in the case of an expression like *trainspotter*, except that now the Individual is headed by a configurational head consisting of a two-place verbal predicate (*spot*) and its two arguments (an Actor and an Undergoer):

(148) a trainspotter

RL: $(1x_1: [(f_1: spot_V) (x_1)_A (x_2: (f_2: train))_U]^x)$

ML: $(Np_1: [(Gw_1: a) (Nw_1: [(Ns_1: train) (Ns_2: [(Vs_2: spot) (Naff_1: er)]^{Ns})]^{Nw})]^{Np})$

The derivation process illustrated here is called **synthetic compounding**, a process which, like syntactic derivation, is assumed to take place in the grammar rather than in the lexicon. More precisely, the process of synthetic compounding takes place at the interface between the Representational Level and the Morphosyntactic Level, as the verbal lexeme *spot* is adapted to its morphosyntactic function as head of a Noun Phrase by the addition of the element -er. The Actor argument is once again co-referential with the expression as whole; as such it can no longer be expressed separately. The Undergoer element, *train*, is incorporated into the Nominal Word, where it appears as a Nominal Stem.

Which elements can be incorporated is, to some extent, semantically determined. Since in the case of -er nominalizations the resulting lexeme designates the same Individual as the Actor argument in the predication heading the nominalization, the Actor cannot be incorporated. Neither is it possible to incorporate the Recipient argument, if present: a State-of-Affairs like *He lends money to friends* cannot be nominalized as a *friend lender* (whereas a *money lender* is fine). Location arguments (location, direction) can, however, be incorporated (*partygoer, city dweller*).

> Think of some more examples of synthetic compounding and try and find out which further arguments (and modifiers) can be incorporated.

5.7.6. The ordering of core units

Since English allows only one argument to be incorporated, the ordering of core elements within the Word is quite simple. Consider the following example:

(149)   trainspotters

(Np$_1$: [(Nw$_1$: [(Ns$_1$: train) (Ns$_2$: [(Vs$_2$: spot) (Naff$_1$: er)] ^{Ns}) (Gaff$_1$: pl)] ^{Nw})] ^{Np})

P^I P^F

[P^I P^F]

^{U}train   spotter $^{\sigma x}$pl

As the only element corresponding to a non-core unit in this Word, the plural Affix is the first element to be assigned a position (P^F), after which the compound *trainspotter* is placed in P^I. Within this compound, the element *spotter*, formed on the basis of the predicate *spot*, is first placed in position (going to P^F), after which the Undergoer argument *train* is placed in P^I.

> ### Alignment of elements within Words in other languages
>
> Whereas in English incorporation of arguments is restricted to cases of synthetic compounding (like *trainspotter/trainspotting* or *partygoer*), in other languages (so-called incorporating languages) incorporation of arguments and modifiers is a common process. Incorporating languages differ, however, in the kind of arguments and modifiers that can undergo this process. Moreover, it once again turns out that the factors triggering this process may be interpersonal, representational, or morphosyntactic.
>
>   Let us first consider Nivkh, a language that allows the incorporation of Undergoers as well as various kinds of Locations (Source, Recipient, Direction). Incorporation is, however, only allowed if the incorporated element has the same information value as the verb. Compare, for instance, examples (150a) and (150b) (see Savel'eva 1966: 125, cited in Mattisen 2003: 107; see also Hengeveld and Mackenzie 2008: 406):

(150) a. T'a   ku-ñivɣ-əz-ja.
PROH DEM-person.call-IMP.sg
'Don't call that person.'

   b. Ku-ñivx   t'a   j-əz-ja.
DEM-person PROH 3.sg.U-call-IMP
'That person, don't call him/her.'

In (150a), the Undergoer *ku-ñivx* 'that person' and the verb *əz* 'call' are both assigned Focus function; as a result, the Undergoer is incorporated. In (150b), the verb still has Focus function, but the Undergoer is now the Topic; consequently, the Undergoer cannot be incorporated.

In other languages, however, it is representational (semantic) factors that determine whether or not an element can be incorporated. In Southern Tiwa, for instance, incorporation of inanimate (intransitive) Subjects is obligatory (e.g. *k'uru* 'dipper' in example (151)), while incorporation of animate Subjects (e.g. *musa* 'cat' in example (152)) is not allowed (examples from Allen et al. 1984: 293–301):

(151) a. I-k'uru-k'euwe-m
B-dipper-old-PRES
'The dipper is old.'

   b. *K'uru i-k'euwe-m
(Allen et al. 1984: 299; B = gender class 3 + singular marker)

(152) a. Musan i-k'euwe-m.
cats   B-old-PRES
'The cats are old.'

   b. *I-musa-k'euwe-m.
(Allen et al. 1984: 300; B = gender class 1 + plural marker)

5.7.7. Dummy elements

As pointed out above, English has a separate set of Derivational Affixes consisting of bound Morphemes introduced during the process of syntactic derivation. Consider the following examples (see also Section 5.7.2):

(153)   a diver

RL: $(1x_1: [(f_1: dive_V) (x_1)_A]^x)$

ML: $(Np_1: [(Gw_1: a) (Nw_1: (Ns_1: [(Vs_1: dive) \textbf{(Naff}_1\textbf{: er)}]^{Ns})^{Nw})]^{Np})$

(154)   They have *legalized* soft drugs

RL: $(past\ ep_1: (perf\ e_1: [(f_1: legal_A) (x_1)_{Ag} (x_2)_U]^e)^{ep})$

ML: $(Cl_1: [(Np_1: (Nw_1: they))_{Subj} (Vp_1: [(^fVw_1: have) (^{nonf}Vw_2: [(Vs_1:$
$[(As_1: legal) \textbf{(Vaff}_1\textbf{: ize)}]^{Vs}) (Gaff: past)]^{Vw})]^{Vp}) (Np_2: (Nw_2: soft$
$drugs))_{Obj}]^{Cl})$

In these examples a Derivational Affix (*-er*, *-ize*) is added to a Word to prepare the verbal lexeme *dive* and the adjectival lexeme *legal* for use in a syntactic slot for which they were not designed. These Affixes do not represent lexical information; nor do they correspond to any operators or function at the Interpersonal or Representational Levels. Instead they function as dummy elements, allowing lexemes to be used in a non-prototypical manner. Like all dummy elements, they will be the last elements to be assigned a position:

(155)   a diver

P^I P^{I+1}

$[P^I$ $P^{I+1}]$

a   div-   er

5.7.8. Compounding, derivation, and affixation: summary

We started this section by looking at four different kinds of complex words (illustrated in example (134)). In the course of this section it will have become clear that these kinds of complex words are the result of different word formation processes, and as such are provided with different analyses in FDG. To facilitate comparison, the four kinds of complex words and their FDG analysis are listed here once more.

1. Compounding

Semantically transparent compounds, like *filename, kitchen chair*, or *toothpaste* are formed productively at the Representational Level, where they are analysed as one complex Property consisting of two individual Properties, one of which functions as the head, the other as a modifier. At the Morphosyntactic Level the complex Property corresponds to a single Word, consisting of two Stems:

(156)   filename

    RL: $(f_1: (f_2: name_N: (f_3: file_N)\ ^f)\ ^f)$

    ML: $(Nw_1: [(Ns_1: file)\ (Ns_2: name)]\ ^{Nw})$

Compounds that are semantically opaque (e.g. *honeymoon* or *pineapple*), on the other hand, are listed in the lexicon, from where they are retrieved as single lexemes.

2. Lexical derivation

The productive formation of a new lexeme by the addition of a prefix or suffix with lexical content is taken care of in the lexicon. A derived lexeme like *undelete*, for instance, can be seen as the outcome of a lexeme formation rule taking a movement verb as its input and another verb, with the opposite meaning (designating the reverse movement), as its output:

(157)   Reverse movement verb formation:

    Input: $delete_V$

    Output: $[un\text{-}delete]_V$

    Meaning: the action designated by the output verb is the reverse of the action designated by the input verb

Once again, non-transparent formations (like *unfrock* 'to remove someone from their position as a priest') will simply be stored as separate lexemes; the same may be assumed for certain frequently used derivations (*unhappy*, *unkind*).

3. Syntactic derivation

The productive derivation of new lexemes of another word class through the addition of a suffix without lexical content is regarded as taking place in the grammar. During this formation process a lexeme of a particular class is placed in a slot usually reserved for lexemes of another class. Through a process of coercion, the lexeme is prepared for its non-prototypical morphosyntactic role. An example was given in (137), here repeated as (158), where the adjective *ferocious* is used to modify a verbal Property (rather than a nominal Property). Note that the result is a mismatch between a lexeme at the Representational Level and the corresponding Word at the Morphosyntactic Level:

(158)   barked *ferociously*

    RL: $(f_1: bark_V: (\mathbf{f_2: ferocious_A})\ ^f)$

    ML: $(Vp_1: (Vw_1: barked))\ (Advp_1: (\mathbf{Advw_1: [(As_1: ferocious)\ (Ad\text{-}vaff_1: ly)]}\ ^{Advw})\ ^{Advp})$

4. Affixation

Finally, complex words may consist of a lexeme and a Grammatical Affix. In that case, the result is not a new lexeme, but simply a form of an existing lexeme. The Affixes in question are triggered by representational operators such as tense, aspect, or plural. An example is given in (159) (cf. (143c)):

(159)   dogs

RL: $(\mathbf{m}\ x_1: (f_1: dog_N))$

ML: $(Np_1: (Nw_1: [(Ns_1: dog)\ (Aff_1: \mathbf{pl})]^{\ Nw})^{\ Np})$

5.8. Summary

- In this chapter we have looked at how information from the Interpersonal and Representational Levels is encoded morphosyntactically, that is, in the form and order of units at the Morphosyntactic Level.
- As at the higher levels of representation, morphosyntactic units (or layers) are hierarchically organized, from Linguistic Expressions (Le), to Clauses (Cl), Phrases (Xp), and Words (Xw), all the way down to Stems (Xs) and Affixes (Xaff) (Section 5.2).
- It was demonstrated that there are a number of general principles (iconicity, domain integrity, functional stability) that maximize the parallelism between the levels by establishing a direct relation between function (Formulation) and form (Encoding) (Section 5.1). In addition, however, there were shown to be cases where the relation between Formulation and Encoding is not straightforward. Such mismatches, it was argued, occur in all languages, leading to a reduction in the degree of transparency (Section 5.3).
- The rest of the chapter was devoted to a discussion of the various layers of the Morphosyntactic Level. Each layer was discussed in terms of its internal structure and the principles governing the ordering of units; where relevant, such matters as alignment, agreement and subordination were discussed (Sections 5.4–5.7)
- It was shown that many of the important morphosyntactic principles and distinctions apply to each of the layers, for example the general ordering principles, the difference between core elements and non-core elements, the difference between lexical and grammatical elements, and the presence of dummy elements.

• In addition, attention was paid to a number of specific aspects of English belonging to one particular layer only, such as raising (at the layer of the Clause; Section 5.5.7.4), the distinction between relative and content Clauses (at the layer of the Phrase; Section 5.6.6), and word formation, derivation, and inflection (at the layer of the Word; Section 5.7.8).

Exercises

1. As mentioned in Section 5.1, there are three general principles that help to establish a direct relationship between the morphosyntactic units and units at the higher two levels: iconicity, domain integrity, and functional stability. There are, however, also many cases where one of these principles is violated.

a. For each of the following examples decide which principle is/which principles are violated
b. Try and think of a reason (or reasons) for violating these principles.

(i)   The conclusion is inescapable that in Bernicia a very small and largely aristocratic Anglian element ruled over a predominantly British population (ICE-GB, written, students' essays)
(ii)   My dogs were frantic, and *so was I* (BYU-BNC, miscellaneous)
(iii) ... they call anything a burger that you slap into a roll (ICE-GB, spoken, direct conversation)
(iv)   Before she died, she wrote another book—The Tenant of Wildfell Hall—about a woman who left her cruel husband. (BNY-BNC, written, fiction)

2.* In FDG, a fully transparent language is a language where there is a one-to-one relationship between units at all the different levels of representation (see Section 5.3, example (15)). Every language, however, has a certain degree of non-transparency, brought about by the presence of one-to-many and many-to-one relationships between units at the different levels (e.g. examples (17)–(19)).

a. Provide a morphosyntactic analysis of the sentence in (i)
b. Identify all non-transparent elements in this sentence and describe the source of their non-transparency.

(i)   His great-aunt has finally popped her clogs.   (to pop one's clogs = to die)

3. Provide a morphosyntactic representation of the following sentences, indicating all Linguistic Expressions, Clauses, Phrases, and Words, as well as any syntactic functions:

  (i)   Peter told me that he would probably be late for class.
  (ii) Unfortunately, it hasn't rained for three months.
  (iii) The parents of my boyfriend don't really like me.
  (iv) Presumably, the burglar had tripped over some toys.

4.* Provide representations of the following sentences at the Interpersonal, Representational, and Morphosyntactic Levels:

  (i)   Who has eaten all the chocolates?
  (ii) He sort of begged me for forgiveness.
  (iii) Thank you all for coming.
  (iv) Jenny is my best friend.

5. For each of the following Clauses, decide the order in which the Clausal elements are placed and to which positions they go (e.g. example (61)).

  (i)   Luckily, we may get another chance tomorrow.
  (ii) Last night we watched a film together.
  (iii) Allegedly, his brother illegally imported exotic birds from Australia.

6. For each of the following Phrases (as well as the Phrases or Clauses within these Phrases), decide the order in which each of the elements are placed and to which position they go (e.g. example (105)).

  (i)   an amazingly tasty soup
  (ii) an old friend from university
  (iii) the first film I ever saw
  (iv) a long hot summer
  (v)   on a sort of hill

7. Using the ordering rules discussed in this chapter, explain why the following sentences are not acceptable.

  (i)   Probably, yesterday she met him.
  (ii) We will meet next year often.
  (iii) He bought yesterday a new car.
  (iv) Often have I seen him.

8. Identify the dummy elements in the following sentences and indicate which obligatory position they fill.

(i)   Did Jane sneeze?
(ii) It is six o'clock.
(iii) There are many foxes in London.
(iv) Nick and Hugh were the lucky ones.

9.**

a. Indicate for each of the italicized elements in the following sentences, whether they involve lexical derivation (by means of a lexical formation rule) or syntactic derivation (coercion):

(i)   The *truck driver*, unhurt, *fanned* himself with his flat cap. (COCA, written, fiction)
(ii) *Suddenly* the *idiocy* of these thoughts struck her. (BYU-BNC, written, fiction prose)
(iii) She had *toyed* with the idea of doing volunteer work with the *homeless*, but had done nothing about it. (BYU-BNC, written, fiction prose)

b. How would you analyse the Words *youngish* and *nothingy* in the following sentences? (See also Chapter 3, Section 3.8.4.)

(i)   He was a very kind, *youngish*, amiable scholar of great distinction, and a power in the university. (BYU-BNC, written, biography)
(ii) in a lot of other contact-based dance work you can actually cheat and not – give your weight fully or uhm take weight fully and it becomes a bit – sort of *nothingy* (ICE-GB, spoken, direct conversation)

c. Provide a morphological representation of the compound *truck driver* and indicate in which order the component elements are placed and to which positions they go.

10* According to the analysis in Section 5.7.5, both *trainspotter* and *trainspotting* would be analysed by means of synthetic compounding. Which feature at the Representational Level triggers the different forms?

11.* As pointed out in Section 5.7.5, noun incorporation in English is restricted but not impossible (Feist 2013). Thus, although we do not have such forms as *to celloplay* or *to birdwatch*, we do find such forms as *to babysit* and *to fundraise*. Which word formation process(es) would you say are involved in the creation of these forms?

12.** Consider the sentence in (i):

(i)   My father met Douglas, my new boyfriend, for the first time last week.

a. How would you analyse the element *my new boyfriend* at the Interpersonal Level?
b. How does this affect the order in which the elements are placed at the layer of the Clause?
c. Provide a representation of (i) indicating which clausal position each element takes and in which order they are placed.

Suggestions for further reading

Word order phenomena are discussed by Hannay and Martínez-Caro (2008), who deal with clause-final focus constructions in English and Spanish, and by Hengeveld (2013), who provides an update on the FDG approach to clausal constituent order. Specific morphosyntactic topics are dealt with in García Velasco (2013b), which provides an account of raising in FDG, and Keizer (2009b), which offers an FDG analysis of reported speech. Word formation processes are dealt with in García Velasco (2009), which discusses the process of conversion in an FDG framework, as well as in García Velasco and Keizer (2014), which deals with the place of derivational morphology in the FDG model. Finally, morphosyntactic alternations are discussed by Mackenzie (2011, 2012), who develops a dialogic FDG to deal with situations with two or more interlocutors.

6

The Phonological Level

6.1. Introduction	252	6.6. Phonological Words	269
6.2. The organization of the Phonological Level	255	6.7. Feet and Syllables	273
		6.8. Summary	279
6.3. Utterances	257	Exercises	280
6.4. Intonational Phrases	259	Suggestions for further reading	282
6.5. Phonological Phrases	263		

This chapter deals with the last of the four levels of representations that make up the Grammatical Component, the Phonological Level. Like the representations at the Morphological Level, Phonological Level representations form the output of the operation of Encoding (in this case phonological Encoding): it receives its input from the higher three levels and translates this input into the appropriate phonological form. The representations thus created subsequently feed into the Articulator, which is situated outside the Grammatical Component. Like the other levels, the Phonological Level is hierarchically organized into different layers; these will be discussed in a top-down order, from the highest layer (the Utterance, Section 6.3) to the lowest (the Syllable, Section 6.7). Once again, however, we will start with a short introduction and a section on the overall organization of the Phonological Level (Sections 6.1 and 6.2). Throughout the chapter, reference will be made to units of higher levels to indicate how the pragmatic, semantic, morphosyntactic, and phonological properties of an utterance interact. Finally, it needs to be mentioned that the variety of English used for analysis in this chapter is RP. This is merely a matter of convenience;

as a typological model, FDG applies equally well to all other varieties of English, as well as to all other languages.

6.1. Introduction

The Phonological Level receives its input from the three higher levels; it is here that the representations from the Interpersonal, Representational, and Morphosyntactic Levels are translated into phonological representations. In turn, the Phonological Level of representation feeds into the operation of Articulation, which converts these representations into acoustic, written, or signed output. Like the Morphological Level, the task of the Phonological Level is to encode information from the operation of (interpersonal and representational) Formulation. In addition, however, many phonological processes are sensitive to the morphosyntactic features of an expression; in those cases, the Phonological Level also receives input from the Morphosyntactic Level. Let us begin by considering these different kinds of input in some more detail.

Together with the Interpersonal Level, the Phonological Level is obligatory in the production of a linguistic expression: whereas it is possible for expressions to lack semantic (representational) content or morphosyntactic structure, the communicative function of language requires each utterance (i) to signal, in some form or other, the Speaker's intention in using that expression, and (ii) to have a phonological form, irrespective of how this form is eventually communicated (by speaking, writing, or signing). Thus, whereas in the majority of cases all four levels of representation are involved in the production of an utterance, as in example (1), there are cases where all that is needed is the relevant interpersonal and phonological information. An example is given in (2), where the production of the vocative *hey* only requires interpersonal information (specification of the Illocution, in this case the interjection itself, and the presence of the two speech participants) and phonological information. (For the moment, the phonological representations are simply given in phonemic form, without internal structure.)

(1)   The train arrived.
   IL: $(A_1: [(F_1: \text{DECL}) (P_1)_S (P_2)_A (C_1: [(T_1) (R_1)]^C)]^A)$
   RL: $(p_1: (\text{pres } ep_1: (e_1: [(f_1: \text{arrive}_V) (x_1: (f_2: \text{train}_N))_U]^e)^{ep})^P)$
   ML: $(Cl_1: [(Np_1: [(Gw_1: \text{the}) (Nw_1: \text{train})]^{Np})_{Subj} (Vp_1: (Vw_1: \text{arrived}))]^{Cl})$
   PL: / ðə'treɪnə'raɪvd /

(2) Hey!

    IL: $(A_1: [(F_1: \text{hey}) (P_1)_S (P_2)_A]^A)$

    PL: / heɪ /

Representations at the Phonological Level can also be sensitive to information from the Representational Level. This is, for instance, the case in morphosyntactically ambiguous expressions whose ambiguity can only be resolved through intonation. An example is given in (3):

(3) Right now, they are looking for two suspects, *a man and a woman with blond hair* driving a black SUV. (Internet)

The italicized phrase in this example allows for two readings: one in which both the man and the woman have blond hair and one in which it is only the woman who is blond. These two readings are distinguished at the Representational Level, where the prepositional phrase *with blond hair* either modifies both parts of the coordination (*a man with blond hair and a woman with blond hair*) or only the second part (*a woman with blond hair*). At the Morphosyntactic Level, however, these two readings lead to the same representation. It is only at the Phonological Level that the use of different intonation patterns can help to indicate which of the two readings is the intended one (see Section 6.5 for more details).

    The phonological form of elements may also be triggered by morphosyntactic information, for instance in those cases where suppletive forms are used or where a placeholder is present at the Morphosyntactic Level. As pointed out in Section 5.2, many elements (Words) receive their final phonemic form at the Morphosyntactic Level (the first stage of Encoding). An exception, however, is made for those elements whose form is not entirely predictable at this stage of the grammar, either because they are irregular (realized by means of suppletive forms), or because their realization depends on their phonological environment (in the case of allomorphs); in those cases, the final form is determined only at the Phonological Level. Consider the sentence in (4):

(4) Shakespeare wrote many sonnets.

    IL: $(A_1: - (C_1: [(T_1) (R_1: \text{Shakespeare}) (R_2)]) - {}^C)$

    RL: $(p_1: (\text{past } ep_1: (e_1: [(f_1: \text{write}_V) (x_1)_A (\text{many } x_2: (f_2: \text{sonnet}_N))_U]^e)^{ep})^P)$

    ML: $(Cl_1: [(Np_1: (Nw_1: / \,\text{'ʃeɪkspɪə} / \,))_{Subj} (Vp_1: (Vw_1: \text{write-past}))$
              $(Np_1: [(Gw_1: / \,\text{'meni} / \,) (Nw_1: / \,\text{'sɒnɪt} / \text{-pl})]^{Np})_{Obj}]^{Cl})$

    PL: / 'ʃeɪkspɪə'rəʊt'menɪ'sɒnɪts /

Here we see that at the Morphosyntactic Level only the proper name *Shakespeare* (introduced at the Interpersonal Level), the quantifier *many* (expressing an operator at the Representational Level) and the Nominal Word *sonnet* are given in their phonological form. The phonological form of the remaining elements, the past tense of *write* and the plural ending of *sonnet*, is determined at the Phonological Level: in the former case because we are dealing with a suppletive form (*wrote*) and in the latter because the (regular) plural ending has different allomorphs (/ s /, / z / and / ɪz /). The correct phonological form of these elements is thus triggered by information from the Morphosyntactic Level: the presence of the 'past' marker on the verb *write* and the plural placeholder 'pl' following the noun *sonnet*.

Finally, the actual phonetic form of an element may depend on the occurrence of a number of a-functional phonological processes that are not triggered by information from any of the higher levels. Such processes, including assimilation, elision, and linking, are optional and unpredictable (depending on the context, speed of delivery, idiolect of the Speaker). As such, these processes are not represented within the Grammatical Component, but are seen as taking place in the Output Component (OC), during the Operation of Articulation. Some examples are given in (5a), where the final sound of the numeral *ten* is optionally assimilated, and in (5b), where elision of the final sound of *ask* is possible but not required:

(5)   a.   ten pounds

    ML: $(Np_1: [(Gw_1: ten) (Nw_1: paʊnd\text{-}pl)]^{Np})$

    PL: / tenpaʊndz /

    OC: [tenpaʊndz] or [tempaʊndz]

    b.   asked

    ML: $(Vw_1: ɑːsk\text{-}past))$

    PL: / ɑːskt /

    OC: [ɑːskt] or [ɑːst]

From the preceding it will be clear that the task of Encoding is shared between the Morphosyntactic Level and the Phonological Level. In some cases, Encoding takes place at only one of these levels; in that case the two levels supplement each other. The difference between Subject and Object function, for instance, is coded at the Morphosyntactic Level only, through a combination of form (in the case of pronouns) and placement vis-à-vis the verb. The pragmatic functions Focus and Contrast, on the other hand, are often coded by phonological (prosodic) means only. The same is true for irony; in (6), for instance, the difference between a literal and a figurative (ironic) use of the sentence *That's just great* can be coded by using different intonation patterns (represented roughly by the use of small capitals to indicate prosodic prominence):

(6)   A: Peter will come to the meeting tonight.
B_1: That's just GREAT.
B_2: That's JUST great.

In other cases, however, both levels contribute to the coding of an utterance. Examples are canonical Interrogatives and cleft sentences, where interpersonal information (Illocution, pragmatic function) is coded by means of a combination of morphosyntactic properties (word order) and phonological properties (prosodic features).

Finally, let us consider the relation between the Phonological Level and the Output Component. Like all representations in the Grammatical Component, representations at the Phonological Level are abstract and digital in nature, based on oppositions imposed by the linguist, and as such, by definition, a simplification of reality. Once these abstract representations have been fed into the Output Component, the Articulator will 'translate' this digital information into (concrete, measurable) analogue form, exhibiting highly unpredictable properties resulting from individual differences between language users (such as differences in pitch and loudness in the case of acoustic output) and a-functional contextual influences (such as emotional states or physical conditions like a cold, nervousness, or exhaustion) (Hengeveld and Mackenzie 2008: 8, 421). The transition from Phonological Level to Output Component thus marks the conversion from phonological form into phonetic form.

After this very general characterization of the Phonological Level, the next section will deal with the internal organization of this level, introducing the various phonological layers, as well as the primitives relevant to each of these layers. Subsequently, each layer will be discussed in more detail.

6.2. The organization of the Phonological Level

At the Phonological Level, six basic units are distinguished, which are hierarchically organized as follows (note that, in accordance with convention, variables at this level are represented in small capitals):

(7) $(\pi\ U_1$: [$]^{U)}$ Utterance

$(\pi\ IP_{1-n}$: [$]^{IP)}$ Intonational Phrase

$(\pi\ PP_{1-n}$: [$]^{PP)}$ Phonological Phrase

$(\pi\ PW_{1-n}$: [$]^{PW)}$ Phonological Word

$(\pi\ F_{1-n}$: [$]^{F)}$ Foot

$(\pi\ S_{1-n}$: [...] $^{S)}$ Syllable

The highest phonological layer is that of the Utterance (U_1), which is made up of one or more Intonational Phrases (IP_1), which in turn consist of one or more Phonological Phrases (PP_1). Each Phonological Phrase contains one or more Phonological Words (PW_1), which consist of one or more Feet (F_1), which contain one or more Syllables (S_1). Each of these units has its own phonological properties: Utterances, for instance, are separated from each other by clearly perceptible pauses, while Intonational Phrases are characterized by the presence of a pitch change and Feet by the presence of a stressed Syllable.

When we compare the phonological layers to the units distinguished at the other three levels certain default relations can be recognized. Thus the higher phonological layers typically correspond with interpersonal units: Utterances often correlate with Moves, Intonational Phrases with Discourse Acts, and Phonological Phrases with Referential or Ascriptive Subacts. Phonological Words, on the other hand, often correspond to (lexical or grammatical) Words at the Morphosyntactic Level. These correspondences are, however, only tendencies, and exceptions can easily be found. In (8), for instance, the contracted form *won't* is analysed at the Morphosyntactic Level as two separate Words; at the Phonological Level, however, these two Words correspond to a single Phonological Word:

(8)   Jack won't come.
ML: $(^fVw_1$: will) $(Gw_1$: not)
PL: $(PW_1$: / wəʊnt /)

The fact that there is not always a one-to-one relationship between phonological units and units at the higher levels shows the need for distinguishing these phonological units (Nespor and Vogel 1986: 2; see also Hengeveld and Mackenzie 2008: 428).

Try to think of more examples of mismatches between phonological units and units at the higher levels of representation.

Like the other levels, the Phonological Level has its own set of primitives. First of all, there are the phonological templates (prosodic patterns) that apply at each phonological layer, specifying the possible configurations of phonological units available in a specific language. In addition to these suprasegmental sequences, there is a set of segmental sequences for the expression of configurations of Morphemes (such as / wəʊnt / for *will + not*, or / rəʊt / for 'write-past') or placeholders (such as / s /, / z / or / ɪz / for 'pres-3sg'). Together these segmental sequences can be said to make up the 'grammatical lexicon' that Speakers have at their disposal for the Phonological encoding of expressions. Finally, the Phonological Level makes use of a small number of operators, such as 'fall', 'rise', or 'stress', which have their effect in the Output Component (Hengeveld and Mackenzie 2008: 422). Each of these primitives will be discussed in more detail in the remaining sections of this chapter.

6.3. Utterances

Utterances are the largest stretches of speech at the Phonological Level. They can typically be recognized by the fact that they are separated from other Utterances by a substantial pause, which is always intentional (and will not be misinterpreted as a hesitation). In spoken language, Utterances often correspond to Moves at the Interpersonal Level. This, however, only really works for shorter Moves—when Moves are longer, distinguishing Utterances on phonological grounds will become more difficult.

By way of illustration, consider the following short dialogue, consisting of a number of short turns:

(9) A: Did you have a good weekend?
   B: Yes, we went to the Salzkammergut.
   A: I've never been there. Is it beautiful?

In FDG each of the three turns in (9) can be analysed as consisting of one Utterance (although other analyses are certainly possible). Thus, on a neutral reading, A's opening Move constitutes a single prosodic unit, preceded and followed by a pause (introduced by Speaker A; overlap with B's answer is of course possible). B's answer can also easily be expressed as one Utterance, as the two parts (the single element *yes* and the clause *we went to the Salzkammergut*) are typically not separated by a (substantial) pause. The same is true for A's reaction: despite the fact that A's contribution clearly consists of two Discourse Acts (a declarative and an interrogative), these two Discourse Acts can be regarded as one Move, expressed by means of a single phonological unit, without internal pauses.

Generally speaking, the global intonation pattern of a sequence is determined by the Illocution of a Discourse Act: although A's second turn in (9) forms one prosodic unit, we can still recognize two distinct intonation patterns: one falling (*I've never been there*) and the other rising (*Is it beautiful?*). This means that this particular Utterance consists of two Intonational Phrases, each with its own intonational pattern (but see also Section 6.4). In addition, however, Utterances can be specified (optionally) by the intonational operators 'fall' (f) and 'rise' (r), which have the effect of strengthening the falling or rising intonation of the Utterance as a whole. Consider in this respect the two short passages in (10) and (11):

(10)   a.   ... *They lived happily for many years.* But then things started to go wrong ...

   b. $(U_1:$ (f $IP_1:$ / ðeɪˈlɪvdˈhæpəlifəˈmeniˈjɪəz / ^{IP}) ^{U})

(11)   a.   ... the next day they got married. *And they lived happily ever after.*

   b.   (f $U_1:$ (f $IP_1:$ / ðeɪˈlɪvdˈhæpəliˈevəˈɑːftə / ^{IP}) ^{U})

Let us assume that the two sentences in (10a) occur in the middle of a story (that is, in the middle of a Move). In all likelihood, both sentences would be pronounced with the slightly falling intonation characteristic of declarative sentences. This intonation pattern would in that case be triggered by the presence of a fall operator on the Intonational Phrase, as represented in (10b). Now think of the two sentences in example (11) as forming the end of a story (or Move). Once again both sentences will be pronounced with the falling tone associated with declaratives. The last sentence, however, is likely to be pronounced with a lower pitch (or larger pitch fall) on the final stressed Syllable, indicating finality (the end of the Move). This extra low pitch is triggered by the presence of an additional fall marker at the layer of the Utterance, as represented in (11b).

From the brief discussion above, it has become clear that Utterances consist of one or more Intonational Phrases and may be specified by an operator. They can therefore be represented by the following general schema:

(12) $(\pi\ U_1:\ [(\pi\ IP_1) \ldots (\pi\ IP_n)]\ ^U)$

6.4. Intonational Phrases

The second layer at the Phonological level is that of the Intonational Phrase (IP₁). Intonational Phrases can be recognized on the basis of internal and external properties. Internally, they are characterized by the fact that they contain a nucleus, that is, a pitch movement which is realized on one Syllable and which serves to characterize the Intonational Phrase as a whole. Externally, they are typically separated from other Intonational Phrases by a short pause (shorter than the pause between two Utterances) (Hengeveld and Mackenzie 2008: 432).

Whereas Utterances typically coincide with Moves at the Interpersonal Level, Intonational Phrases usually correspond to a Discourse Act. Example (13), for instance, consists of two Discourse Acts, which can plausibly be regarded as corresponding to two Intonational Phrases, with the Syllables in small capitals carrying the nuclei and the hyphen indicating a brief pause. Note that in the phonological representation given in (13), both Intonational Phrases contain the fall operator 'f', triggering the default intonation for Declarative Illocutions. In English the falling tone is usually expressed on the last stressed Syllable of the Intonational Phrase, in this case the second Syllable of *against* and the first Syllable of *Andrew*.

(13) Her father advised aGAINST this – and so did ANdrew. (BNY-BNC, written newspaper)

IL: (M₁: [(A₁: [(F₁: DECL) (P₁)S (P₂)A (C₁)] ᴬ) (A₂: [(F₂: DECL) (P₁)S (P₂)A (C₂)] ᴬ)] ᴹ)

PL: (U₁: [(f IP₁: / hə'faðərəd'vaɪzdə'genstðɪs / ᴵᴾ) (f IP₂: / ənd'səudɪd 'ændruː / ᴵᴾ)] ᵁ)

There are, however, also cases where this one-to-one relationship between Discourse Acts and Intonational Phrases is overridden. In rapid speech, for instance, the two Discourse Acts in (13) can be expressed as one Intonational Phrase; in that case, there will be no pause separating the two Discourse Acts and there will be only one Syllable with pitch movement (the first Syllable of *Andrew*). This leads to the phonological representation in (14), where two Discourse Acts correspond to one Intonational Phrase.

(14) Her father advised against this and so did ANdrew.

IL: (M₁: [(A₁: [(F₁: DECL) (P₁)S (P₂)A (C₁)] ᴬ) (A₂: [(F₂: DECL) (P₁)S (P₂)A (C₂)] ᴬ)] ᴹ)

PL: (U₁: (f IP₁: / hə'faðərəd'vaɪzdə'genstðɪsənd'səudɪd'ændruː / ᴵᴾ) ᵁ)

A similar mismatch may occur in example (9) above, repeated here for convenience:

(9)   A: Did you have a good weekend?
   B: Yes, we went to the Salzkammergut.
   A: I've never been there. Is it beautiful?

Here, too, it is possible for the two Discourse Acts in A's second turn to be expressed as one Intonational Phrase. In that case, the entire Utterance contains only one nucleus (expressed on the first Syllable of *beautiful*). Further evidence for such an analysis can be found in the fact that (in non-rhotic varieties of English) a final *r* in the spelling is not pronounced before a pause (*there* being pronounced as / ðeə /); if, however, words ending in *r* are immediately followed by a vowel, a linking-*r* may be introduced (*there is* being pronounced as / ðeərɪz /). Since it is possible to introduce such a linking-*r* between the *there* and *is* in (9) (as shown in (15)), it is clear that there is no need for a pause between the two Discourse Acts, which means that they can be assumed to form one Intonational Phrase.

(15)   (U₁: / ˈaɪvnevəˈbiːnðeərɪzɪtˈbjuːtɪfʊl / ᵁ)

The opposite is also possible: one Discourse Act can be expressed as two (or more) Intonational Phrases. An example is given in (16), where the element *however*, expressing the interpersonal operator 'contrast', is treated as a separate Intonational Phrase:

(16)   However, her father advised against this.
   IL: (contr A₁: [(F₁: DECL) (P₁)ₛ (P₂)ₐ (C₁)] ᴬ)
   PL: (U₁: [(f IP₁: / hauˈevə / ᴵᴾ) (f IP₂: / həˈfaðərədˈvaɪzdəˈgenstðɪs / ᴵᴾ)] ᵁ)

When the element *however* breaks up the Discourse Acts to which it belongs, as in example (17), the two parts of the Discourse Act preceding and following *however* can each be expressed by means of an Intonational Phrase. In that case, a single Discourse Act can correspond to three Intonational Phrases:

(17)   Her father, however, advised against this.
   IL: (contr A₁: [(F₁: DECL) (P₁)ₛ (P₂)ₐ (C₁)] ᴬ)
   PL: (U₁: [(f IP₁: / həˈfaðə / ᴵᴾ) (r IP₂: hauˈevə / ᴵᴾ) (f IP₃: ədˈvaɪzdə ˈgenstðɪs / ᴵᴾ)] ᵁ)

As we can see in examples (16) and (17), the element *however* can have either a falling or a rising intonation (represented by the IP operators 'f' anf 'r', respectively). There are, however, also Discourse Acts that are typically characterized by a rising intonation. *Yes–no* interrogatives are, of course, an obvious example: in (18), for instance, the Interrogative Illocution triggers the presence of a 'rise' operator on the Intonational Phrase, resulting in a rising pitch on the last stressed Syllable of the Intonational Phrase:

(18)   Have you ever seen The Third Man?
  IL: $(M_1: (A_1: [(F_1: \text{INTER}) (P_1)_S (P_2)_A (C_1)]^A)^M)$
  PL: $(U_1: [(r \text{ IP}_1: / \text{hævjʊ'evə'siːnðə'ðɜd'mæn} /^{IP})]^U)$

Note, however, that in English not all interrogatives have a rising intonation. *Wh*-interrogatives (or Content interrogatives), for instance, tend to be expressed with a falling intonation: since their status as interrogative is already marked morphosyntactically (by the presence of a *wh*-word), there is no need for a specific intonation pattern to distinguish them from declaratives.

Do all *wh*-interrogatives in English have a falling intonation? If not, how would you account for the exceptions?

Phonological encoding of content interrogatives in other languages

Whereas in English content interrogatives are coded morphosyntactically rather than phonologically, in other languages such interrogatives, too, are marked by a rising intonation. In Mandarin Chinese, for instance, where the questioned element in content interrogatives has the same form as the indefinite pronoun, different intonation patterns are needed to distinguish content interrogatives from declaratives (Haspelmath 1997: 171; Hengeveld and Mackenzie 2008: 435):

(19) Tā   bǎ   shénme   shū   diū   le.
          3.sg   ACC   what/something   book   throw   PFV
          'She threw away a certain book.' (**f** IP$_1$)
          'What books did she throw away? (**r** IP$_1$)

In English, it is not only *yes–no* interrogatives that are associated with a rising intonation; conditional clauses, like the *if*-clause in (20), may also be realized with a rising intonation. Note that since these clauses are analysed as dependent Discourse Acts (with the rhetorical function Condition, triggering the presence of the r-operator), the two Intonational Phrases in (19) neatly coincide with two Discourse Acts:

(20)   if you're tired just go to sleep on the couch (BYU-BNC, written, non-academic)

IL: $(M_1: [(A_1: [(F_1: DECL) (P_1)_S (P_2)_A (C_1)] ^A)_{Cond} (A_1: [(F_1: IMP) (P_1)_S (P_2)_A (C_1)] ^A)] ^M)$

PL: $(U_1: [(r IP_1: / 'ɪfjʊə'taɪəd / ^{IP}) (f IP_2: / 'dʒʌst'gəʊtʊ'sliːpɒnðə'kaʊtʃ / ^{IP})] ^U)$

The analyses proposed in this section can also be applied to question tags. It is well known that in English question tags can, broadly speaking, perform two functions. When uttered with a rising intonation, they are interrogative in nature: the Speaker wants to check the correctness of his/her statement and asks the Addressee for confirmation. When the tag is expressed with a falling intonation, however, the Speaker indicates that he/she expects the Addressee to agree with the preceding statement, the overall effect being one of reinforcement. Given the fact that question tags cannot be used independently, but at the same time have their own intonation pattern, it is plausible to analyse them as separate, dependent Discourse Acts, which either have the rhetorical function of Confirmation (triggering a rising intonation) or the rhetorical function of Reinforcement (triggering a falling intonation). The two analyses are given in (21a) and (21b), respectively. Note that in both cases, the question tag has an Interrogative Illocution, needed to trigger the correct morphosyntactic form (inversion of Subject and finite verb); thus, it is the combination of the Interrogative Illocution and the rhetorical function that yields the appropriate form.

(21)   a. That was rather good, wasn't it? (rising intonation)

IL: $(M_1: [(A_1: [(F_1: DECL) (P_1)_S (P_2)_A (C_1)] ^A) (A_2: [(F_2: INTER) (P_1)_S (P_2)_A (C_2)] ^A)_{Conf}] ^M)$

PL: $(U_1: [(f IP_1: / 'ðætwɒːzrɑːðə'gʊd / ^{IP}) (r IP_2: / 'wɒːzntɪt/ ^{IP})] ^U)$

b. That was rather good, wasn't it? (falling intonation)

IL: $(M_1: [(A_1: [(F_1: DECL) (P_1)_S (P_2)_A (C_1)] ^A) (A_2: [(F_2: INTER) (P_1)_S (P_2)_A (C_2)] ^A)_{Reinf}] ^M)$

PL: $(U_1: [(f IP_1: / 'ðætwɒːzrɑːðə'gʊd / ^{IP}) (f IP_2: / 'wɒːzntɪt/ ^{IP})] ^U)$

In this section we have seen how the distinction of separate Intonational Phrases can help us to account for the various global patterns of intonation found in English Utterances. In doing so, we have ignored, for the moment, many of the complexities involved in the realization of these Utterances. In order to tackle these complexities, we have to move to the next phonological layer, that of the Phonological Phrase.

6.5. Phonological Phrases

In a stress language like English, Phonological Phrases are characterized by the fact that they contain one Syllable that is more strongly stressed than any other stressed Syllables within that Phrase; this will be referred to as the nuclear Syllable. By way of illustration, consider once more the sentence in (3), repeated here as (22):

(22)   Shakespeare wrote many sonnets.
   IL: $(A_1: - (C_1: [(T_1) (R_1: Shakespeare) (R_2)_{Foc}]^C) - ^A)$
   PL: $(U_1: (f IP_1: [(PP_1: / \,'ʃeɪkspɪə /) (PP_2: / \,'rəʊt /) (PP_3: / \,'meni'sɒnɪts /)]^{IP})^U)$

In this example the Intonational Phrase IP_1 is analysed as containing three Phonological Phrases. The first two of these Phrases contain one stressed Syllable, which thus functions as the nuclear Syllable. The third Phonological Phrase contains two stressed Syllables, the second of which, the first Syllable of *sonnet*, is stressed more strongly than the first (the first Syllable of *many*); it is therefore the second stressed Syllable that functions as the nuclear Syllable. This is, in fact, a property of English: in the default case, it is the last stressed Syllable in a Phonological Phrase that functions as the nuclear Syllable.

   Similarly, since English is characterized by **End Focus**, it is typically the nuclear Syllable of the final Phonological Phrase within an Intonational Phrase that carries the tone (displays the pitch movement) characterizing the Intonational Phrase: thus the fall operator 'f' on the Intonational Phrase in example (22) is expressed on the nuclear Syllable of the third Phonological Phrase (the first Syllable of *sonnet*). Obviously, this default pattern can be overridden, for instance by the presence of the pragmatic function Contrast on the elements *Shakespeare, wrote* or *many* (see also below).

   Note finally that in the case of polysyllabic words, the position of (primary and secondary) stress is fixed: this information is carried over from the higher levels of representation (the Interpersonal Level in the case of the proper noun *Shakespeare*, the Representational level in the case of the lexeme *sonnet* and the Morphosyntactic Level in the case of Grammatical Morpheme *many*); in turn, these levels have received this information from the (grammatical) lexicon, where these primitives are stored together with their stress pattern.

   Just like Utterances and Intonational Phrases, Phonological Phrases typically coincide with a certain type of unit at the Interpersonal Level, in this case the (Referential or Ascriptive) Subact within the Communicated Content. This is indeed what we find in example (22), where each of the Phonological Phrases corresponds to a Subact: the first and third Phonological Phrase to Referential Subacts (R_1 and R_2, respectively), the second Phonological Phrase to an Ascriptive Subact (T_1). This is, however, not always the case. Thus, the sentence in (22) could also be realized as two Phonological Phrases, as represented in (23):

(23) Shakespeare wrote many sonnets.

(u$_1$: (f IP$_1$: [(PP$_1$: / ˈʃeɪkspɪə /) (PP$_2$: / rəʊtmeniˈsɒnɪts /)] ^{IP}) ^{U})

Like Utterances and Intonational Phrases, Phonological Phrases can also contain a fall or rise operator. Where present, these operators combine with the fall or rise operator on the Intonational Phrase to produce full falls and rises or complex tones (fall–rise or rise–fall). Consider in this respect the two very similar Utterances in (24):

(24) a. Sit down.

IL: (M$_1$: (A$_1$: [(F$_1$: IMP) (P$_1$)$_S$ (P$_2$)$_A$ (C$_1$: (T$_1$))] ^{A}) ^{M})

PL: (u$_1$: (**f** IP$_1$: (PP$_1$/ ˈsɪt ˈdaʊn /) ^{IP}) ^{U})

b. Sit DOWN!

IL: (M$_1$: (**emph** A$_1$: [(F$_1$: IMP) (P$_1$)$_S$ (P$_2$)$_A$ (C$_1$: (T$_1$))] ^{A}) ^{M})

PL: (u$_1$: (f IP$_1$: (**f** PP$_1$/ ˈsɪt ˈdaʊn /) ^{IP}) ^{U})

The two examples in (24) represent two possible ways of pronouncing the same string of words. In example (24a) the sequence *sit down* is pronounced with a slightly falling tone normally associated with requests expressed in the form of an Imperative. In (24a) this intonation pattern, triggered by the fall operator 'f' on the Intonational Phrase, is used to politely invite the Addressee to take a seat. In (24b), however, the presence of the Emphatic operator on the Discourse Act results in a different intonation pattern, brought about by an extra fall operator at the layer of the Phonological Phrase, which strengthens the falling intonation of the Intonational Phrase, resulting in a full fall on the element *down*. Obviously, this intonation pattern encodes a different intention: rather than being invited to take a seat, the Addressee is now ordered to do so.

Reinforcement of a falling or rising tone may also be triggered by strong emotions. In (25a), for instance, the full fall, brought about by the combination of two fall operators, may express a strong feeling of disapproval, while in (25b) the full rise, triggered by the combination of two rise operators, is caused by feelings of disbelief or shock:

(25)   a.   Awful!

IL: (**emph** A$_1$: [(F$_1$: DECL) (P$_1$)$_S$ (P$_2$)$_A$ (C$_1$)] ^{A})

PL: (U$_1$: (**f** IP$_1$: (**f** PP$_1$: / 'ɔ:fəl /)))

b.   Really??

IL: (**emph** A$_1$: [(F$_1$: INTER) (P$_1$)$_S$ (P$_2$)$_A$ (C$_1$)] ^{A})

PL: (U$_1$: (**r** IP$_1$: (**r** PP$_1$: / 'rɪəli /)))

It is, however, also possible for two different operators (a fall and a rise) to co-occur, one at the IP layer and the other at the PP layer, the result being either a fall–rise or a rise–fall. An example of a fall–rise can be found in example (20), here repeated as (26):

(26)   *if you're tired* just go to sleep on the couch (BYU-BNC, written, non-academic)

(U$_1$: (**r** IP$_1$: [(PP$_1$: / 'ɪf /) (**f** PP$_2$: / jʊə'taɪəd /)] ^{IP}) . . . ^{U})

In this example the presence of a conditional modifier at the Representational Level (*if you are tired*) is marked both morphosyntactically, by the use of the Grammatical Morpheme *if*, and phonologically, by a global rising intonation pattern on the Intonational Phrase corresponding to this modifier (IP$_1$). The rising tone is expressed on the nuclear Syllable of the final Phonological Phrase of the Intonational Phrase, that is, on the element *tired*. This Phonological Phrase, however, also has its own operator, a fall. The combination of the rise operator on the Intonational Phrase (indicating a global rising intonation) and the fall operator on the Phonological Phrase (indicating a local falling intonation) brings about a fall–rise tone on the relevant Syllable. Note that when a combination of two operators results in a complex tone, it is always the higher operator (in this case the IP operator 'rise') that determines the final direction of the pitch movement.

The fall–rise intonation pattern may also serve to indicate tentativeness on the part of the Speaker. In the following short dialogue, for instance, use of a fall–rise tone on the element *yes* functions as an indication of limited agreement:

(27)   A: The Third Man is a great film, don't you think?

B: Yes . . .

(U$_1$: (**r** IP$_1$: (**f** PP$_1$: / jes /)))

The rise–fall intonation pattern, like the full fall, typically indicates a Speaker's emotional involvement; the emotions involved may be positive (approval, excitement) or negative (disapproval, irritation). An example is given in (28), where a rise–fall on the stressed Syllable (typically extended to the preceding and following Syllables) expresses a strong feeling of approval (possibly strengthened by an Emphatic operator at the Interpersonal Level):

(28)   A: There's no class today.
      B: Terrific!
         (U_1: (**f** IP_1: (**r** PP_1: / tə'rɪfɪk /)))

So far we have seen that it is typically the Illocution which triggers the global intonation patterns of an Intonational Phrase, realized as a pitch movement on the nuclear Syllable of the final Phonological Phrase, while other kinds of Interpersonal or Representational information (the presence of an emphasis operator or of a specific type of modifier) can have a local effect on this intonation pattern. In addition, intonation can be sensitive to the presence of pragmatic functions. Typically, however, this kind of information does not bring about a movement in pitch, but instead tends to result in relative pitch differences. Compare, for instance, the two examples in (29):

(29)   a. (Who did you trust?) I trusted Sue.
      IL: (A_1: [(F_1: DECL) (P_1)$_S$ (P_2)$_A$ (C_1: [(T_1) (R_1: [+S -A])
           (R_2: Sue)$_{FOC}$] ^{C})] ^{A})
      PL: (U_1: (**f** IP_1: [(PP_1: / aɪ'trʌstɪd/) (PP_2: / 'su: /)] ^{IP}) ^{U})
     b. Sue I trusted.
      IL: (A_1: [(F_1: DECL) (P_1)$_S$ (P_2)$_A$ (C_1: [(T_1) (R_1: [+S -A])
           (R_2: Sue)$_{CONTR}$] ^{C})] ^{A})
      PL: (U_1: (**f** IP_1: [(**h** PP_1: / 'su: /) (PP_2: / aɪ'trʌstɪd /)] ^{IP}) ^{U})

In (29a) we find a declarative Discourse Act with a Focus element in final position. Since in English it is typically the nuclear Syllable of the final Phonological Phrase that carries the tone, the pitch movement in (29a) is automatically expressed on the Focus element. This means that the pragmatic function does not have to be coded separately by an operator on the Phonological Phrase containing the Focus. In (29b), on the other hand, the element *Sue* is assigned the pragmatic function of Contrast. This is coded both morphosyntactically, by placement in initial position, and phonolo-gically, by the presence of a (level) high tone (represented by the operator 'h'). This does not affect the expression of the fall operator on the Inton-ational Phrase, which is still realized on the nuclear Syllable of the last Phonological Phrase (i.e. the first Syllable of *trusted*).

   There are, however, also cases where the operator on the Intonational Phrase is not expressed on the nuclear Syllable of the final Phonological Phrase. An example is the sentence in (30):

(30)   I have ALWAYS trusted Sue.

IL: (A$_1$: [(F$_1$: DECL) (P$_1$)$_S$ (P$_2$)$_A$ (C$_1$: [(T$_1$) (T$_2$)$_{FOC}$ (R$_1$: [+S -A]) (R$_2$: Sue)] ^{C})] ^{A})

PL: (U$_1$: (**f** IP$_1$: [(PP$_1$: / aɪv'ɔːlwəz /) (**l** PP$_2$: / 'trʌstɪd'suː /)] ^{IP}) ^{U})

In this sentence, Focus assignment to the adverb *always* results in the fall operator on the Intonational Phrase being realized on the nuclear Syllable within the Phonological Phrase corresponding to this Subact, despite the fact that it is not the final Phonological Phrase. The low tone operator 'l' on the last Phonological Phrase has the effect of keeping the pitch low after the fall has been realized, blocking the application of the pitch change on this Phrase (Hengeveld and Mackenzie 2008: 439).

Let us end this section by looking at two more examples showing how the Phonological Phrase can be used to express distinctions made at the higher levels of representation. The first concerns the phonological coding of irony, an example of which was given in (6), repeated here as (31):

(31)   A: Peter will come to the meeting tonight.

B$_1$:   That's just GREAT.

(U$_1$: (**f** IP$_1$: [(PP$_1$: / 'ðæts /) (PP$_2$: / dʒʌst'greɪt /)] ^{IP}) ^{U})

B$_2$:   That's JUST great.

(U$_1$: (**f** IP$_1$: [(PP$_1$: / 'ðæts /) (**h** PP$_2$: / 'dʒʌst /) (PP$_3$: / 'greɪt /)] ^{IP}) ^{U})

The first response to A's remark (B$_1$) is meant literally and displays the default intonation contour for declarative sentences, with a fall on the nuclear Syllable of the final Phonological Phrase (corresponding to the Focus element *great*). This is also the case in the second response, which is meant to be ironic. The difference between the responses is, however, that whereas the first consists of two Phonological Phrases, the second contains three Phonological Phrases: in B$_2$ the particle *just* forms by itself a Phonological Phrase specified by a high tone operator. This specific intonation pattern is used to signal to the Addressee that the Utterance is to be interpreted as ironic.

The second example concerns the kind of ambiguity present in the construction given in (3), here repeated as (32):

(32)   Right now, they are looking for two suspects, *a man and a woman with blond hair* driving a black SUV. (Internet)

As pointed out in Section 6.1, the italicized phrase in this example is ambiguous: either both the man and the woman have blond hair or only the woman. These two readings are distinguished at the Representational

Level, where the Phrase *with blond hair* modifies either both parts of the coordination (*a man with blond hair and a woman with blond hair*) or the second part only (*a woman with blond hair*). These two readings are represented in (33a) and (33b), respectively:

(33)   a. $(1x_1: (f_1: man_N): (f_2)^x)$ and $(1x_2: (f_3: woman_N): (f_2: -with \ blond \ hair-)^x)$
         b. $(1x_1: (f_1: man_N)^x)$ and $(1x_2: (f_3: woman_N): (f_2: - with \ blond \ hair -)^x)$

In (33a), both parts of the coordination contain the modifier *with blond hair*, represented by the variable f_2. The lexical information, however, is only contained in the second part of the coordination; in the first part this variable appears without a head, thus accounting for the fact that the Property is predicated without being expressed. In (33b), however, the modifier is present only in the second part of the coordination, which means that the Property in question is only predicated of the second Individual (x_2).

In English, this difference in scope can, but need not, be reflected in morphosyntactic form. Thus, expressions like *a man with blond hair and a woman with blond hair* (corresponding to (33a)) or *a woman with blond hair and a man* (corresponding to (33b)) could also have been used, but may have been considered less satisfactory by the Speaker.

Think of possible reasons why the two alternative word orders given above may have been considered less appropriate by the Speaker of the passage in (32).

In addition, however, English offers the possibility of resolving the ambiguity by means of intonation. One way of doing this is to realize both representations in (33) by means of different two Phonological Phrases, but to draw the boundary between these phrases at different places. In (34a), for instance, the first PP consists of the string *a man and a woman*, while the second Phonological Phrase contains the modifier *with blond hair*. In this representation, /wʊ/ is the nuclear Syllable of the first Phonological Phrase, and /heə/ that of the second. In (33b), on the other hand, the first Phonological Phrase consists only of the element *man* (which must therefore be the nuclear Syllable), while the second Phonological phrase consists of the string *and a woman with blond hair* (with /heə/ once more serving as the nuclear Syllable).

(34)   a. $-$ (PP$_1$: / ə'mænəndə'wʊmən / ^{PP}) (PP$_2$: / wɪð'blɒnd'heə / ^{PP}) $-$
         b. $-$ (PP$_1$: / ə'mæn / ^{PP}) (PP$_2$:/ əndə'wʊmənwɪð'blɒnd'heə / ^{PP}) $-$

In the course of this section it has been shown that it is justified to divide Intonational Phrases into Phonological Phrases, since certain distinctions made at the higher levels of representation can only be made at this lower phonological layer. There are, however, still a number of phonological phenomena that cannot be explained at the layer of the Phonological Phrase. This means that we need to distinguish yet another layer, that of the Phonological Word. In other words, Phonological Phrases have further internal complexity, as indicated in the following general schema:

(35) $(\pi \text{ PP}_1: [(\text{PW}_1) \dots (\text{PW}_n)]^{\text{PP}})$

6.6. Phonological Words

The exact characterization of a Phonological Word depends on the (type of) language we are dealing with. In a stress language like English, the defining feature of a Phonological Word is the presence of one primary stress. This means that there is a default relation between lexemes and Phonological Words.

Since English has variable stress, that is, since the position of the primary stress in a lexeme is not predictable, stress patterns are specified in the Lexicon as part of a lexeme's pronunciation and must be learnt by the Speaker. As the position of the stress is not fully governed by rules, stress needs to be indicated at the Phonological Level; this happens at the layer of the Phonological Word, as illustrated in (36):

(36) a. terrific
  (PW$_1$: / təˈrɪfɪk /)
 b. horrible
  (PW$_1$: / ˈhɒrɪbl /)
 c. individual
  (PW$_1$: / ˌɪndɪˈvɪdjʊəl /)

> ### Word stress in other languages
>
> Apart from languages with variable stress, such as English, German, and Russian, there are also many languages with **fixed stress**. In such languages the position of the stress is fully predictable, as it is always located on the same Syllable within a word. In Hungarian, Icelandic, and Czech, for instance, stress always falls on the first Syllable of a word, in Turkish stress falls on the last Syllable, while in Polish and Welsh it is the
>
> *(continued)*

penultimate Syllable that is stressed. Since in these languages the position of the stress is governed by a simple rule, there is no need to indicate stress on the Phonological Word. In languages like Italian, where stress usually falls on the penultimate Syllable and where exceptions are orthographically marked (as in *città* 'city'), stress will only be indicated in the case of exceptions.

In addition, there are languages that lack word stress altogether; such languages have what is referred to as **prosodic stress**. In Acehnese, for instance, stress always falls on the last Syllable of the Phonological Phrase, regardless of the internal structure of the Phrase (Durie 1985: 30). This means that in this language there is no need to assume a layer in between the Phonological Phrase and the Syllable; Acehnese, in other words, has no Phonological Words. A similar claim has been made with regard to French: although it may seem that the stress always falls on the last Syllable of a lexeme, it could also be claimed that stress actually falls on the last Syllable of the Phonological Phrase; lexemes uttered in isolation could then be regarded as forming by themselves a Phonological Phrase, in which case the final Syllable of the lexeme is also the final Syllable of the Phrase (see Jun and Fougeron 2000 (who call it Accentual Phrase) and Post 2000).

In English, there is not only a default relation between Phonological Words and lexemes, but also between Phonological Words and morphosyntactic Words. This is illustrated in the following example, where there is a one-to-one relationship between the Words (both lexical and grammatical) on the Morphosyntactic Level and the Phonological Words at the Phonological Level. In this particular respect, English thus has a relatively high degree of transparency (see Section 5.3)

(**37**)   Shakespeare wrote many sonnets.

ML: (Cl_1: [(Np_1: (Nw_1: / 'ʃeɪkspɪə /))$_{Subj}$ (Vp_1: (Vw_1: write-past)) (Np_1: [(Gw_1: / 'meni /) (Nw_1: / 'sɒnɪts /-pl)] ^{Np})$_{Obj}$] ^{Cl})

PL: (U_1: (f IP_1: [(PP_1: (PW_1: / 'ʃeɪkspɪə /)) (PP_2: (PW_2:/ 'rəʊt /) (PP_3: [(PW_3:/ 'meni /) (PW_4: / 'sɒnɪts /)] ^{PP})] ^{IP}) ^{U})

There are, however, also instances where there is no direct relation between Words at the Morphosyntactic level and Phonological Words. One of these exceptions is the occurrence of clitics, illustrated in example (38) (see also example (8) above):

(38) a. We*'ll* win.

ML: $(Cl_1: [(Np_1: (Nw_1: we)) (Vp_1: [(^{fin}Vw_2: will) (^{non-f}Vw_3: / 'win /)] ^{Vp})] ^{Cl})$

PL: $(U_1: (f IP_1: [(PP_1: (PW_1: / wɪl /)) (PP_2: (PW_2:/ 'win /))] ^{IP}) ^{U})$

b. You*'ve* lost.

ML: $(Cl_1: [(Np_1: (Nw_1: you)) (Vp_1: [(^{fin}Vw_2: have.2.sg) (^{non-f}Vw_3: lose.past-part)] ^{Vp})] ^{Cl})$

PL: $(U_1: (f IP_1: [(PP_1: (PW_1: / juv /)) (PP_2: (PW_2:/ 'lɒst /))] ^{IP}) ^{U})$

As already mentioned in Section 5.5.3.2, clitics are elements that behave morphosyntactically as separate words (usually function words), but which phonologically depend on (are attached to) another word. In FDG terms this means that a clitic functions as a (grammatical) Word at the Morphosyntactic Level, but at the Phonological Level fuses with another Word (its host) to form one Phonological Word. Thus, in (37), the elements *'ll* and *'ve* are clitics: they function as Verbal Words at the Morphological Level, but at the Phonological Level they attach to the preceding Word (*we* and *you*, respectively) to form one Phonological Word.

Within the category of clitics, a further distinction can be made between enclitics, which follow their host (like *'ll* and *'ve* in (38)) and proclitics, which precede their host. In English, clitics tend to follow their host; occasionally, however, proclitics also seem to occur. In American English, for instance, the combination of *you* + *all* has come to be used as a second person plural pronoun (distinguishable from the second person singular form, *you*).[1] The frequent use of this combination has resulted in the reduction of the first element to / j /; this element could thus be regarded as a proclitic, phonologically dependent on the following element *all*:

(39) "*Y'all* are one of us now. This won't cost *y'all* a thing." (COCA, written, fiction)

ML: $(Nw_1: you) (Gw_2: all)$

PL: $(PW_1: / 'jɔːl /)$

It might, however, also be claimed that the combination of *you* and *all*, sometimes also pronounced as /jɑːl/, has grammaticalized to such an extent that it is now actually one morphosyntactic Word (a new pronoun); in that

---

[1] Note that this phenomenon can also be found in British English, where the second person plural pronoun takes the form *you-guys*. Alternative forms are *yous(e)* and *you-lot*.

case, the one-to-one relation between morphosyntactic Word and Phonological Word has been restored.

Another example of a mismatch between Words at the Morphosyntactic Level and Phonological Words can be found in (40a), where the complex morphosyntactic Word *ex-president* corresponds to two Phonological Words, each with a primary stress. In (40b), on the other hand, the simplex morphosyntactic Word *express*, pronounced with one primary stress, corresponds to one Phonological Word.

(40)   a. ex-president
         ML: (Nw$_1$: (ekspresident))
         PL: (pw$_1$: / 'eks /) (pw$_2$:/ 'president /)
       b. express
         ML: (Nw$_1$: / ɪkspres /)
         PL: (pw$_1$: / ɪk'spres /)

In analogy with example (40), provide the morphological and phonological representations of *non-stop* and *nonsense*.

The relation between Phonological Words and (morphosyntactic) Words in other languages

Languages differ in the degree to which Words at the Morphosyntactic Level correspond to Phonological Words. Generally speaking, there is a good correlation in isolating, agglutinating, and fusional languages (Hengeveld and Mackenzie 2008: 443–4). Thus we have seen that in English, a largely isolating language with some fusional elements, there is indeed a default relation between morphosyntactic Words and Phonological Words. Taking stress as a criterion, the same is true for an agglutinating language like Turkish, where morphosyntactic Words, regardless of their internal complexity, have only one primary stress. The morphosyntactically highly complex Word in (41), for instance, has only one primary stress, on the final Syllable; as such it corresponds to one Phonological Word (Hengeveld and Mackenzie 2008: 444, example from Kabak and Vogel 2001: 316).

(41)   kitap-lık-lar-ım-ız-'dan
        book-case-PL-1-PL-ABL
        'from our bookcases'

In polysynthetic languages, on the other hand, complex Words may contain more than one primary stress. An example from Yimas is given in (42) (example from Foley 1991: 80, given here in simplified form):

(42) Mamparŋkat   ta-mpu-'park-mpi-'kapik-mpi-'wark-ra.
     branches   NEG-they-split-SEQ-break-SEQ-tie-SEQ-PL
     'They didn't split the branches, split them and tie them.'

In Yimas, the presence of the negative element *ta* at the beginning of the sequence *ta-mpu-'park-mpi-'kapik-mpi-'wark-ra* shows that we are dealing with one Verbal Word. At the Phonological Level, however, this sequence contains a number of primary stresses, which means that it corresponds to more than one Phonological Word.

Just like morphological Words, Phonological Words have internal structure. In the next section we will look at three units smaller than the Phonological Word: Feet, Syllables, and Phonemes.

6.7. Feet and Syllables

In this section we will look at the two lowest layers at the Phonological Level: the Foot and the Syllable. Within the Phonological Word, these two kinds of units are hierarchically ordered: Phonological Words consist of one or more Feet, which in turn consist of one or more Syllables:

(43) $(\text{PW}_1: [(\text{F}_1) \ldots (\text{F}_n)]^{\text{PW}})$
       $(\text{F}_1: [(\text{S}_1) (\text{S}_2)]^{\text{F}})$

In what follows, these two types of units will be discussed in turn, starting with the larger of the two, the Foot.

Feet are characterized by the presence of one strong Syllable and (in most cases) one weaker Syllable. Strong Syllables are Syllables with either primary or secondary stress. Thus a word like *introspective* consists of two Feet, both of which consist of two Syllables, one of which is strong (stressed):

(44)   introspective

$(\text{PW}_1\!: [(\text{F}_1\!: [(\text{ss}_1\!: / \text{in} /)\,(\text{s}_2\!: / \text{trəʊ} /)]^{\,\text{F}})\,(\text{sF}_2\!: [(\text{ss}_3\!: / \text{spek} /)\,(\text{s}_4\!: / \text{tɪv} /)]^{\,\text{F}})]^{\,\text{PW}})$

From the phonological representation in (44) we see that strong Syllables are provided with the operator 's'; primary stress (as opposed to secondary stress) is brought about by the presence of another 's' operator on the layer of the Foot. Thus, in (44), the presence of an 's' operator on the second Foot (F_2) and on the first Syllable within that Foot (s_4) has the accumulative effect of primary stress on the Syllable / spek /; secondary stress, on the other hand, is brought about by the presence of a strong Syllable in a weak Foot (e.g. the strong Syllable / ɪn / in the weak Foot F_1 in (44)).[2]

Feet are important in so-called stress-timed languages, that is, languages (like English) where stressed Syllables tend to occur at relatively regular intervals of time, irrespective of whether any (and if so, how many) unstressed Syllables occur in between. This means that all Feet are more or less of equal length, a property referred to as **isochronicity**. Consider the following examples:

(45)   a.   two pears

$(\text{PP}_1\!: [(\text{PW}_1\!: (\text{sF}_1\!: (\text{ss}_1\!: / \text{tuː} /)))\,(\text{PW}_1\!: (\text{sF}_2\!: (\text{ss}_2\!: / \text{peəz} /)))]^{\,\text{PP}})$

   b.   twenty peaches

$(\text{PP}_1\!: [(\text{PW}_1\!: (\text{sF}_1\!: [(\text{ss}_1\!: / \text{twen} /)\,(\text{s}_2\!: / \text{ti} /)]^{\,\text{F}})^{\,\text{PW}})\,(\text{PW}_2\!: (\text{sF}_2\!: [(\text{ss}_3\!: / \text{piː} /)$
$(\text{s}_4\!: / \text{tʃəz} /)]^{\,\text{F}})^{\,\text{PW}})]^{\,\text{PP}})$

The phrases in (45a) and (45b) both contain two Phonological Words containing two Feet. In (45a) each Foot contains only one Syllable, in (45b) both Feet consist of two Syllables. Since all Feet have equal duration, the two Syllables in (45a) are about twice as long as the two Syllables in (45b).

Cross-linguistically, a distinction can be made between **trochaic Feet** (where the first Syllable is strong) and **iambic Feet** (where the second Syllable is strong). It is generally assumed that English, along with the vast majority of languages, has only trochaic Feet, as illustrated in (46a) and (46b), where the first Syllable is strong (as indicated by the 's' operator on the first Syllable):

---

[2] With the introduction of the operator 's' at the layer of the Foot and the Syllable, stress marks have become redundant. From now on they will therefore no longer be included in the representations.

(46) a. friendly

(PW$_1$: (SF$_1$: [(SS$_1$: / frend/) (S$_2$: / li /)] ^{F}) ^{PW})

b. childish

(PW$_1$: (SF$_1$: [(SS$_1$: / tʃaɪl /) (S$_2$: / dɪʃ /)] ^{F}) ^{PW})

Not all Syllables, however, need to be part of a Foot. In a word like *polite*, for instance, the first (unstressable) Syllable is 'unfooted'; the second (strong) Syllable forms, by itself, a Foot. In a word like *dependent*, too, the first Syllable is unfooted; here, the second and third Syllables form a trochaic Foot. As soon as we add the prefix *in-*, however, the Syllable / də / forms a Foot with the stressed prefix, as shown in examples (47a) and (47b):

(47) a. dependent

(PW$_1$: [(S$_1$: / dɪ /) (SF$_1$: [(SS$_2$: / pen /) (S$_3$: / dənt /)] ^{F})] ^{PW})

b. independent

(PW$_1$: [(F$_1$: [(SS$_1$: / ɪn /) (S$_2$: / dɪ /)] ^{F}) (SF$_2$: [(SS$_3$: / pen/) (S$_4$: / dənt /)] ^{F})] ^{PW})

Provide a phonological representation of the word *oversensitive*.

The position of the primary (and, if present, secondary) stress, is, as we have seen in the previous section, a property of the lexeme, and as such is stored in the lexicon. Nevertheless, the actual realization of primary and secondary stress may depend on the phonological environment. In English, for instance, it is possible for the primary and secondary stress within a Phonological Word to be reversed, a process known as iambic reversal (e.g. Spencer 1996: 258ff.; Hogg and McCully 1987: 132ff.). This process is triggered by the presence of a stress clash (two stressed Syllables in a row) and results in a more even distribution of primary stresses within a Phonological Phrase. Thus, the primary stress in the Phonological Word *fourteen*, when used in isolation, is on the second Syllable (the stressed Syllable in a strong Foot), while the first Syllable (contained within a weak Foot) has secondary stress (example (48a)). However, when *fourteen* is followed by a Phonological Word with a trochaic Foot, like *peaches* in (48b), the primary stress is placed on the first Syllable of *fourteen*. Similarly, in (49), the position of the primary stress depends on whether the adjective *rent-free* is used predicatively (as in (49a)) or attributively (as in (49b)).

(48) a. fourTEEN

(PW$_1$: [(F$_1$: (SS$_1$: / fɔː /)) (SF$_2$: (SS$_2$: / tiːn /))] ^{PW})

b. FOURteen PEAches

(PW$_1$: [(SF$_1$: (SS$_1$: / fɔː /)) (F$_2$: (SS$_2$: / tiːn /))] ^{PW})

(49) a. Our flat is *rent-FREE*.

$(\text{PW}_1: [(\text{F}_1: (\text{ss}_1: / \text{ rent } /)) (\text{sF}_2: (\text{ss}_2: / \text{ fri: } /))]^{\text{PW}})$

b. This is a *RENT-free* flat

$(\text{PW}_1: [(\text{sF}_1: (\text{ss}_1: / \text{ rent } /)) (\text{F}_2: (\text{ss}_2: / \text{ fri: } /))]^{\text{PW}})$

Note that iambic reversal may also take place when there is no apparent stress clash, as in example (50b); here, however, it could be argued that the unstressable Syllable / dɪd / is too weak to resolve the clash between the first Syllable of *minded* and the first Syllable of *person*:

(50) a. That was very *noble-MINded* of you.

$(\text{PW}_1: [(\text{F}_1: [(\text{ss}_1: / \text{ nəʊ } /) (\text{s}_2: / \text{ bl } /)]^{\text{F}}) (\text{sF}_2: [(\text{ss}_3: / \text{ maɪn } /) (\text{s}_4: / \text{ dɪd } /)]^{\text{F}})]^{\text{PW}})$

b. You are a *Noble-minded* PERson.

$(\text{PW}_1: [(\text{sF}_1: [(\text{ss}_1: / \text{ nəʊ } /) (\text{s}_2: / \text{ bl } /)]^{\text{F}}) (\text{F}_2: [(\text{ss}_3: / \text{maɪn} /) (\text{s}_4: / \text{ dɪd } /)]^{\text{F}})]^{\text{PW}})$

These examples and their phonological representations show that the process of iambic reversal involves the reversal of a strong and a weak Foot within a Phonological Word, that is, the 'shifting' of the 's' variable from the second to the first Foot.

Feet, as we have seen, consist of one or more Syllables, which in turn may consist of a single phoneme or of an uninterrupted sequence of phonemes. When a Syllable consists of one phoneme only, this phoneme forms the peak (or head) of the Syllable. In addition, Syllables may have an onset (one or more consonants preceding the peak) and/or a coda (one or more consonants following the peak). In English, Syllables can consist of a peak only (a vowel, V), an onset and a peak (CV), a peak and a coda (VC), and an onset, peak, and coda (CVC). In most cases, the peak is a vowel; in addition, however, peaks take the form of a syllabic consonant. Some examples are given in (51):

(51)

peak only:	'I' / aɪ / ; 'a' / ə /
onset + peak:	'you' / ju: / ; 'sky' / skaɪ /
peak + coda	'am' / æm / ; 'ask' / ɑ:sk /
onset + peak + coda:	'rain' / reɪn / ; 'strand' /strænd /
onset + syllabic consonant:	'no.**ble**' / bl̩ /

The Syllable is the domain of phonotactic rules, that is, language-specific rules that determine which (combinations) of sounds are allowed in each part of the Syllable. Such rules usually take the form of constraints. In English, for instance, open Syllables (i.e. Syllables ending in a peak) must have a peak consisting of a long vowel, a diphthong, or a schwa. If the peak is a short vowel, it must be followed by a coda; if the peak is a syllabic consonant, it must be preceded by an onset. Apart from these restrictions, English is relatively flexible, as Syllables can, but need not, have an onset and/or a coda, and both the onset and the coda can consist of (sometimes quite complicated) consonant clusters (e.g. CCCVC, as in *spring* or CVCCCC, as in *texts*).

Syllable structure in other languages

In many languages the internal structure of Syllables is much more constrained than in English. Thus, some languages require the presence of an onset; in Axininca Campa, for instance, onsets are obligatory in non-word-initial Syllables. In this language, a word-internal epenthetic / t / is inserted wherever otherwise an initial vowel would occur. Thus in a word like *iŋkoma-i* 'he will paddle', / t / is inserted at the beginning of the last Syllable, yielding *iŋkomati* (McCarthy and Prince 1993: 30).

There are also language-specific constraints on the presence and form of codas. Hawaiian, for instance, does not have closed Syllables, while Japanese, too, has a strong preference for open Syllables, allowing only a limited number of sounds to occur in the coda. Similarly, in French, final consonants in spelling are often not pronounced before a pause or another consonant. When, however, such a Syllable is followed by a word beginning with a vowel, some of these (latent) consonants are expressed as the onset of the following Syllable, a process known as liaison. Some instances of liaison can be found in (52):

(52) les   anciens   élèves
      the   former   pupils
      ML: $(Np_1: [(Gw_1: le.pl) (Ap_1: (Aw_1: anciens.pl)) (Nw_1: elɛv.pl)]^{Np})$
      PL: $(PP_1: [(s_1: / le /) (s_2: / zɑ̃ /) (ss_3: / sjɛ̃ /) (s_4: / ze /) (ss_5: / lɛv /)]^{PP})$

Here we see that the final (latent) consonants of the morphosyntactic Words *les* and *anciens* are pronounced as the onset of the following Syllables (s_2 and s_4, respectively). As a result, there is no one-to-one relationship between units at the Morphosyntactic and the Phonological Level.

The next question that arises is how to divide larger phonological units (Phonological Words or Phonological Phrases) into Syllables; in other words, how do we know where to draw the boundaries between two Syllables? In many cases, we can simply rely on our intuition: words like *father* and *arise*, for instance, can quite easily be divided into Syllables (/fɑ.ðə/ and /ə.raɪz/). In other cases, however, it is much more difficult to decide where one Syllable ends and the next begins. Take, for instance, a word like *extreme*. Given that the first Syllable must end in a consonant cluster allowed in English (thus ruling out / ɪkstr.i:m /) and that second Syllable must begin with a consonant cluster allowed in English (thus ruling out / ɪ.kstri:m/), there are three possible ways of dividing this word into Syllables:

(53)   extreme
      a.   / ɪk.stri:m /
      b.   / ɪks.tri:m /
      c.   / ɪkst.ri:m /

One way of deciding which option to choose is to apply the so-called Maximal Onsets Principle, which states that the onset of the second Syllable should consist of as many consonants as possible (in the English system) (e.g. Roach 2009: 61). In the case of *extreme*, this would lead to the structure given in (53a).

> Provide an analysis of the syllabic structure of the following two words:
> (a) *astound*; (b) *rustic*.

However, when applied to such words as *better* or *squalor*, which have a short vowel in the first Syllable, this strategy turns out to be problematic. Application of the Maximal Onsets Principle will lead to the following division into Syllables:

(54) a.   better
        / be.tə /
     b.   squalor
        / skwɒ.lə /

Remember, however, that in open Syllables in English the peak has to consist of a long vowel, a diphthong, or a schwa, a requirement not fulfilled in (54). The alternative would be to add a coda to the first Syllable (/ bet.ə /, / skwɒl.ə /); this, however, would not only violate the Maximal Onsets Principle, but would also be strongly counterintuitive. Another solution that has been offered is to assume that the consonants /t/ and /l/ in these examples are ambisyllabic, that is, that they belong to both Syllables. This would lead to the following representations:

(54) a. better
    / bet.tə /
    (PW$_1$: [(SF$_1$: [(SS$_1$: / bet /) (S$_2$: / tə /)] ^{F})] ^{PW})
  b. squalor
    / skwɒl.lə /
    (PW$_1$: [(SF$_1$: [(SS$_1$: / skwɒl /) (S$_2$: / lə /)] ^{F})] ^{PW})

The analysis in (54) solves both problems: the Maximal Onsets Principle is adhered to, while at the same time the first Syllable is closed. It does, however, create a new problem, since we now have two consonants in the phonological structure of these Words, even though only one is pronounced. In order to prevent the ambisyllabic consonant from being pronounced twice, a process of degemination is assumed to take place in the Output Component (during Articulation), reducing the two consonants to a single phoneme. Note, however, that this process is blocked in those cases where the consonant in question is part of two different units at the Morphosyntactic Level. Thus, degemination does not take place between separate Morphemes in derived Words like *soulless* or in compounds like *night train*; here the coda of the first Syllable and the onset of the second Syllable are both pronounced.

(55) a. soulless
    (AW$_1$: [(NS$_1$: / səʊl /) (Aaff$_1$: / lɪs /)] ^{AW})
    (PW$_1$: (SF$_1$: [(SS$_1$: / səʊl /) (S$_2$: / lɪs /)] ^{F}) ^{PW})
  b. night train
    (NW$_1$: [(NS$_1$: / naɪt /) (NS$_2$: / treɪn /)] ^{NW})
    (PW$_1$: (SF$_1$: [(SS$_1$: / naɪt /) (S$_2$: / treɪn /)] ^{F}) ^{PW})

This means that the Articulator must be sensitive not only to information from the Phonological Level, but in some cases also to information from the Morphosyntactic Level.

6.8. Summary

• As the last of the four levels of representation, the Phonological Level receives its input from the three higher levels. Like the Morphological

Level, it has the function of encoding information from the Interpersonal and Representational Levels; in addition, the phonological form of elements may be triggered by morphosyntactic information.

- As part of the Grammatical Component, the Phonological Level deals with the phonemic form of utterances, representing only that interpersonal and representational information that is predictably and systematically encoded in phonological form in any specific language. Optional, non-predictable processes are taken care of by the Articulator, which produces the phonetic form of an utterance on the basis of input received from the Phonological Level and different kinds of contextual information (Section 6.1).
- The Phonological Level is hierarchically organized into Utterances, Intonational Phrases, Phonological Phrases, Phonological Words, Feet, and Syllables; in addition, it has its own set of primitives (prosodic templates and phonological operators). Although default relations exist between phonological units and higher-level units (e.g. between Discourse Acts and Intonational Phrases, and between (morphosyntactic) Words and Phonological Words), mismatches do occur, thus justifying the presence of a separate level (Section 6.2).
- The detailed discussions of the various layers provided in Sections 6.3–6.7 also allowed for a number of general observation, such as the fact that Illocutions trigger different global intonation patterns, whereas higher-level operators (e.g. Irony or Emphasis) trigger local intonation patterns; or the fact that where Illocutions and operators trigger movements in pitch, pragmatic functions trigger relative differences in pitch.
- Finally, in the course of the chapter a number of specific phonological features of English were discussed, such as linking and the realization of question tags (Section 6.4), end focus, reinforcement, irony, and complex tones (Section 6.5), stress patterns and clitics (Section 6.6), and isochronicity, iambic reversal, ambisyllabicity, and degemination (Section 6.7).

Exercises

1. In the following short dialogue, the element *really* can be pronounced in different ways, depending on the Speaker's intentions (given between brackets).

(i)   A: Peter thinks you're marvellous.
(ii) B: Really! (expressing surprise)
        Really. (expressing irony)

Provide representations at the Interpersonal and Representational Levels
that bring out the difference between the two realizations of *really*.

2.* Provide the complete phonological representations of the following
words and comment on the differences between them (with regard to stress
pattern and Syllable structure):

(i)   'post-'hoc
(ii) 'postscript
(iii) ˌpost'pone
(vi) 'posthumous

3. For each of the phrases below:

a. Provide a phonological representation
b. Explain why iambic reversal can / cannot take place.

(i)   New York City
(ii) Eastern Europe
(iii) polite request
(vi) big-mouthed brat

4.* Provide complete phonological representations of the following
utterances (after deciding on a plausible intonation pattern; note that
more than one intonation pattern may be possible). The analyses of sample
sentences given in Chapter 7 may prove useful.

(i)   I will NOT take the blame!
(ii) Why me?
(iii) That's a bit of an understatement.
(iv) Thomas put the dictionary back in the bookcase.

5.** In Section 6.7 the consonant / t / in a word like *better* was assumed
to be ambisyllabic; this made it possible for the Maximal Onsets Principle to
be adhered to, while at the same time the first Syllable (containing a short
vowel) is closed (see example (56)). Such an analysis, however, proves to be
problematic in the case of words like *carry* and *worry* (in their RP pronunciation). Explain the problem and think of a possible solution.

6.** In Section 6.3 an analysis of question tags is offered in which they are regarded as separate Discourse Acts at the Interpersonal Level. Alternative analyses, however, are also conceivable. Can you think of such an alternative? (Hint: think of different ways of representing question tags at the Interpersonal Level).

Suggestions for further reading

Of the four levels of analysis, the Phonological Level is by far the least developed. So far, only a few publications have been devoted specifically to this level. One of these is O'Neill (2012), which deals with initial consonant mutation in Irish Gaelic. O'Neill (2014) discusses the interaction between the Contextual Component and the Grammatical Component by analysing different speech channels of communication in Pirahã. Seinhorst (2014) looks at the place of phonetics in FDG. Finally, in her discussion of *the thing is*-constructions in English, Keizer (2013) provides a phonological analysis of these constructions.

7

Sample representations

7.1. Example 1   283   7.3. Example 3   294

7.2. Example 2   290

In the preceding chapters a great many examples have been given to illustrate the kind of phenomenon dealt with in a particular section. Typically, these examples were then provided with a representation to show how FDG deals with the phenomenon in question. For the sake of clarity, all these representations were, however, given in simplified form, providing details only of those levels and layers relevant to the discussion.

In this final chapter, three sentences used in previous chapters will be provided with complete analyses at all four levels, including all relevant layers at each level. Each representation will be followed by a brief discussion of some specific aspects of the analysis. Although far from exhaustive, these discussions, together with the representations and, of course, the information given in previous chapters, provide a more complete picture not only of the way in which each element within these sentences is analysed at the four different levels, but also of how the four levels of analysis are related and how they complement each other to provide a satisfactory account of all pragmatic and semantic aspects of an utterance as reflected in its morphosyntactic and phonological form.

7.1. Example 1

(1) I hear you are planning to take your entire family to Ireland. (= Chapter 3, example (82A))

7.1.1. Interpersonal Level

At the Interpersonal Level, the sentence in (1) can be given the following representation:

(2) $(M_1: [(A_1: [(F_1: \text{DECL})$
           $(P_1)_S$
           $(P_2)_A$
           $(C_1: [(T_1)$
                (T_2)
                $(+\text{id } R_1: [\text{-S, } +A]^{R})$
                $(+\text{id } R_2: [(T_3) (T_4) (+\text{id } R_3: [\text{-S, } +A]^{R})]^{R})_{FOC}$
                $(R_4: \text{Ireland})]:$
          I-hear $^{C})]^{A})]^{M})$

The representation in (2) consists of a contentive communicative Discourse Act whose configurational head contains a Declarative Illocution, two Speech Participants, and a Communicated Content. Within the Communicated Content, we find two independent Ascriptive Subacts, T_1 and T_2, evoking the Properties *plan* and *take*. In addition, there are three Referential Subacts, evoking the entities described as *you* (R_1), *your entire family* (R_2), and *Ireland* (R_4). Lacking descriptive content, the proper name *Ireland* is represented as the lexical head of the relevant Referential Subact. The pronoun *you*, also devoid of semantic content, is analysed as a combination of features, [-S +A], indicating that we are dealing with a deictic Act of Reference picking out the Addressee. The Referential Subact corresponding to *your entire family* consists of two Ascriptive Subacts (T_3 and T_4, evoking the Properties *family* and *entire*), as well as another Referential Act (R_3), corresponding to the possessive pronoun *your* (see Hengeveld and Mackenzie 2008: 116). Note that although the pronouns *you* and *your* refer to the same entity (see Section 7.1.1), this entity is referred to twice, at different moments in time; we are therefore dealing with two separate Referential Subacts, as indicated by the different indices. As the element providing the most salient information, R_2 (*your entire family*) is assigned the pragmatic function Focus.

Finally, note that the expression *I hear* is not analysed as a separate Discourse Act; instead it is analysed as a fixed expression serving the interpersonal function of indicating that the Speaker received the information conveyed from someone else. As such, this expression is analysed as a (reportative) modifier at the layer of the Communicated Content. The reason for analysing the expression as a modifier rather than an operator is that modification (although restricted) is possible (*I hear from John that ...*).

7.1.2. Representational Level

At the Representational Level, example (1) will be given the following representation:

(3)   (p_1: (pres ep$_2$: (prog e$_1$: [(f$_1$: plan$_V$)
                (1 ^{s}x$_1$)$_A$
                (e$_2$: [(f$_2$: take$_V$)
                        (1 ^{s}x$_1$)$_A$
                        (1 ^{coll}x$_2$: [(f$_3$: family: (f$_4$: entire) ^{f})
                            (1 ^{s}x$_1$)$_{Ref}$] ^{x})$_U$
                        (l$_1$)$_{Dir}$] ^{e})$_U$] ^{e}) ^{ep}) ^{P})

First of all, note that since the expression *I hear* is analysed as an interpersonal modifier it is not represented at the Representational Level. What is represented at the Representational Level corresponds to the information contained within the configurational head of the Communicated Content. This information is now analysed as a Propositional Content consisting of a single Episode (ep$_1$), specified by the present tense operator (pres). The head of this Episode is the State-of-Affairs e$_1$, specified by the progressive aspect operator (prog). This State-of-Affairs has a configurational head consisting of a verbal Property (*plan*), a singular, countable Actor argument (x$_1$), and an Undergoer argument which takes the form of another State-of-Affairs (e$_2$). The Actor argument, x$_1$, corresponds to the Referential Subact R$_1$ at the Interpersonal Level; since it is realized as a pronoun (*you*), and since pronouns have no semantic (descriptive) content, it takes the form of a headless Individual (just a variable, no Property).

   As already mentioned, the Undergoer argument of the first State-of-Affairs is itself an (embedded) State-of-Affairs (e$_2$). This State-of-Affairs consists of the three-place verbal Property *take* and its three arguments, an Actor (x$_1$), an Undergoer (x$_2$), and a Location (l$_1$). Note that the Actor argument is coindexed with the Actor argument of the higher State-of-Affairs, reflecting the fact that the same Individual is involved in both predications. The second occurrence of this Actor does not, however, correspond to a Referential Subact at the Interpersonal Level; as a result, the Actor of the embedded State-of-Affairs is not expressed (only implied) and the verb appears in the infinitival form.

The second argument of the embedded State-of-Affairs (x_2) corresponds to a collective Individual designated by the head *family* and the modifier *entire*. Since family is a relational predicate (a family is always someone's family), it takes an argument with the semantic function Reference. This argument designates the same Individual as the Actor argument of both States-of-Affairs (x_1). This argument corresponds to an identifiable Referential Subact at the Interpersonal Level, (R_3: [−S, +A]), which, together with the semantic function Reference, triggers the possessive pronoun *your*.

Lastly, the third argument of *take* has the form of a headless Location, as the non-descriptive proper name *Ireland* has already been specified at the Interpersonal Level.

7.1.3. Morphosyntactic Level

The interpersonal and representational representations provided in (2) and (3) trigger the following morphosyntactic representation:

(4) $(Le_1: [(^{dep}Cl_1:$ $[(Np_1: (Nw_1: / aɪ /))_{Subj}$
$(Vp_1: (^fVw_1: hear))] ^{Cl})$
$(Cl_2: [(Np_2: (Nw_2: you))_{Subj}$
$(Vp_2: [(^fVw_2: be.pres.2.sg)$
$(^{non-f}Vw_3: / plæn-ɪŋ /)] ^{Vp})$
$(Cl_3: [(Gw_1: to)$
$(Vp_3: (^{nonf}Vw_4: / teɪk /))$
$(Np_3: [(Gw_2: your) (Ap_1: (Aw_1: entire))$
$(Nw_3: / fæmli /)] ^{Np})_{Obj}$
$(Adpp_i: [(Adpw_1: to) (Np_4:$
$(Nw_4: / aɪələnd /))] ^{Adpp})] ^{Cl})_{Obj}] ^{Cl})] ^{Le})$

Despite the fact that the expression *I hear* is not analysed as a Discourse Act at the Interpersonal Level, nor as a predication at the Representational Level, it is given clausal status at the Morphosyntactic Level, due to the fact that it consists of a pronoun in the nominative form filling the Subject position and a finite verb. Such an analysis reflects the in-between status of the expression in question, as a fixed expression with the outward appearance of a regular Clause. Note, however, that the expression does not have the status of a main Clause but that of a dependent Clause, combining with an independent Clause (Cl_2) without being a constituent of the independent Clause. What we have here is therefore an example of cosubordination.

Apart from this, the representation in (4) is quite straightforward. Note that there are two Objects: the Noun Phrase *your entire family*, which functions as the Object of the verb *take*, and the embedded Clause Cl_3 (*to take your entire family to Ireland*), which functions as the Object of the verb *plan*.

Finally, the finite verb *are*, triggered by the Progressive aspect operator, is not yet given in its final form; instead it is represented by a combination of the infinitival form of the dummy element *be* and the placeholders 'pres', '2', and 'pl' (the latter two features copied from the Subject to achieve person and number agreement), triggering the appropriate from at the Phonological Level.

As for the placement of the various elements, the application of the ordering principles introduced in Chapter 5 yield the following results:

(5) P^{pre} $| P^I$ P^M P^{M+1} P^{M+2}

    $^{\Sigma C}$I hear ^{Subj}you ^{Vf}be.pres.2.sg $^{Vnon-f}$planning ^{Obj}[to take ... to Ireland]

    1   4   2   3   5

As the only interpersonal element, the Communicated Content modifier *I hear* is the first element to be placed in position, going to P^I. Next, the placeholder 'pres', expressing the Episodical tense operator, is placed in the Clause medial position, where it is joined by the auxiliary *be*, triggered by the Progressive operator. Next, the main verb is placed in P^{M+1}. Finally, the Subject is placed in initial position and the Clausal Object in P^{M+2}.

The ordering of the elements in the Clausal Object can be accounted for as follows. First the presence of an Undergoer in the form of a (tense-less) State-of-Affairs triggers the placement of the particle *to* in position P^I, followed by the elements realizing the State-of-Affairs itself in P^{I+1}. Within the State-of-Affairs, the predicate is the first element to be placed in position, going to P^I. Next the argument *to Ireland* is placed in P^F. Note that placement of this element precedes placement of the Object *your entire family*, since its form and position are triggered by the semantic function Direction. Finally, the Object Phrase is placed in P^{I+1}.

(6) P^I P^{I+1}

      $[P^I$ P^{I+1} $P^F]$

    to $^{Vnon-f}$take ^{Obj}[your entire family] ^{Dir}[to Ireland]

Within the Noun Phrase *your entire family*, it is the possessive pronoun *your*, combining information from the Interpersonal Level (the Referential Subact operator '+identifiable') and the Representational Level (the semantic function Reference at the layer of the Individual), that is first placed in position (P^I). Subsequently, the modifier *entire*, as a non-core representational unit, is assigned position P^{I+1}. Then the head of the Noun Phrase is placed in position P^{I+2}.

(7) P^I P^{I+1} P^{I+2}

$^{\pi R/sf\text{-}x}$your $^{\sigma x}$entire   family

Within the Adpositional Phrase *to Ireland*, the Adposition *to*, expressing the semantic function Direction, is first placed in position, followed by the head of the Phrase, *Ireland*.

(8) P^I P^{I+1}

$^{sf\text{-}l}$to   Ireland

7.1.4. Phonological Level

The representations at the three higher levels of analysis lead to the following possible representation at the Phonological Level:

(9) $(U_1:$ (f $IP_1:$ [$(PP_1:$ $(PW_1:$ [$(S_1:$ / aɪ /) $(F_1:$ $(ss_2:$ / hɪə /))] $^{PW})$ $^{PP})$

$(PP_2:$ $(PW_2:$ [$(s_3:$ / jə /) $(F_2:$ [$(ss_4:$ / plæn /)

$(s_5:$ / nɪŋ /)] $^F)$] $^{PW})$ $^{PP})$

$(PP_3:$ $(PW_3:$ [$(s_6:$ / tə /) $(F_3:$ $ss_7:$ / teɪk /)] $^{PW})$ $^{PP})$

(f $PP_4:$ [$(PW_4:$ $(F_4:$ $(ss_8:$ / jʊər /))$^{PW})^1$ $(PW_5:$ [$(s_9:$ / ɪn /)

$(F_5:$ $(ss_{10}:$ / taɪə /))] $^{PW})$

$(PW_6:$ $(F_6:$ [$(ss_{11}:$ / fæm /) $(s_{12}:$ / li /)] $^F)$ $^{PW})$] $^{PP})$

(l $PP_5:$ [$(PW_7:$ [$(s_{13}:$ / tə /) $(F_7:$ [$(ss_{14}:$ / aɪə /)

$(s_{15}:$ / lənd /)] $^F)$] $^{PW})$] $^{PP})$] $^{IP})$ $^U)$

As pointed out in Chapter 6, there are a number of default relations between units at the higher three Levels and the Phonological Level. Thus, the

---

[1] Wells (1990: 78–9) argues that in syllables ending in / r / preceded by a long vowel or diphthong, the / r / occurs in syllable-final position (since its realization is that of syllable-final / r /, which is different from syllable-initial / r /).

Intonational Phrase IP_1 corresponds to a Discourse Act at the Interpersonal Level (A_1 in example (2)). At the Morphological Level, however, this Discourse Act consists of two Clauses, which results in a mismatch not only between the Interpersonal Level and the Morphosyntactic Level, but also between the Morphosyntactic Level and the Phonological Level. Note further that, whereas PP_3, PP_4, and PP_5 are in a one-to-one relationship with a Subact at the Interpersonal Level (T_2, R_2, and R_4, respectively), this does not hold for PP_2, which corresponds to two interpersonal units (R_1 and T_1).

Mismatches can also be found at the layer of the Phonological Word. As mentioned in Chapter 6, these typically correspond to a lexeme at the Interpersonal or Representational Level. This is obviously the case for the lexemes *entire* and *family*, and arguably for *Ireland* and *take*, which, in addition to a lexeme, also include an unstressed grammatical element (the particle *to* and the preposition *to*, both realized as unfooted syllables). In other cases, however, clear mismatches occur, as in the case of the possessive pronoun *your*, which does not contain any lexical information, but which—due to a certain degree of prosodic prominence (as reflected in its status as a separate Foot (F_4))—is nevertheless realized as a separate Phonological Word (PW_4). Note that the unstressed pronouns *I* and *you* do not form separate Words or Feet; instead they are realized as unfooted syllables within a larger Phonological Word (PW_1 and PW_2, respectively).

As can be seen from the representation in (9) the phoneme / n / in *planning* is analysed as ambisyllabic: since the first syllable of *planning* contains a short vowel it must have a coda; according to the Maximal Onsets Principle, however, the phoneme / n / belongs to the second syllable. This problem is solved by analysing the phoneme / n / as belonging to both syllables. To prevent the phoneme from being pronounced twice, a process of degemination will take place in the Articulator (see Chapter 6, Section 6.7).

The representation in (9) further contains three operators. The fall operator (f) at the layer of the Intonational Phrase is triggered by the Declarative Illocution at the Interpersonal Level and leads to a global falling intonation pattern. The second fall operator, specifying PP_4 (*your entire family*), is triggered by the pragmatic function Focus at the Interpersonal Level (assigned to the Referential Subact R_2). Together these fall operators result in a strong fall on the strong syllable of last the Phonological Word within this phrase, the first syllable of *family* (s_{11}). The low operator (l) on the final Phonological Phrase (PP_5) causes this final phrase (normally the locus of the pitch change) to be pronounced at a low level tone, reflecting the presupposed status of the information contained in this phrase.

7.2. Example 2

(10) The 1989 flooding of Lake Torrens was a rare event (COCA, written, magazine) (= Chapter 4, (70a))

7.2.1. Interpersonal Level

At the Interpersonal Level the sentence in (10) may be given the following interpersonal representation:

(11) $(M_1: (A_1: [(F_1: DECL)$
$(P_1)_S$
$(P_2)_A$
$(C_1: [(T_1: [(T_2) (T_3)] ^T)_{FOC}$
$(+id R_1: [(T_4) (R_2: Lake Torrens)$
$(R_3: 1989)] ^R)] ^C)] ^A) ^M)$

In Chapter 4 (Section 4.5.4), sentences like (10) were analysed as classificational sentences, consisting of an Ascriptive Subact and a Referential Subact. In (11), the Referential Subact (R_1) evokes the referent of the expression *the 1989 flooding of Lake Torrens*, the Ascriptive Subact (T_1) evokes the Property described as *a rare event*, which is ascribed to the referent of R_1. The Ascriptive Subact T_1 consists of two separate Ascriptive Subacts, evoking the Properties *event* and *rare*; the Referential Subact R_1 consists of an Ascriptive Subact (T_4), evoking the Property *flood*, and two more Referential Subacts, evoking the referents of the expressions *Lake Torrens* (R_2) and *1989* (R_3). Since the lexemes used to describe these referents are uniquely identifying, non-descriptive elements, they are specified at the Interpersonal Level. Note also that because these elements are unique, they do not contain the identifiability operator '+id', since their identifiable status need not be marked morphosyntactically (by the presence of a definite determiner). Finally, the pragmatic function Focus is assigned to the Ascriptive Subact T_1.

7.2.2. Representational Level

At the Representational Level, the sentence in (10) will be analysed as in (12):

(12) $(p_1: (past ep_1: (e_1: [(1 ep_2: (f_1: event): (f_2: rare) ^{ep})$
$(1 ep_3: [(f_3: flood_V) (^s x_1)_U]: (t_1) ^{ep})_U] ^e) ^{ep}) ^P)$

The representation in (12) consists of a single Propositional Content, corresponding to the Communicated Content at the Interpersonal Level. This Propositional Content consists of an Episode situated in the past. The Episode consists of a single State-of-Affairs (e_1), which, in turn, consists of two Episodes, (ep_2) and (ep_3), one of which (ep_2, corresponding to an Ascriptive Subact at the Interpersonal Level) functions as the non-verbal predicate, while the other (ep_3, corresponding to the Referential Subact at the Interpersonal Level) functions as the argument of this predicate. Since we are dealing with a classificational construction, this argument is being classified as belonging to the set designated by the non-verbal predicate (i.e. event designated by ep_3, i.e. *the 1989 flooding of Lake Torrens*, is classified as belonging to the set of rare events). Since the argument undergoes a process of classification, it is assigned the semantic function Undergoer.

When we look at the internal structure of the non-verbal predicate (ep_2), we find that it contains the singular operator '1', indicating that we are dealing with a single set. This set is then described by two Properties: the head of the Episode, *event* (f_1), and the modifier *rare* (f_2). As to be expected, these Properties both correspond to a headless Ascriptive Subact (T_2 and T_3, respectively).

The internal structure of the argument (ep_3) is slightly more complicated, consisting of the number operator '1', a configurational head and a modifier. The configurational head contains the verbal predicate *flood* and its Undergoer x_1 (the entity undergoing the process of flooding; i.e. *Lake Torrens*). This argument is represented as a headless Individual, since it contains no descriptive information (the proper name *Lake Torrens* already being given at the Interpersonal Level). The modifier of this Episode takes the form of a headless Time (t_1), expressed as *1989*.

Although designating Episodes, neither ep_2 nor ep_3 are specified for tense. Both, moreover, contain the operator '1'. As a result, both these events will be expressed as Noun Phrases at the Morphosyntactic Level. For the non-verbal predicate, ep_2, this is unproblematic, as it contains a nominal head (*event*). The argument ep_3, however, consists of a configurational head consisting of the verbal predicate *flood* and its argument *Lake Torrens*. Since verbal predicates normally do not function as the head of a Noun Phrase, the verbal predicate *flood* needs to be prepared for expression in a non-default morphosyntactic slot. This is done by adding the suffix *-ing*, thus allowing the verbal predicate to be expressed as a Nominal word. Similarly, the Undergoer argument (*Lake Torrens*) is adapted to its role as complement of a Nominal Word: instead of appearing as a Noun Phrase (the default form of the Undergoer of a verbal predicate), it appears in the form of an Adpositional Phrase (*of Lake Torrens*). What we have here, in other words, is a case of syntactic derivation.

7.2.3. Morphosyntactic Level

The interpersonal and representational analyses of the sentence in (10) lead to the following representation at the Morphosyntactic Level:

(13) (Le$_1$: [(Cl$_1$: [(Np$_1$: [(Gw$_1$: def.sg)
                              (Nw$_1$: [(Vs$_1$: / flʌd /) (Naff$_1$: / ɪŋ /)] ^{Np})
                              (Adpp$_i$: [(Adpw$_1$: of)
                              (Np$_2$: (Nw$_2$: / leɪktɒrəns /))] ^{Adpp})] ^{Np})$_{Subj}$
                    (Vp$_1$:   (^{f}Vw$_1$: be.past.3.sg))
                    (Np$_3$: [(Gw$_2$: indef.sg)
                              (Ap$_1$: (Aw$_1$: rare))
                              (Nw$_3$: / ɪvent /)] ^{Np})] ^{Cl})] ^{Le})

As explained in the previous section, the Nominal Word *flooding* is the result of a process of syntactic derivation. At the Morphosyntactic Level, this is reflected by the internal structure of this Word, which consists of a Verbal Stem / flʌd / and a Nominal (or nominalizing) Affix / ɪŋ /.

The second interesting feature of the representation in (13) is the presence of the support element *be*, introduced as a dummy element for expressing the operator tense in the absence of a verbal predicate. The dummy verb *be* is given in its infinitival form, followed by the placeholders for tense, person, and number (the latter two features being copied from the Subject to obtain person and number agreement); together these elements trigger the appropriate suppletive form at the Phonological Level.

Finally, it needs to be pointed out that whereas the 'def' placeholder (Gw$_1$) is triggered by the presence of the '+id' operator in the Referential Subact corresponding to the Noun Phrase *the 1989 flooding of Lake Torrens* at the Interpersonal Level, the indefinite placeholder 'indef' (Gw$_2$) in the Noun Phrase corresponding to the non-verbal predicate *a rare event* (Np$_3$) is triggered by the fact that this is a classificational sentence (distinguishing them from, for instance, identificational sentences, which consist of two definite Noun Phrases).

In placing the Morphosyntactic units of this Linguistic Expression in their appropriate position, we begin by putting the past tense placeholder (triggered by the highest non-core element, i.e. the tense operator) in its typical Clause-medial position. Next, the non-verbal predicate is placed in position P^{M+1}, after which the Subject is placed in P^I. Finally, the dummy verb *be* is inserted in the finite verb slot:

(14) P^I $\qquad\qquad\qquad\qquad\qquad\qquad\quad$ P^M $\qquad\qquad\quad$ P^{M+1}

$\quad$ ^{Subj}[the 1989 flooding of Lake Torrens] $\quad$ ^{Vf}be.past.3.sg $\quad$ ^{pred}[a rare event]

Within the Noun Phrase *the 1989 flooding of Lake Torrens*, the placeholder 'def' (triggered by an Interpersonal operator) is first placed in position, going to P^I. Next the placeholder 'sg' (triggered by the singularity operator '1') goes into P^M. Then the modifier *1989* is placed in the relative position P^{I+1}. Subsequently, the predicate *flooding* is placed in P^M (joining the singularity placeholder), and its argument, the Adpositional Phrase *of Lake Torrens*, in P^{M+1}:

(15) P^I $\quad$ P^{I+1} $\quad$ P^M $\qquad\qquad$ P^{M+1}

$\quad$ $^{\pi R}$def $\quad$ $^{\sigma ep}$1989 $\quad$ flooding.$^{\pi ep}$sg [of Lake Torrens]

Within the Adpositional Phrase the adposition *of*, expressing a semantic function, is first placed in P^I; then the head is placed in P^{I+2}:

(16) P^I $\qquad$ P^{I+1}

$\quad$ $^{sf-x}$of $\quad$ Lake Torrens

Finally, the placement of elements within the Noun Phrase *a rare event* is as follows:

(17) P^I $\qquad\qquad$ P^{I+1} $\qquad$ P^{I+2}

$\quad$ $^{\pi R}$indef $\quad$ $^{\sigma ep}$ rare $\quad$ event.$^{\pi ep}$sg

7.2.4. Phonological Level

The phonological representation of the sentence in (10) is given in (18):

(18) $(U_1: (^F IP_1: [(PP_1: [(PW_1: [(S_1: / ðə /) (F_1: [(SS_2: / flʌd /) (S_3: / dɪŋ /)]^F)]^{PW})$
$(PW_2: [(S_4: / əv /)$
$(F_2: (SS_5: / leɪk /))$
$(SF_3: [(SS_6: / tɒr /) (S_7: / rəns /)]^F)]^{PW})]^{PP})$
$(PP_2: [(PW_3: (F_4: [(SS_8: / wɒz /) (S_9: (/ zə /))]^F)^{PW})$
$(PW_4: (F_5: (SS_{10}: / reər /)))^2$
$(PW_5: [(S_{11}: / ɪ /) (F_6: (SS_{12}: / vent /))]^{PW})]^{PP})]^{IP})^U)$

In (18) we find three instances of ambisyllabicity (followed by degemina-tion): the / d / in *flooding*, the / r / in *Torrens*, and the / z / in *was a*. As for the coding of the pragmatic function Focus, note that in this case this does not lead to an extra fall operator in the relevant Phonological Phrase (PP$_2$). This is not necessary, since the fall operator of the Intonational Phrase is by default expressed on the most strongly stressed syllable of the final Phrase (in this case the second syllable of *event*).

7.3. Example 3

(19)   Martha reportedly struck her makeup artist with a brush (COCA, spoken, talk show) (= Chapter 4, (81b))

7.3.1. Interpersonal Level

At the Interpersonal Level the sentence in example (19) may be represented as follows:

(20) $(M_1: (A_1: [(F_1: DECL)$
$(P_1)_S$
$(P_2)_A$
$(C_1: [(T_1)$
$(R_1: Martha)$
$(+id R_2: [(T_2: [(T_3) (T_4)]^T) (+id R_3)]^R)$
$(-id R_4: (T_5))$
reportedly $^C)_{FOC}]^A)^M)$

The interpersonal analysis of this sentence is fairly straightforward, consist-ing of a declarative Discourse Act A$_1$, containing a focal Communicated

---

[2] Compare to the analysis of *your* in example (9).

Content C_1. The configurational head of this Communicated Content consists of three Subacts: the Ascriptive Subact T_1 (evoking the Property *strike*) and three Referential Subacts (R_1, evoking the entity described as *Martha*, R_2, evoking the identifiable entity described as *her makeup artist*, and R_4, evoking the unidentifiable entity described as *a brush*). Of these, R_2 has a configurational head, made up of the Ascriptive Subact *makeup artist* (T_2) and the Referential Subact corresponding to the possessive pronoun *her* (which, since it is anaphoric, is represented as a headless Referential Subact R_3). The Ascriptive Subact T_2 also has a configurational head, consisting of the Ascriptive Subacts T_3 and T_4, representing the Properties *makeup* and *artist*.

Finally, the Communicated Content is modified by the reportative adverb *reportedly*, indicating that the Speaker obtained this information from someone else.

7.3.2. Representational Level

At the Representational Level the sentence in (19) will be analysed as in (21):

(21) $(p_1: (\text{past ep}_2: (e_2:[$ $(f_1: \text{strike}_V)$

           $(1\ {}^s x_1)_A$

           $(1\ {}^s x_2: (f_2: (f_3: \text{artist}_N: (f_4: \text{makeup}_N)\ ^f)\ ^f):$

                $(1\ {}^s x_1)_{Ass}\ {}^X)_U]:$

      $(f_5: [(f_6: \text{with}_{Adp}) (1\ {}^s x_3: (f_7: \text{brush}_N))_{Ref}]\ ^f)\ ^e)\ ^{ep})\ ^P)$

Two aspects of this representation merit some attention. In the first place, the Undergoer argument x_2 is represented as an Individual with a compositional lexical head f_2, expressed as the compound noun *makeup artist*. Note that within this compositional head, the Property *artist* (f_3) functions as the head, while the Property *makeup* (f_4) functions as a modifier; we are, in other words, dealing with an endocentric compound (see Chapter 4, Section 4.6.2). The Individual x_2 further contains a modifier with the semantic function Associative. This modifier, a singular headless Individual co-indexed with the Actor, is expressed as *her*.

The second interesting aspect of the representation in (21) is the manner modifier *with a brush*, here represented as a Property (f_5) with a configurational head consisting of a predicate, the lexical adposition *with* (f_6), and its Reference argument, the Individual *a brush* (x_3).

7.3.3. *Morphosyntactic Level*

The interpersonal and representational representations of example (19) trigger the morphosyntactic representation given in (22):

(22) (Le$_1$: [(Cl$_1$: [(Np$_1$:   (Nw$_1$: / mɑ:θə /))$_{Subj}$
                     (Advp$_i$: (Advw$_1$: / rɪpɔ:tɪdli /))
                     (Vp$_1$:   (^{f}Vw$_1$: strike.past))
                     (Np$_2$: [(Gw$_1$: her)
                               (Nw$_2$: [(Ns$_1$:/ meɪkʌp /)
                                   (Ns$_2$: / ɑ:tɪst /)] ^{Nw})] ^{Np})$_{Obj}$
                     (Adpp$_1$: [(Adpw$_1$: / wɪð /)
                               (Np$_3$: [(Gw$_2$: indef.sg)
                                   (Nw$_3$: / brʌʃ /)] ^{Np})] ^{Adpp})] ^{Cl})] ^{Le})

The placement of constituents within each layer of this representation is specified in examples (23)–(27):

(23) P^I P^M P^{M+1} P^{M+2} P^F
      ^{Subj}Martha $^{\Sigma C}$reportedly ^{Vf}strike-past ^{Obj}[her makeup artist] ^{oe}[with a brush]

(24) P^I P^{I+1}
      $^{\pi R/\sigma x}$her   [makeup artist]

(25) P^I P^{I+1}
      ^{of}makeup   artist

(26) P^I P^{I+1}
      with ^{Ref}[a brush]

(27) P^I P^{I+1}
      $^{\pi R}$indef   brush.$^{\pi x}$sg

Note that in (25) the first element of the compound, the modifier *makeup*, is also the first element to be placed, going to P^I, followed by the head (*artist*), in P^{I+1}. In (26), the predicate *with* is the first element to be assigned a position, going to P^I, followed by the argument *a brush*, in P^{I+1}.

7.3.4. Phonological Level

The phonological representation of example (19) is given in (28):

(28) $(U_1$: (f IP$_1$: [(PP$_1$:   (PW$_1$: (F$_1$: [(ss$_1$: / mɑ: /) (s$_2$: / θə /)] ^{F}) ^{PW}) ^{PP})

(PP$_2$:   (PW$_2$: [(s$_3$: / rɪp /) (F$_2$: [(ss$_4$: / pɔ: /) (s$_5$: / tɪd /)] ^{F})

(s$_6$: / li /)] ^{PW}) ^{PP})

(PP$_3$: [(PW$_3$: (F$_3$: [(ss$_7$: / strʌk /) (s$_8$: / hə /)] ^{F}) ^{PW})

(PW$_4$: [(PW$_5$: [(sF$_4$: (ss$_9$: / meɪk /)) (F$_5$: (ss$_{10}$: / ʌp /))] ^{PW})

(PW$_6$: (F$_6$: [(ss$_{11}$: / ɑ: /) (s$_{12}$: / tɪst /)] ^{F}) ^{PW})] ^{PP})

(PP$_4$: [(PW$_7$: (F$_7$: [(ss$_{13}$: / wɪð /) (s$_{14}$: / ə /)]) ^{PW})

(PW$_8$: (F$_8$: (ss$_{15}$: / brʌʃ /)))] ^{PP})] ^{IP}) ^{U})

An interesting feature of this representation is the fact that the Phonological Word *reportedly* (PW$_2$) contains two unfooted syllables, due to the fact that it contains only one stressed syllable. This stressed syllable (s$_4$, / pɔ: /) forms a Foot with the following unstressed syllable (s$_5$, / tɪd /). The unstressed syllables preceding and following this Foot (s$_3$, / rɪp /, and s$_6$, / li /) are not part of a Foot.

Also note the complex phonological structure of the compound *makeup artist*, which is represented as a Phonological Word (PW$_4$), which in turn consists of two more Phonological Words (PW$_5$, *makeup*, and PW$_6$, *artist*). Since both syllables of the first of these Phonological Words (*make* and *up*) are stressed, they form two Feet; since primary stress is on the first Foot, this Foot is marked by the operator 'strong'. The second Phonological Word (*artist*) consists of a single Foot consisting of two Syllables, the first of which is stressed. The overall effect is that of three levels of stress within the compound as a whole, with the primary stress going to the first syllable (/ meɪk /), with secondary stress on the next two Syllables (/ ʌp / and / ɑ: /), and with a final unstressed Syllable (/ tɪst /).

Glossary

absolute tense (RL): a grammatical means to specify the time of occurrence of an Episode in relation to the time of speaking, independently from any other Episodes. English has three absolute tenses: present, past, and future, each of which can combine with phasal aspect (e.g. progressive and perfect aspect). See also **relative tense**.

absolutive-ergative alignment: see **alignment**.

Affix (ML): Affixes are Morphemes that can only be used in combination with a Stem and which cannot function as the head of a Word (e.g. bound Morphemes like the plural or past tense ending). In English, two kinds of Affixes can be distinguished: purely grammatical Affixes (such as the plural and tense endings) and derivational (lexical) Affixes, introduced during the process of syntactic derivation (e.g. *-er*, *-ize*, *-ly*). See also **Stem, syntactic derivation**.

agreement (ML): a mechanism causing certain properties of one element to be copied onto one or more other elements. Two kinds of agreement can be distinguished: argument agreement (which takes place between two elements at the same layer, e.g. between subject and finite verb) and operator agreement (where the form of an element at a lower layer is determined by an operator at a higher layer, e.g. *consecutio temporum*).

alienable possession (RL): possessive relation between two entities, each of which can exist (be evoked) independently from the other; e.g. *Udo's bike, my dog*. In these constructions the possessor (*Udo, I*) functions as a modifier with the semantic function Associative. See also **inalienable possession**.

alignment (ML): process whereby interpersonal and representational units are mapped onto (or aligned with) morphosyntactic units; particularly relevant in the assignment of the syntactic functions Subject and Object. English makes use of a nominative–accusative alignment system, in which the syntactic function Subject is assigned to the Actor or Undergoer argument in a one-place predication frame, as well as to the Actor argument in a two-place predication frame; these elements appear in the nominative form; the Undergoer in a two-place predication frame, on the other hand, is assigned Object function and appears in the accusative form. Other languages use an absolute–ergative alignment system, which means that the Actor argument of a one-place predication frame and the Undergoer arguments of one- and two-place predication frames receive the same morphosyntactic treatment; these elements appear in the Absolutive form. The Actor in a two-place predication frame appears in the Ergative form. See also **interpersonal alignment, morphosyntactic alignment, representational alignment**.

ambisyllabicity (PL): an ambisyllabic consonant is a consonant which, although it is expressed only once, is analysed as belonging to two adjacent Syllables (e.g. / t / in *better*). See also **degemination.**

anaphoricity (RL): the term anaphoricity is used to indicate an identity relation between two units at the Representational Level, e.g. co-reference between two Individuals (*the house–it*) or Properties (*a blue car–a red one*).

anaphoric pronoun (IL/RL): pronoun used to refer to an entity previously introduced in the discourse (e.g. *he/she/it, they, this/that* or *one*). See also **deictic pronoun.**

approximator (IL): lexical or grammatical element used to indicate that the Property evoked can only be ascribed approximately to the referent in question (e.g. *sort-of, more or less, so to speak*). See also **exactness marker.**

argument (RL): a component of a configurational head at the Representational Level; within this head arguments function as dependents of the predicate. A sentence like *Ellie reads many books*, for instance, describes an SoA with a configurational head containing a verbal predicate (*read*) and two arguments (an Actor, *Ellie*, and an Undergoer, *many books*). Nominal predicates can also have arguments; in that case the relation between predicate and argument is typically one of inalienable possession (e.g. *Miriam's sister*).

argument agreement (ML): see **agreement.**

Ascriptive Subact (IL): see **Subact of Ascription.**

Aside (IL): a rhetorical function assigned to a dependent Discourse Act serving the communicative function of providing background information about one of the entities evoked within the nuclear Discourse Act. Asides are typically expressed as non-restrictive relative clauses or appositive elements. See also **rhetorical function.**

assimilation: process whereby a sound belonging to one word becomes similar or identical to a sound belonging to a neighbouring word; e.g. *ten pounds*: [tenpaʊndz] → [tempaʊndz]. When this process is optional and unsystematic, as in English, it is assumed to take place in the Output Component.

auxiliary verb (RL): Grammatical Morpheme, typically triggered by the presence of a representational operator, e.g. *have* (triggered by the phasal aspect operator 'perfect') or *may* (triggered by the epistemic modality operator 'probability').

categorical sentence (IL): a sentence which provides new information about an element related to the ongoing discourse. Represented at the Interpersonal Level by a content frame containing (at least) one Subact with the pragmatic function Topic and one with the pragmatic function Focus: $(C_1: [(SA_1)_{TOP} \ldots (SA_N)_{FOC}])$. See also **thetic sentence.**

classificational sentence (RL): copular sentence which at the Representational Level consists of an Undergoer argument and a non-verbal predicate designating the class to which the Undergoer belongs, e.g. *Robert is a teacher*. See also **existential, identificational,** and **relational sentence.**

Clause (ML): the second-highest layer at the Morphosyntactic Level, part of a Linguistic Expression and consisting of a sequenced combination of Words (Xw), Phrases (Xp), and other (embedded) Clauses. Clauses are the default expression of Discourse Acts and SoAs.

clitic (ML): an element that behaves morphosyntactically as a separate word (usually a function word), but which phonologically depends on (is attached to) another word; e.g. the element *'ll* in *We'll do it*.

coda (PL): part of the Syllable consisting of one or more consonants following the peak (optional in English). See also **onset, peak**.

coercion (RL/ML): process whereby the class of a lexeme is adapted to the requirements of its syntactic position. Coercion applies to lexemes that are used in a non-default position at the Representational Level and need to be prepared for their function at the Morphosyntactic Level. A verbal lexeme (*play*), for instance, can be used as the head of an Individual, a position typically taken by nominal lexemes; in that case the class of the verbal lexeme is adapted: *play* → *player*. See also **syntactic derivation**.

collective noun (RL): nominal lexeme used to describe a non-countable, inherently plural, homogeneous Individual, e.g. *police, cattle*. See also **count noun, mass noun**.

Communicated Content (IL): interpersonal layer capturing everything a Speaker wishes to evoke. Communicated Contents are part of the configurational head of a Discourse Act; they consists of one or more Subacts.

competence: a Speaker's abstract knowledge about the (syntactic) structure of his/her native language. See also **performance**.

Concession (IL): a rhetorical function assigned to a dependent Discourse Act serving the communicative function of indicating that the Speaker is aware of the fact that the content of the preceding Discourse Act may not have been expected. See also **rhetorical function**.

configurational head: a head consisting of two or more non-hierarchically related units.

consecutio temporum **(ML):** type of operator agreement whereby the past tense marking of the main Clause is copied onto the embedded Clause.

content frame (IL): interpersonal core unit; the configurational head of the Communicated Content, consisting of one or more Subacts. See also **predication frame**.

Content interrogatives: see *Wh*-**interrogative**.

Contrast (IL): pragmatic function assigned to Subacts signalling the Speaker's desire to bring out certain differences between two or more Communicated Contents or between a Communicated Content and other contextually available information. See also **pragmatic function**.

coordination (ML): one of the basic configurations (macrotemplates) of the Linguistic Expression, consisting of two or more Clauses, each of which can be used independently.

copular verb (ML): dummy element introduced at the Morphosyntactic Level to express tense and number distinctions in the absence of a verbal element (main verb or auxiliary).

copulative compound (RL): type of compound consisting of two lexemes with equal status, which both apply directly to the entity designated; e.g. *sofa-bed*, *bittersweet*.

core unit (IL/RL): unit at the Interpersonal or Representational Level that forms the core of that level in that it contains information that is essential. At the Interpersonal Level the core unit is the configurational head of the Communicated Contents (the content frame); at the Representational Level, the core unit is the configurational head of the State-of-Affairs (the predication frame). See also **non-core unit**.

Correction (IL): a rhetorical function assigned to a dependent Discourse Act serving the communicative function of clarifying (part of) the preceding (nuclear) Discourse Act. See also **rhetorical function**.

co-subordination (ML): one of the basic configurations (macrotemplates) of the Linguistic Expression, consisting of two or more Clauses (neither part of the other), only one of which can be used independently.

count noun (RL): nominal lexeme typically (but not exclusively) used to describe a countable, heterogeneous Individual, e.g. *car*, *boy*, *party*. See also **mass noun**, **collective noun**.

Declarative (IL): one of the basic abstract Illocutions of English, providing the formal means to provide information; e.g. *Hella lives in Amsterdam*. See also **Illocution**.

degemination: process taking place in the Output Component, whereby two consonants are reduced to a single phoneme. In English, degemination is triggered in the case of ambisyllabicity to prevent the ambisyllabic consonant from being pronounced twice. See also **ambisyllabicity**.

deictic pronoun (IL): pronoun used to refer to an entity present in the discourse situation: the Speaker (I, we), Addressee (you), or a third party (he/she/they; this/that, etc). See also **anaphoric pronoun**.

deontic modality (RL): type of event-oriented modality indicating what is obligatory or permitted according to a certain moral code or legal system, specifying general rules of conduct. In English, deontic modality is expressed grammatically by means of a modal auxiliary (e.g. *have to*, *need to*), represented as an operator at the layer of the State-of-Affairs.

deontic participant-oriented modality (RL): type of participant-oriented modality indicating a moral obligation on the part of one of the participants in a State-of-Affairs. In English, deontic participant-oriented modality is expressed grammatically by means of a modal auxiliary (e.g. *may*), triggered by an operator at the layer of the State-of-Affairs. See also **participant-oriented modality, facultative participant-oriented modality**.

dependence (IL/RL): relation between two units within a configurational head at any of the four levels, one of which functions as the nucleus, the other as the dependent; e.g. between a nuclear and a dependent Discourse Act within the Move, or between a predicate and (one of) its argument(s) within the State-of-Affairs. The dependent unit is assigned a (rhetorical or semantic) function reflecting the relation between the two units. See also **equipollence**.

descriptive grammar: grammar describing the function and form of language as it is used.

Designation (RL): process taking place at the Representational Level, where the different layers designate (single out) entities from the extra-linguistic world (States-of-Affairs, Individuals, Properties, etc.) by specifying the semantic aspects of these entities. See also **Evocation**, **semantic categories**.

dialect: language variety spoken in a specific geographic area.

Discourse Act (IL): interpersonal layer constituting the smallest identifiable unit of communication. Discourse Acts form part of a Move; within the Move, they can be nuclear (used independently from another Discourse Act) or dependent (subsidiary to another Discourse Act). As for their internal structure, they have a configurational head consisting of an Illocution, the Speech Participants, and a Communicated Content. Discourse Acts are the basic unit of analysis in FDG. Their default relation is with the Clause at the Morphosyntactic Level and with the Intonational Phrase at the Phonological Level, but they may also correspond to larger or smaller units at both levels. See also **nucleus**, **dependence**, and **equipollence**.

domain integrity: the principle of domain integrity dictates that units of information that belong together at the Interpersonal and Representational Levels are also placed next to each other at the Morphosyntactical Level (e.g. modifiers at a particular layer are placed immediately before or after the head of that layer).

dummy element (ML): an a-functional morphosyntactic element, i.e. an element which does not correspond to any specific unit at the Interpersonal or Representational Level, introduced at the Morphosyntactic Level to fill an obligatory position; e.g. the dummy subject *it* in *It rains*.

dynamic State-of-Affairs (RL): State-of-Affairs containing an Actor argument which is actively and volitionally involved in the State-of-Affairs in question (e.g. *John left*, *Mary closed the door*). See also **non-dynamic State-of-Affairs**.

elision: process whereby under certain circumstances sounds are not pronounced; e.g. *asked*: [ɑːskt] → [ɑːst]. When this process is optional and unsystematic, as in English, it is assumed to take place in the Output Component.

embedding (RL): process whereby a State-of-Affairs or Propositional Content functions as an argument within another State-of-Affairs; e.g. *That she passed the exam surprised me, I know that she stole the exam papers*.

Encoding: one of the two operations taking place in the Grammatical Component. During the operation of Encoding the pragmatic and semantic representations produced during Formulation are converted into language-specific morphosyntactic representations (Morphosyntactic Encoding) and phonological representations (Phonological Encoding). See also **Formulation**.

end focus (IL/ML): the tendency to place new or salient information at the end of a Clause or Phrase.

end weight (ML): the tendency to place long or complex information at the end of a Clause or Phrase.

endocentric compound (RL): type of compound consisting of two lexemes, one of which (the rightmost component) functions as the head, indicating the entity designated, and the other as a modifier, specifying some additional property of this entity; e.g. *file name, blackboard.*

Episode (RL): a representational layer representing a coherent sequence of events characterized by unity of participants, time, and location. Episodes are part of a Propositional Content and consist of one or more States-of-Affairs.

epistemic modality (RL): type of modality that allows a speaker to indicate the likelihood that an SoA will take place. See **subjective epistemic modality, objective epistemic modality**.

equiordination (ML): one of the basic configurations (macrotemplates) of the Linguistic Expression, consisting of two mutually dependent units of the same type, i.e. two Clauses (Clausal equiordination) or two Phrases (Phrasal equiordination).

equipollence: equipollent units have the same status within a higher unit; e.g. two independent (nuclear) Discourse Acts within a Move (same communicative status) or two coordinated Clauses within a Linguistic Expression (same formal status). See also **dependence**.

event-oriented modality (RL): type of modality that allows a Speaker to indicate the likelihood or desirability of the SoA's taking place; e.g. objective epistemic modality and deontic modality.

evidential modality (RL): type of modality that allows a Speaker to indicate the (non-verbal) source of the contents of a proposition. Can be expressed lexically by such Propositional Content modifiers as *in my experience*. See also **experiential evidentiality, inferential evidentiality**.

Evocation (IL): action performed at the Interpersonal Level, where Speakers, by using Subacts of Ascription and Reference, evoke the communicatively relevant Properties and Referents within a Discourse Act. See **Subact of Ascription, Subact of Reference, Designation**.

exactness marker (IL): lexical or grammatical element used to indicate that the Property evoked applies exactly to the referent. See also **approximator**.

Exclamative (IL): one of the minor abstract Illocutions of English, providing the formal means to express the Speaker's strong feelings about something or someone (delight, anger, surprise, excitement, etc.); e.g. *What a mess!* See also **Illocution**.

existential sentence (RL): a copular sentence introduced by the dummy element *there*, consisting at the Representational Level of a single argument designating an entity whose existence is asserted, e.g. *There is only one candidate*. Existential sentences do not contain a predicate. See also **classificational, identificational**, and **relational sentence**.

exocentric compound (RL): type of compound consisting of two lexemes, one of which (the rightmost component) functions as the head, and the other as a modifier, specifying some additional property of this entity. Unlike with endocentric compounds, however, the head does not literally describe the entity designated, but does so by means of metonymy; e.g. *skinhead, farmhand*.

experiential evidentiality (RL): subtype of evidential modality, indicating that the source of a Propositional Content is the Speaker's own experience. Typically expressed by means of a propositional modifier (e.g. *in my experience, from what I've seen,* etc.). See also **evidential modality, inferential evidentiality**.

extra-clausality (ML): one of the basic configurations (macrotemplates) of the Linguistic Expression, consisting of a Noun Phrase and a Clause, whereby only the Clause can be used independently.

facultative participant-oriented modality (RL): type of participant-oriented modality indicating that a participant has the ability to participate in the designated State-of-Affairs. In English, facultative participant-oriented modality can be expressed grammatically by means of the auxiliaries *can* and *be able to*. See also **participant-oriented modality, deontic participant-oriented modality**.

fixed stress (PL): in a language with fixed stress, the position of the stress is fully predictable, as it is always located on the same Syllable within a word.

Focus (IL): pragmatic function assigned to Subacts presenting new information, either to fill a gap in the Addressee's knowledge (NewFoc) or to correct the Addressee's knowledge (CorFoc). See also **pragmatic function**.

Foot (PL): phonological layer, characterized by the presence of one strong Syllable and (in most cases) one weak Syllable; in English, the strong Syllable is always the first Syllable in a Foot. One or more Feet make up a Phonological Word. See also **iambic Foot, trochaic Foot**.

Formulation: one of the two operations taking place in the Grammatical Component. During the operation of Formulation information from the Conceptual Component is translated into the appropriate language-specific pragmatic and semantic representations. These pragmatic and semantic representations form the input to the operation of Encoding. See also **Encoding**.

frame (IL/RL): one of the primitives available during the operation of Formulation, defining the possible combinations of elements at each layer.

function: in FDG, units can be assigned a (rhetorical, pragmatic, semantic, or syntactic) function; these functions represent grammatically expressed information about the relation between the units to which they are assigned and other units within the same layer. See also **rhetorical function, pragmatic function, semantic function, syntactic function**.

functional stability: principle stating that units within a certain interpersonal or representational layer tend to be placed in the same position with regard to each other (e.g. modifiers indicating size precede those indicating colour: *a big black car*).

gradience: the lack of clear-cut distinctions between categories. Gradience in linguistics is often caused by (gradual) changes in language (e.g. grammaticalization or lexicalization).

Grammatical Word (ML): a morphosyntactic unit that does not correspond to any lexical information at the Interpersonal or Representational Level. There are three types of Grammatical Word: (i) auxiliaries (triggered by interpersonal and representational operators); (ii) pronouns (corresponding to non-lexical interpersonal and/or representational units); and (iii) dummy elements (which do not correspond to any interpersonal or representational information). See also **Lexical Word**.

grammaticalization: process whereby a lexical item (e.g. a verb or a noun) gradually changes into a grammatical item (e.g. a particle or an affix); e.g. the grammatical free Morpheme *will*, which developed out of the Old English lexical verb *willan* 'to want'.

habitual aspect (RL): type of phasal aspect indicating that a State-of-Affairs occurs or occurred habitually. In English, habitual aspect indicating a past habit is expressed grammatically by means of the habitual auxiliary *used to* (e.g. *Sue used to visit me every day*). Represented as the operator 'hab' at the layer of the State-of-Affairs. See also **phasal aspect**.

Hortative (IL): one of the minor abstract Illocutions of English, providing the formal means to encourage the Speaker and Addressee to perform some action; e.g. *Let's go home*. See also **Illocution**.

hypothetical modality (RL): subtype of subjective epistemic modality, expressed at the layer of the Propositional Content, allowing a Speaker to create a possible world in which another Propositional Content is true. Can be expressed grammatically by means of the subordinator *if* (***If it rains**, we won't go.*).

iambic Foot (PL): a Foot in which the second Syllable is strong.

iambic reversal (PL): situation in which the stress is placed on the second Syllable of what would otherwise have been a trochaic Foot, in order to obtain a more even rhythm. See **iambic Foot, trochaic Foot**.

iconicity: in semiotics the notion of iconicity is used to describe a perceived non-arbitrary relation between the form of a linguistic expression and the extra-linguistic world designated by that expression. In FDG it is used to describe a direct relation between function (Formulation) and form (Encoding), i.e. between interpersonal and representational units on the one hand, and morphosyntactic and phonological units on the other.

identificational sentence (RL): copular sentence which at the Representational Level consists of two arguments designating the same entity e.g. *Violet is the winner/The winner is Violet*. Identificational sentences do not contain a predicate. See also **classificational, existential**, and **relational sentence**.

Illocution (IL): interpersonal layer representing the conventionalized means available in a language to indicate the Speaker's communicative intentions. Illocutions typically have an abstract head (e.g. Declarative, Interrogative, and Imperative), but may also be headed by lexical items (e.g. vocatives or performative verbs). Illocutions are an obligatory part of the configurational head of the Discourse Act.

Imperative (IL): one of the basic abstract Illocutions of English, providing the formal means to express an order; e.g. *Go away!* See also **Illocution, Prohibitive**.

inalienable possession (RL): possessive relation between two entities which do not exist (cannot be evoked) independently from each other; e.g. *Miriam's sister, my body*. In these constructions the possessor (*Miriam, I*) functions as an argument of the nominal predicate (*sister, body*) with the semantic function Reference. See also **alienable possession**.

incorporation (ML): process whereby the argument of a verbal predicate at the Representational Level is expressed as part of the Verbal Word corresponding to the verbal predicate. In English, incorporation is highly constrained: there is no productive process to form such Verbal Words as **to birdwatch* or **to celloplay*. Incorporation does, however, freely take place when it goes hand in hand with a process of syntactic derivation, yielding such compounds as *birdwatcher* or *cello player*. See also **synthetic compounding**.

Individual (RL): a representational layer representing a concrete, tangible entity occupying a (unique) portion of space. In English, three subtypes of Individual can be distinguished: countable Individuals (typically described by means of a count noun, e.g. *car*), non-countable Individuals or masses (typically described by means of a mass noun; e.g. *water*) and collections of Individuals (typically described by means of a collective noun, e.g. *police*). See also **count noun, mass noun, collective noun**.

inferential evidentiality (RL): subtype of evidential modality, indicating that the Speaker has inferred the contents of a proposition from external (e.g. visual) evidence. Typically expressed by means of a propositional modifier (e.g. *I see you've decided to stay.*). See also **evidential modality, experiential evidentiality**.

ingressive aspect (RL): type of phasal aspect indicating the start of a new State-of-Affairs. In English, ingressive aspect may be expressed periphrastically by means of the expression *got to* (e.g. *Gunther got to believing he could do it*). Represented as the operator 'ingr' at the layer of the State-of-Affairs. See also **phasal aspect**.

innateness: the quality of being already present in a person or animal when they are born. The ability to learn a language is often regarded as an innate characteristic of human beings. See also **language faculty, language universal**.

interjection (IL): lexical item with little semantic contents, typically functioning as a direct expression of a Speaker's emotions; e.g. *ouch!, yuck!*

Interpellative (IL): one of the minor abstract Illocutions of English, providing the formal means to attract an Addressee's attention; e.g. *Hey, Julia!* See also **Illocution**.

interpersonal alignment (ML): alignment system in which the morphosyntactic behaviour of elements, i.e. their form and the order in which they appear, can be explained in terms of the interpersonal features of these elements (e.g. pragmatic functions, referentiality, identifiability, etc.). See also **alignment**.

Interrogative (IL): one of the basic abstract Illocutions of English, providing the formal means to elicit information from an Addressee. See also **Illocution**, *Wh*-**interrogative**, *Yes–no* **interrogative**.

Intonational Phrase (PL): phonological layer, recognizable by the presence of a single pitch change (nucleus), triggered by a specific Illocution at the Interpersonal Level. Intonational Phrases are part of an Utterance and consist of one or more Phonological Phrases; they typically correlate with Discourse Acts at the Interpersonal Level.

isochronicity (PL): situation in which stressed Syllables occur at regular intervals of time (which means that Feet are of more or less equal length). Languages characterized by this property are referred to as stress-timed languages.

language acquisition device: see **language faculty**.

language faculty: part of the brain (from the anatomical, neural perspective) or mind (from the mental, cognitive perspective) that makes it possible for human beings to learn language (also referred to as the language acquisition device). Often claimed to be innate and unique to human beings. See also **innateness, language universal**.

language universal: a linguistic feature common to all languages. All language universals together are claimed to form the universal grammar, sometimes equated with the language faculty (cognitive perspective). See also **language faculty**.

Lexeme (IL/RL): one of the primitives available during the operation of Formulation; a meaningful element providing the descriptive information needed for successful communication.

Lexical Word (ML): a morphosyntactic unit that corresponds to lexical information at the Interpersonal or Representational Level. Lexical Words are divided into Verbal Words, Nominal Words, Adjectival Words, Adverbial Words, and Adpositional Words. Lexical Words function as the head of a Phrase, with the syntactic category of the Lexical Word determining the type of Phrase. See also **Grammatical Word**.

Linguistic Expression (ML): the highest layer at the Morphosyntactic Level, typically consisting of one or more lower-layer morphosyntactic units (Clauses, Phrases, or Words). Linguistic Expressions can be subcategorized according to their internal structure, yielding a number of macrotemplates: **coordination, listing, cosubordination, extra-clausality, clausal equiordination,** and **phrasal equiordination**.

linking (PL): process whereby a sound (e.g. / r /) is introduced to link two words; e.g. *four apples*: [fɔ æpəlz] → [fɔræpəlz].

listing (ML): one of the basic configurations (macrotemplates) of the Linguistic Expression, consisting of two or more coordinated Phrases.

Location (RL): minor semantic category relevant for English, designating a 'portion of space' where a physical entity (Individual) or event (State-of-Affairs) can be located. Locations typically function as modifiers (*the book **on the table**; John* *bought the book **in London***), but may also function as arguments (*John put the book **on the table***; *John lives **in London***).

macrotemplate (ML): one of a limited number of abstract morphosyntactic templates (linearly ordered combinations of Morphosyntactic units) representing an infinite number of specific templates. See also **microtemplate**.

mass noun (RL): nominal lexeme typically (but not exclusively) used to describe a non-countable, homogeneous Individual, e.g. *water*, *butter*, *fun*. See also **count noun**, **collective noun**.

Maximal Onsets Principle (PL): principle which states that the onset of a non-first Syllable of a word should consist of as many consonants as possible (in a specific language).

microtemplate (ML): one of an infinite number of specific morphosyntactic templates (linearly ordered combinations of Morphosyntactic units) allowed in a language. See also **macrotemplate**.

mitigation (IL): the weakening of the force of an Illocution by the Speaker, typically with the intention of expressing tentativity (*That is **perhaps** not a good idea*) or politeness (***Please** wait behind the red line*). Mitigating elements are analysed as operators or modifiers at the layer of the Illocution. See also **reinforcement**.

modifier (IL/RL): lexical element providing optional information about the entity represented by a particular layer.

Morpheme (ML): lowest layer at the Morphosyntactic Level. Morphemes can be subclassified along two parameters: free vs. bound and lexical vs. grammatical. Free lexical Morphemes are Stems, elements with lexical content that can be used independently; free grammatical Morphemes are auxiliary verbs. Bound Morphemes (lexical or grammatical) are Affixes. See also **Stem, Affix, auxiliary verb**.

morphosyntactic alignment (ML): alignment system in which the morphosyntactic behaviour of elements, i.e. their form and the order in which they appear, can be explained in terms of the morphosyntactic features of these elements (e.g. syntactic functions, complexity). See also **alignment**.

Motivation (IL): a rhetorical function assigned to a dependent Discourse Act serving the communicative function of indicating the Speaker's motivation for uttering the nuclear Discourse Act. See also **rhetorical function**.

Move (IL): the highest interpersonal layer and as such "the largest unit of interaction relevant to grammatical analysis" (Hengeveld and Mackenzie 2008: 50). Moves either start an interaction, provoking a reaction from the Addressee, or are themselves a reaction to another Move. Moves consist of one or more Discourse Acts.

nesting: increasing the complexity of a layer by embedding a unit within a unit at that layer, e.g. *my neighbour's son's fiancée*. See also **stacking**.

neutralization (ML): process whereby units with different pragmatic and semantic features appear in the same form and position at the Morphosyntactic Level; e.g. the expression of an Actor and an Undergoer argument in a one-place predication (*The man$_A$ smiled* / *The man$_U$ fell*).

nominative–accusative alignment: see **alignment**.

non-core unit (IL/RL): all interpersonal and representational information that is not part of the core unit at the relevant level (content frame and predication frame); i.e. all functions, operators, and modifiers of layers outside the core unit. See also **core unit**.

non-dynamic State-of-Affairs (RL): State-of-Affairs containing an Undergoer argument which is not actively and volitionally involved in the State-of-Affairs in question (e.g. *John is ill, Maria likes singing*). See also **dynamic State-of-Affairs**.

nuclear Syllable (PL): the Syllable with the strongest stress in a Phonological Phrase; this stress is often triggered by the presence of a pragmatic function (Focus, Contrast) at the Interpersonal Level.

nucleus (PL): a pitch movement (fall, rise, etc.) realized on one Syllable within an Intonational Phrase.

Object (ML): one of the two syntactic functions in English, assigned at the Morphosyntactic Level to one of the arguments at the Representational Level, singling out this argument for special morphosyntactic treatment (in terms of position, argument agreement, and case). The default candidate for Object assignment is the Undergoer, but English also allows Object function to be assigned to Locations (Recipients). See also **Subject**.

objective epistemic modality (RL): type of event-oriented modality indicating the existence of a logical possibility (ranging from completely certain to highly unlikely) without involving any judgement by the Speaker. In English, objective epistemic modality is expressed grammatically by means of a modal auxiliary (e.g. *may, must*), represented as an operator at the State-of-Affairs. See also **subjective epistemic modality**.

Object-to-Subject raising (ML): process whereby the Undergoer argument of an embedded State-of-Affairs, normally expressed as the Object of a subordinate Clause, is realized as the Subject of the main Clause; e.g. *It is easy to solve this problem* vs. *This problem is easy to solve*. See also **Subject-to-Subject raising**.

onset (PL): part of the Syllable, consisting of one or more consonants preceding the peak (optional in English). See also **coda, peak**.

open Syllable (PL): Syllable ending in a peak (i.e. a Syllable without a coda).

operator: a type of primitive available during the operations of Formulation and Encoding, representing grammatically expressed information at each layer.

operator agreement (ML): See **agreement**.

Optative (IL): one of the minor abstract Illocutions of English, providing the formal means to express a wish; e.g. *May she be very happy*. See also **Illocution**.

Orientation (IL): a rhetorical function assigned to a dependent Discourse Act serving the communicative function of drawing the Addressee's attention to a part of the following (nuclear) Discourse Act. See also **rhetorical function**.

participant-oriented modality (RL): type of modality indicating the possibility or desirability of a State-of-Affairs taking place from the point of view of one of the participants. See also **facultative participant-oriented modality, deontic participant-oriented modality**.

parts-of-speech (RL): the classes of lexemes distinguished in a language on the basis of their function at the Representational Level. FDG distinguishes three major (although not universal) parts-of-speech: verb, noun, and adjective.

peak (PL): obligatory part of the Syllable; usually a vowel, but may also take the form of a syllabic consonant. See also **coda, onset**.

perfect aspect (RL): type of phasal aspect indicating the result or relevance of a State-of-Affairs that started in the past. In English, perfect aspect is expressed grammatically by means of the perfect auxiliary *have* and the past participle form of the main verb (e.g. *Iris has left for Vienna*). Represented as the operator 'perf' at the layer of the State-of-Affairs. See also **phasal aspect**.

performance: a Speaker's actual use of language in a concrete situation. See also **competence**.

performative verb (IL): by using a performative verb, a Speaker does not describe an event in the real (extra-linguistic) world; instead, by using these verbs, a Speaker performs the action designated by the verb. Sentences with performative verbs cannot be checked against any non-linguistic world, and cannot be given a truth value (i.e. they cannot be denied); instead, they are evaluated pragmatically, in terms of felicitousness. Some examples of performative sentences are *I hereby open the meeting*; *I insist that you leave*; *I promise I will be there*.

phasal aspect (RL): type of aspect specifying the internal temporal structure (or phases of development) of a State-of-Affairs. In English, phasal aspect tends to be expressed grammatically (through a combination of an auxiliary and an inflectional ending on the main verb; e.g. *Lotti was laughing*, *Iris has arrived in Vienna*). See also **progressive aspect, perfect aspect, habitual aspect, ingressive aspect,** and **prospective aspect**.

Phonological Phrase (PL): phonological layer, characterized by the presence of one Syllable (the nuclear Syllable) that is more stressed than any other stressed Syllables within that Phrase. Phonological Phrases are part of an Intonational Phrase and consist of one or more Phonological Words; they typically correlate with a Subact at the Interpersonal Level.

Phonological Word (PL): phonological layer, characterized (in English) by the presence of one primary stress. Phonological Words are part of Phonological Phrase and consist of one or more Feet; they typically correlate with a lexeme at the Representational Level and a Word at the Morphosyntactic Level.

Phrase (ML): morphosyntactic layer, typically part of a Clause, but may also be part of a Linguistic Expression or another Phrase. Phrases are headed by Lexical Words, whereby the category of the Lexical Word determines the category of the Phrase (Verb Phrase, Noun Phrase, etc.).

polar interrogative: see *yes–no* **interrogative**.

pragmatic function (IL): function assigned to a Subact within a Communicated Content or the Communicated Content as a whole, reflecting the communicative status of the unit to which it is assigned in terms of saliency in and/or relevance to the ongoing discourse; e.g. **Topic, Focus, Contrast**.

predicate (RL): part of the predication that designates a Property of an argument or a relation between arguments. Predicates typically take the form of a verb but may also be non-verbal (e.g. the nominal or adjectival predicate in a copular construction).

predication (RL): the configurational head of a State-of-Affairs, typically consisting of a predicate and one or more arguments. See also **predicate, argument**.

predication frame (RL): representational core unit; the configurational head of a State-of-Affairs, typically consisting of a predicate and one or more arguments. See also **content frame**.

Prescriptive grammar: grammar intended to instruct users how a language should be used.

presentative construction (IL/RL): construction used to introduce a new entity into the discourse. In English, presentative constructions may take the form of an existential sentence introduced by the dummy element *there* (e.g. *There was a big explosion*).

Principle of Formal Encoding: basic principle in FDG, according to which only those pragmatic and semantic distinctions are included (represented) in the Grammatical Component of a language that are systematically reflected in morphosyntactic or phonological form.

progressive aspect (RL): type of phasal aspect indicating that a State-of-Affairs is (was) in progress either at the time of speaking or during the occurrence of another State-of-Affairs. In English, progressive aspect is expressed grammatically by means of the progressive auxiliary *be* and the present participle form of the main verb (e.g. *Lotti was laughing*). Represented as the operator 'prog' at the layer of the State-of-Affairs. See also **phasal aspect**.

Prohibitive (IL): a type of Illocution, providing the formal means to order an Addressee not to carry out a certain action. This type of Illocution is not found in English, which uses a negated Imperative for this purpose (*Don't fidget!*). See also **Imperative**.

Property (IL/RL): a basic unit of analysis at the Representational Level, providing the descriptive information needed to designate (sets of) entities. Typically headed by a lexeme. Properties are evoked by a Subact of Ascription at the Interpersonal Level.

Propositional Content (RL): the highest representational layer, representing the content of a proposition, i.e. information that can be known, believed, claimed, questioned, hoped or wished for. Propositional Contents consist of one or more Episodes.

prosodic stress (PL): languages with prosodic stress lack word stress; instead stress always falls on a fixed Syllable within the Phonological Phrase. In such languages, there is no need to assume a layer in between the Phonological Phrase and the Syllable (i.e. these languages do not have Phonological Words).

prospective aspect: type of phasal aspect indicating that a State-of-Affairs is about to begin. In English, prospective aspect is expressed periphrastically by means of the expression *be about to* (e.g. *Arne was about to volunteer*). Represented as the operator 'ingr' at the layer of the State-of-Affairs. See also **phasal aspect**.

prototype theory: theory developed in cognitive psychology (in particular by Eleanor Rosch), according to which people categorize entities by comparing them to a prototype (i.e. a prototypical member, or best example, of a category). Prototype theory does not depend on, or assume, the existence of strict divisions, but can accommodate gradience and fuzziness.

question tag: reduced form of a question which can only be used in combination with a (preceding) declarative Discourse Act, and whose form depends on the formal aspects of this Discourse Act. Question tags are typically used to ask for confirmation of the Propositional Content expressed in the Discourse Act (rising intonation) or to signal that the Speaker assumes the Addressee to agree with this Propositional Content (falling intonation). Some examples of question tags are *You haven't said anything, **have you?*** and *It's rather cold, **isn't it**.*

quotative (IL): subtype of reportative expression or marker indicating (direct or indirect) reported speech; e.g. *John would be late, **or so he said**; I was **like** No way!*

raising (ML): a process whereby a unit that semantically belongs to a subordinate Clause is 'raised' to (placed in) a position in the main Clause; see also **Subject-to-Subject raising, Object-to-Subject raising**.

Referential Subact: see **Subact of Reference**.

reinforcement (IL): the strengthening of the force of an Illocution by the Speaker, either with a positive effect (***Do** sit down*; *He is **really, really** brilliant*) or with a negative effect (***Do** shut up!*). Reinforcing elements are analysed as operators or modifiers at the layer of the Illocution. See also **mitigation**.

relational sentence (RL): copular sentence which at the Representational Level consists of an Undergoer argument and a non-verbal predicate introduced by a preposition relating the predicate to the Undergoer, e.g. *This letter is from John.* See also **classificational, existential,** and **identificational sentence**.

relative tense (RL): a grammatical means to specify the time of occurrence of an SoA in relation to the tense of the Episode of which it forms part. See also **absolute tense**.

reportative (IL): modifier or operator at the layer of the Communicated Content indicating that the Speaker has received the Communicated Contents from a third party; e.g. ***I hear** you are getting married.*

representational alignment (ML): alignment system in which the morphosyntactic behaviour of elements, i.e. their form and the order in which they appear, can be explained in terms of the representational features of these elements (e.g. semantic functions, animacy, person, etc.). See also **alignment**.

rhetorical function (IL): function assigned to a dependent Discourse Act indicating the relation between this Discourse Act and the Nuclear Discourse Act to which it is subsidiary; e.g. **Motivation, Orientation, Correction**.

semantic categories (RL): basic unit of analysis at the Representational Level, where each layer represents a different semantic category (Propositional Contents, Episodes, States-of-Affairs, Individuals, etc.). Semantic categories form a subset of all the ontological categories in the extra-linguistic world in that only those ontological categories that are linguistically relevant for a particular language are represented by a semantic category.

semantic function (RL): function assigned to a unit (argument or modifier) at the Representational Level specifying the role of the entity designated by this unit within the specific layer. At the layer of the State-of-Affairs, FDG recognizes three macro-functions: Actor, Undergoer, Location. Further subtypes may be distinguished when needed in a language (e.g. Recipient, Beneficiary, Comitative, Instrument, Time, Reason, Associative, Reference, etc.).

sociolect: language variety spoken by the members of a specific social group.

Speech Participants (IL): participants in a Discourse Act (representing Speaker and Addressee). Represented at the Interpersonal Level as part of the configurational head of the Discourse Act.

stacking: increasing the complexity of a layer by adding units at the same layer, e.g. through coordination (*an apple, a pear, and some kiwis*). See also **nesting**.

State-of-Affairs (RL): representational layer representing an entity (state, event) that (typically) involves one or more participants and which happens (or does not happen) at a particular time and place. States-of-Affairs are part of an Episode and have a configurational head (the predication) consisting of a predicate and one or more arguments. See also **predication frame, predicate, argument**.

Stem (ML): a Morpheme with lexical content that can be the sole element within a Word. Stems typically function as the head of a Lexical Word and can be divided into Verbal Stems, Nominal Stems, Adjectival Stems, Adverbial Stems, and Adpositional Stems. See also **Affix**.

stress-timed language (PL): language in which stressed Syllables occur at regular intervals of time (which means that Feet are of more or less equal length).

Subact of Ascription (IL): the Evocation of a property by the Speaker at the Interpersonal Level; part of the Communicated Content.

Subact of Reference (IL): the Evocation of a referent by the Speaker at the Interpersonal Level; part of the Communicated Content.

Subject (ML): one of the two syntactic functions in English, assigned at the Morphosyntactic Level to one of the arguments at the Representational Level, singling out this argument for special morphosyntactic treatment (in terms of position, argument agreement, and case). The default candidate for Subject assignment is the Actor, but

English also allows Subject function to be assigned to Undergoers and Locations (Recipients). See also **Object**.

Subject-to-Subject raising (ML): process whereby the Actor argument of an embedded State-of-Affairs, normally expressed as the Subject of a subordinate Clause, is realized as the Subject of the main Clause; e.g. *We believe that **John** has stolen the money* vs. ***John** is believed to have stolen the money*. See also **Object-to-Subject raising**.

subjective epistemic modality (RL): type of modality specifying the extent to which a Speaker (or some other participant) is committed to the truth of a proposition (ranging from complete certainty to strong doubt). In English, subjective epistemic modality is typically expressed by means of a modifier at the layer of the Propositional Content (*certainly, probably, possibly*, etc.). See also **objective epistemic modality**.

suppletive form (PL): irregular form within a paradigm; i.e. an inflected form that cannot be predicted on the basis of the rules of the language; e.g. irregular past tenses (*ate, went*) or plural forms (*oxen, geese*).

syllabic consonant (PL): consonant that functions as the peak of a Syllable; e.g. the second Syllable / bl̩ / in *noble*.

Syllable (PL): lowest phonological layer which functions as the domain of phonotactic rules, i.e. language-specific rules that determine which (combinations) of sounds are allowed in each part of the Syllable. Syllables typically make up a Foot (either by themselves or together with another Syllable), but may also function as an independent unit within the Word (unfooted Syllable). Syllables may carry stress (primary or secondary) or be unstressed.

syntactic derivation (RL/ML): word formation process taking place in the grammar whereby new lexemes of another word class are derived through the addition of a suffix without lexical content, in order to prepare this lexeme for expression at the Morphosyntactic Level; e.g. *play* → *player, happy* → *happily, legal* → *legalize*. See also **coercion, synthetic compounding**.

syntactic function (ML): function assigned at the Morphosyntactic Level, relevant for languages with morphosyntactic alignment. By assigning a syntactic function (Subject, Object) to an argument at the Representational Level, this argument is singled out for special morphosyntactic treatment (in terms of case, position, agreement, etc.).

synthesis (ML): process whereby two or more interpersonal and/or representational units are fused into one morphosyntactic unit. Synthesis reduces the transparency of a construction or language (e.g. unidentifiable and singular expressed as *a*). See also **transparency**.

synthetic compounding (RL/ML): word formation process taking place in the grammar whereby a predication used as the head of an Individual is prepared for use at the Morphosyntactic Level. This process involves both syntactic derivation and incorporation of the original Undergoer argument; the resulting noun designates the original Actor argument of the predication; e.g. *fundraiser, trainspotter*). See also **incorporation, syntactic derivation**.

template (ML/PL): one of the primitives available during the operation of Encoding. Morphological templates specify, for the language in question, the order in which elements can appear at each morphosyntactic layer; phonological templates represent the possible intonation and stress patterns of a language.

thetic sentence (IL): a sentence which provides new information only. Thetic sentences are represented at the Interpersonal Level by a content frame containing one or more Subacts (SA) with the pragmatic function Focus: $(C_1: [(SA_1) \ldots (SA_N)]_{FOC})$. See also **categorical sentence**.

Time (RL): minor semantic category relevant for English, designating the time of occurrence of a (sequence) of event(s). Times typically function as modifiers at the layer of the Episode (absolute time: *I met Sarah yesterday*) or the State-of-Affairs (relative time: *I met Sarah after lunch*).

Topic (IL): pragmatic function assigned to Subacts signalling how the Communicated Content relates to the gradually constructed record in the Contextual Component. In most cases Topics contain information that is given in (or inferable from) the Contextual Component. See also **pragmatic function**.

transparency: in FDG, the transparency of a construction or a language is defined in terms of the number of one-to-one (i.e. transparent) relations between units at the different levels.

trochaic Foot (PL): a Foot in which the first Syllable is strong.

Utterance (PL): highest phonological layer, recognizable by the fact that they are separated from each other by clearly perceptible pauses. Utterances consist of one or more Intonational Phrases, and typically correlate with Moves at the Interpersonal Level.

valency (RL): term used to describe the number and kind of participants (arguments) a Predicate (Property) combines with in a Predication. A distinction is made between quantificational valency, specifying the number of participants within a Predication, and qualificational valency, specifying the semantic roles of the participants in the State-of-Affairs designated. A verb like *buy* in *Ellie bought a new book*, for instance, takes two arguments (quantificational valency) with the semantic functions Actor and Undergoer (qualificational valency).

variable stress (PL): in a language with variable stress, the position of the primary stress in a lexeme is not predictable. This means that stress patterns are specified in the Lexicon and must be learnt by the Speaker.

vocative (IL): construction used by a Speaker to address or draw the attention of an Addressee (e.g. *Hey!, Peter!*). See also **Interpellative**.

Wh-interrogative (or content interrogatives) (IL): type of Interrogative Discourse Act (containing a *Wh*-element) intended to elicit specific information from the Addressee; e.g. *Who were you talking to?* or *Where do you live?*

Word (ML): morphosyntactic layer, part of a Phrase, Clause, or Linguistic expression; consisting of one or more Morphemes. A distinction is made between Lexical Words (typically corresponding to a lexeme at the Representational Level) and Grammatical Words (typically triggered by interpersonal or representational operators). See also **Grammatical Word, Lexical Word**.

Yes–no **(polar) interrogative (IL):** type of Interrogative Discourse Act intended to elicit either an affirmative (*yes*) or a negative (*no*) answer from the Addressee (affirming or negating the Propositional Content contained in the question); e.g. *Did you see anyone?*

List of languages

Acehnese (ace): a Chamic language in the Austronesian family spoken in Indonesia

Aghem (agq): a Grassfields language in the Niger-Congo family spoken in the North West Region of Cameroon

Axininca Campa (cni): a Southern Maipurean language spoken in Peru

Basque (eus): a language isolate spoken in Spain and France

Czech (ces): a Slavic language in the Indo-European family spoken in the Czech Republic

Dutch (nld): a Germanic language in the Indo-European family spoken in the Netherlands and Belgium (Flanders)

French (fra): a Romance language in the Indo-European family spoken in France and Belgium (Wallonia)

Garo (grt): a Tibeto-Burman language in the Sino-Tibetan family spoken in India

Georgian (kat): a Kartvelian (Southern-Caucasian) language spoken in Georgia

German (deu): a Germanic language in the Indo-European family spoken in Germany, Austria, and Switzerland

Hawaiian (haw): a Polynesian language in the Austronesian family spoken in Hawaii

Hungarian (hun): a Uralic language spoken in Hungary

Icelandic (isl): a Germanic language in the Indo-European family spoken in Iceland

Italian (ita): a Romance language in the Indo-European family spoken in Italy

Jamul Tiipay (dih): a language in the Yuman family spoken in Southern California

Japanese (jpn): a Japonic language spoken in Japan

Javanese (jav): a language in the Austronesian family spoken in Indonesia

Kham: a group of Tibeto-Burman languages in the Sino-Tibetan family spoken in Nepal

Kisi (kiz): a Bantu language in the Niger-Congo family spoken in Tanzania

Korean (kor): a language isolate spoken in South Korea

Koryak (kpy): a northern Chukotko-Kamchatkan language spoken in Eastern Russia

Leti (lti): a Southwest Maluku language in the Austronesian family spoken on the island of Leti in Maluku, Indonesia

Mandarin Chinese (cmn): a Chinese language in the Sino-Tibetan family spoken in China

Nivkh (niv): a language isolate spoken in Eastern Russia

Oromo (Borana) (gax): a Cushitic language in the Afro-Asiatic family spoken in Kenya

Pawnee (paw): a Northern Caddoan language in the Caddoan family spoken in north central Oklahoma

Polish (pol): a Slavic language in the Indo-European family spoken in Poland

Portuguese (por): a Romance language in the Indo-European family spoken in Portugal

Russian (rus): a Slavic language in the Indo-European language family spoken in Russia

Saramaccan (srm): an English-based creole language spoken in Surinam

Scottish Gaelic (gla): a Celtic language in the Indo-European family spoken in Central and Northern Scotland

Shipibo (shp): a Panoan language spoken in Peru

Spanish (spa): a Romance language in the Indo-European family spoken in Spain

Southern Tiwa (tix): a Tanoan language on the Kiowa-Tanoan family spoken in New Mexico

Tagalog (tgl): a Philippine language in the Austronesian family spoken in the Philippines

Tariana (tae): a Northern Maipurean language in the Maipurean family spoken in Amazonas, Brazil

Tauya (tya): a Madang language in the Trans-New Guinea family spoken in Papua New Guinea

Tidore (tvo): a North Halmahera language in the West Papuan family spoken on the island of Tidore, Indonesia

Tsafiki (Colorado) (cof): a Southern Barbacoan language in the Barbacoan family spoken in Ecuador

Turkish (tur): a Turkic language in the Altaic family spoken in Turkey

Tuvaluan (tvl): a Polynesian language in the Austronesian family spoken in Tuvalu

Wambon (wms): a Central and South New Guinea language in the Trans New Guinea family spoken in Irian Jaya, Indonesia

Welsh (cym): a Celtic language in the Indo-European family spoken in Wales

Yimas (yee): a Lower Sepik language in the Ramu-Lower Sepik family spoken in Papua New Guinea

Descriptions principally based on Ethnologue (<www.ethnologue.com>, accessed 6 June 2014).

Abbreviations between brackets refer to the ISO code.

Bibliography

AARTS, BAS. 2007. *Syntactic Gradience: The Nature of Grammatical Indeterminacy*. Oxford: Oxford University Press.

AARTS, BAS, DAVID DENISON, EVELIEN KEIZER, and GERGANA POPOVA (eds). 2004. *Fuzzy Grammar: A reader*. Oxford: Oxford University Press.

AIKHENVALD, ALEXANDRA Y. 2003. *A Grammar of Tariana, from Northwest Amazonia* (Cambridge Grammatical Descriptions). Cambridge: Cambridge University Press.

ALLEN, BARBARA J., DONNA B. GARDINER, and DONALD G. FRANTZ. 1984. Noun incorporation in Southern Tiwa, *IJAL* 50, 292–311.

ALTURO, NÚRIA, EVELIEN KEIZER and LLUÍS PAYRATÓ (eds). 2014a. *The Interaction between Context and Grammar in Functional Discourse Grammar*. Special Issue of *Pragmatics* 24(2).

ALTURO, NÚRIA, EVELIEN KEIZER, and LLUÍS PAYRATÓ. 2014b. Introduction. In Núria Alturo, Evelien Keizer, and Lluís Payrató (eds), *The Interaction Between Context and Grammar in Functional Discourse Grammar*. Special Issue of *Pragmatics* 24(2), 185–201.

AUSTIN, JOHN L. 1962. *How to do Thing with Words*, Lecture 1. Oxford: Oxford University Press.

BARÐDAL, JÓHANNA. 2001. *Case in Icelandic: A Synchronic, Diachronic and Comparative Approach*. Lundastudier i Nordisk språkvetenskap A 57. Doctoral dissertation, Department of Scandinavian Languages, University of Lund.

BESNIER, NIKO. 1988. Semantic and pragmatic constraints on Tuvaluan raising. *Linguistics* 26: 747–78.

BIBER, DOUGLAS, STIG JOHANSSON, GEOFFREY LEECH, SUSAN CONRAD, and EDWARD FINEGAN. 1999. *Longman Grammar of Spoken and Written English*. Harlow: Longman.

BÓGORAS, WALDEMAR. 1917. *Koryak texts* (Publications of the American Ethnological Society 5). Leiden: Brill.

BÖRJARS, KERSTI. 2006. Description and theory. In Bas Aarts and April McMahon (eds), *The Handbook of English Linguistics*. Oxford: Blackwell. 9–32.

BRINTON, LAUREL J. and ELIZABETH C. TRAUGOTT. 2005. *Lexicalization and Language Change*. Cambridge: Cambridge University Press.

BURLING, ROBBINS. 2004. *The Language of the Modhupur Mandi Garo*. Vol I: Grammar. New Delhi: Bibliophile South Asia & Morganville NJ: Promilla.

BUTLER, CHRISTOPHER S. 2003. *Structure and Function: A Guide to Three Major Structural-Functional Theories*. Amsterdam & Philadelphia: John Benjamins.

BUTLER, CHRISTOPHER S. 2008. Interpersonal meaning in the noun phrase. In Jan Rijkhoff and Daniel García Velasco (eds), *The Noun Phrase in Functional Discourse Grammar* (Trends in Linguistics). Berlin & New York: Mouton de Gruyter, 221–61.

BUTLER, CHRISTOPHER S. and FRANCISCO GONZÁLVEZ-GARCÍA. 2005. Situating FDG in functional-cognitive space: An initial study. In María Á. Gómez-González, and J. Lachlan Mackenzie (eds), *Studies in Functional Discourse Grammar* (Linguistic Insights, 26). Berne: Peter Lang, 109–58.

BUTLER, CHRISTOPHER S., RAQUEL HIDALGO DOWNING, and JULIA DAVID (eds). 2007. *Functional Perspectives on Grammar and Discourse. In Honour of Angela Downing*. Amsterdam & Philadelphia: John Benjamins.

BRYANT, GREG A. and JEAN E. FOX TREE. 2002. Recognizing verbal irony in spontaneous speech, *Metaphor and Symbol* 17(2): 99–117.

BYBEE, JOAN L. 1985. *Morphology: A Study of the Relation between Meaning and Form*. Amsterdam & Philadelphia: John Benjamins.

CANN, RONNIE. 1993. *Formal Semantics: An Introduction*. Cambridge: Cambridge University Press.

CHILDS, G. TUCKER. 1995. *A Grammar of Kisi: A Southern Atlantic Language* (Mouton Grammar Library 16). Berlin & New York: Mouton de Gruyter.

CHOMSKY, NOAM. 1957. *Syntactic Structures*. The Hague: Mouton.

CHOMSKY, NOAM. 1965. *Aspects of the Theory of Grammar*. Cambridge MA: MIT Press.

CHOMSKY, NOAM. 1968. *Language and Mind*. New York: Harcourt, Brace & World.

CHOMSKY, NOAM. 1986. *Knowledge of Language: Its Nature, Origin and Use*. New York: Praeger.

CONNOLLY, JOHN H. 2004. The question of discourse representation in Functional Discourse Grammar. In J. Lachlan Mackenzie, and María Á. Gómez-González (eds), *A New Architecture for Functional Grammar*, Berlin: Mouton de Gruyter, 89–116.

CONNOLLY, JOHN H. 2007. Context in Functional Discourse Grammar. *Alfa: Revista de Lingüística* 51(2): 11–33.

CONNOLLY, JOHN H. 2014. The contextual component within a dynamic implementation of the FDG Model: Structure and Interaction. In Núria Alturo, Evelien Keizer, and Llís Payrato (eds), *The Interaction between Context and Grammar in Functional Discourse Grammar*. Special issue of *Pragmatics* 24(2): 229–48.

CORNISH, FRANCIS. 2004. Absence of ascriptive predication, Topic and Focus: The case of 'thetic' clauses. In Henk Aertsen, Mike Hannay, and Rod Lyall (eds), *Words in their Places: A Festschrift for J. Lachlan Mackenzie*, Amsterdam: Vrije Universiteit Amsterdam. 211–27.

CORNISH, FRANCIS. 2009. *Text* and *discourse* as *context*: discourse anaphora and the FDG contextual component. In Evelien Keizer and Gerry Wanders (eds), *Web Papers in Functional Discourse Grammar* 82: 97–115. Available at <http://home.hum.uva.nl/fdg/working_papers/WP-FDG-82_Cornish.pdf>.

CROFT, WILLIAM. 1995. Autonomy and functional linguistics. *Language* 71: 490–532.

CROFT, WILLIAM. 1999. What some functionalists can learn from some formalists. In Michael Darnell, Edith A. Moravcsik, Frederick J. Newmeyer, Michael Noonan, and Kathleen Wheatley (eds), *Functionalism and Formalism in Linguistics*. Volume 1: general papers. Amsterdam & Philadelphia: John Benjamins.

CRYSTAL, DAVID. 1967. English. *Lingua* 17: 24–56.

DICKINSON, CONNIE 2002. *Complex Predicates in Tsafiki*. Doctoral dissertation, University of Oregon.

DIK, SIMON C. 1997a. *The Theory of Functional Grammar. Part I: The Structure of the Clause*. 2nd rev edn. Edited by Kees Hengeveld. Berlin & New York: Mouton de Gruyter.

DIK, SIMON C. 1997b. *The Theory of Functional Grammar. Part II: Complex and Derived Constructions*. Edited by Kees Hengeveld. Berlin & New York: Mouton de Gruyter.

DONNELLAN, KEITH S. 1966. Reference and definite descriptions. *The Philosophical Review* 77: 281–304.

DOWTY, DAVID. 1991. Thematic proto-roles and argument selection. *Language* 673: 547–619.

DURIE, MARK. 1985. *A Grammar of Acehnese: On the Basis of a Dialect of North Aceh* (Verhandelingen van het Koninklijk Instituut voor Taal-, Land- en Volkenkunde 112). Dordrecht & Cinnaminson: Foris.

ENGELENHOVEN, AONE VAN. 2004. *Leti, a Language of Soutwest Maluku* (Verhandelingen van het Koninklijk Instituut voor Taal-, Land- en Volkenkunde 211). Leiden: KITLV Press.

ETXEPARE, RICARDO. 2003. Valency and argument structure in the Basque verb. In José Ignacio Hualde and Jon Ortiz the Urbina (eds), *A Grammar of Basque*. Berlin & New York: Mouton de Gruyter.

EVANS, VYVYAN and MELANIE GREEN. 2006. *Cognitive Linguistics: An Introduction*. Edinburgh: Edinburgh University Press.

FAUST, NORMA. 1973. *Lecciones para el aprendizaje del idioma Shipibo-Conibo*. Lima, Peru: Summer Institute of Linguistics and Yarinacocha: Instituto Lingüístico de Verano.

FEIST, JIM. 2013. Noun incorporation in English. *Functions of Language* 20(2): 159–84.

FINCH, GEOFFREY. 2003. *How to Study Linguistics*. 2nd edn. Basingstoke: Palgrave Macmillan.

FOLEY, WILLIAM A. 1991. *The Yimas Language of New Guinea*. Stanford: Stanford University Press.

FOLEY, WILLIAM A. 2005. Semantic parameters and the unaccusative split in the Austronesian language family. *Studies in Language* 29(2): 385–430.

FOLEY, WILLIAM A. and ROBERT D. VAN VALIN. 1984. *Functional Syntax and Universal Grammar*. Cambridge: Cambridge University Press.

GARCÍA VELASCO, DANIEL. 2008. Functional Discourse Grammar and extraction from complex noun phrases. In Jan Rijkhoff and Daniel García Velasco (eds),

The Noun Phrase in Functional Discourse Grammar (Trends in Linguistics). Berlin & New York: Mouton de Gruyter, 321–63.

GARCÍA VELASCO, DANIEL. 2009. Conversion in English and its implications for Functional Discourse Grammar. In Kees Hengeveld and Gerry Wanders, *The Representational Level in Functional Discourse Grammar*. *Lingua* 119(8): 1164–85.

GARCÍA VELASCO, DANIEL. 2013a. Degree words in English: a Functional Discourse Grammar account. *Revista Canaria de Estudios Ingleses* 67 (Special Issue): 79–96.

GARCÍA VELASCO, DANIEL. 2013b. Raising in Functional Discourse Grammar. In J. Lachlan Mackenzie and Hella Olbertz (eds), *Casebook in Functional Discourse Grammar*, Amsterdam & Philadelphia: John Benjamins. 249–76.

GARCÍA VELASCO, DANIEL and KEES HENGEVELD. 2002. Do we need predicate frames? In Ricardo Mairal Usón and María Jesús Pérez Quintero (eds), *New Perspectives on Argument Structure in Functional Grammar* (Functional Grammar Series 25). Berlin & New York: Mouton de Gruyter, 95–123.

GARCÍA VELASCO, DANIEL, and EVELIEN KEIZER. 2014. Derivational morphology in Functional Discourse Grammar. In María de los Ángeles Gómez González, Francisco José Ruiz de Mendoza Ibáñez, and Francisco Gonzálvez-García (eds), *Theory and Practice in Functional-Cognitive Space*. Amsterdam & Philadelphia: John Benjamins, 151–77.

GARCÍA VELASCO, DANIEL, and GERRY WANDERS (eds) 2012. Introduction: The morphosyntactic level in Functional Discourse Grammar. In Daniel García Velasco and Gerry Wanders (eds), *The Morphosyntactic Level in Functional Discourse Grammar*. *Language Sciences* 34(4). 384–99.

GRICE, H. PAUL 1975. Logic and conversation. In Peter Cole and Jerry L. Morgan (eds), *Speech Acts: Syntax and Semantics 3*. New York: Academic Press, 41–58.

GROOT, CASPER DE. 1981. Sentence-intertwining in Hungarian. In A. Machtelt Bolkestein, Henk A. Combé, Simon C. Dik, Casper de Groot, Jadranka Gvozdanovic, Albert Rijksbaron, and Co Vet (eds), *Predication and Expression in Functional Grammar*. London: Academic Press, 41–62.

HAABO, VINIJE. 2002. *Grammatica en fonetiek van het Saramaccaans*. Ms., Wageningen.

HALLIDAY, MICHAEL A. K. 1978. *Language as Social Semiotic: The Social Interpretation of Language and Meaning*. London: Edward Arnold.

HALLIDAY, MICHAEL A. K. 1994. *An Introduction to Functional Grammar*, 2nd edn. London: Edward Arnold.

HALLIDAY, MICHAEL A. K. 1997. Linguistics as metaphor. In Anne-Marie Simon-Vandenbergen, Kristin Davidse, and Dirk Noël (eds), *Reconnecting Language: Morphology and Syntax in Functional Perspectives*. Amsterdam & Philadelphia: John Benjamins. 3–37.

HANNAY, MICHAEL. 1985. *English Existential in Functional Grammar* (Functional Grammar Series). Dordrecht: Foris Publications.

HANNAY, MICHAEL and EVELIEN KEIZER. 2005. A discourse-treatment of non-restrictive apposition in an FDG of English. In María Á. Gómez-González and J. Lachlan

Mackenzie (eds), *Studies in Functional Discourse Grammar* (Linguistic Insights, 26). Berne: Peter Lang, 159–94.

HANNAY, MICHAEL and KEES HENGEVELD. 2009. Functional Discourse Grammar: Pragmatic aspects. In Frank Brisard, Jan-Ola Östman, and Jef Verschueren (eds), *Grammar, Meaning and Pragmatics* (Handbook of Pragmatics Highlights 5). Amsterdam & Philadelphia: John Benjamins, 91–116.

HANNAY, MICHAEL and ELENA MARTÍNEZ-CARO. 2008. Last things first? A FDG approach to clause-final focus constituents in English and Spanish. In María A. Gómez-González, J. Lachlan Mackenzie, and Elsa González-Álvarez (eds), *Languages and Cultures in Contrast and Comparison*. Amsterdam & Philadelphia: John Benjamins, 33–68.

HANNAY, MICHAEL and GERARD STEEN (eds). 2007 *Structural-Functional Studies in English Grammar. In Honour of Lachlan Mackenzie*. Amsterdam: John Benjamins.

HASPELMATH, MARTIN. 1997. *Indefinite Pronouns* (Oxford Studies in Typology and Linguistic Theory). Oxford: Oxford University Press.

HEINE, BERND and HEIKE NARROG. 2010. Introduction. In Bernd Heine and Heike Narrog (eds), *The Oxford Handbook of Linguistic Analysis*. Oxford: Oxford University Press.

HEINE, BERND and HEIKE NARROG (eds). 2010. *The Oxford Handbook of Linguistic Analysis*. Oxford: Oxford University Press.

HEINE, BERND and HEIKE NARROG (eds). 2011. *The Oxford Handbook of Grammaticalization*. Oxford: Oxford University Press.

HENGEVELD, KEES. 1992. Parts of speech. In Michael Fortescue, Peter Harder, and Lars Kristoffersen (eds), *Layered Structure and Reference in a Functional Perspective*. Amsterdam & Philadelphia: John Benjamins. 29–55. Reprinted in Matthew Anstey and J. Lachlan Mackenzie (eds), 2005. *Crucial Readings in Functional Grammar*. Amsterdam & Philadelphia: John Benjamins, 79–106.

HENGEVELD, KEES. 2008. Prototypical and non-prototypical noun phrases in Functional Discourse Grammar. In Jan Rijkhoff, and Daniel García Velasco (eds), *The Noun Phrase in Functional Discourse Grammar* (Trends in Linguistics). Berlin & New York NY: Mouton de Gruyter, 43–62.

HENGEVELD, KEES. 2011. The grammaticalization of tense and aspect. In Bernd Heine and Heike Narro (eds), *The Oxford Handbook of Grammaticalization*. Oxford: Oxford University Press, 580–94.

HENGEVELD, KEES. 2013. A new approach to clausal constituent order. In J. Lachlan Mackenzie and Hella Olbertz (eds), *Casebook in Functional Discourse Grammar*. Amsterdam: John Benjamins, 15–38.

HENGEVELD, KEES and EVELIEN KEIZER. 2011. Non-straightforward communication. *Journal of Pragmatics* 43: 1962–76.

HENGEVELD, KEES and J. LACHLAN MACKENZIE. 2008. *Functional Discourse Grammar: A Typologically-based Theory of Language Structure*. Oxford: Oxford University Press.

HENGEVELD, KEES and J. LACHLAN MACKENZIE. 2010. Functional Discourse Grammar. In Heine Bernd and Heike Narrog (eds), *The Oxford Handbook of Linguistic Analysis.* Oxford: Oxford University Press, 367–400.

HENGEVELD, KEES and J. LACHLAN MACKENZIE. 2014. Grammar and context in Functional Discourse Grammar. In Núria Alturo, Evelien Keizer, and Lluís Payrató (eds), *The Interaction between Context and Grammar in Functional Discourse Grammar.* Special Issue of *Pragmatics* 24(2): 203–27.

HENGEVELD, KEES and HELLA OLBERTZ. 2012. Didn't you know? Mirativity does exist! *Linguistic Typology* 16: 487–503.

HENGEVELD, KEES and NIELS SMIT. 2009. Dynamic formulation in Functional Discourse Grammar. In Kees Hengeveld and Gerry Wanders (eds), *Semantic Representation in Functional Discourse Grammar. Lingua* 119(8): 1118–30.

HOGG, RICHARD and CHRIS B. MCCULLY. 1987. *Metrical Phonology: A Coursebook.* Cambridge: Cambridge University Press.

HOPPER, PAUL J. and ELIZABETH C. TRAUGOTT. 1993. *Grammaticalization.* Cambridge: Cambridge University Press.

HYMES, DELL H. 1972. On communicative competence. In John B. Pride and Janet Holmes (eds), *Sociolinguistics: Selected Readings.* Harmondsworth: Penguin, 269–93.

JAKOBSON, ROMAN. 1960. Closing statement: Linguistics and poetics. In Thomas A. Sebeok (ed.), *Style in Language.* Cambridge MA: MIT Press, 350–77.

JUN, SUN-AH, and CÉCILE FOUGERON. 2000. A phonological model of French intonation. In Antonis Botinis (ed.), *Intonation: Analysis, Modeling and Technology.* Dordrecht: Kluwer Academic, 209–42.

KABAK, BARIS and IRENE VOGEL. 2001. The phonological word and stress assignment in Turkish. *Phonology* 18: 315–60.

KEIZER, EVELIEN. 1992. Predicates as referring expressions. In Michael Fortescue, Peter Harder, and Lars Kristoffersen (eds), *Layered Structure and Reference in a Functional Perspective.* Amsterdam & Philadelphia: John Benjamins. 1–27. Reprinted in Matthew Anstey and J. Lachlan Mackenzie (eds), 2005. *Crucial Readings in Functional Grammar.* Berlin & New York: Mouton de Gruyter, 109–36.

KEIZER, EVELIEN. 2007a. *The English Noun Phrase: The Nature of Linguistic Categorization.* Cambridge: Cambridge University Press.

KEIZER, EVELIEN. 2007b. The grammatical-lexical dichotomy in Functional Discourse Grammar. *Alfa—Revista de lingüística* 51(2) (Advances in Functional Discourse Grammar): 35–56.

KEIZER, EVELIEN. 2008a. Reference and Ascription in FDG: An inventory of problems and some possible solutions. In Jan Rijkhoff and Daniel García Velasco (eds), *The Noun Phrase in Functional Discourse Grammar* (Trends in Linguistics). Berlin & New York: Mouton de Gruyter, 181–220.

KEIZER, EVELIEN. 2008b. English prepositions in Functional Discourse Grammar. *Functions of Language* 152: 216–56.

KEIZER, EVELIEN. 2009a. Verb-preposition constructions in Functional Discourse Grammar. In Kees Hengeveld and Gerry Wanders (eds), *The Representational Level in Functional Discourse Grammar*. Special issue of *Lingua* 1198: 1186–211.

KEIZER, EVELIEN. 2009b. The interpersonal level in English. In Miriam van Staden and Evelien Keizer (eds), *Interpersonal Grammar: A Cross-linguistic Perspective*. Special issue of *Linguistics* 47(4): 845–66.

KEIZER, EVELIEN. 2012. Proforms in Functional Discourse Grammar. In Daniel García Velasco and Gerry Wanders (eds), *The Morphosyntactic Level in Functional Discourse Grammar*. Special issue of *Language Sciences* 34(4): 400–20.

KEIZER, EVELIEN. 2013. The *X is (is)* construction: an FDG account. In J. Lachlan Mackenzie and Hella Olbertz (eds), *Casebook in Functional Discourse Grammar*. Amsterdam & Philadelphia: John Benjamins, 213–48.

KEIZER, EVELIEN. 2014. Context and cognition in Functional Discourse Grammar: What, where and why? In Núria Alturo, Evelien Keizer, and Llúis Payrato (eds), *The Interaction between Context and Grammar in Functional Discourse Grammar*. Special issue of *Pragmatics* 24(2): 399–423.

KEIZER, EVELIEN and MIRIAM VAN STADEN. 2009. Introduction. In Miriam van Staden and Evelien Keizer (eds), *Interpersonal Grammar: A Cross-linguistic Perspective*. Special issue of *Linguistics* 47(4): 799–824.

KENESEI, ISTVÁN, ROBERT M. VAGO, and ANNA FENYVESI. 1998. *Hungarian* (Descriptive Grammars). London & New York: Routledge.

KORNFILT, JAKLIN. 1997. *Turkish* (Descriptive Grammars). London: Routledge.

KROON, CAROLINE. 1995. *Discourse Particles in Latin* (Amsterdam Studies in Classical Philology 4). Amsterdam: Gieben.

LABOV, WILLIAM. 1973. The boundaries of words and their meanings. In Charles-James Bailey and Roger W. Shuy (eds), *New ways of Analyzing Variation in English*. Washington DC: Georgetown University Press, 340–73.

LAKOFF, GEORGE. 1987. *Women, Fire and Dangerous Things: What Categories Reveal about the Mind*. Chicago & London: University of Chicago Press.

LEE, SUN-HEE. 2001. Argument composition and linearization: Korean complex predicates and scrambling. *Ohio State University Working Papers in Linguistics* 56: 53–78.

LEUFKENS, STERRE. 2013. Time reference in English indirect Speech. In J. Lachlan Mackenzie and Hella Olbertz (eds), *Casebook in Functional Discourse Grammar*. Amsterdam & Philadelphia: John Benjamins, 189–212.

LEVELT, WILLEM J. M. 1989. *Speaking*. Cambridge MA: MIT Press.

LI, CHARLES N. and SANDRA A. THOMPSON. 1981. *Mandarin Chinese: A Functional Reference Grammar*. Berkeley, Los Angeles & London: University of California Press.

LYONS, JOHN. 1977. *Semantics*, 2 vols. Cambridge: Cambridge University Press.

MCCARTHY, JOHN and ALAN S. PRINCE. 1993. *Prosodic Morphology I: Constraint Interaction and Satisfaction*. Technical Report #3, Rutgers University Center for Cognitive Science.

MacDonald, Lorna. 1990. *A Grammar of Tauya* (Mouton Grammar Library 6). Berlin & New York: Mouton de Gruyter.

Mackenzie, J. Lachlan. 2005. Places and things. In Matthew Anstey and J. Lachlan Mackenzie (eds), *Crucial Readings in Functional Grammar*. Berlin & New York: Mouton de Gruyter, 141–65. Also appeared in Michael Fortescue, Peter Harder, and Lars Kristoffersen (eds), 1992. *Layered Structure and Reference in a Functional Perspective*. Amsterdam & Philadelphia: John Benjamins, 253–76.

Mackenzie, J. Lachlan. 2009. Aspects of the interpersonal grammar of Gaelic. *Interpersonal Grammar: A Cross-linguistic Perspective*. Special issue of *Linguistics* 47(4): 885–911.

Mackenzie, J. Lachlan. 2011. The study of semantic alternations in a dialogic Functional Discourse Grammar. In Pilar Guerrero Medina (ed.), *Morphosyntactic Alternations in English: Functional and Cognitive Perspectives*. London: Equinox, 38–61.

Mackenzie, J. Lachlan. 2012. Cognitive adequacy in a dialogic Functional Discourse Garammar. In Daniel García Velasco and Gerry Wanders (eds), *The Morphosyntactic Level in Functional Discourse Grammar*. Special issue of *Language Sciences* 34(4): 421–32.

Mackenzie, J. Lachlan. 2013a. The family of secondary predications in English: An FDG view. *Revista Canaria de Estudios Ingleses* 67 (Special Issue): 43–58.

Mackenzie, J. Lachlan. 2013b. Spatial adpositions between lexicon and grammar. In J. Lachlan Mackenzie and Hella Olbertz (eds), *Casebook in Functional Discourse Grammar*. Amsterdam & Philadelphia: John Benjamins, 67–93.

Mackenzie, J. Lachlan and Evelien Keizer. 1991. On assigning pragmatic functions in English. *Pragmatics* 1(2): 169–215.

Mackenzie, J. Lachlan and Hella Olbertz. 2013. Introduction. In J. Lachlan Mackenzie and Hella Olbertz (eds), *Casebook in Functional Discourse Grammar*. Amsterdam & Philadelphia: John Benjamins, 1–14.

Mattissen, Johanna. 2003. *Dependent-Head Synthesis in Nivkh: A Contribution to a Typology of Polysynthesis* (Typological Studies in Language 57). Amsterdam: Benjamins.

Miller, Amy. 2001. *A Grammar of Jamul Tiipay*. Berlin & New York: Mouton de Gruyter.

Nespor, Marina and Irene Vogel. 1986. *Prosodic Phonology*. Dordrecht & Riverton: Foris Publications.

Olbertz, Hella. 1998. *Verbal Periphrases in a Functional Grammar of Spanish*. Berlin & New York: Mouton de Gruyter.

Olbertz, Hella. 2007. *Dizque* in Mexican Spanish: The subjectification of reportative meaning. *Rivista di Linguistica* 19(1): 151–72.

Olbertz, Hella. 2012. The place of exclamatives and miratives in grammar—A Functional Discourse Grammar view. *Linguística* (Rio de Janeiro) 8: 76–98.

O'Neill, Gareth. 2012. Initial consonant mutation in Irish Gaelic: A Functional Discourse Grammar analysis. MA thesis, University of Amsterdam.

O'NEILL, GARETH. 2014. Humming, whistling, singing, and yelling in Pirahã: Context and channels of communication in FDG. In Núria Alturo, Evelien Keizer, and Lluís Payrato (eds), *The Interaction between Context and Grammar in Functional Discourse Grammar*. Special issue of *Pragmatics* 24(2), 349–75.

PARKS, DOUGLAS R. 1976. *A Grammar of Pawnee*. New York: Garland.

PÉREZ QUINTERO and MARÍA JESÚS. 2013. Grammaticalization vs. lexicalization: The Functional Discourse Grammar view. *Revista Canaria de Estudios Ingleses* 67 Special Issue: 97–121.

POLANYI, LIVIA and REMKO SCHA. 1983. On the recursive structure of discourse. In Konrad Ehlich and Henk van Riemsdijk (eds), *Connectedness in Sentence, Discourse and Text*. Tilburg: Tilburg University, 141–78.

POST, BRECHTJE. 2000. *Tonal and Phrasal Structures in French Intonation*. The Hague: Holland Academic Graphics.

QUIRK, RANDOLPH, SIDNEY GREENBAUM, GEOFFREY LEECH, and JAN SVARTVIK. 1985. *A Comprehensive Grammar of the English Language*. London: Longman.

REINHART, TANYA. 1975. Whose main clause? Point of view in sentences with parentheticals. In Susumu Kuno (ed.), *Harvard Studies of Syntax and Semantics: Vol. 1*. Cambridge MA: Dept. of Linguistics, Harvard University, 127–71.

RIJKHOFF, JAN. 2002. *The Noun Phrase*. Oxford: Oxford University Press.

RIJKHOFF, JAN. 2008. Layers, levels and contexts in Functional Discourse Grammar. In Daniel García Velasco, and Jan Rijkhoff (eds), *The Noun Phrase in Functional Discourse Grammar*. Berlin & New York: Mouton de Gruyter, 63–115.

ROACH, PETER. 2009. *English Phonetics and Phonology*. Cambridge: Cambridge University Press.

ROSCH, ELEANOR. 1978. Principles of categorization. In Eleanor Rosch and Barbara B. Lloyd (eds), *Cognition and Categorization*. Hillsdale NJ: Lawrence Erlbaum, 27–48.

SAMPSON, GEOFFREY. 2005. *The 'Language Instinct' Debate*. London: Continuum.

SAUSSURE, FERDINAND DE. 1915/1974. *Course in General Linguistics*. New York: Fontana.

SAVEL'EVA, V. N. 1966. *Review of Grammatika nivxskogo jazyka* [Nivkh grammar], 2 vols. Moscow & Leningrad: Nauka.

SEARLE, JOHN R. 1969. *Speech Acts*. Cambridge: Cambridge University Press.

SEINHORST, KLAAS. 2014. Phonetics in Functional Discourse Grammar. *Web papers in Functional Discourse Grammar* 87. Available at <http://home.hum.uva.nl/fdg/working_papers/WP-FDG-87.pdf>.

SIMON-VANDENBERGEN, ANNE-MARIE, KRISTIN DAVIDSE, and DIRK NOËL (eds). 1997. *Reconnecting Language: Morphology and Syntax in Functional Perspectives*. Amsterdam & Philadelphia: John Benjamins.

SMIT, NIELS. 2010. FYI. Theory and typology of information packaging. Doctoral dissertation, University of Amsterdam.

SPENCER, ANDREW. 1996. *Phonology*. Oxford: Blackwell.

STADEN, MIRIAM VAN. 2000. Tidore: A linguistic description of a language of the North Moluccas. Doctoral dissertation, University of Leiden.

STADEN, MIRIAM VAN, and EVELIEN KEIZER (eds). 2009. *Interpersonal Grammar: A Cross-linguistic Perspective.* Special issue of *Linguistics* 47(4).

STROOMER, HARRY. 1987. *A Comparative Study of Three Southern Oromo Dialects in Kenya: Phonology, Morphology and Vocabulary* (Cushitic Language Studies 6). Hamburg: Buske.

TAVERNIERS, MIRIAM and STAVROS KELEPOURIS. 2013. An FDG analysis of the English resultative construction. Paper presented at the Fourth International Workshop on Functional Discourse Grammar, Vienna, 5–6 September.

TAYLOR, JOHN R. 2003. *Linguistic Categorization.* Oxford: Oxford University Press.

VAN DER AUWERA, JOHAN. 1997. Co-subordination. *Working Papers in Functional Grammar* 63.

VAN DE VELDE, FREEK. 2009. The emergence of modification patterns in the Dutch noun phrase. In Miriam van Staden and Evelien Keizer (eds), *Interpersonal Grammar: A Cross-linguistic Perspective.* Special issue of *Linguistics* 47(4): 1021–49.

VAN VALIN, ROBERT D. 1991. Functionalist linguistic theory and language acquisition. *First Language* 11: 7–40.

VAN VALIN, ROBERT D. 1993. Synopsis of role and reference grammar. In Robert D. Van Valin (ed.), *Advances in Role and Reference Grammar.* Amsterdam: John Benjamins, 1–164.

VAN VALIN, ROBERT D. 2001. *An Introduction to Syntax.* Cambridge: Cambridge University Press.

VAN VALIN, ROBERT D. and RANDY J. LAPOLLA. 1997. *Syntax: Structure, Meaning and Function.* Cambridge: Cambridge University Press.

VANDELANOTTE, LIEVEN. 2004. Deixis and grounding in speech representation. *Journal of Pragmatics* 363: 489–520.

VRIES, LOURENS DE. 1985. Topic and focus in Wambon discourse. In A. Machtelt Bolkestein, Casper de Groot, and J. Lachlan Mackenzie (eds), *Syntax and Pragmatics in Functional Grammar.* Dordrecht: Foris, 155–80.

WATTERS, DAVID E. 2002. *A Grammar of Kham* (Cambridge Grammatical Descriptions). Cambridge: Cambridge University Press.

WATTERS, JOHN R. 1979. Focus in Aghem: A study of its formal correlates and typology. In Larry Hyman (ed.), *Aghem Grammatical Structure.* Los Angeles: University of Southern California, 137–97.

WELLS, JOHN. 1990. Syllabification and allophony. In Susan Ramsaran (ed.), *Studies in the Pronunciation of English, A Commemorative Volume in Honour of A.C. Gimson.* London and New York: Routledge, 76–86. Also available at <http://www.phon.ucl.ac.uk/home/wells/syllabif.htm>.

Index

absolute time 121–2, 142
Acehnese 192, 270
Actor, *see* semantic function
Addressee, *see* Speech Participant
adposition 136–7, 161–2, 176, 218, 222, 224, 288
  grammatical 236–7
adposititional phrase 136–7, 176, 197, 218, 224, 230, 288, 290
adjective 88–9, 95, 129, 146–7, 150–1, 156–7, 164, 174, 176, 180, 224, 233–5, 244
Admonitive 62–3
adverb 151, 164, 179–80; *see also* modifier
Affix 237
  Derivational 237–8, 240–2, 243–4
  Grammatical 237–40, 246
agglutinating language 272
Aghem 78
agreement, *see* Clause; Phrase
alignment 191–2
  interpersonal 192
  representational 192–3
  morphosyntactic 193–4
  nominative–accusative 195
  absolute–ergative 196–7
  see also Clause; Phrase; word
allomorph 176–7, 208, 238, 253–4
ambisyllabicity 279, 281, 289, 294
anaphoric reference 27, 34, 36, 37–8, 39, 41, 91, 94; *see also* head, absent; head, empty
apposition 56, 71
approximation, *see* operator

argument 125, 164–6, 223; *see also* valency
Articulation 21–2, 254–5, 279
Ascriptive Subact 32–3, 83–90, 139–40, 147, 220
  head 85–7
  modifier 87–9
  operator 89–90
Aside 55–6, 60, 174–5
aspect
  habitual 144
  ingressive 144
  nominal 151–2
  perfect 144, 219, 226, 238
  progressive 144, 212, 238, 285
  prospective 144
assimilation 254
Auxiliary 84, 236; *see also* aspect
Axininca Campa 277

Background 74–5
Basque 196
Beneficiary, *see* modifier; semantic function

categorical sentence 76
categorization 10, 11, 17
causative 131–2
cause, *see* modifier
Clause 37, 175–8, 184–217
  agreement 207–8, 214
  alignment 191–9, 199
  dummy 204–7
  linear ordering 184–91, 199–204
  placeholder 201, 206, 208, 216, 287

cleft construction 74, 77, 100, 255
clitic 192–3, 199, 223, 270–1
coda 276–7, 278–9, 289
coercion 233, 241, 245, 249
collective noun 152
Comment 74–6
Communicated Content 32–3, 72–82,
    115–16, 139, 185, 210–11
  head 73–9
  modifier 79–82, 210–11
  operator 82
communicative intention, *see* Speaker's
    intention
competence 7–8
complement clause 208, 209
complexity 198–200
complex tone 264–5
compound 149–50, 231, 235, 240–2,
    244–5, 295
  synthetic compounding 241–2, 249
Conceptual Component 21, 22, 23–5
Concession 55–6
Condition 261
Confirmation 262
consecutio temporum 214
content frame 79, 185
context 9, 11, 13–14; *see also*
    Contextual Component
Contextual Component 21, 22, 25–7;
    see also context
Contrast, *see* pragmatic functions
coordination 182
copular construction 84, 129, 136–40, 226
  classificational 137, 139–40, 141,
    290–2
  identificational 137–8, 139–40
  relational 136–7, 139
core unit, *see* linear ordering
Correction 55
cosubordination 182, 287
count noun 152–3
Czech 269

Declarative 25, 39, 55–6, 61–2, 213,
    258–61, 266
definiteness 26, 39, 46, 95; *see also*
    identifiability
deictic expression 26, 93, 120–1, 159, 284
degemination 279, 289
demonstrative 159, 181
dependence 53–4
derivation, *see* compound; lexical
    derivation; syntactic derivation
descriptive linguistics 2–3
designation 34, 103, 104
direct speech 213
discourse 13
Discourse Act 12, 14, 21, 32–3, 52–60, 213
  head 57–8
  function 53–7
  modifier 58–9
  operators 59–60
domain integrity 174, 175, 199, 247
dummy element 85–6, 94, 180, 233, 236,
    287, 292
  it 76, 130, 205, 215, 217
  be 138, 217, 226, 287, 292–3
  do 100, 184, 205–6
  one 226
  so 227
  there 205
  see also Clause; Phrase; Word
duration, *see* modifiers
Dutch 67, 72, 80, 206–7

elision 254
embedding 140–1, 285; *see also*
    complement clauses
emergence 9
emphasis 59, 87, 90
Encoding 22, 29–30, 173–4, 254
  morphosyntactic 29–30, 173–4
  phonological 29–30
end focus 263
end weight 198–9

Episode 34, 106, 112–13, 117–23, 211–12
  head 119–21
  modifier 121–3, 211
  operator 123, 211
equiordination 183
equipollence 53–4
Evocation 34, 85
Exclamative 61–2
existential sentence 138; *see also*
  presentative construction
extra-clausality 183, 187

factuality 108–9
falling tone 38–9, 48, 53, 258–70, 289, 294
feature copying 227–8
features 70, 92–3
Focus, *see* pragmatic function
Foot 38, 256, 273–9
  iambic 274–6
  trochaic 274–5
formal paradigm, *see* paradigm
Formulation 22, 29
frame 22, 30, 33, 35; *see also* content
  frame; predication frame
French 72, 225, 270, 277
frequency, *see* modifier
function 31, 47; *see also* pragmatic
  function; rhetorical function;
  semantic function; syntactic function
Functional Grammar 21
functional paradigm, *see* paradigm
functional stability 174, 175, 247
functions of language 5–7
fusional language 272

Garo 123
genre 27
Georgian 151
German 72, 82, 135
gradience 10, 13
Grammatical Component 20–1, 22–4,
  28–39
grammaticalization 4

Hawaiian 277
head 31, 47, 106–7
  absent 107, 109–10, 119, 125, 148,
   154, 162
  abstract 61–4, 66, 69, 70, 92–3, 103
  configurational 57–8, 73, 107, 120–1,
   123–5, 126–35, 149, 155–6, 163,
   222, 223, 233, 241
  empty 70, 85–6, 92, 94, 107, 110, 120,
   126, 129, 148, 155, 162–3
  lexical 64–6, 70, 92, 94, 107, 111–12,
   120, 126, 146, 148–9, 155, 163
Hortative 61–2
Hungarian 78, 215, 269

iambic reversal 275–6, 280
Icelandic 135, 269
iconicity 173, 174, 247
identifiability 26–7, 46, 95–6; *see also*
  definiteness; operator
idiom 235
if-clause 98, 116, 261
Illocution 33, 55, 60–8, 258
  head 61–6
  modifier 66–8
  operator 68
  see also Declarative; Exclamative;
   Hortative; Imperative;
   Interpellative; Interrogative;
   Optative
Imperative 30, 55, 61–2, 64, 68,
  100–1, 264
implicature 24–5, 64
incorporation 240–2, 249
indirect speech act 24–5, 64
Individual 34, 105, 152–9
  head 154–6
  modifiers 156–8
  operators 158–9
innateness 8–9, 11
instrument, *see* modifiers; semantic
  functions
interjection 57, 65, 98, 252

Interpersonal Level 32–4, 40, 44–97,
    252, 284–5, 290, 294–5; *see also*
    Ascriptive Subact; Communicated
    Content; Discourse Act; Illocution;
    Move; Referential Subact; Speech
    Participant
Interpellative 61–2
Interrogative 55, 61–2, 64, 255,
    260–1, 262
intonation 30, 38–9, 48, 55–6, 58–9,
    253, 255, 258–68, 289; *see also*
    prosody; template (phonological)
Intonational Phrase 38, 53, 256, 259–62
Irony 59, 267
isolating language 272
isochronicity 274
Italian 270

Jamul Tiipay 63
Japanese 72, 277
Javanese 72

Kham 78, 90
Kisi 192
Korean 191
Koryak 119

language
    acquisition 4; *see also* innateness;
        language faculty
    change 4
    evolution 4
    faculty 9; *see also* language acquisition
    universal 9, 30
layer 31, 32, 33–4, 35, 47
Leti 90
levels of
    analysis, *see* levels of, representation
    representation 22; *see also*
        Interpersonal Level;
        Morphosyntactic Level;

Phonological Level;
    Representation Level
lexeme 22, 30, 35, 146–7, 232–5
    formation rule 234–5, 245, 248
lexical derivation 234, 245, 249
liaison 277
linear ordering 184–91, 199–204,
    219–25, 237–40
    core unit 184–5, 199–204, 219, 242–3
    non-core unit 184–5, 187–91, 219,
        237–40
Linguistic Expression 37, 175–7, 181–4
    template 182–3
linking 254, 260
listing 182
Location 34, 106, 159–66, 221–2
    head 162–3
    modifier 164–6
    operator 166
Locative, *see* semantic function

Mandarin Chinese 62–3, 131, 191, 261
manner adverb, *see* modifier
mass noun 152
Maximal Onsets Principle 278–9,
    281, 289
metonymy 149
mitigation 33, 68
modality
    deontic 145
    event-oriented 145
    experiential 114
    hypothetical 116–17
    inferential 1–14, 116
    objective epistemic 145
    participant-oriented 145
    subjective epistemic 113–14, 116
modifier 31, 36, 46, 47, 67, 142–3,
    164–6, 210
    absolute time 121–2, 142
    approximation 88

attitude 46, 79, 87, 94–5, 113–14
beneficiary 143
cause 54, 142
degree 150
duration 142
exactness 88–9
experiential 114
frequency 142
inferential 114
instrument 143
manner 67, 150, 179–80
place 142
placement of 187–90, 221
purpose 142
reality status 142
relative time 142
reportative 80–1, 115–16, 285
Morpheme 22, 29, 31, 176, 231, 257, 279
Grammatical 22, 31, 176
Morphosyntactic Level 20–1, 36–8, 173–250, 253, 286–8, 292–3, 296
see also Clause; Linguistic Expression; Morpheme; Phrase; Word
Motivation 54
Move 32, 47, 48–52, 210, 257
head 49–50
modifier 50–1
operator 51–2, 210

negation 16, 146, 205–6, 236
nesting 178
neutralization 195–8
Nivkh 242–3
nominalization 240
noun phrase 176, 178, 218–27, 233, 241
Nucleus (Discourse Act) 54–5
number, *see* operator

Object, *see* syntactic function
onset 276–7

operator 22, 29, 31, 35, 36, 46, 47, 210, 257
anterior 144
approximation 89–90, 222
deontic modality, *see* modality
distance 159
dubitative 117
emphasis 90
epistemic modality, *see* modality
event-oriented modality, *see* modality
exactness 90
fall 257–60, 263–7
habitual aspect, *see* aspect
high tone 266–7
hypothetical modality 116
identifiability 46, 95–6, 221
ingressive aspect, *see* aspect
intonational 258
low tone 266–7
mitigation 33, 68
number 71, 158–9, 221
numeral 158–9, 166
participant-oriented modality, *see* modality
perfect aspect, *see* aspect
phasal aspect, *see* aspect
polarity 146
politeness 72
progressive aspect, *see* aspect
prospective aspect, *see* aspect
quantity 158–9, 166
rise 257–8, 260–1, 264–5
reportative 80–1
reinforcement 33, 68
simultaneous 144
stress 274
tense 123, 143–4
Optative 61–2
Orientation 55
Oromo 151–2
Output Component 21, 22, 28, 254–5, 279

paradigm 5, 10–13, 18–19
part-of-speech 146
Pawnee 117
peak 276–8
performance 8
performative verb 64–5, 68–70, 99
Phonological Phrase 38, 256, 263–9
Phonological Level 20–1, 38–9, 176,
    252–82, 288–9, 293–4, 297;
    see also Foot; Intonational Phrase;
    Phoneme; Phonological Phrase;
    Phonological Word; Syllable;
    Utterance
Phonological Word 38, 269–73, 276
  vs. morphological Word 270–3
phonotactic rule 276–7
Phrase 37, 176–9, 218–31; see also
    Adpositional phrase, Noun phrase,
    Verb phrase
  agreement 227–8
  dummy 219
  placeholder 217, 221–2, 292–3
pitch 53, 256, 258–9, 261, 263,
    265–7, 289
place adverbial, see modifier
placeholder 37, 201, 257, 287, 292–3;
    see also Clause; Phrase; Word
polarity, see operator
Polish 191, 269
polysynthetic language 273
Portuguese 112
possession
  alienable 158
  inalienable 155–6, 158, 223
pragmatic adequacy 12
pragmatic function 46, 73, 199–200,
    216, 266
  Focus 46, 73–9, 192, 194, 216–17,
    264
  Topic 73–9, 194, 216–17
  Contrast 74–9, 266
predicate 125

non-verbal 126, 129; see also copular
    construction
predication 125
predication frame 128–9, 130–2, 155,
    185
preposition, see adposition
presentative construction 77; see also
    existential sentence
prescriptive linguistics 2
primitive 28, 29, 30–1, 35–6, 38–9, 62,
    176, 257
Principle of Formal Encoding 15, 21,
    24, 41, 61, 74, 133
Prohibitive 30, 63, 100
pronoun 66, 95, 154–5, 158, 160–1,
    164–6, 226, 236, 285; see also
    anaphoric reference; deictic
    expression; head, absent; head,
    empty
proper name 66, 86–7, 94, 153–4, 284
Property 34, 105, 146–52
  head 148–50
  modifier 151–2
  operator 151–2
Propositional Content 34, 105, 108–15,
    165–6, 210–11
  head 109–12
  modifier 113–16, 210–11, 212
  operator 116–17
prosody 74, 254–5, 257–8
prototypicality 10
purpose, see modifier

raising 214–17
Reinforcement 262
relational noun 155, 222–3
reality status, see modifier
  question tag 262, 281
  question word 96
  quotative 81
Referential Subact 33, 46, 72, 83–4,
    90–6, 139–40, 147, 220

head 46, 92–4
 modifier 94–5
 operator 95–6
register 27
Representational Level 32, 34–6, 103–71,
     253, 285–6, 290–2, 295; *see also*
     Propositional Content; Episode;
     State-of-Affairs; Property;
     Individual; Location; Time
reinforcement 33, 68
relative clause, *see also* subordination
     clause
 headless 156
 non-restrictive 56
 restrictive 158, 164, 229–31
relative time, *see* modifier
reportative 80
Resultative, *see* semantic function
rhetorical function 44, 54–7; *see also*
     Aside; Concession; Condition;
     Confirmation; Correction;
     Motivation; Orientation;
     Reinforcement
rising tone 258, 261, 264–5

Saramaccan 132
scope 67
Scottish Gaelic 63, 112
semantic category 105
semantic function 132–5, 199–200
 Actor 133–5, 194–8
 Associative 157
 Beneficiary 143
 Direction 287
 Instrument 143
 Locative 133–5
 Reference 156, 161
 Resultative 141
 Source 137, 222
 Undergoer 133–5, 194–8
semantics 34; *see also* Representational
     Level

serial construction 131
Shipibo 82
sort-of 89
Southern Tiwa 243
Source, *see* semantic function
Spanish 16, 71, 228
Speaker, *see* Speech Participant
Speaker's intention 12, 21, 23–5, 40–1,
     44, 60–2, 64–6, 98, 173
specificity 95–6
Speech Participant 33, 68–72
 head 70
 modifier 71
 operator 71–2
stacking 178
State-of-Affairs 34, 105–6, 124, 212
 complex 140–2
 (non)dynamic 133–5
 head 125–36
 modifier 142–3, 212
 operator 143–6
Stem 237–9, 241
stress 30, 59, 75, 256–9, 263, 269–70,
     272–6, 289, 294, 297
style 27
Subact, *see* Ascriptive Subact,
     Referential Subact
Subject, *see* syntactic function
subordination; *see also* relative clause
 within the Clause 208–17
 within the Phrase 229–31
suppletion 22, 29, 31, 253–4
syllabic consonant 276–7
Syllable 38, 256, 263, 273–9
 nuclear 263, 268
 unfooted 275, 289, 297
syntactic derivation 234–5, 237–8,
     240–1, 245, 292
syntactic function 194–9, 199–204
 Object 36, 192, 197–8, 199–204
 Subject 36, 192–7, 199–204
synthesis 181

Tagalog 193

Tariana 77

Tauya 119

template 22, 29, 30, 36

  morphosyntactic 178

  phonological 257

tense 123

  absolute 123, 211

  relative 143

tone, *see* operator

theoretical model 3

thetic sentence 76

Tidore 78, 118–19

Time 34, 106, 159–66

  head 162–3

  modifier 164–6

  operator 164–6

top-down approach 29, 186, 219

Topic, *see* pragmatic function

transparency 178–81, 217, 232–3, 246

truth value 64

Tsafiki 239

Turkish 131, 269, 272

Tuvaluan 215

Undergoer, *see* semantic function

Utterance 38, 53, 256, 257–8

valency

  qualificational 132–5

  quantificational 128–32

variable 31, 32, 45, 47, 105–6

verbal phrase 176, 184

vocative 65–6, 70, 252–3

Wambon 77

weather verb 85, 205; *see also* valency

Welsh 269

Word 37, 176–8, 231–46

  alignment 240–2

  dummy 238, 243–4

  formation 231, 244–6; *see also* compound; lexical derivation; syntactic derivation

  Grammatical 184, 235–7

  Lexical 235–7

  order, *see* linear ordering

  placeholder 257

  vs. lexeme 232–5

  vs. Phonological 256, 270–3